LOCAL GOVERNMENT, LAND USE, AND THE FIRST AMENDMENT

PROTECTING FREE SPEECH AND EXPRESSION

AMERICAN BAR ASSOCIATION
Section of State and
Local Government Law

Printed in the United States of America.

21 20 19 18 17 5 4 3 2 1

ISBN: 978-1-63425-918-7
e-ISBN: 978-1-63425-919-4

Library of Congress Cataloging-in-Publication Data

Names: Connolly, Brian J., editor.
Title: Local government, land use, and the First Amendment / Brian J.
    Connolly, editor.
Description: Chicago : American Bar Association, 2017. | Includes index.
Identifiers: LCCN 2017029540 | ISBN 9781634259187
Subjects: LCSH: Land use—Law and legislation—United States. | United
    States. Constitution. 1st Amendment. | Zoning law—United States. | Local

    government—Law and legislation—United States.
Classification: LCC KF5698 .L63 2017 | DDC 346.7304/4—dc23 LC record
available at https://lccn.loc.gov/2017029540

www.ShopABA.org

To those who work daily to ensure that individuals'
rights to free speech and free exercise of religion
are vindicated. And to my family.
—Brian J. Connolly

Contents

Foreword

by Daniel R. Mandelker

Howard A. Stamper Professor of Law
Washington University in St. Louis
St. Louis, Missouri

Sixteen years ago, I had the privilege to serve as co-editor, along with my student Rebecca Rubin, of a book published by the American Bar Association (ABA) titled *Protecting Free Speech and Expression: The First Amendment and Land Use Law.* When we set to work on that publication, our intent was to publish a groundbreaking book that distilled, in an accessible, practitioner-friendly format, a massive amount of First Amendment case law in a way that local governments could find useful. That publication was the Section of State and Local Government's first known attempt to publish a "one-stop-shop" volume that could serve as a desk reference or practice guide for the many First Amendment issues associated with zoning and planning.

In the several decades before we published *Protecting Free Speech and Expression*, local governments had increasingly frequent run-ins with the First Amendment because of Supreme Court decisions extending First Amendment protection to commercial speech. Local government regulation of signs and outdoor advertising and efforts to control the spread of adult businesses closely intertwined with constitutional doctrine that was previously inapplicable in these areas. In 1977, the Supreme Court decided *Linmark Associates v. Township of Willingboro*, the Court's first application of First Amendment principles to outdoor signs—in that case, real estate "for sale" signs. Just a year earlier, the Court considered *Young v. American Mini-Theatres*, which signaled the birth of First Amendment doctrine associated with zoning regulation of adult businesses, including bookstores, theaters, and live entertainment venues. In subsequent decades, the Court continued to expand the First Amendment's reach into local government affairs with cases such as *Metromedia v. City of San Diego*, relating to billboard advertising; *Members of City Council of Los Angeles v. Taxpayers for*

Vincent, addressing placement of signs in the public right-of-way; *Renton v. Playtime Theatres, Inc.,* confirming the "secondary effects" doctrine for adult business regulation; *City of Ladue v. Gilleo,* considering the suppression of political signs; and *City of Erie v. Pap's A.M.,* concerning the regulation of nude dancing establishments.

These legal developments, associated primarily with private individuals' rights to speak on privately owned property, followed the Court's earlier work of developing what became known as the public forum doctrine, which set parameters on governments' ability to control or regulate speech in government-controlled areas. Beginning as early as the 1930s, in *Hague v. Committee for Industrial Organization,* the Supreme Court recognized that the government's right to control speech on government property was subject to First Amendment limitations. Later cases, including *Heffron v. International Society for Krishna Consciousness; Perry Education Association v. Perry Local Educators' Association; Clark v. Community for Creative Non Violence; Ward v. Rock Against Racism; United States v. Kokinda, Burson v. Freeman,* and many others, clarified the distinctions between the traditional, designated, limited, and even nonpublic fora that we know today.

Moreover, following the Supreme Court's landmark decision in *Roe v. Wade,* which legalized abortion, the public forum doctrine cases were both amplified and confused by a series of cases beginning in the 1990s involving public protests at and around reproductive health clinics. These included *Madsen v. Women's Health Center, Inc.; Schenck v. Pro-Choice Network of Western New York;* and in 2000, *Hill v. Colorado.* By 2000, the combination of these cases had a profound impact on local governments, addressing and limiting the ways in which governments could regulate speech activities on local streets, in public parks, in and around government buildings, and even near controversial uses such as abortion clinics.

During this entire time, the Supreme Court made parallel efforts to clarify and strengthen its doctrine concerning the religion clauses of the First Amendment, developing tests and standards of review for analyzing government restrictions on religious land uses. In 1963, the Court developed the now-familiar *Sherbert* test for analyzing government limitations on the free exercise of religion, which began to infiltrate into local zoning approvals and conditions for houses of worship and their ancillary uses. Seven years later, in 1970, the Court adopted the broadly used *Lemon* test for deciding when a government exceeded its Establishment Clause limitations, which, over succeeding decades, began to affect local government activities such as legislative prayer and local government-sponsored holiday displays and parades. Then in 2000, on the eve of *Protecting Free Speech and Expression*'s publication, Congress adopted the Religious Land Uses and Institutionalized Persons Act (RLUIPA). RLUIPA was Congress's second attempt at a statute intended to preserve heightened scrutiny for local land use regulations that burdened religion, reversing the hotly debated 1990 Supreme Court decision in *Employment Division v. Smith*. RLUIPA concluded, for the time being, a decade-long back-and-forth between the Supreme Court and Congress concerning the appropriate standard of review for government regulations that burden religion.

Our goal in producing *Protecting Free Speech and Expression* back in 2001 was to develop a book that collapsed Supreme Court case law, as well as some lower court interpretations of these cases, into a review that would be accessible and informative to lawyers, planners, and other parties to the local land use process. Plenty of case citations provided opportunities for further research. We recognized the First Amendment's increasing influence on local government decision-making and the court decisions that reviewed local government actions. By the beginning of the twenty-first century, the First Amendment had become a powerful weapon for individuals and groups that wished to challenge long-recognized police power efforts, such as zoning, maintenance of public spaces, and policing. *Protecting Free Speech and Expression* was our most significant attempt yet at distilling these messages from the courts for our colleagues in local government decision-making.

As we went about developing *Protecting Free Speech and Expression*, we sought out some of the most respected legal academics and practitioners to help us write the book. Our authors reflected the best available in terms of both knowledge and authorship. Our academic contributors included Bob Sedler from Wayne State University in Detroit and Alan Weinstein and Kevin O'Neill from Cleveland State University in Cleveland. Our practitioner contributors included Scott Bergthold, one of the nation's leading minds on adult business regulation, and Randal Morrison, one of the leaders on sign regulation. We also had chapters from Nancy Stroud, Shelley Ross Saxer, Katherine Stone, and Neil Lehto. It was a great group of authors, and their contributions led to a collection of chapters that made the book a success.

In the intervening sixteen years since the launch of *Protecting Free Speech and Expression*, the law of the First Amendment as applied to local government has continued to evolve, as have some of the practical issues associated with land use and local government regulation. Four legal and technical developments are worth noting.

First, when we wrote *Protecting Free Speech and Expression* in 2001, we had no experience with RLUIPA's implementation. The statute was just a year old when we released the book, and it was anyone's guess on how courts would respond to the law, or even whether it was constitutional. Now, with the constitutional question answered affirmatively, we have a robust volume of case law interpreting RLUIPA as it relates to local government powers. Many religious congregations have utilized the provisions of RLUIPA to challenge local government decisions successfully, mostly in the realm of zoning. RLUIPA has proven to be a powerful legal stick for religious congregations that experience alleged discrimination at the hands of local government regulators.

Second, advances in technology have changed aspects of local government regulation in the free speech arena. By the late 1990s, the Internet was beginning to change the regulation of adult businesses. Local governments in the 1970s and 1980s strove to stem the proliferation into stable residential neighborhoods of adult bookstores, live entertainment venues, and adult novelty shops. By the time we published *Protecting Free Speech and Expression*, the Internet was bringing about a revolution in adult entertainment that allowed individuals to access such entertainment and purchase novelty items from home computers or even mobile phones. The advent of Internet pornography and online shopping, which offers individuals greater access to entertainment options while simultaneously providing more privacy, has lessened the demand for brick-and-mortar adult businesses that may have deleterious effects on surrounding neighborhoods.

This development puts less pressure on local governments to control these establishments through zoning.

In addition, sign codes have had to respond to new sign technologies. Billboard advertisers, which into the 1990s had to send work crews out every time they changed copy on a sign, developed digital technology allowing billboards to shine more brightly and be changed from a remote computer control. This technology allows billboard advertisers to lease a sign face to multiple advertisers at once because sign messages scroll across the sign face several times in a day. The same technology now allows local businesses to display "ticker" messages or even videos on signs along public streets. Although digital sign technology offers greater flexibility and more avenues for advertising products and services, such technology has sometimes come at the expense of community aesthetic character and traffic safety. Local governments face steep political pressure to make sign codes more permissive for digital technology, and they confront legal challenges when they deny advertisers the right to display electronic signage.

Third, the Supreme Court's clarification and reinforcement of the content neutrality doctrine in the 2015 case of *Reed v. Town of Gilbert* was a watershed moment in First Amendment jurisprudence relating to local governments. Whether a regulation of speech is content neutral is generally the determining factor in whether it is upheld under intermediate scrutiny or is overturned on strict scrutiny. After developing the content neutrality doctrine in the early 1970s in *Police Department of Chicago v. Mosley*, Supreme Court statements on content neutrality became clouded by several decades of public forum cases, including the 2000 case of *Hill v. Colorado*. The federal courts of appeals split on whether the content neutrality analysis should look only at the government's purpose in enacting a regulation or whether content neutrality required courts to analyze whether the regulation was facially content based. The more flexible purpose-based approach gave local governments much wider leeway to regulate signs and other speech in a commonsense, category-oriented manner. *Reed* confirmed that the stricter approach should govern, which threw most U.S. sign codes into a state of questionable constitutionality and forced local governments to reconsider their approaches to speech regulation.

Fourth, the advent of the government speech doctrine has provided a new regulatory "escape valve" for local governments that engage in their own speech activities. The formal announcement of a doctrine regarding "government speech," and the exemption of government speech from First Amendment limitations except for Establishment Clause considerations, came in 2009 in *Pleasant Grove City v. Summum*. The Supreme Court then had the opportunity to provide further clarification of the government speech doctrine in *Walker v. Texas Division, Sons of Confederate Veterans* in 2015. The Supreme Court has now held that donated public monuments and state license plates are government speech, and lower courts have followed suit in expanding government speech boundaries. Issues previously decided as public forum doctrine cases are now being decided as government speech cases, or are at least requiring courts to consider the government speech doctrine as part of their regular forum analysis.

Because of these changes in the law, the ABA Section of State and Local Government in 2014 began considering whether an update to *Protecting Free Speech and Expression* should be undertaken. I elected to bow out of the editorial role for the update, and the Section set about to find an editor for the updated book. Section leadership set its collective eyes on Brian Connolly as a potential editor, and we are pleased that he agreed. At that time, Connolly had established himself as one of the land use bar's rising stars and one of the leading authors and practitioners in the area of sign regulation. Just three years prior, Connolly served as the lead co-author of the *Michigan Sign Guidebook*, an impressive volume that provides practical advice on sign regulation for communities in Michigan and beyond. We were familiar with Connolly's work and were pleased that he agreed to serve as the editor of the updated publication. He has now spent more than two years working with authors, writing a chapter of his own, and making this book ready for publication.

The first task in preparing the new publication required an outline that reflected the changes that had occurred in the law. It places special emphasis on several issues, including billboard advertising; electronic and digital signage; political advertising; "vice" advertising of tobacco, liquor, and other products; RLUIPA case law; speech by governmental agencies;

and street and sidewalk speech, including panhandling and solicitation. Some of these topics have their own chapters, whereas others are discussed in chapters with a broader scope.

The second task was identifying authors to assist in the update. Connolly elected to contact all of our authors from *Protecting Free Speech and Expression* to request updates, or in most cases complete rewrites, for their chapters. I'm pleased to see that several individuals accepted his invitation. Bob Sedler provided an excellent overview, as well as a chapter on live adult entertainment establishments. Nancy Stroud contributed a conclusion to the book. Randal Morrison, Alan Weinstein, Scott Bergthold, and Kevin O'Neill have again contributed their collective expertise in the areas of sign regulation, religious land use issues, adult business licensing and regulation, and public forum matters, respectively. Connolly also brought several new authors into the fold, including several rising stars of the State and Local Government Section. These include Chris Brown of Mansfield, Ohio, on electronic and digital signage and Evan Seeman of Robinson & Cole on the constitutional issues associated with religious land use regulation. Jerry Hicks and Joe Cerullo of Sacramento, California, have additionally contributed a chapter on government speech. Connolly's Denver, Colorado, colleague Tom Macdonald has written on street and sidewalk speech, and Connolly himself has authored a new chapter on artwork and architecture. The authors of the updated volume reflect a collection of some of the best-regarded practitioners and academics in the areas of local government and First Amendment law, and I am thrilled to see such a great group of people collaborate on this project.

The new book, now called *Local Government, Land Use, and the First Amendment: Protecting Free Speech and Expression,* is a tour de force of the current First Amendment law as applied to local governments. There are four main parts. The first part includes three chapters that cover private speech issues on private property, including Morrison's chapter on outdoor sign and advertising regulation, Brown's chapter on electronic and digital signs, and Connolly's own chapter on artwork and architecture regulation. These chapters contain excellent discussions of some of the core issues associated with regulation of speech on private property, such as content neutrality. They consider the Supreme Court's recent decision in *Reed v. Town of Gilbert* and devote significant attention to methods local governments should consider when regulating signs and other media of speech to avoid constitutional problems. The second part of the book contains two chapters, one by Seeman and the other by Weinstein, covering religious land use issues under the Free Exercise and Establishment Clauses of the First Amendment as well as RLUIPA. Since the passage of RLUIPA, developments in the application of the religion clauses of the First Amendment to local government have not been significant, but Seeman's chapter covers several important "constitutional basics" that require attention. As before, Weinstein's chapter on RLUIPA provides an excellent overview of the statute, and this time contains an impressive volume of case law interpreting RLUIPA and its effect on local government regulatory practices.

The third part of the book reviews the law of adult business regulation. Bergthold provides a chapter that discusses adult business regulation generally, giving a thorough overview of the case law and the all-important secondary effects doctrine that allows local governments to regulate adult businesses specially. Sedler provides an update to his chapter on adult live entertainment establishments, giving a more closely tailored overview of constitutional limitations associated with local government regulation of what happens inside a strip club or similar establishment.

Finally, the fourth part of the book contains chapters that discuss speech by both private individuals and government on public property. Hicks and Cerullo's chapter on government speech outlines some of the very recent case law that has developed the government speech doctrine, providing guidance to local governments on when government agencies' speech becomes government speech with exemptions from First Amendment limitations. O'Neill and Macdonald provide chapters on the public forum doctrine. O'Neill covers the application of the public forum doctrine to government permitting programs, especially as they relate to mass protests, demonstrations, and parades. Macdonald covers the applicability of the public forum doctrine to nonpermitted speech, such as that by sidewalk performers or individuals engaging in panhandling and solicitation of donations.

Local Government, Land Use, and the First Amendment is published at an interesting moment in history. Despite the prevalence of new forms of citizen engagement, such as the Internet and social media, traditional forms of protest and demonstration and older methods of communication, such as political yard signs, remain powerful methods for communicating ideas and messages. The Black Lives Matter movement has shed light on police brutality and community safety in minority communities here in the United States, primarily through marches, parades, and demonstrations. Our international engagements are testing the limits of religious tolerance, along with many reports of religious discrimination in neighborhoods around the nation.

In many ways, First Amendment guarantees are felt most closely in local communities and by local governments, as individuals most often respond to current events and engage politically in their hometowns. Our country's political course is often the result of what happens locally. Some of our most significant Supreme Court decisions on the interpretation of the First Amendment arose from "neighborhood" issues. Local governments' adherence to—or failure to adhere to—our country's deeply held First Amendment values will remain of paramount importance. Although there is no way of predicting our political future, I am confident that, in *Local Government, Land Use, and the First Amendment*, the editor and authors have provided a "go-to" resource for the local government lawyers, planners, elected officials, community leaders, and citizens who address all these values "on the ground." I hope you find the following chapters interesting, thought-provoking, and most of all, useful in your daily work.

Acknowledgments

The editor wishes to acknowledge the following individuals for their assistance in preparing this book: John Baker, Daniel Mandelker, Dwight Merriam, Andrew Peters, Brittany Wiser, Margo Brown. The editor additionally wishes to acknowledge the members of the publications committee of the Section of State and Local Government for their assistance in reviewing and providing insightful comments on early drafts of this book.

About the Editor and Authors

Editor

Brian J. Connolly is a planner and lawyer at Otten Johnson Robinson Neff + Ragonetti, P.C. in Denver, Colorado. There, he represents public- and private-sector clients in matters relating to zoning, planning, development entitlements, and other complex regulatory issues. Connolly additionally specializes in the First Amendment and land use issues associated with outdoor sign and advertising regulation, as well as fair housing matters in local planning and zoning. Prior to practicing law, Connolly was an urban planner in the planning department of Westchester County, New York. He has served as lead co-author of two books, including *Group Homes: Strategies for Effective and Defensible Planning and Regulation* (ABA Publishing 2014), addressing the planning and local zoning issues associated with group homes for people with disabilities, and *The Michigan Sign Guidebook: The Local Planning and Regulation of Signs* (Scenic Michigan 2011), which discusses the legal aspects—particularly the First Amendment issues—relating to outdoor sign and advertising regulation. Connolly serves on the advisory board of the Rocky Mountain Land Use Institute, he was one of twenty-eight experts in land use law serving as reporters for the national land use law publication *Planning & Environmental Law*, and he is the editor of Rocky Mountain Sign Law (www.rockymountainsignlaw. com), a blog on free speech and land use issues. He frequently writes on planning and land use law topics, including fair housing, sign regulation, aesthetics, and other matters, and Connolly is a regular speaker at conferences on these topics, including at national and state conferences of the American Planning Association, American Bar Association, International Municipal Lawyers Association, and Rocky Mountain Land Use Institute. Connolly holds a J.D., magna cum laude, from the University of Michigan Law School and a Master of Regional Planning and Bachelor of Science in urban and regional studies, both from Cornell University.

Authors

Scott D. Bergthold has a municipal law practice focused on the drafting and defense of adult business regulations in state and federal courts. He has successfully handled litigation on zoning, licensing, regulatory, and alcohol matters for cities and counties in more than twenty states. Bergthold is a frequent lecturer for state municipal leagues and the International Municipal Lawyers Association. For more than a decade, he has been the principal author of *Local Regulation of Adult Businesses* (West), and he has authored articles for *ABA State and Local Law News*, *Land Use Law & Zoning Digest*, and *Municipal Lawyer*. He served as lead brief writer for the city in *City of Littleton v. Z.J. Gifts D-4, LLC*, 541 U.S. 774 (2004), and he has been lead counsel in adult business litigation in seven federal appellate courts and numerous state supreme courts.

Christopher Lake Brown is the deputy law director at the City of Mansfield, Ohio. He is primarily engaged in civil matters but sometimes assists with the prosecution of crimes. As a municipal attorney, he sees a variety of state and local government law issues, including Section 1983 claims, labor and employment disputes, public records law, zoning and planning, and real estate issues including transfers of city-owned land and foreclosures. Brown is active in the ABA, Ohio State Bar Association (OSBA), and his local bar association. He is currently the ABA Young Lawyers Division (YLD) Committees director, co-chair of the ABA Section of State and Local Government Law's Young Lawyers Committee, secretary of the OSBA Young Lawyers Section, and president of the Richland County Bar Association. He is also active in the Ohio Municipal Attorneys Association. Chris has authored articles for *ABA State and Local Law News* and is a frequent speaker at conferences on municipal law topics. In 2016, he was awarded the ABA Section of State and Local Government Law's Jefferson B. Fordham Up & Comer Award. Brown earned his B.A. in English from the Ohio State University and his J.D. from the University of Cincinnati College of Law.

Joseph Cerullo, Jr. is a senior deputy city attorney for the City of Sacramento, California. He holds a J.D. and an M.B.A., both from the University of Southern California, and a B.S. from California State University, Long Beach.

Gerald C. Hicks is a supervising deputy city attorney with the City Attorney's Office in Sacramento, California. Hicks has served the Sacramento City Attorney's Office since February 1998. He has made presentations before the League of California Cities, California State Association of Counties, and International Municipal Lawyer's Association on various topics, including the Americans with Disabilities Act and the First Amendment. Hicks received B.A. degrees from California State University Sacramento in history and communications. He received his law degree from McGeorge School of Law in 1990, graduating magna cum laude. He was assistant comment editor of the *Pacific Law Journal* from 1989–1990.

J. Thomas Macdonald is a lawyer in the Denver, Colorado, firm of Otten Johnson Robinson Neff + Ragonetti, P.C. Macdonald represents clients in complex litigation involving land use and governmental regulation. Macdonald is well known for his expertise concerning constitutional limitations on the local governments' authority to regulate land use. He has extensive experience with First Amendment challenges to land use regulation. Macdonald received his J.D. from the University of Colorado School of Law, where he graduated first in his class and Order of the Coif, and his B.A. from the University of Colorado–Boulder.

Randal R. Morrison is director of litigation with Sabine & Morrison, a public agency law firm in San Diego, California. His practice has focused on the law of signs, public forum, and government speech since 1993. He is admitted to practice before the U.S. Supreme Court, four of the federal courts of appeal, and trial courts (both state and federal) in several states. He often consults with local governments on sign code updates and sign-related litigation, including cases filed by billboard companies. Morrison graduated from the University of the Pacific, McGeorge School of Law, Order of the Coif, "with great distinction." West Publishing named one of his briefs "Trial Court Brief of the Day" on December 29, 2010. Morrison co-authored an *amicus* brief for the National League of Cities in the Supreme Court case *Reed v. Town of Gilbert*. He has also arbitrated international trademark with the International Chamber of Commerce in London. Morrison operates the website www.signlaw.com and occasionally publishes a newsletter, distributed free by e-mail only, summarizing the latest court decisions in the law of signs and related topics. Before attending law school, he was a music programmer and radio broadcaster with ABC in Chicago and several stations in the Denver–Boulder market. He is a regular speaker at conventions of public-sector attorneys and professional land use planners.

Kevin Francis O'Neill is an associate professor at Cleveland-Marshall College of Law, where he teaches courses on First Amendment rights, civil procedure, and evidence. O'Neill joined the full-time faculty in August 1996 after a year-long stint as a visiting professor. His scholarship focuses on the Speech Clause of the First Amendment, with particular emphasis on public protest and forum free access issues. He is the co-author (with Howard E. Katz) of *Strategies and Techniques of Law School Teaching* (Aspen 2009). Prior to entering academia, O'Neill served four years (1991 to 1995) as the legal director for the American Civil Liberties Union (ACLU) of Ohio. He was responsible for supervising all ACLU litigation in the State of Ohio, trying selected cases himself, lecturing on constitutional issues at conferences and seminars, and explaining law and ACLU policy to the news media. During his tenure at the ACLU, O'Neill focused special attention on First Amendment issues, reproductive freedom, police misconduct, and government mistreatment of the homeless. He continues to serve as an ACLU volunteer attorney on First Amendment cases. Acting in that capacity, he negotiated a settlement in September 2001 that restored to Ohio death row inmates the traditional privilege to deliver a last dying speech. Prior to joining the ACLU in May 1991, O'Neill was a trial lawyer at the national law firms of Smith & Schnacke (now Thompson, Hine & Flory) and Arter & Hadden (now Tucker, Ellis & West). During his seven years in commercial litigation, O'Neill represented clients in a broad range of locales— from California to Saudi Arabia. His work has spanned all phases of trial and appellate practice, including cases decided by the Ohio and U.S. Supreme Courts. O'Neill obtained a Bachelor of Arts degree from San Francisco State University in 1977. In the years following his graduation, he worked on the editorial staff of the *Los Angeles Herald-Examiner*, where he wrote a column on consumer affairs. He returned to Cleveland, his hometown, in 1981 to attend law school at Case Western Reserve University, obtaining his law degree in 1984.

Robert Allen Sedler is a distinguished professor at Wayne State University Law School, where he teaches courses on constitutional law and conflict of laws. Sedler earned his A.B. degree from the University of Pittsburgh in 1956 and his law degree from the same university in 1959. He is a member of Phi Beta Kappa and Order of the Coif. In 2005, he was elected to the Wayne State University Academy of Scholars, which is the highest recognition that may be bestowed upon faculty members by their colleagues. He served as president of the academy during the 2007–2008 academic year. Sedler has published extensively in both of his fields, and there have been many citations to his works by courts and academic commentators. In 1994, he published a book on American constitutional law for the *International Encyclopedia of Laws*. The book was updated and republished in 2000, 2005, and 2012. It was updated and republished in 2014 with the title *Constitutional Law in the United States*. Sedler has litigated a large number of civil rights and civil liberties cases in Michigan, Kentucky, and elsewhere, mostly as a volunteer lawyer for the American Civil Liberties Union (ACLU). Cases he has litigated in Michigan include the Dearborn Parks case, the racial discrimination in adoption and foster care case, and a challenge to the suspicionless drug testing of welfare recipients. He served as a member of the Social Action Commission of the Union for Reform Judaism from 2003 to 2009 and is a member of its Amicus Brief Committee. Sedler was named a Gershenson Distinguished Faculty Fellow at Wayne State for 1985–1987 and received the Donald H. Gordon Award for Excellence in Teaching in 1988. From 2000 to 2005, he held the Gibbs Chair in

Civil Rights and Civil Liberties. He also has received awards from the NAACP Kentucky Conference in 1975, ACLU of Kentucky in 1976, NAACP Metropolitan Detroit Branch in 1986, Southwestern Michigan ACLU in 1988, Metropolitan Detroit ACLU in 1994, Oakland County ACLU in 2002 (together with Rozanne Sedler), and Metropolitan Detroit Chapter of the American Jewish Committee in 2012 (together with Rozanne Sedler). He was the chairperson of the Michigan State Bar Constitutional Law Committee from 1981 to 1987 and of the Legal Education Committee from 1988 to 1994. In 2012, he was awarded the State Bar of Michigan John W. Reed Michigan Lawyer Legacy Award, which is presented periodically to an educator from a Michigan law school whose influence on lawyers has elevated the quality of legal practice in the state.

Evan J. Seeman is a member of the Real Estate + Development Group at the law firm of Robinson & Cole LLP in Hartford, Connecticut, where he practices land use, real estate, and municipal law. Seeman advises clients on how to meet requirements for land development, real property disputes, and other administrative and real estate issues that arise in land use and environmental matters. He represents developers, landowners, municipalities, corporations, and advocacy groups in administrative proceedings before municipal and state agencies, as well as in litigation in the state and federal courts. Seeman helps municipalities avoid religious land use conflicts under the Religious Land Use and Institutionalized Persons Act (RLUIPA) and the U.S. Constitution, and he defends municipalities when litigation ensues. He is a contributing editor to RLUIPA Defense (www.rluipa-defense .com), and he frequently writes and speaks on RLUIPA. Seeman also handles cases involving eminent domain, inverse condemnation, fair housing, equal protection, zoning appeals, wetlands regulation, littoral and riparian water rights, coastal management, easements, restrictive covenants, and property rights. He is the chair-elect of the American Planning Association's Planning and Law Division, and he previously served as the division's secretary and treasurer. He previously served as the chair of the Planning and Zoning and Municipal Law Sections of the Connecticut Bar Association's Young Lawyers Section.

Nancy E. Stroud practices land use law of counsel to the firm of Lewis, Stroud & Deutsch in Boca Raton, Florida. Her extensive experience in the field includes representation of local government as well as private clients. She is certified by the American Institute of Certified Planners and an active member of the national, state, and local planning associations. She regularly lectures and publishes on land use topics for professional and lay organizations. Among her publications, she is co-author of the LexisNexis land use treatise *Planning and Control of Land*

Development: Cases and Materials (9th ed.), one of the leading land use textbooks for law students. She holds a J.D. and Master of Regional Planning from the University of North Carolina at Chapel Hill and a Bachelor of Science cum laude in sociology (certificate in urban studies) from the Indiana University, Bloomington.

Alan C. Weinstein holds a joint faculty appointment at the rank of professor with Tenure in the Cleveland-Marshall College of Law and the Maxine Goodman Levin College of Urban Affairs at Cleveland State University in Cleveland, Ohio, and also serves as director of the colleges' J.D./M.P.A. and J.D./M.U.P.D. Dual Degree Programs and Law and Public Policy Program. He is a nationally recognized expert on planning law who frequently lectures at planning and law conferences and has published over eighty books, treatise revisions, and law journal articles. He is a past chair of the Planning and Law Division of the American Planning Association (APA), was one of the twenty-eight planning law experts who served as reporters for the APA's monthly journal *Planning and Environmental Law*, and served from 1982 to 2000 as chair of the Sub-Committee on Land Use and the First Amendment in the American Bar Association's Section of State and Local Government Law. Weinstein has also counseled/represented clients or served as an expert on a broad range of First Amendment issues. Weinstein holds a B.A. in international relations from the University of Pennsylvania, a J.D. from the University of California–Berkeley, and a Master of City Planning from the Massachusetts Institute of Technology.

The First Amendment and Land Use
An Overview

Robert Allen Sedler
Distinguished Professor of Law
Wayne State University
Detroit, Michigan

I. Introduction

The First Amendment changes everything. The Supreme Court has interpreted the First Amendment's guarantee of freedom of expression very expansively, and the constitutional protection for freedom of expression is perhaps the strongest protection afforded to any individual right under the Constitution. It is also fair to say that the constitutional protection for freedom of expression in the United States is seemingly unparalleled in the constitutional systems of other democratic nations and that in the United States, as a constitutional matter, the value of freedom of expression generally prevails over other democratic values.[1]

What this means in practice is that laws or governmental actions that clearly would be upheld under other constitutional provisions are more likely to be invalidated when they also implicate the interest in freedom of expression. For the litigating lawyer challenging the constitutionality

---

[1] *See generally* Robert A. Sedler, *Essay on Freedom of Speech: The United States Versus the Rest of the World*, 2006 MICH. ST. L. REV. 377 (2006).

of a law or governmental action, it is almost always preferable to assert that challenge on First Amendment grounds, and for the defending lawyer, the defense against such a challenge is usually the most difficult one to make.

So it is with respect to First Amendment challenges to land use regulation. The customary judicial deference to legislative judgment that appears in due process and equal protection challenges to land use regulation is completely absent when the regulation affects the use of the land for expressive purposes. Thus, aesthetic considerations that are relied upon to sustain the constitutionality of regulations relating to the appearance of residential property are not sufficient to justify bans on lawn signs containing political or even commercial messages.[2] Bans on billboards, which can generally be justified as advancing legitimate traffic safety and aesthetic concerns, run into First Amendment problems when they make exceptions that allow billboards to convey some messages but not others.[3] A city's seemingly reasonable decision to avoid a proliferation of newsracks on the public streets by excluding newsracks that contain only advertising and promotional materials has been held to violate the First Amendment.[4] And even the government's efforts to prohibit or regulate the operation of the commercial sex industry are constrained by the First Amendment when those efforts reach sexual expression in "adult bookstores" and nude dancing establishments.[5]

---

[2] *See, e.g.,* City of Ladue v. Gilleo, 512 U.S. 43, 53 (1994); Linmark Assocs., Inc. v. Willingboro Twp., 431 U.S. 85, 93 (1977); Cleveland Area Bd. of Realtors v. City of Euclid, 88 F.3d 382, 388 (6th Cir. 1996); Arlington Cnty. Republican Comm. v. Arlington Cnty., 983 F.2d 587, 594 (4th Cir. 1993).

[3] *See* Metromedia, Inc. v. City of San Diego, 453 U.S. 490, 513 (1981).

[4] *See* City of Cincinnati v. Discovery Network, Inc., 507 U.S. 410, 430–31 (1993).

[5] As we will see, however, what the First Amendment protects is only the message of sexuality conveyed by sexually oriented entertainment. The government may extensively regulate the location and operation of adult entertainment establishments to deal with the undesirable secondary effects associated with the operation of adult entertainment establishments. But precisely because sexually oriented entertainment is protected by the First Amendment, locational restrictions must allow for ample alternative avenues where sexually oriented entertainment can take place, *see, e.g.,* City of Renton v. Playtime Theatres, Inc., 475 U.S. 41, 52 (1986); Schad v. Borough of Mt. Ephraim, 452 U.S. 61, 71–72 (1981); Young v. Am. Mini Theatres, Inc., 427 U.S. 50, 71 fn. 34 (1976), and regulations on the presentation of sexually oriented entertainment cannot prevent the entertainer from conveying the message of sexuality. *See, e.g.,* City of Erie v. Pap's A.M., 529 U.S. 277, 292–93 (2000).

The First Amendment does indeed change everything when land use regulation extends to expressive activity taking place on the land. The regulation then becomes subject to constitutional challenge under what I refer to as the "law of the First Amendment."[6]

II. The "Law of the First Amendment"

The "law of the First Amendment" consists in large part of concepts, principles, specific doctrines, and precedents that the Supreme Court has developed over the years in the process of deciding First Amendment cases. In practice, the constitutional protection of freedom of expression is very much a matter of identification and application. In many cases, once the appropriate concept, principle, specific doctrine, or precedent has been identified and applied, the parameters for the resolution of the First Amendment issue have been established, and the result is often fairly clear.

A. The Chilling Effect Concept and the "Overbreadth" Doctrine

The concepts, principles, specific doctrines, and precedents of the "law of the First Amendment" often interact with each other. The chilling effect concept, which is the most fundamental and pervasive concept in the "law of the First Amendment," has been the basis for a number of principles and specific doctrines of the "law of the First Amendment." It has been the basis for the overbreadth or void-on-its-face doctrine. In order to prevent a chilling effect on expression resulting from the existence and threatened enforcement of overbroad or vague laws regulating or applicable to acts or expression, such laws may be challenged on their face for substantial overbreadth or vagueness without regard to whether the activity of the party challenging the law is itself constitutionally protected. The "overbreadth" doctrine is very important in practice, not only because it permits a First

---

[6] *See generally* Robert A. Sedler, *The First Amendment in Litigation: The "Law of the First Amendment,"* 48 WASH. & LEE L. REV. 457 (1991); Robert A. Sedler, *The "Law of the First Amendment" Revisited,* 58 WAYNE L. REV. 1003 (2013).

Amendment challenge by a party whose own activity is not constitutionally protected but also because the constitutional analysis does not go beyond the terms of the law itself. To illustrate, whereas the state can prohibit completely nude dancing in adult entertainment establishments, it cannot prohibit complete nudity in other entertainment venues, such as in plays being performed in legitimate theaters.[7] This being so, a law prohibiting any person from appearing in a state of nudity in any place where the general public is invited by its terms would reach nudity in live theatrical performances with serious literary, artistic, or political value. Thus, the law is void on its face for overbreadth. It can be successfully challenged by the operator of an adult entertainment establishment featuring completely nude dancing notwithstanding that the state can constitutionally prohibit completely nude dancing in such establishments.[8] It should be noted, however, that an overbreadth challenge is not available to challenge laws regulating commercial speech, such as advertising.[9] The constitutionality of these laws is determined under the commercial speech doctrine, and a party engaged in commercial speech cannot assert an overbreadth challenge to a law on the ground that it also reaches constitutionally protected noncommercial speech.[10]

B. The Narrow-Specificity Principle

The narrow-specificity principle also derives from the chilling effect concept. As the Supreme Court has stated, "[b]ecause First Amendment freedoms need breathing space to survive, government may regulate in the area only with narrow specificity."[11] Thus, any regulation of expression is always subject to challenge on the ground that it sweeps more broadly than is necessary to advance the legitimate governmental interests at stake.

Under the narrow-specificity principle, absolute prohibitions on expressive activity will frequently be found unconstitutional because the

---

[7] See City of Erie, 529 U.S. at 293–94.
[8] See generally Triplett Grille, Inc. v. City of Akron, 40 F.3d 129 (6th Cir. 1994).
[9] See Bd. of Trustees of State Univ. of N.Y. v. Fox, 492 U.S. 469, 481 (1989).
[10] See id. at 481–82.
[11] NAACP v. Button, 371 U.S. 415, 433 (1963).

asserted governmental interest could be advanced by less drastic means than an absolute prohibition. Applying the narrow-specificity principle, the Supreme Court has held unconstitutional a prohibition of all live entertainment in a city's small commercial zones.[12] It has also held unconstitutional an absolute ban on door-to-door canvassing and solicitation in residential neighborhoods[13] and a municipal law that required individuals to obtain a permit prior to engaging in door-to-door advocacy and to display the permit on demand.[14] In this situation, the government can protect householder privacy by limiting unannounced visitation or solicitation to reasonable times and by enforcing the householder's posting of a "no visitation" or "no solicitation" sign.[15] The narrow-specificity principle is the basis of that component of the commercial speech doctrine that requires that the regulation may not be more extensive than is necessary to advance the governmental interest at stake.[16]

C. The Content Neutrality Principle

Perhaps the most important First Amendment principle in terms of its applicability in actual litigation is the principle of content neutrality. Under this principle, the government may not proscribe any expression because of its content, and an otherwise valid regulation will violate the First Amendment if it discriminates between different types of expression

---

[12] *See, e.g.*, Schad v. Borough v. Mt. Ephraim, 452 U.S. 61, 76–77 (1981).

[13] *See, e.g.*, Martin v. City of Struthers, 319 U.S. 141, 147–49 (1943).

[14] *See, e.g.*, Watchtower Bible & Tract Soc'y of N.Y. v. Vill. of Stratton, 536 U.S. 150, 168 (2002).

[15] This being so, any regulation of door-to-door canvassing and solicitation can be challenged as unreasonably restricting the times available for canvassing and solicitation. *See generally* Wisc. Action Coal. v. City of Kenosha, 767 F.2d 1248 (7th Cir. 1985). The law in *Wisconsin Action Coalition* limited solicitation to the hours between 8:00 A.M. and 8:00 P.M. The court held that it was not reasonable for the city to prohibit solicitation before 9:00 P.M. *See id.* at 1258. A number of cases have held that it is not reasonable to limit solicitation to the daylight hours. *See generally* Ass'n of Cmty. Orgs. for Reform Now v. City of Frontenac, 714 F.2d 813 (8th Cir. 1983); N.J. Citizen Action v. Twp. of Edison, 797 F.2d 1250 (3d Cir. 1986).

[16] While the Court had upheld a ban on door-to-door commercial solicitation before promulgating the commercial speech doctrine, now that commercial speech is clearly within the protection of the First Amendment, an absolute ban on commercial door-to-door solicitation would likely be invalidated under this component of the commercial speech doctrine. *See, e.g.*, Project 80's Inc. v. City of Pocatello, 942 F.2d 635, 638 (9th Cir. 1991).

based on their content. Analytically, there are two aspects to the principle of content neutrality, viewpoint neutrality and category neutrality.

Under the viewpoint neutrality aspect of the principle, to which the Supreme Court has recognized no exceptions, the government cannot regulate expression in such a way as to favor one viewpoint over another viewpoint. That being so, the First Amendment renders unconstitutional a law prohibiting the display of any sign in front of a foreign embassy that "tends to bring the foreign government into public odium or disrepute."[17] The law violated the viewpoint neutrality component of the content neutrality principle because it prohibited displays that were critical of the foreign government and not displays that were favorable to it.[18] The viewpoint neutrality component of the content neutrality principle was also the basis of the Court's invalidation of state and federal laws prohibiting the burning of the American flag because the laws authorized burning as a proper means of disposing of a torn or soiled flag and so were directed toward the content of the message conveyed by the burning.[19]

Under the category neutrality aspect of the principle, the government generally cannot regulate in such a way as to discriminate between different categories of expression. Applying the category neutrality aspect of the principle, the Court has held unconstitutional a law prohibiting drive-in movie theaters from showing films containing nudity when the screen was visible from the highway because the law singled out one kind of film for differential treatment based on its content.[20] The Court has also held unconstitutional a billboard ban that exempted from its coverage billboards containing some kinds of noncommercial messages but not others,[21] as well as a law prohibiting picketing in front of a school while school is in session but making an exception for picketing in connection with a labor dispute.[22]

---

[17] Boos v. Barry, 485 U.S. 312, 315 (1988).

[18] *See id.* at 319.

[19] *See* Texas v. Johnson, 491 U.S. 397, 418 (1989); United States v. Eichman, 496 U.S. 310, 312, 315–16 (1990).

[20] *See* Erznoznik v. City of Jacksonville, 422 U.S. 205, 211–12 (1975).

[21] *See* Metromedia, Inc. v. City of San Diego, 453 U.S. 490, 514–15 (1981).

[22] *See* Police Dep't v. Mosley, 408 U.S. 92, 99 (1972).

The Court has recognized two exceptions to the principle of category neutrality, both of which are applicable to land use regulation. First, in order to deal with the undesirable secondary consequences resulting from the concentration of adult entertainment establishments in a particular area, the government can enact zoning regulations specifically applicable to such establishments.[23] Typically, these regulations require that such establishments be located at some distance from each other and at some distance from residential areas. These regulations are constitutional as long as they provide ample alternative avenues of communication by allocating sufficient land in the community where adult entertainment establishments can locate.[24] Similarly, the Court has held that the government can adopt regulations specifically applicable to nude dancing in adult entertainment establishments, such as a requirement that female dancers wear "pasties" and "G-strings" in order to deal with the undesirable secondary effects purportedly associated with completely nude dancing in these establishments.[25]

Second, because commercial speech receives less constitutional protection than noncommercial speech, the Court has held that a billboard ban exempting some kinds of commercial billboards from its coverage does not violate the First Amendment. However, the ban was found to be unconstitutional insofar as it included some noncommercial billboards within its coverage because, under the First Amendment, the state cannot give more protection to commercial speech than it gives to noncommercial speech.[26]

The Court has recently applied the content neutrality principle to hold unconstitutional a sign regulation that regulated the size of signs with reference to the subject matter of the signs, with some signs permitted to

---

[23] *See* City of Renton v. Playtime Theatres, Inc., 475 U.S. 41, 49 (1986).
[24] *See id.* at 53–54 (1986); Young v. Am. Mini Theatres, Inc., 427 U.S. 50, 62-63 (1976).
[25] *See* City of Erie v. Pap's A.M., 529 U.S. 277, 294 (2000).
[26] *See* Metromedia, 453 U.S. at 513; In *City of Ladue v. Gilleo*, 512 U.S. 43 (1994), the Court held unconstitutional a municipal ordinance that prohibited signs in residential areas, including political signs, while making exceptions for "for sale" signs.

be higher and other signs required to be lower depending on the subject matter of the signs.[27]

D. The Prior Restraint Doctrine

The prior restraint doctrine applies to any effort by the government to enjoin or otherwise impose an advance prohibition on expression. Because a prior restraint directly interferes with the ability of the public to receive the information, it has a freezing effect on expression. It is presumptively unconstitutional and imposes on the government a very heavy burden of justification. The Supreme Court has held unconstitutional as an impermissible prior restraint a state public nuisance law authorizing an injunction against the "habitual use of premises for the commercial exhibition of obscene motion pictures."[28] The operator of the premises would run the risk of violating the injunction if a court should subsequently find that particular materials sold there were in fact obscene and therefore would be chilled from selling materials on the borderline between permissible pornography and impermissible obscenity.[29] Any injunction against the dissemination or sale of obscenity must be limited to works that have previously been found to be obscene by a judicial determination in an adversary proceeding.[30] On the other hand, as the previous discussion indicates, the prior restraint doctrine only applies to the issuance of an injunction against the dissemination of constitutionally protected expression. An enterprise engaged in the "business of expression" is still subject to generally applicable laws, and if premises are used for illegal purposes,

---

[27] *See* Reed v. Town of Gilbert, 135 S. Ct. 2218, 2228 (2015). Under the ordinance, "ideological signs" could be up to twenty square feet and were not subject to any placement or sign restrictions; "political signs" could be up to thirty-two square feet but could only be displayed during an election season; "temporary directional signs" were limited to no more than four signs of six square feet that could be displayed no more than twelve hours before the "qualifying event" and one hour after. *Id.* at 2224–25.

[28] *See* Vance v. Universal Amusement Co., Inc., 445 U.S. 308, 321 (1980) (White, J., dissenting).

[29] *See* Bantam Books, Inc. v. Sullivan, 372 U.S. 58, 69–70 (1963) (invalidating as an informal prior restraint a state's use of a governmental commission that would identify objectionable books, notify the bookstore of the commission's duty to recommend obscenity prosecutions to the attorney general, and distribute the commission's list of objectionable books to the local police departments, which usually visited the bookstore to determine if the store had stopped selling the objectionable books).

[30] *See* Kingsley Books, Inc. v. Brown, 354 U.S. 436, 445 (1957)

such as prostitution or other prohibited sexual activity, the premises can be shut down as a public nuisance in accordance with state law.[31]

Analytically, any system of governmental licensing of expression, such as one requiring a license to operate an "adult use" or to provide entertainment in a liquor-licensed establishment, involves a prior restraint. The Court has dealt with governmental licensing of expression by imposing very specific requirements for such licensing. The licensing law must be content neutral and must contain narrow, objective, and definite standards that control the discretion of the licensing official. If the law fails to contain such standards, it is void on its face for overbreadth, and a party subject to the law is not required to apply for a license as a condition for challenging its constitutionality.[32]

In addition, the First Amendment imposes procedural requirements on the operation of licensing systems to prevent any delay or chilling of expression. The official decision to grant, suspend, or revoke the license must be made within a specified and reasonable period of time, and there must be the possibility of expeditious judicial review in the event that the license is erroneously denied.[33] The First Amendment requirements for

---

[31] *See* Arcara v. Cloud Books, Inc., 478 U.S. 697, 707 (1986); *see also* Michigan ex rel. Wayne Cnty. Prosecuting Attorney v. Dizzy Duck, 535 N.W.2d 178 (1995). In the remand of *Arcara*, the New York Court of Appeals held that the closure order violated the freedom of expression guarantee of the state constitution. *See* People ex rel. Acara v. Cloud Books, Inc., 503 N.E.2d 492 (N.Y. 1986).

[32] For illustrative cases invalidating licensing and permit laws due to a lack of constitutionally adequate standards, *see* City of Lakewood v. Plain Dealer Publ'g Co., 486 U.S. 750 (1988); Hynes v. Mayor and Council of Borough of Oradell, 425 U.S. 610 (1976); Shuttlesworth v. City of Birmingham, 394 U.S. 147 (1969); Staub v. City of Baxley, 355 U.S. 313 (1958); Lowell v. City of Griffin, 303 U.S. 444 (1938). The government may not impose unconstitutional conditions on the granting of a license for expression, such as a requirement that a liquor-licensed establishment applying for an entertainment license agree not to perform topless dancing. *See generally* G & V Lounge v. Mich. Liquor Control Comm'n.

[33] *See* City of Littleton v. Z.J. Gifts D-4, L.L.C., 541 U.S. 774, 781 (2004); FW/PBS, Inc. v. City of Dallas, 493 U.S. 215, 227–28 (1990); Freedman v. Maryland, 380 U.S. 51, 58–59 (1965). In *City of Littleton* the Court held that the state's ordinary judicial review procedures would suffice to assure prompt judicial access and a prompt judicial decision provided that the state courts remained sensitive to the need to prevent First Amendment harms. The Court upheld the facial validity of an adult entertainment licensing law that included an appeal as of right to a state court pursuant to the state's civil procedure rules. In *Thomas v. Chicago Park District*, 534 U.S. 316 (2002), the Court held that the *Freedman* procedures did not apply to a content neutral licensing requirement for assemblies involving more than 50 persons in a public park even when the ordinance grants city officials 14 days to decide whether a permit should be issued.

a permissible system of licensing apply fully to licensing requirements for access to governmental property for purposes of expression, such as a parade permit law,[34] a permit for placing newsracks on governmental property,[35] and a permit for the leasing of a municipal theater for a theatrical presentation.[36]

E. The Commercial Speech Doctrine

The constitutionality of governmental regulation of commercial speech, such as product advertising, is determined under the commercial speech doctrine. The application of the commercial speech doctrine requires a four-part analysis. First, the commercial speech must concern lawful activity and must not be misleading. Assuming that the commercial speech in question meets this requirement, three factors must be evaluated to determine the constitutionality of the particular regulation of commercial speech: (1) the governmental interest asserted to justify the regulation must be substantial, (2) the regulation must directly advance the asserted governmental interest, and (3) the regulation may not be more extensive than is necessary to serve that interest.[37]

Applying the commercial speech doctrine, the Supreme Court has held that a city could not ban the placement of "for sale" signs on the lawns of private homes, despite the city's claim that such a practice was necessary to prevent "panic selling" in racially mixed neighborhoods.[38] At the same time, emphasizing that commercial speech receives less First Amendment protection than noncommercial speech, the Court found that a ban on commercial billboards directly advanced governmental interests in aesthetics and traffic safety.[39]

---

[34] *See generally* Shuttlesworth v. City of Birmingham, 394 U.S. 147 (1969).

[35] *See* City of Lakewood v. Plain Dealer Publ'g Co., 486 U.S. 760 (1988).

[36] *See generally* Se. Promotions, Ltd. v. Conrad, 420 U.S. 546 (1975).

[37] *See* Cent. Hudson Gas & Elec. Co. v. Pub. Serv. Comm'n, 447 U.S. 557, 566 (1980).

[38] *See* Linmark Assocs., Inc. v. Willingboro Twp., 431 U.S. 85, 93–94 (1977).

[39] *See* Metromedia, Inc. v. City of San Diego, 453 U.S. 490, 507–08 (1981). As pointed out previously, in this case, the Court made an exception to the category neutrality aspect of the content neutrality principle and held that the exemption of some kinds of commercial speech from the billboard ban did not violate the First Amendment. *See supra* note 21 and accompanying text.

In a very important commercial speech case, the Court invalidated a state law regulating the location of billboards advertising tobacco products and point-of-sale restrictions on the placement of signs for tobacco products.[40] The law prohibited any outdoor advertising of tobacco products that was directed toward or visible in any location within a one thousand-foot radius of any public playground, playground area in a public park, elementary school, or secondary school and required that retail stores selling tobacco products located within one thousand feet of such playgrounds, playground areas, or schools must place point-of-sale advertising at least five feet above the floor.[41] The Court found that the location regulation violated the tailoring component of the commercial speech doctrine because it would prevent the placing of any billboards advertising tobacco in some cities.[42] It also found that the point-of-sale restrictions would not prevent children from seeing the signs, so the restrictions failed the doctrine's components of direct advancement of a substantial government interest and were more extensive than necessary.

F. The Public Forum and Reasonable Time, Place, and Manner Doctrines

The First Amendment applies to governmentally owned property when the government denies or regulates access to governmental property that is sought for purposes of expression. The constitutionality of governmental action in this context is determined by the public forum doctrine and the cognate reasonable time, place, and manner doctrine. Access to governmentally owned property, such as public streets, for purposes of expression may also affect the activity taking place on privately owned property adjacent to the streets.

If the governmentally owned property in question constitutes a public forum, there must be universal access to that property for purposes

---

[40] *See* Lorillard Tobacco Co. v. Reilly, 533 U.S. 525 (2001).
[41] *Id.* at 534–36.
[42] *Id.* at 561–62.

of expression by all persons and groups, subject only to reasonable time, place, and manner regulations.[43] Public streets and parks are traditional public forums that must be open to the public for purposes of expression.[44] Any other governmentally owned property constitutes a public forum only if the government has designated it as such, either generally or for limited purposes.[45] Whenever governmental property has been designated as a public forum, access to that property is governed by the reasonable time, place, and manner doctrine in the same manner as access to a traditional public forum.

In order for a regulation to be sustained as a reasonable time, place, and manner limitation, it must (1) be content neutral,[46] (2) serve a significant governmental interest, and (3) leave open ample alternative avenues of communication.[47] In practice, the Supreme Court has more

---

[43] *See* Perry Educ. Ass'n v. Perry Local Educ. Ass'n, 460 U.S. 37, 45 (1983).

[44] *See* Hague v. Comm. for Indus. Org., 307 U.S. 496, 515 (1939).

[45] Examples of a limited public forum are the facilities of a state university available for use by student groups, *see* Widmar v. Vincent, 454 U.S. 263 (1981), and school board meetings open to the public, *see* Madison Sch. Dist. v. Wisc. Emp't Relations Comm'n, 429 U.S. 167 (1976).

[46] Any distinction between different groups or persons seeking access to a public forum, such as denying access to groups engaging in religious expression, violates the principle of content neutrality and is unconstitutional. *See, e.g.*, Lamb's Chapel v. Ctr. Moriches Union Free Sch. Dist., 508 U.S. 384 (1993) (finding that where a school district permitted after-hours use of school facilities for "social, civic and recreational purposes" by private organizations, it could not prohibit such use of school facilities by a private organization seeking to show a religious film); Capitol Square Review Advisory Bd. v. Pinette, 515 U.S. 753 (1995) (holding that where the plaza in front of state capitol had been dedicated as a public forum, the city could not deny access to the Ku Klux Klan seeking to display a Christian cross during the Christmas season). The difference between a content neutral and content based regulation is illustrated by comparing the two regulations relating to picketing in front of a foreign embassy that were involved in *Boos v. Barry*, 485 U.S. 312 (1988). The content neutral one prohibited the congregation of persons within five hundred feet of a foreign embassy "when the police reasonably believe that such congregation poses a threat to the security or peace of the embassy" and was upheld as a reasonable time, place, and manner regulation. The content based one prohibited the display of any sign in front of a foreign embassy that "tends to bring the foreign government into public odium," thereby prohibiting only displays that were critical of the foreign government and not displays that were favorable to it, and so it was found unconstitutional. *See* note 16, *supra*, and accompanying text.

[47] *See* Heffron v. Int'l Soc'y for Krishna Consciousness, 452 U.S. 640, 648–55 (1981).

often than not upheld content neutral regulations as being reasonable time, place, and manner limitations,[48] although some content neutral regulations have been found to be unreasonable.[49]

---

[48] See *Krishna Consciousness*, 452 U.S. at 648–55 (upholding a regulation requiring that the sale or distribution of merchandise, including written materials, at a state fair take place only from a booth on the fairgrounds, which could be rented by any person on a first-come, first-serve basis, with the rental charge based on the size or location of the booth); Ward v. Rock against Racism, 491 U.S. 781, 791–92 (1989) (validating a municipal regulation requiring that musical performance in a public park bandshell make use of the sound system and a sound technician provided by the city); Frisby v. Schultz, 487 U.S. 474 (1988) (finding constitutional a ban on "focused picketing" in front of the home of a doctor who performed abortions that did not otherwise prevent picketing in the neighborhood or walking a route in front of an entire block of houses); Clark v. Cmty. for Creative Non Violence, 468 U.S. 288, 294–95 (1984) (validating a National Park Service rule prohibiting overnight sleeping in a small public park near the White House as applied to prohibit "tenting" in connection with a demonstration intended to call attention to the plight of the homeless); Grayned v. City of Rockford, 408 U.S. 104 (1972) (validating a prohibition of "any noise or diversion on school grounds while school is in session that tends to disturb the peace or good order of such school session," as applied to a public sidewalk adjacent to the school).

There is no First Amendment requirement that the government permit expression in the form of demonstrations or parades to take place in a public forum, such as the public streets or parks. *See, e.g.,* Thomas v. Chicago Park Dist., 534 U.S. 316, 318–23 (2002). However, if the government chooses to permit concerted expression to take place in a public forum, as, for example, by opening up the public streets for parades, the First Amendment comes into play and imposes significant limits on how the government can regulate access to a public forum. *See, e.g.,* Gregory v. City of Chicago, 394 U.S. 111, 113 (1969) (overturning disorderly conduct convictions of peaceful protestors who refused to curtail a lawful demonstration when onlookers became disorderly). The most significant limit, of course, is the principle of content neutrality, which prohibits any distinctions between groups seeking access to the public forum and requires that any licensing law contain narrow, objective, and definite standards controlling the discretion of the licensing officials. *See* the discussion, *supra,* notes 17–27, and accompanying text.

[49] See United States v. Grace, 461 U.S. 171, 183–84 (1983) (rejecting absolute ban on all displays and leafletting on a sidewalk in front of the Supreme Court building), *but see* Cox v. Louisiana, 379 U.S. 559, 555 (1965) (upholding a ban on picketing "on or near a courthouse with the intent of interfering with, obstructing or impeding the administration of justice") *and* Madsen v. Women's Health Ctr., Inc., 512 U.S. 753, 776 (1994) (analyzing injunction creating three-hundred-foot buffer zone around the homes of those who worked in an abortion clinic).

In *Schneider v. Irvington*, 308 U.S. 147 (1939), the Court held that a city's interest in preventing littering was not of sufficient importance to justify a ban on distributing political leaflets in the public streets. This case was relied on in *Krantz v. City of Fort Smith*, 160 F.3d 1214 (8th Cir. 1998), to invalidate a law prohibiting people from placing handbills or advertisements on the windshield wipers of unattended vehicles parked on the public streets. In *Valentine v. Chrestensen*, 316 U.S. 52 (1942), the Court upheld the constitutionality of a leafletting ban as applied to commercial advertisements, on the assumption that commercial speech was not protected by the First Amendment. Today, the constitutionality of such a restriction would have to be evaluated under the commercial speech doctrine, and the question would be whether this was a reasonable time, place, and manner limitation of commercial speech. *See* note 14, *supra.*

Most governmentally owned property is not a public forum, and the constitutionality of restrictions on access to such property is evaluated under a general reasonableness test. The test recognizes the government's entitlement to reserve the property for its intended uses, communicative or otherwise, but at the same time prevents the government from declaring the property completely "off limits" for expression. The government may impose category-type restrictions relating to the purpose for which the property is being used, such as by excluding partisan political activity and protest activity from military bases.[50] It may not impose category-type restrictions that are unrelated to the purpose for which the property is being used, such as by prohibiting picketing in front of a school building while school was in session but permitting peaceful picketing of a school in connection with a labor dispute.[51]

The government may also prohibit expressive activity that is basically incompatible with the normal activity of a particular place at a particular time. Thus, the government could prohibit making a speech in the reading room of a public library, but it could not prohibit a silent vigil where persons sat on the floor of a reading room to protest the library's policies.[52] The government may prohibit the posting of signs on government owned property, such as utility poles and lampposts, in order to prevent "visual

---

[50] *See generally* Greer v. Spock, 424 U.S. 828 (1976); United States v. Albertini, 472 U.S. 675 (1985). The reasonableness of this category-type restriction relates to the fact that the United States has had a long tradition of a politically neutral military establishment. This being so, the military could properly exclude partisan political activity from the base, although it allowed other activity, such as charitable solicitation, to take place there. It may be noted that the government must maintain strict viewpoint neutrality in regard to access to the nonpublic forum. If, for example, the military allowed the president to speak on a military base during a political campaign, it could not refuse to allow a speech on the base by a candidate of the opposite political party.

[51] *See* Police Dep't v. Mosley, 408 U.S. 92, 95 (1972).

[52] *See* Brown v. Louisiana, 383 U.S. 131 (1965), where the Court held that the government could not prohibit a silent "sit-in" at a public library to protest its policy of racial segregation. *Id.* at 141–42. In *United States v. Am. Library Ass'n Inc.*, 539 U.S. 194, 205–206 (2003), the Court specifically held that a public library was not a designated public forum. In that case the Court also upheld on its face a provision of the Children's Internet Protection Act (CIPA), 20 U.S.C. § 9134(f)(1), requiring public libraries receiving federal assistance to install software filters to block obscene or child pornographic images and to "prevent minors from obtaining access to material that is harmful to them." The law permitted disabling the filters for "other lawful purposes," and the filtered programs at issue permitted disabling during use by an adult.

clutter,"[53] and the U.S. Postal Service, which owns the mailboxes on a homeowner's property, may prohibit the deposit of unstamped materials in the mailboxes.[54]

As a practical matter, where the nonpublic forum is physically open, such as an airport terminal, the Court's application of the general reasonableness test does not appear to differ significantly from its application of the reasonable time, place, and manner doctrine to the public forum. Thus, although the Court has held that an airport terminal concourse is not a public forum, it has held unconstitutional an absolute ban against "all First Amendment activity" at the terminal.[55] It has also held unconstitutional a ban on the distribution of literature in a terminal but has upheld a ban on the solicitation and receipt of funds in a terminal.[56]

In a series of cases, the Court has dealt with the constitutionality of limitations on anti-abortion protests on the public streets in front of abortion clinics. These limitations are designed to protect the privacy of women seeking abortions, but at the same time, they interfere with the ability of anti-abortion protestors not only to express their opposition to abortion but also to try to dissuade women entering the clinics from having an abortion. The Court's application of the reasonable time, place, and manner doctrine in this context has represented an effort to balance the First Amendment rights of protestors with the privacy rights of the woman seeking to obtain an abortion. The Court has held unconstitutional the issuance of injunctions prohibiting anti-abortion protestors from attempting to counsel women entering abortion clinics who indicated that they did not wish to be counseled, making uninvited approaches, and displaying observable images of aborted fetuses.[57] On the other hand, the Court has upheld as a reasonable time, place, and manner regulation an injunction

---

[53] *See* Members of City Council v. Taxpayers for Vincent, 466 U.S. 789, 817 (1984).

[54] *See* U.S. Postal Serv. v. Council of Greenburgh Civic Ass'n, 453 U.S. 114, 132–33 (1981).

[55] *See* Bd. of Airport Comm'rs v. Jews for Jesus, 482 U.S. 569, 575 (1987).

[56] *See* Int'l Soc'y for Krishna Consciousness, Inc. v. Lee, 505 U.S. 672, 685 (1992). At the time this case was decided, nonpassengers could go through the concourses to the gates. With current airport security, expressive activity at airports would likely be limited to the ticketing and baggage-claim areas of the terminal.

[57] *See* Schenck v. Pro-Choice Network of W. N.Y., 519 U.S. 357, 383–84 (1997); Madsen v. Women's Health Ctr., Inc., 512 U.S. 753, 776 (1994).

establishing a thirty-six foot buffer zone around abortion clinics and a state law prohibiting anti-abortion protestors within one hundred feet of an abortion clinic from coming within eight feet of a person going to the clinic, without that person's consent, in an effort to dissuade her from having an abortion.[58] But it has recently held unconstitutional a state law that barred anti-abortion protestors from entering a fixed thirty-five-foot buffer zone in front of an abortion clinic.[59]

III. Land Use and the Religion Clauses

Governmental regulation affecting the use of land for religious purposes by religious institutions is potentially subject to constitutional challenge under the freedom of religion clauses of the First Amendment. The First Amendment provides twofold protection to freedom of religion under the Establishment Clause, which requires that the government pursue a policy of complete official neutrality toward religion,[60] and under the Free Exercise Clause, which protects the religious freedom of individuals and religious institutions from improper governmental interference. In practice, the Supreme Court has given an expansive interpretation to the Establishment Clause but a fairly narrow interpretation to the Free Exercise Clause. This narrow interpretation of the Free Exercise Clause has resulted in very limited constitutional protection for religious institutions against zoning laws and other land use regulations that interfere with the use of their religious property. However, Congress has responded to this limited constitutional protection with the enactment of the Religious Land Use and Institutionalized Persons Act of 2000 (RLUIPA).[61] Under RLUIPA, if

---

[58] See Hill v. Colorado, 530 U.S. 703, 726–27 (2000); Madsen, 512 U.S. at 776.

[59] See McCullen v. Coakley, 134 S. Ct. 2518, 2537 (2014). It should be noted that picketing and protests in front of abortion clinics are protected by the First Amendment because they take place on adjacent public streets and sidewalks. The picketing and protests would lose their First Amendment protection if they carried over onto the clinics' privately owned property because the protestors would then be engaging in an illegal trespass, and conduct that is otherwise illegal does not become any less so when it is carried out for purposes of expression. See Giboney v. Empire Storage and Ice Co., 336 U.S. 490, 502 (1949).

[60] Walz v. Tax Comm'n of City of N.Y., 397 U.S. 664, 676–77 (1970).

[61] 42 U.S.C. §§ 2000cc–2000cc-5.

a land use regulation substantially burdens the free exercise of religion, the government must show that the burden serves a compelling governmental interest by the least drastic means.[62] In addition, RLUIPA prohibits discrimination against religious institutions and provides that a land use regulation may not totally exclude religious assemblies or unreasonably limit religious assemblies, institutions, or structures within the state.[63]

A. Establishment Clause Issues

The overriding principle of the Establishment Clause is that the government must maintain a course of complete official neutrality toward religion. The government cannot favor religion over nonreligion, and it cannot favor one religion over another religion.[64] But precisely because the constitutional principle is one of complete official neutrality toward religion, the government is not required to be hostile to religion and may interact with religious institutions in a neutral way. This principle is illustrated in simple form by police officers directing traffic when churches let out after Easter services in the same way as they direct traffic exiting from a large concert or sporting event. Regulations affecting the use of land for religious purposes by religious institutions create Establishment Clause problems only when the regulation has the effect of preferring religion over nonreligion or preferring one religion over another religion. When the government enacts a law applying equally to religious and nonreligious activity, such as a tax exemption for land owned by "religious, charitable, and educational institutions," the law is considered a neutral law for Establishment Clause purposes and is constitutionally permissible. This concept is true because the benefit from the tax exemption encompasses all nonprofit institutions and does not give a preference to religious institutions over nonreligious institutions. On this basis, the Court has upheld this exemption against an Establishment Clause challenge, notwithstanding that it provides a very substantial financial benefit to the religious institutions.[65] For the same

---

[62] 42 U.S.C. § 2000cc(a).
[63] 42 U.S.C. § 2000cc(b).
[64] *See* Wallace v. Jaffree, 472 U.S. 38, 60 (1985).
[65] *See Walz*, 397 U.S. at 679–80.

reason, zoning laws that prohibit the location of businesses serving liquor or engaged in adult uses near residences, schools, and houses of worship are constitutionally permissible. On the other hand, a state law giving houses of worship the power to prevent the issuance of a liquor license to a business that would be located within five hundred feet of the house of worship was found to be a preference for religion and thus violative of the Establishment Clause.[66]

The Establishment Clause also prohibits governmental action that fosters excessive entanglement with religion. This means that the civil courts cannot become involved in deciding questions of religious doctrine or policy and must defer to the resolution of those questions by the highest tribunal of a hierarchical church authority. This principle was applied in disputes over church property with each of the contending groups asserting that it represented the "true faith." The Establishment Clause prevented the civil courts from deciding this religious question and required that the courts defer to the determination of which group had the "true faith" that had been made by the highest authority of a hierarchical church structure.[67] However, where the form of church organization is congregational rather than hierarchical, the courts may, consistent with the Establishment Clause, apply general principles of contract and property law to determine which of the contending groups is entitled to the church property.[68]

B. RLUIPA and Land Use Challenges by Religious Institutions

As stated previously, the Supreme Court has given a fairly narrow interpretation to the Free Exercise Clause. This narrow interpretation of the Free Exercise Clause has resulted in very limited constitutional protection for religious institutions against zoning laws and other land use regulations that interfered with the use of their religious property. Reflecting this narrow interpretation of the Free Exercise Clause, the Court has held that the Free

---

[66] *See* Larkin v. Grendel's Den, Inc., 459 U.S. 116, 127 (1982).
[67] *See* Presbyterian Church v. Hull Mem'l Presbyterian Church, 393 U.S. 440, 447 (1969); Kedroff v. St. Nicholas Cathedral, 344 U.S. 94, 116 (1952); Watson v. Jones, 80 U.S. 679, 727 (1871).
[68] *See* Jones v. Wolf, 443 U.S. 595, 602–03 (1979).

Exercise Clause does not require the government to provide a religiously based exemption from laws of general application.[69] At the same time, the Court has held that the government may, consistent with the Establishment Clause, take action that is precisely tailored to protect the religious freedom of individuals and religious institutions. And it does not matter that the failure of the government to take such an action would not violate the Free Exercise Clause. Usually these actions have involved religiously based exemptions from generally applicable laws, such as the exemption for "religious entities" from the religious discrimination provisions of civil rights laws, which enable a religious institution to employ individuals of the same religion to carry out the work of the institution. The Court has held that these religiously based exemptions are constitutionally permissible.[70]

RLUIPA was enacted under the spending power of Congress and applies to state and local governmental programs and activities receiving federal assistance, which would include a very substantial number of programs. With respect to institutionalized persons, RLUIPA provides that institutional regulations that impose a substantial burden on the religious practices of institutionalized persons are invalid unless they can be justified under the rigorous compelling governmental interest standard as being precisely tailored to advance a compelling governmental interest. With respect to religious institutions, as stated previously, RLUIPA imposes the same compelling governmental interest standard for land use regulations that substantially burden the free exercise of religion, such as a zoning regulation that prevents a church from building a new structure.

In a case involving the refusal of a state prison to make an exception to prison regulations so as to permit a nontraditional religious sect to hold religious services and engage in religious activities, the Court held that RLUIPA applied and that RLUIPA itself did not violate the Establishment Clause.[71] In light of that decision, lower courts have upheld the land use

---

[69] See Emp't Div. v. Smith, 494 U.S. 872, 890 (1990). There the Court held that the Free Exercise Clause did not require the state to exempt from the application of its substance abuse laws the use of peyote in the religious ceremonies of the Native American Church.

[70] See Corp. of the Presiding Bishop v. Amos, 483 U.S. 327, 339 (1987).

[71] Cutter v. Wilkinson, 544 U.S. 709, 720 (2005).

provisions of RLUIPA,[72] and these provisions have enabled religious institutions to challenge successfully a number of land use regulations affecting the use of their religious property.[73]

IV. A Concluding Note

The First Amendment imposes some significant constitutional limitations on the government's power to regulate the use of land. In the chapters that follow, the authors will discuss in greater detail the application of the First Amendment to a number of areas of land use regulation. As the chapters will demonstrate, lawyers involved with land use regulation and other matters of local concern must take the First Amendment into account and must understand how the First Amendment imposes these significant constitutional limitations on land use regulation by the government.

---

[72] *See, e.g.*, Westchester Day Sch. v. Vill. of Mamaroneck, 504 F.3d 338, 353–56 (2d Cir. 2007).

[73] *See, e.g.*, Bethel World Outreach Ministries v. Montgomery City Council, 706 F.3d 548 (4th Cir. 2013); Fortress Bible Church v. Feiner, 694 F.3d 208 (2d Cir. 2012); Centro Familiar Cristiano Buenas Nuevas v. City of Yuma, 651 F.3d 1163 (9th Cir. 2011). As two commentators have observed: "[o]ver the twelve years since its enactment, RLUIPA has proven its worth. Churches have brought numerous successful lawsuits protecting their core First Amendment rights and many cases have settled. Local officials are now on notice that they cannot treat churches as a disfavored land use, despite the issues with NIMBY neighbors, tax collection, or commercial districts, or fear of Muslims or other prejudices among their constituents." Douglas Laycock & Luke W. Goodrich, *RLUIPA: Necessary, Modest, and Under-Enforced*, 39 FORDHAM URB. L. J. 1021, 1023 (2012).

2

Sign Regulation
Private Signs on Private Property

Randal R. Morrison
Sabine & Morrison
San Diego, California

This chapter is dedicated in memory of William D. Brinton for his decades of work protecting the scenic landscapes of our nation.

I. Chapter Overview

This chapter focuses on the application of the First Amendment and its corollaries in state constitutions, to local governments' regulation of private speech on signs. In most cases, the sign is located on private property, although a few cases—notably, governmentally sponsored public art projects—concern private signs that may be displayed on public or private property. In any event, the "speaker" is a private party, even if that party is participating in an event sponsored or controlled by some governmental entity.

Other chapters of this book identify other areas in which the First Amendment limits local governments' regulation of a particular activity, including religious land uses, art and architecture, and adult businesses. However, as any study of case law will demonstrate, local governments' regulation of outdoor signage is perhaps the area of local government activity that most directly implicates First Amendment concerns and is the subject of a large portion of First Amendment litigation involving local governments.

Regulation of signs on private property was the subject of the Supreme Court's historic 2015 decision in *Reed v. Town of Gilbert.*[1] That case is the Court's most recent statement on the core First Amendment concept of content neutrality, and the case's outcome has dramatic implications for local government regulation of signs and other land uses that carry the protection of the First Amendment. *Reed* and its progeny are discussed in detail later in this chapter.

This chapter first delves into some foundational material on sign regulation, including the reasons local governments regulate signs and the legal basis for modern sign regulation. The chapter then discusses some of the First Amendment basics of sign regulation—particularly, the all-important issue of content neutrality. The balance of the chapter covers many of the special First Amendment problems that arise in the context of sign regulation, including issues of on-site and off-site signage, bans and exceptions, the commercial speech doctrine, political signs, and residential neighborhood signage.

II. Foundations of Sign Regulation

A. Protection for Outdoor Signage Under the U.S. Constitution

Writing for the majority in *City of Ladue v. Gilleo,*[2] Justice John Paul Stevens provided the following overview of outdoor signs, noting both the particular problems that they cause for municipal regulation as well as the First Amendment protections afforded to them:

> While signs are a form of expression protected by the Free Speech Clause, they pose distinctive problems that are subject to municipalities' police powers. Unlike oral speech, signs take up space and may obstruct views, distract motorists, displace alternative uses for land, and pose other problems that legitimately call for regulation. It is now well-understood that governments may regulate the physical

---

[1] 135 S. Ct. 2218 (2015).
[2] 512 U.S. 43 (1994).

characteristics of signs, just as they can, within reasonable bounds and absent censorial purpose, regulate audible expression in its capacity as noise. However, because regulation of a medium inevitably affects communication itself, it is not surprising that we have had occasion to review the constitutionality of municipal ordinances prohibiting the display of certain outdoor signs.[3]

Although Justice Stevens authored this opinion in 1994, it still stands as an accurate assessment of both the problems of outdoor signs and the protections afforded them. This chapter is thus based on the premise that outdoor signs are (1) a form of speech protected by the First Amendment and similar rights under state constitutions, and (2) a form of land use that requires regulation primarily by local governments[4] for the purpose of protecting the safety of the public and beautifying the community. Free speech does not mean that citizens must tolerate the visual shouting match that excessive signage can produce.[5]

The First Amendment to the U.S. Constitution states:

> Congress shall make no law respecting an establishment of religion, or prohibiting the free exercise thereof; or abridging the freedom of speech, or of the press; or the right of the people peaceably to assemble, and to petition the Government for a redress of grievances.[6]

Nearly all sign-related litigation involves claims of Free Speech Clause violation. Less common, but still important, are claims arising from the religion clauses and the Free Press Clause. Politicians, protestors, preachers, and ordinary people all have equal free speech rights, whether

---

[3] *Id.* at 48.

[4] Signs along federally funded highways are subject to the Highway Beautification Act, 23 U.S.C. § 131 (1965), which is enforced by the states under state-level statutory corollaries. Any state that does not maintain effective control of outdoor advertising could be subject to the loss of 10 percent of its allotment of federal highway funds. *See* South Dakota v. Goldschmidt, 635 F.2d 698, 699 (8th Cir. 1980); United Outdoor Adver. Co. v. Bus., Transp., and Hous. Agency, 746 P.2d 877, 879–80 (Cal. 1988).

[5] Cox v. State of Louisiana, 379 S. Ct. 536 (1965) ("The rights of free speech and assembly, while fundamental in our democratic society, still do not mean that everyone with opinions or beliefs to express may address a group at any public place and at any time.")

[6] U.S. Const., amend. I.

those rights are exercised by picketing on a public sidewalk,[7] criticizing the local government by scrawling huge letters across the facade of a home,[8] or giving directions to the next meeting place of a religious congregation.[9]

Prominent examples of Free Speech Clause sign cases before the U.S. Supreme Court include the following: *Linmark Associates, Inc. v. Township of Willingboro*,[10] invalidating a prohibition on real estate "for sale" signs; *Metromedia, Inc. v. City of San Diego*,[11] holding that although a city could ban billboards (defined as off-site signs), it could not favor commercial speech over noncommercial speech and it could not favor particular types of noncommercial messages over others; *City of Ladue v. Gilleo*,[12] outlawing a restriction on yard signs containing a war protest message; *Burson v. Freeman*,[13] upholding a restriction on political signs and electioneering near polling places on election day as narrowly tailored to serve compelling governmental interests in preventing voter fraud and intimidation; and *Reed v. Town of Gilbert*,[14] rejecting a local government's sign rules (size, location, and display duration) that varied according to message type, including political, ideological, and "qualifying event" signs.

B. Protection for Outdoor Signage Under State Constitutions

Although the predominant share of litigation involving outdoor sign regulation is brought under the Federal Constitution—and often in federal court[15]—it is important to consider state constitutional limitations on the

---

[7] *See, e.g.*, Police Dep't v. Mosley, 408 U.S. 92 (1972).
[8] *See, e.g.*, Brown v. Town of Cary, 706 F.3d 294 (4th Cir. 2013).
[9] *See, e.g.*, Reed v. Town of Gilbert, 135 S. Ct. 2218 (2015).
[10] 431 U.S. 85 (1977).
[11] 453 U.S. 490 (1981).
[12] 512 U.S. 43 (1994).
[13] 504 U.S. 191 (1992).
[14] 135 S. Ct. 2218 (2015). Before reaching the Supreme Court, the sign code of Gilbert, Arizona, had been repeatedly validated: 587 F.3d 966 (9th Cir. 2009) (upholding denial of a preliminary injunction to the plaintiff), 832 F. Supp. 2d 1070 (D. Ariz. 2011) (granting summary judgment in favour of the Town), 707 F.3d 1057, 1068 (9th Cir. 2013) ("The definition of content neutral has evolved over the last few decades, . . .").
[15] Challenges brought under the First Amendment may be heard in state courts. *See, e.g.*, Veterans of Foreign Wars v. City of Steamboat Springs, 575 P.2d 835 (Colo. 1978).

regulation of speech. Such formulations may result in interpretations that differ significantly from federal court interpretations.

For example, the Oregon courts have interpreted that state's constitution to mean that local governments cannot distinguish between on-site and off-site signs[16]—that is, the regulation of signage on the basis of whether the message relates to an event or activity occurring on the premises where the sign is located—and have also rejected regulatory distinctions between commercial and noncommercial speech.[17] Both of these distinctions, which are common in local sign codes, are permissible under the Federal First Amendment, so long as noncommercial speech has at least equal display rights as commercial speech.[18] The commercial–noncommercial distinction is discussed in detail later in the chapter.

Although state constitutions vary significantly on some points, all contain a corollary to the First Amendment, often within a declaration of rights or bill of rights.[19] Virtually all grant free speech and free press rights on *all subjects* to *all persons*. For example, the New York State Constitution, section 8, states: "Every citizen may freely speak, write, and publish his sentiments on all subjects, being responsible for the abuse of that right; and no law shall be passed to restrain or abridge the liberty of speech or of the press."[20] This provision was widely copied in many later state constitutions, such as in the Texas Constitution:

> Every person shall be at liberty to speak, write or publish his opinions on any subject, being responsible for the abuse of that privilege; and no law shall ever be passed curtailing the liberty of speech or of the press . . . .[21]

---

[16] *See* Outdoor Media Dimensions, Inc. v. Dep't of Transp., 132 P.3d 5, 16–17 (Or. 2006) (finding state outdoor advertising law's distinction between on-premises and off-premises signage to constitute a content based restriction in violation of state constitution's guarantee of free speech).

[17] Ackerley Commc'ns, Inc. v. Multnomah Cnty., 696 P.2d 1140 (Or. Ct. App. 1985).

[18] *See* Metromedia, Inc. v. City of San Diego, 453 U.S. 490, 512–13 (1981).

[19] *See generally* Peter P. Miller, Note, *Freedom of Expression Under State Constitutions*, 20 Stan. L. Rev. 318 (1968).

[20] N.Y. Const., art. I § 8 (2016).

[21] Tex. Const., art. I § 8 (2015).

The corollary provision from the California Constitution reads:

> Every person may freely speak, write and publish his or her sentiments
> on all subjects, being responsible for the abuse of this right. A law may
> not restrain or abridge liberty of speech or press.[22]

And the Oregon formulation is:

> No law shall be passed restraining the free expression of opinion,
> or restricting the right to speak, write, or print freely on any subject
> whatever; but every person shall be responsible for the abuse of this
> right.[23]

III. Purpose And Intent: Why Regulate Signs?

The typical sign ordinance commonly recites that it is adopted to serve
public interests in safety and aesthetics. Although those two interests are
ubiquitous, and sufficient in the absence of content based regulations,[24]
other interests can be and sometimes are listed, including the following:
protecting the right of free speech; advancing the sign-related goals of
the city's general plan; lessening of driver distraction; protecting the city's
appearance; improving property values; protecting the visibility triangle
at intersections; controlling "spillover effects" from one sign affecting
neighboring properties; enhancing the local economy; providing direction,
destination, and location information; and accommodating the need for
functional information such as credit cards accepted, hours of operation,
and safety warnings.[25]

---

[22] CAL. CONST., art. I § 2(a) (2015).

[23] OR. CONST., art. I § 8 (2015).

[24] *See* Metromedia, Inc. v. City of San Diego, 453 U.S. 490, 508–09 (1981) ("Nor can there be substantial doubt that the twin goals that the ordinance seeks to further— traffic safety and the appearance of the city—are substantial governmental goals.").

[25] *See, e.g.*, SAN CARLOS, CAL., MUNICIPAL CODE § 18.22.140.C (2016), *available at* http://www .codepublishing.com/CA/SanCarlos/html/SanCarlos18/SanCarlos1822.html.

Many courts interpret sign codes in light of the governmental interests to be served, which are commonly stated in the Purpose and Intent section of the sign code.[26]

IV. Foundations of Modern Sign Regulation

The modern law of signs is built upon a body of legal doctrines developed over many decades by the U.S. Supreme Court, lower federal courts, and state courts. There are several principal building blocks of modern-day sign regulation, beginning in the early twentieth century. These building blocks include the following:

- The validation by the Court of zoning as a legitimate exercise of the police power that does not necessarily violate the due process, liberty, or property rights guaranteed by the Fourteenth Amendment.[27]
- The acceptance by federal and state courts of community aesthetics as a valid basis and rationale for zoning and land use control, including redevelopment.[28]
- The extension of the First Amendment, which by its literal terms applies only to Congress, through the Fourteenth Amendment

---

[26] *See, e.g.,* KH Outdoor, LLC v. City of Trussville, 458 F.3d 1261, 1267 (11th Cir. 2006); Neighborhood Enters., Inc. v. City of St. Louis, 644 F.3d 728, 735 (8th Cir. 2011).

[27] *See* Vill. of Euclid v. Ambler Realty Co., 272 U.S. 365, 388 (1926). Two years after *Euclid,* the U.S. Supreme Court clarified the doctrine, finding that a zoning regulation that was unreasonable constituted a violation of the Due Process Clause of the Fourteenth Amendment. *See* Nectow v. City of Cambridge, 277 U.S. 183, 188 (1928).

[28] *See* Berman v. Parker, 348 U.S. 26, 33 (1954) ("It is within the power of the legislature to determine that the community should be beautiful as well as healthy, spacious as well as clean, well-balanced as well as carefully patrolled."). *Berman* was followed shortly thereafter by state court decisions that validated aesthetics as a basis for land use regulation as a matter of state law. *See generally* J. F. Ghent, Annotation, *Aesthetic Objectives or Considerations as Affecting Validity of Zoning Ordinance,* 21 A.L.R. 3d 1222 (1968).

to actions of state governments[29] and subsequently to local governments.[30]

- The gradual abrogation by the Court of the early-twentieth century holding that commercial speech did not have First Amendment protection,[31] the corresponding development of an intermediate level of constitutional protection for advertising and commercial speech,[32] and the formalization of the constitutional standard of review for commercial speech regulations.[33]

- The development of the "time, place, and manner" test for regulations deemed "content neutral,"[34] the strict scrutiny test for content based regulations,[35] and the related concept that regulation aimed at controlling the secondary effects of certain forms of speech, particularly the "speech" of sexually oriented businesses

[29] *See, e.g.,* Gitlow v. New York, 268 U.S. 652, 666 (1925); Near v. Minnesota, 283 U.S. 697, 707 (1931) ("It is no longer open to doubt that the liberty of the press, and of speech, is within the liberty safeguarded by the due process clause of the Fourteenth Amendment from invasion by state action."). As late as 1922, the U.S. Supreme Court stated in dicta that the First Amendment's free speech guarantees were inapplicable to the states, *Prudential Ins. Co. v. Cheek,* 259 U.S. 530, 543 (1922) ("[A]s we have stated, neither the Fourteenth Amendment nor any other provision of the Constitution of the United States imposes upon the States any restrictions about 'freedom of speech' or the 'liberty of silence'"), but *Gitlow* appears to have overruled such statements.

[30] *See, e.g.,* Lovell v. Griffin, 303 U.S. 444, 450 (1938) ("It is also well settled that municipal ordinances adopted under state authority constitute state action and are within the prohibition of the [First] amendment.").

[31] *See* Valentine v. Chrestensen, 316 U.S. 52, 54 (1942).

[32] *See* Linmark Assocs., Inc. v. Twp. of Willingboro, 431 U.S. 85, 92 (1977); Va. State Bd. of Pharmacy v. Va. Citizens Consumer Council, Inc., 425 U.S. 748, 762 (1976) ("Our question is whether speech which does 'no more than propose a commercial transaction,' is so removed from any 'exposition of ideas,' and from 'truth, science, morality, and arts in general, in its diffusion of liberal sentiments on the administration of Government,' that it lacks all protection. Our answer is that it is not.") (citations omitted); Bigelow v. Virginia, 421 U.S. 809 (1975) (holding unconstitutional a state law prohibiting newspaper ads for abortion services that were illegal where advertised but legal where offered).

[33] *See* Cent. Hudson Gas & Elec. Corp. v. Public Serv. Comm'n of N.Y., 447 U.S. 557, 566 (1980).

[34] *See* Ward v. Rock Against Racism, 491 U.S. 781, 791 (1989) (upholding sound-level limits applied to protest music in a public park); Clark v. Cmty. for Creative Non Violence, 468 U.S. 288, 293 (1984) (upholding a National Park Service regulation prohibiting camping in certain parks); Prime Media, Inc. v. City of Brentwood, 398 F.3d 814, 818 (6th Cir. 2005) (stating the time, place, and manner test as follows: the sign rules "are valid provided [1] that they are justified without reference to the content of the regulated speech, [2] that they are narrowly tailored [3] to serve a significant governmental interest, and [4] that they leave open ample alternative channels for communication of the information.").

[35] *See* Reed v. Town of Gilbert, 135 S. Ct. 2218, 2231 (2015); Burson v. Freeman, 504 U.S. 191, 198 (1992).

(see chapters 7 and 8), is not necessarily content based and does not invoke strict scrutiny.[36]

- Recognition by the Court of the right to display real estate signs on residential properties[37] and the right to privacy on residential properties.[38]
- The development by the Court of the public forum doctrine, classifying public property according to its historical or designated use and identifying the appropriate spectra of government regulations of speech for each class of public property.[39]
- The expansion of the government speech doctrine, which allows governments to deliver their official messages to the public without opening a forum and without owing an equal opportunity to members of the public who may disagree and to maintain government control of access even when private suggestions are invited.[40]

---

[36] See City of Renton v. Playtime Theatres, Inc., 475 U.S. 41, 52 (1986).

[37] See, e.g., Linmark, 431 U.S. 85, 96–97 (1977); City of Ladue v. Gilleo, 512 U.S. 43, 54–55 (1994).

[38] See, e.g., Frisby v. Schultz, 487 U.S. 474, 484 (1988) (upholding local ban on focused picketing on public sidewalk in front of private residence); but see Snyder v. Phelps, 562 U.S. 443 (2011) (invalidating jury award for intentional infliction of emotional distress caused to father of fallen military service member by religious group displaying "God Hates Fags" message).

[39] See, e.g., Ark. Ed. Television Comm'n v. Forbes, 523 U.S. 666, 675 (1998) (finding candidate debate on government-owned public television was nonpublic forum; government could exclude independent candidate from televised debate; detailed explanation of public forum categories and corresponding rules; importance of journalistic judgment and the need to avoid dilution of content with too many participants); Burson v. Freeman, 504 U.S. 191, 196–97 (1992) (validating under strict scrutiny a prohibition on signs and politicking within one hundred feet of the polls on election day); United States v. Kokinda, 497 U.S. 720, 730 (1990) (validating a ban on signature gathering on U.S. Postal Service sidewalk); Boos v. Barry, 485 U.S. 312, 334 (1988) (invalidating code provision preventing speech on certain topics near embassies); Members of City Council v. Taxpayers for Vincent, 466 U.S. 789, 814–15 (1984) (validating a prohibition on the placement of political advertising on public right-of-way); Lehman v. City of Shaker Heights, 418 U.S. 298, 302–303 (1977) (upholding a limitation on the placement of political advertising on public train cars); Hague v. C.I.O., 307 U.S. 496, 516–17 (1939) (acknowledging the ancient right of citizenship to use streets and parks for expression of opinions); Children of the Rosary v. City of Phoenix, 154 F.3d 972, 976–77 (9th Cir. 1998) (detailing the historical development of public forum on government vehicles; city could restrict advertising on its buses to commercial messages only, so as to avoid controversy while receiving revenue from ads); Pruneyard Shopping Ctr. v. Robins, 447 U.S. 74 (1980) (holding that state constitutional provision permitting individuals to exercise free speech and petition rights on the property of a privately owned shopping center to which public is invited did not violate the shopping center owner's rights).

[40] See, e.g., Walker v. Tex. Div., Sons of Confederate Veterans, 135 S. Ct. 2239, 2246 (2015) (finding that specialty license plates constitute government speech); Pleasant Grove City v. Summum, 555 U.S.

(footnote continued on next page)

All of the foregoing doctrinal developments guide and influence the modern-day regulation of signs, and many will be referred to throughout the balance of this chapter.

V. Analysis of Sign Regulations Under The First Amendment

A. Reasonable Limitations

The U.S. Supreme Court has long held that the First Amendment "does not guarantee the right to communicate one's views at all times and places or in any manner that may be desired,"[41] that expressive activities may be reasonably limited,[42] and that each medium is "a law unto itself."[43]

The principal legal issues of sign regulation are when, how, and why the right to speak by way of sign display may be limited by regulation for the public good and if the justification is sufficient.[44] Although the foundation concept—reasonable limitation in conformance with the nature of the place[45]—seems simple enough, applying that general concept to specific disputes has vexed many courts and produced a substantial body of case

---

(footnote continued from previous page)

460, 467 (2009) (holding that Ten Commandments monument became government speech when private donation was accepted for permanent mounting in public park; no legal duty to offer similar display right to private group with different message, arguably religious in nature); People for the Ethical Treatment of Animals v. Gittens, 396 F.3d 416 (D.C. Cir. 2005) (reviewing a public art program directly sponsored by City of Washington, D.C.; city could refuse entry for display that, in the view of the administrator, did not meet the "light and whimsical" standard, which had been announced in advance); Mitchell v. Motor Vehicle Admin., 126 A.3d 165 (Md. Ct. Spec. App. 2015) (rescission of custom vanity plates was proper because message contained profanity in Spanish language); *but see* Wooley v. Maynard, 430 U.S. 705, 716 (1977) (holding that state could not require driver to display state motto "Live Free or Die" on license plate).

[41] Heffron v. Int'l Soc. for Krishna Consciousness, Inc., 452 U.S. 640, 647 (1981).

[42] *See* Clark v. Cmty. for Creative Non Violence, 468 U.S. 288, 295 (1984).

[43] Kovacs v. Cooper, 336 U.S. 77, 97 (1949) (Jackson, J., concurring); *See also* Metromedia, Inc. v. City of San Diego, 453 U.S. 490, 501, 527–28 (Brennan, J., concurring).

[44] *See, e.g.*, Reed v. Town of Gilbert, 135 S. Ct. 2218, 2226 (2015).

[45] *See, e.g.*, Wells v. City and Cnty. of Denver, 257 F.3d 1132, 1148 (10th Cir. 2001) (addressing Christmas-themed holiday displays on grounds of public buildings), *citing to* Hill v. Colorado, 530 U.S. 703 (2000) (pertaining to abortion protests and clinic buffer zone); *see also* Lamar Corp. v. City of Twin Falls, 981 P.2d 1146 (Idaho 1999) (validating discretion in sign permitting when sufficient guidance factors are stated in the law).

law that is not entirely, if at all, consistent. In the typical First Amendment analysis, a reviewing court will first determine if there is a restriction on speech, which may include written or verbal expression as well as symbolic acts such as flag burning,[46] music or other sounds,[47] solicitation of donations,[48] and visually communicative images on signs. If a restriction on speech is found, the court will then apply the appropriate test for validity. For restrictions that are content based, at least as to noncommercial speech, the test is strict scrutiny.[49]

B. The Power to Regulate

It has long been settled that land use regulation is within the police power of state governments unless a federal statute declares otherwise. This power is typically delegated to local governments, at least as to certain specified subjects, such as sign regulation. This power is normally limited to the territorial jurisdiction of the state or local government. However, for example, Texas grants home rule cities "extraterritorial jurisdiction" as to off-premises signs.[50] And public transportation systems are sometimes granted state charters that exempt them from local regulations,[51] typically to allow the sale of advertising space that will reduce the public subsidy necessary to keep the system solvent and operating. Such programs often have acceptability guidelines that can raise free speech issues. In *Ridley v. Massachusetts Bay Transportation Authority*,[52] addressing the refusal of ads urging reform of marijuana laws and ads considered "demeaning or disparaging," the court there held that the advertising program did not create a designated public forum. In *Children of the Rosary v.*

---

[46] *See generally* Texas v. Johnson, 491 U.S. 397 (1989) (holding that flag burning was protected symbolic protest).

[47] *See generally* Ward v. Rock Against Racism, 491 U.S. 781 (1989) (limits on sound levels for bandshell in city park); Kovacs v. Cooper, 336 U.S. 77 (1949) (limits on sound levels justified by need for tranquility).

[48] *See generally* Int'l Soc'y for Krishna Consciousness, Inc. v. Lee, 505 U.S. 672 (1992); Santa Monica Food Not Bombs v. City of Santa Monica, 450 F.3d 1022 (9th Cir. 2006) (holding distribution of food to homeless to be an activity protected by the First Amendment).

[49] *See* Reed v. Town of Gilbert, 135 S. Ct. 2218, 2226 (2015).

[50] *See, e.g.*, Brooks v. State, 226 S.W.3d 607 (Tex. 2007).

[51] *See, e.g.*, CBS Outdoor, Inc. v. City of New York, 16 N.Y.S.3d 411 (N.Y. Sup. Ct. 2015).

[52] 390 F.3d 65 (1st Cir. 2004).

City of Phoenix,[53] the city-owned bus system accepted only commercial messages so as to avoid controversy, and the court found that ads for an anti-abortion, pro-life group were properly declined.

C. Commercial and Noncommercial Speech

When reviewing a sign rule, a court will first look for a restriction on speech or expressive conduct. Assuming the court finds that such a restriction exists, the analysis typically then turns on whether the regulated speech is commercial or noncommercial. Some background on the distinction between commercial and noncommercial speech is necessary.

For most of the nation's history, commercial advertising—that is, the solicitation of sales of goods and services—was considered outside the protection of the First Amendment. This was true in large part because mere commerce was viewed as beneath the dignity of classical debate on politics, philosophy, art, and science and the roles that such topics had played in the development of Western civilization. This tradition of nonprotection for mere advertising was noted in the 1942 Supreme Court case of *Valentine v. Chrestensen*:

> [T]he Constitution imposes no such restraint on government as respects purely commercial advertising. Whether, and to what extent, one may promote or pursue a gainful occupation in the streets, to what extent such activity shall be adjudged a derogation of the public right of user, are matters for legislative judgment.[54]

However, during the 1970s the Court incrementally extended constitutional protection to commercial speech, albeit to a lower degree than that afforded to noncommercial speech. One of the foundation cases, *Linmark Associates, Inc. v. Township of Willingboro,*[55] concerned on-site residential real estate "for sale" signs. A complete ban on such signs was ruled unconstitutional, primarily because the sale or purchase of a home is among the most

---

[53] 154 F.3d 972 (9th Cir. 1998).
[54] 316 U.S. 52, 54 (1942)
[55] 431 U.S. 85 (1977).

important decisions a family ever makes and also because there is no other place where the sign will be as effective as on the offered property itself.[56]

The evolution of the commercial speech doctrine is described in *Central Hudson Gas & Electric Corporation v. Public Service Commission,*[57] which also formalized the constitutional test; it is restated in the Ninth Circuit's decision in *Ballen v. City of Redmond*:

> [T]he validity of a restriction on commercial speech depends on the following factors: (1) "whether the expression is protected by the First Amendment," which requires the speech to "concern lawful activity and not be misleading"; (2) "whether the asserted governmental interest is substantial"; (3) "whether the regulation directly advances the governmental interest asserted"; and (4) "whether [the regulation] is not more extensive than is necessary to serve that interest.[58]

For a thorough discussion of the commercial–noncommercial distinction, see the California Supreme Court's decision in *Kasky v. Nike, Inc.*, which concludes:

> [W]hen a court must decide whether particular speech may be subjected to laws aimed at preventing false advertising or other forms of commercial deception, categorizing a particular statement as commercial or noncommercial speech requires consideration of three elements: the speaker, the intended audience, and the content of the message.[59]

D. Favoring Commercial Speech

When a speech regulation, including a sign code, has the effect of favoring commercial speech over noncommercial speech, that inversion of the hierarchy of values usually results in invalidation.[60] Many sign codes

---

[56] *Id.* at 96–97.
[57] 447 U.S. 557, 561–63 (1980).
[58] 466 F.3d 736, 742 (9th Cir. 2006)
[59] 45 P.3d 243, 256 (Cal. 2002).
[60] *See* Metromedia, Inc. v. City of San Diego, 453 U.S. 490, 513 (1981); *see also* Ackerley Commc'ns of Mass., Inc. v. City of Somerville, 878 F.2d 513, 517 (1st Cir. 1989).

avoid charges of favoring commercial speech with a "message substitution" provision that freely allows substitution of a noncommercial message in place of a commercial message, without additional permitting, so long as there is no change in the physical structure of the sign. Such a provision has proved decisive in several billboard company challenges to local sign codes.[61] Because courts analyze sign regulations differently based on whether the rules apply to commercial or noncommercial messages on signs, this chapter bifurcates the discussion into those two categories.

E. Noncommercial Speech Regulations

Once the court finds a restriction on noncommercial speech, it then asks whether the regulation is based on the content of the message expressed and applies the appropriate test or level of scrutiny. The Supreme Court decision in *Reed v. Town of Gilbert*[62] firmly holds that content based regulations are reviewed under strict scrutiny—the most exacting form of constitutional review. In contrast, content neutral regulations are reviewed under the less exacting intermediate scrutiny standard. These standards of review are discussed further in the following sections.

1. Content Neutrality Analysis

Police Department of Chicago v. Mosley[63] was the Supreme Court's first discussion of the concept of content neutrality. A local law prohibited picketing near schools but made exceptions from the ban for labor picketing by teachers. In an oft-quoted passage, the *Mosley* majority held that "above all else, the First Amendment means that government has no power to restrict expression because of its message, its ideas, its subject matter, or its content."[64] Generally speaking, *Mosley* was initially understood by courts, legal scholars, and practitioners to mean that the application of a speech regulation could not turn on the message of the subject speech.

---

[61] *See, e.g.*, Outdoor Media Grp., Inc. v. City of Beaumont, 506 F.3d 895, 905 (9th Cir. 2007); Outdoor Sys., Inc. v. City of Mesa, 997 F.2d 604, 612 (9th Cir. 2002).

[62] 135 S. Ct. 2218 (2015).

[63] 408 U.S. 92 (1972).

[64] *Id.* at 95.

Prior to 2015, one of the long-standing conundrums of First Amendment law was whether absolute, facial neutrality was required as to message content or if viewpoint neutrality within a broader category of speech, such as equal treatment for all political signs, was sufficient. Supreme Court cases, as well as a multitude of lower court cases, can be found supporting two variations on the "neutrality" idea, with a third, more highly specific approach evident as well. Some cases applied a "strict" position, holding that if a regulation applies, or applies differentially, based on the message content, then it is content based.[65] These Supreme Court cases were generally followed by federal circuit court cases that rejected sign regulations containing distinctions between types of signs based on the signs' message, including code provisions treating political signs differently from real estate signs.[66]

Conversely, a second group of cases adopted the "viewpoint neutrality" or "functional" position, which understood content neutrality differently. Viewpoint neutrality—equal treatment among and between different sides of an argument—is a core requirement of the First Amendment.[67] For example, in *Members of City Council v. Taxpayers for Vincent*, the Court stated the general principle that "the First Amendment forbids the government to regulate speech in ways that favor some viewpoints or ideas at the expense of others."[68] Viewpoint neutrality—without content neutrality—is good enough for the government to prevail in cases involving

---

[65] *See, e.g.,* Boos v. Barry, 485 U.S. 312, 318–19 (1998) (invalidating a law prohibiting picketing against foreign governments near embassies); Turner Broad. Sys. v. FCC, 512 U.S. 622, 643 (1994) (holding, generally, that laws that distinguish between favored and disfavored speech on the basis of ideas or views expressed are content based); Whitton v. City of Gladstone, 54 F.3d 1400, 1403–04 (8th Cir. 1995) (finding special restrictions on political signs to be content based).

[66] *See, e.g.,* Neighborhood Enters., Inc. v. City of St. Louis, 644 F.3d 728, 736-37 (8th Cir. 2011) (finding code definition of "sign" to be content based, in part because the definition contained exemptions for, inter alia, "[n]ational, state, religious, fraternal, professional and civic symbols or crests" and other sign types); Solantic v. City of Neptune Beach, 410 F.3d 1250, 1264 (11th Cir. 2005) (applying *Metromedia* formulation of content neutrality test to find that permitting exceptions for governmental flags, political signs, real estate signs, construction signs, memorial signs, yard sale signs, and other content based sign types were unconstitutionally content based).

[67] *See, e.g.,* Reed v. Town of Gilbert, 135 S. Ct. 2218, 2230 (2015); Rosenberger v. Rector and Visitors of Univ. of Va., 515 U.S. 819, 829 (1995).

[68] 466 U.S. 789, 804 (1984).

limited or nonpublic forums, as described more fully in chapters 10 and 11.[69] The cases and courts that followed the viewpoint neutrality position held that as long as the government did not adopt a regulation with the purpose of discriminating between forms of content and did not engage in viewpoint discrimination within broader categories of speech, the constitutional requirement of content neutrality was met.[70] In the context of sign cases, the viewpoint neutrality approach was generally friendlier to local governments than other approaches.

Still, some other cases adopted different approaches to content neutrality. Perhaps most significantly, a set of cases adopted the "secondary effects" position, which holds that a regulation aimed at controlling the secondary or neighborhood spillover effects of constitutionally protected but not legally obscene speech, without reference to the content of the regulated speech, is content neutral.[71] The secondary effects approach has rarely been adopted outside of the context of speech by sexually oriented businesses.[72] The secondary effects view of content neutrality is more fully addressed in chapters 7 and 8, dealing with speech by adult businesses.

The Supreme Court's decision in *Reed* clarified and hardened the content neutrality principle. The Gilbert, Arizona, sign code created categories for signs and then assigned differential rules as to size, location, and duration to each category. The Court addressed three categories: "Ideological Signs," which could be a maximum of twenty square feet and were subject to no display time limit; "Political Signs," which could be sixteen or thirty-two square feet depending on location and could be displayed up to sixty days before a primary election and up to fifteen days following a general election; and "Temporary Directional Signs Relating to a Qualifying Event,"

---

[69] *See* Lehman v. City of Shaker Heights, 418 U.S. 298, 304 (1974); Children of the Rosary v. City of Phoenix, 154 F.3d 972, 977–78 (9th Cir. 1998).

[70] *See* Hill v. Colorado, 530 U.S. 703, 721–23 (2000); Reed v. Town of Gilbert, 707 F.3d 1057, 1071 (9th Cir. 2013).

[71] *See generally* City of Erie v. Pap's A.M., 529 U.S. 277 (2000); City of Renton v. Playtime Theaters, 457 U.S. 41 (1986).

[72] *See, e.g.,* Rappa v. New Castle Cnty., 18 F.3d 1043, 1069 (3d Cir. 1994).

allowing a maximum of six square feet and display time limited to twelve hours before the event in question and one hour after.[73]

Justice Thomas's lead opinion for the Court stated, in absolute terms, that a regulation is content based if the "law applies to particular speech because of the topic discussed or the idea or message expressed."[74] According to the Court, the definition for each category in the Gilbert code turned on the message expressed, such as, for political signs, "designed to influence the outcome of an election." As the Court stated,

> [T]he crucial first step in the content-neutrality analysis [is] determining whether the law is content neutral on its face. A law that is content based on its face is subject to strict scrutiny regardless of the government's benign motive, content-neutral justification, or lack of "animus toward the ideas contained" in the regulated speech.[75]

Finding the three categories all content based, Justice Thomas then subjected them to strict scrutiny: "the government must show that a content based distinction 'is necessary to serve a compelling state interest and is narrowly drawn to achieve that end.'"[76] The town offered only aesthetics and traffic safety as justifications; the regulations in question were found to be "hopelessly underinclusive."[77]

The Court noted that the town had other criteria, beyond message categories, for dealing with signs, including, for example, building materials, lighting, moving parts, and portability.[78] In a clarifying concurrence, Justice Alito listed factors that can be used to regulate signs without using content based rules.[79] These factors include size limits, whether signs are freestanding or attached, sign lighting, whether a sign's message is fixed or changing, placement of the sign on private or public property, placement of

---

[73] Reed v. Town of Gilbert, 135 S. Ct. 2218, 2224–25 (2015).
[74] *Id.* at 2227.
[75] *Id.* at 2228.
[76] *Id.* at 2236 (Kagan, J., concurring in the judgment).
[77] *Id.* at 2231.
[78] *Id.* at 2232.
[79] *Id.* at 2233–34 (Alito, J., concurring).

the sign on commercial or residential property, on-premise or off-premise placement, number of signs per mile of roadway, time restrictions for one-time events, and speech by the government itself.

Cases following *Reed* have reaffirmed the Supreme Court's logic in analyzing content neutrality:

- In *Lone Star Security and Video, Inc. v. City of Los Angeles*, the Ninth Circuit Court of Appeals rejected a challenge to the City of Los Angeles's ban on mobile billboards.[80]
- In *Grieve v. Village of Perry*, a village law allowing certain types of commercial messages on signs without a permit, including real estate signs, official signs, name and address signs, and others, but requiring a permit for certain types of noncommercial messages defined by content, was rejected by a magistrate judge.[81]
- In *Marin v. Town of Southeast*, a town code excepted political signs, posted within stated time limits, from permitting, which was sufficient to invalidate the entire code.[82]

Burson v. Freeman[83] is a rare example of a content based sign regulation that survived strict scrutiny. A state law forbade campaign posters, signs, or other campaign materials; electioneering; and solicitation of votes within one hundred feet of the entrance to a polling place on election day.[84] The Court found that the law served compelling interests in preventing voter intimidation and fraud[85] and that narrow tailoring was satisfied by the time and distance limits of the rule.[86]

---

[80] 584 F.3d 1232 (9th Cir. 2016). *See also* Vosse v. City of New York, 144 F. Supp. 3d 627 (S.D.N.Y. 2015), *aff'd* 666 Fed. App'x 11 (2d Cir. 2016).

[81] No. 15-CV-00365-RJA-JJM, 2016 WL 4491713 (W.D.N.Y. Aug. 3, 2016).

[82] 136 F. Supp. 3d 548 (S.D.N.Y. 2015). *See also* Wagner v. City of Garfield Heights, ___ Fed. App'x ___, 2017 WL 129034 (6th Cir. 2017).

[83] 504 U.S. 191 (1992).

[84] *Id.* at 193–94.

[85] *Id.* at 199.

[86] *Id.* at 206.

2. Standard of Review for Content Neutral Regulations

Unlike content based laws, content neutral sign regulations are reviewed under intermediate scrutiny. That test requires the government only to demonstrate that it has a significant or substantial governmental interest—that is, an interest that is less than compelling—and that the regulation is narrowly tailored to serve that interest.[87] In intermediate scrutiny, the tailoring analysis does not impose a least restrictive means test.[88] This test derives from the test applied to time, place, and manner regulations for speech in public places: in general, governmental restrictions on protected speech, whether by sign or otherwise, are constitutionally permissible so long as they can be justified without reference to the content of the speech itself, they are narrowly tailored to serve a substantial governmental interest, and they leave open ample alternative means for communicating the same information.[89] Although this doctrine is often stated or applied in public forum cases, of which the subject is government owned property,[90] it also applies in cases where the government is acting as a regulator of private property. In *Metromedia*,[91] the Supreme Court concluded that governmental interests in traffic safety and aesthetics qualified as substantial regulatory interests, and *Taxpayers for Vincent* reaffirmed that position.[92] Thus, the lower courts have found governmental interests in aesthetics and traffic safety to be sufficient for purposes of intermediate scrutiny analysis.[93]

The federal courts are divided as to the evidence needed to show actual advancement of the public interest in community aesthetics and safety. In *Ackerley Communications of the Northwest Inc. v. Krochalis*,[94] the Ninth Circuit approved Seattle's plan for gradual attrition of billboards, even though the city provided scant proof that the program would actually

---

[87] *See, e.g.*, McCullen v. Coakley, 134 S. Ct. 2518, 2534–35 (2014).
[88] *Id.* at 2535.
[89] *See, e.g.*, Ward v. Rock Against Racism, 491 U.S. 789, 791 (1989).
[90] *See, e.g.*, Members of City Council v. Taxpayers for Vincent, 466 U.S. 789, 813–15 (1984).
[91] 453 U.S. 490, 507 (1981).
[92] *See* 466 U.S. at 815.
[93] *See, e.g.*, Cent. Radio Co., Inc. v. City of Norfolk, 811 F.3d 625, 633 (4th Cir. 2016); Brown v. Town of Cary, 706 F.3d 294 (4th Cir. 2013), *overruled on other grounds*.
[94] 108 F.3d 1095 (9th Cir. 1997).

advance the stated goals of community aesthetics and safety.[95] In contrast, in *Pagan v. Fruchey*,[96] a bare majority of a fifteen-judge en banc panel of the Sixth Circuit rejected the "bald assertions" and "conclusory articulation of governmental interests" that a ban on public parking of cars displaying "for sale" signs would serve community interests.[97] Following the Supreme Court's 2014 ruling in *McCullen v. Coakley*, which included a fairly deep analysis regarding whether Massachusetts had appropriately tailored its buffer-zone law for healthcare clinics to its stated regulatory purposes, some lower courts have engaged in more searching inquiries regarding the evidentiary basis for local speech regulations' purpose statements.[98]

F. Commercial Speech Regulations

As described previously, commercial advertising was long considered to be outside the protection of the First Amendment,[99] but that position evolved in a trio of cases in the 1970s.[100] The end result is the *Central Hudson* test:

> At the outset, we must determine whether the expression is protected by the First Amendment. For commercial speech to come within that

---

[95] *Id.* at 1100. Relying heavily on the Supreme Court's analysis in *Metromedia* and in light of the fact that Seattle's sign code was substantively similar to the San Diego ordinance under challenge in *Metromedia*, the Ninth Circuit determined that it was not necessary to engage in a searching evidentiary analysis to conclude that Seattle's code was correctly premised on the notion that billboard controls would in fact achieve the city's aesthetic and traffic safety goals. This holding in *Krochalis* was cited approvingly in *Naser Jewelers, Inc. v. City of Concord*, 513 F.3d 27 (1st Cir. 2008).

[96] 492 F.3d 766 (6th Cir. 2007).

[97] *Id.* at 777 ("The record before us does not, however, disclose what Glendale's aesthetic objectives are. Perhaps Glendale hopes to avoid unsightly signage cluttering neighborhood streets; perhaps Glendale seeks to avoid having its streets filled with vehicles that may often not be the sort of automobiles people would like to have parked on their neighborhood streets; perhaps 'For Sale' signs posted on cars are simply not in keeping with the character of Glendale's neighborhoods. There are various possibilities, but it is not the place of the reviewing court to supply hypothetical justifications for speech regulation."). The court in *Pagan* relied heavily on the conclusions of the Supreme Court in *Edenfield v. Fane*, 507 U.S. 761 (1993), where the Court determined that at least some evidentiary basis was required in order "to establish that a speech regulation addresses actual harms with some basis in fact," *Pagan*, 492 F.3d at 774.

[98] *See, e.g.*, Bruni v. City of Pittsburgh, 824 F.3d 353 (3d Cir. 2016); Reilly v. City of Harrisburg, 205 F. Supp. 3d 620 (M.D. Pa. 2016); E & J Equities, LLC v. Bd. of Adjustment, 146 A.3d 623 (N.J. 2016).

[99] *See, e.g.*, Valentine v. Chrestensen, 316 U.S. 52, 54 (1942).

[100] Linmark Assocs. Inc. v. Twp. of Willingboro, 431 U.S. 85 (1977); Va. Pharmacy Bd. v. Va. Citizens Consumer Council, 425 U.S. 748, 96 S. Ct. 1817, 48 L. Ed. 2d 346; Cent. Hudson Gas and Elec. v. Pub. Serv. Comm'n, 447 U.S. 557 (1980)

provision, it at least must concern lawful activity and not be misleading. Next, we ask whether the asserted governmental interest is substantial. If both inquiries yield positive answers, we must determine whether the regulation directly advances the governmental interest asserted, and whether it is not more extensive than is necessary to serve that interest.[101]

The Supreme Court refined this test in *Board of Trustees of the State University of New York v. Fox*,[102] stating that the *Central Hudson* test was "substantially similar" to the application of the test for validity of time, place, and manner restrictions upon protected speech and does *not* require least restrictive means.[103]

G. The Law of Billboards

The foundation case for the "law of billboards," *Metromedia v. City of San Diego*,[104] is a prime example of the cloudiness that long permeated the law of signs and that may be clarified by *Reed*. The *Metromedia* plurality opinion stated that "[w]e deal here with the law of billboards,"[105] yet the word *billboard* is not defined, and the various opinions make references to both "on-site billboards" and "off-site billboards." Because of the complexity of the case and its outcome, in his dissent, Justice Rehnquist called the case a "virtual Tower of Babel from which no definitive principles can be clearly drawn."[106] The case was a review of the sign and billboard regulations of San Diego, California, aimed at eliminating billboards from the city without payment of compensation. The decision includes five separate opinions totaling more than ninety pages, and no more than four votes could be garnered to define the legal issues presented, the appropriate method of analysis, or the constitutional test to apply.

---

[101] 447 U.S. 557, 566 (1980).
[102] 492 U.S. 469 (1989).
[103] *Id.* at 477–78.
[104] 453 U.S. 490 (1981).
[105] *Id.* at 501.
[106] *Id.* at 569 (Rehnquist, J., dissenting).

Justices Brennan and Blackmun voted to invalidate the entire ordinance because, in their view, it created a total ban without justification.[107] Chief Justice Burger, who would have upheld the law in total, maintained that "the ordinance here in no sense suppresses freedom of expression, either by discriminating among ideas or topics or by suppressing discussion generally."[108]

Despite the long and highly fractured decision, many lower courts have distilled *Metromedia* to three basic principles: (1) governments can ban billboards and other off-site signs, (2) a sign regulation may not prefer commercial speech over noncommercial speech, and (3) a sign code may not favor certain categories of noncommercial speech over others.

Even after *Reed*, *Metromedia* is still invoked for the different tests that apply to regulations of commercial versus noncommercial speech. With respect to commercial speech, *Metromedia* had a clear majority for each of the following points: the rights of noncommercial and commercial speakers are entitled to differing levels of First Amendment protection, and they are analyzed separately; regulation of commercial speech is analyzed under the four-part test of *Central Hudson*; the prohibition of off-site advertising is directly related to the stated objectives of traffic safety and aesthetics; local governments may conclude that off-site advertising, with its periodically changing content, presents a more serious problem than on-site advertising; and off-site commercial billboards may be prohibited while on-site commercial billboards are permitted.[109]

Metromedia was favorably cited in *Lamar Central Outdoor, Inc. v. City of Los Angeles*, which held that even after *Reed*, the city could still ban billboards without violating the state constitution.[110] And in *City of Corona v. AMG Outdoor Advertising*, the court approved a city's requirements for

---

[107] *Id.* at 526–27 (Brennan, J., concurring).
[108] *Id.* at 562 (Burger, C. J., dissenting).
[109] In *Members of City Council v. Taxpayers for Vincent*, the Court characterized *Metromedia* thus: "seven Justices explicitly concluded that this interest [avoiding visual clutter] was sufficient to justify a prohibition of billboards," 466 U.S. 789, 806 (1984).
[110] 245 Cal. App. 4th 610, 623–26 (2016)

the relocation of existing billboards erected without permits, relying in part on *Metromedia*.[111]

IV. Special Problems In Sign Regulation

A. On-Site/Off-Site Distinction

Sign codes often distinguish between on-site and off-site signs, with the purpose of regulating billboards (off-site) and store signs (on-site) differently. The same criteria are less commonly called on-premises/off-premises, point-of-sale/non point-of-sale, or accessory/nonaccessory distinctions. Although the term *off-site* commonly connotes billboards, signs indicating "Motel 9 next exit" or "Denny's Restaurant straight ahead two miles" are off-site signs, but they may not be billboards.

One of the most vexing theoretical problems of sign regulation is whether and where a sign expressing a noncommercial idea may be considered to be on-site. The narrowest view is that "Vote for Pat Smith" is on-site only at campaign offices for Pat Smith; similarly, "Jesus Saves" would be on-site only at a Christian church. A broader view would consider the sign on-site anywhere a Smith supporter or a Christian exercises his or her signage right. And the broadest view is that an idea has no location at all and thus must be considered "on-site" anywhere.

Although this distinction is obvious enough when the message promotes the sale of goods or services offered for immediate sale at the same location as the sign, defining the location of an idea—such as expression of political or religious views—can be a more difficult call. For example, in *Southlake Property Associates v. City of Morrow*, the court concluded:

> An idea, unlike a product, may be viewed as located wherever the idea is expressed, *i.e.*, wherever the speaker is located. Under this alternative view, all noncommercial speech is onsite. A sign bearing a noncommercial message is onsite wherever the speaker places it.[112]

---

[111] 244 Cal. App. 4th 291 (2016).
[112] 112 F.3d 1114, 1118 (11th Cir. 1997).

Contrast the Eleventh Circuit's view in *Southlake* with the Ninth Circuit's view in *National Advertising Co. v. City of Orange*:

> We interpret Orange's ordinance as prohibiting all signs relating to activity not on the premises on which the sign is located . . . and permitting all signs relating to activity on the premises. Whether the message on the signs is commercial or noncommercial is irrelevant: both commercial and noncommercial signs are permitted if they relate to activity on the premises and prohibited if they do not.[113]

Although it has often been argued that the distinction between on-site and off-site signs is content based—an evaluation of a sign's message to determine whether it relates to the premises on which the sign is located is, after all, an evaluation of the sign's message or content—most courts have rejected the argument, concluding that it is a location criterion selected by the sign owner, based on projected use, either for limited and local display or for a variety of messages from many sponsors.[114]

B. Bans and Exceptions

Despite the plurality opinion in *Metromedia* disapproving of exceptions to a ban on certain forms of signage, some courts have upheld ordinances containing content based exceptions. Examples include *Lavey v. City of Two Rivers*, in which several sign types were exempted from permitting, including construction signs,[115] government signs, house number and name plate signs, interior signs, memorial signs and plaques, "no trespassing" or "no dumping" signs, public notice signs, political signs, real estate signs, vehicular signs, and neighborhood identification signs; *Messer v. City of*

---

[113] 861 F.2d 246, 247 (9th Cir. 1988).

[114] *See, e.g.*, Clear Channel Outdoor, Inc. v. City of Los Angeles, 340 F.3d 810, 814 (9th Cir. 2003) ("[T]he on-site/off-site distinction is, in effect, a distinction between sign-structures dedicated to a limited and local purpose and those made available for a wider range of communicative purposes."). In his concurrence in *Reed v. Town of Gilbert*, 135 S. Ct. 2218, 2233 (2015), Justice Alito wrote that the on-premises/off-premises distinction is a valid content neutral distinction even after *Reed*, and there is reason to believe that six of the nine justices participating in the *Reed* decision agreed with him. *Id.* at 2233.

[115] 171 F.3d 1110, 1113 n. 5 (7th Cir. 1999).

Douglasville, with several exceptions from the permit requirement;[116] and *National Advertising Co. v. Town of Babylon*, where the Second Circuit upheld a general ban with an exemption for real estate signs.[117] These decisions are of questionable validity after *Reed*. However, the turning point in *Reed* was not exemption from a permit requirement but differing rules for size, display time, and locations, based on the message content or category. Several older decisions are arguably inconsistent with *Reed*, including *Flying J Travel Plaza v. Transportation Cabinet*,[118] *Matthews v. Needham*,[119] *State v. Miller*,[120] and *Adams v. City of Newport News*.[121]

C. Favoring Commercial Versus Noncommercial Speech and Message Substitution

Some sign ordinances address the "inversion problem"—also known as "favoring commercial over noncommercial speech"—by including in the sign ordinance a provision stating, in essence, that a noncommercial message of any type may be substituted for any commercial message that is otherwise allowable. Such language led courts to validate sign regulations in *Outdoor Systems v. City of Mesa*,[122] *Major Media of the Southeast v. City of Raleigh*,[123] and *Georgia Outdoor Advertising v. City of Waynesville*.[124] However, in a case where a sign code allowed substitution for on-site but not off-site signs, the First Circuit found that the law "isolated business and property owners as a privileged class" and invalidated the law.[125] Message

---

[116] 975 F.2d 1501 (11th Cir. 1992).

[117] 900 F.2d 551 (2d Cir. 1989).

[118] 928 S.W.2d 344 (Ky. 1996) (invalidating a ban on flashing signs because it made exception for time, date, and weather signs).

[119] 764 F.2d 58 (1st Cir. 1985) (upholding general ban with exceptions for various types of commercial and noncommercial signs, but no exception for political; unconstitutional).

[120] 416 A.2d 821 (N.J. 1980) (upholding law that prohibited political signs but allowed "for sale" and signs identifying churches and governmental signs).

[121] 373 S.E.2d 917 (Va. 1988) (invalidating broad exception for on-site commercial without exception for noncommercial speech).

[122] 997 F.2d 604 (9th Cir. 1993).

[123] 792 F.2d 1269, 1271–72 (4th Cir. 1986).

[124] 833 F.2d 43 (4th Cir. 1987).

[125] *See* Ackerley Commc'ns of Mass., Inc. v. City of Cambridge, 88 F.3d 33 (1st Cir. 1996); *but see* Wheeler v. Comm'r of Highways, 822 F.2d 586 (6th Cir. 1987) (allowing persons who own or lease property to have a sign is not favoring one message over another).

substitution provisions have proven decisive in some billboard company challenges to local sign codes.[126]

Exceptions to a general ban are not the only means of finding improper favoring of commercial speech. Courts have found the same flaw when a permit is required for off-site noncommercial speech but not on-site commercial speech,[127] when the law disallows all noncommercial messages,[128] and when construction signs are allowed to be bigger than political signs or temporary construction signs are allowed a longer display period than election signs.[129]

D. The Site Relevance Theory

In *Rappa v. New Castle County*,[130] the Third Circuit declined to follow *Metromedia* on the issue of exceptions from a general ban and created a new test. The core concept of the "site relevance" theory is that certain messages have special meaning or purpose in particular places and that this relationship between message and location can justify a content based exception if there is no governmental purpose to censor or favor particular messages or speakers.[131] This theory has never been adopted outside the Third Circuit. Even within that circuit, its validity is questionable in light of *Reed*.

E. Punishing Past Speech

In *Ackerley Communications of Massachusetts v. City of Somerville*,[132] the city adopted a "grandfather" provision that exempted existing nonconforming signs from the city's amortization scheme unless they had been used for

---

[126] *See, e.g.*, Outdoor Media Grp., Inc. v. City of Beaumont, 506 F.3d 895, 902 (9th Cir. 2005); Get Outdoors II, LLC v. City of Chula Vista, 407 F.Supp.2d 1172, 1174 (S.D. Cal. 2005).

[127] *See* Desert Outdoor Adver., Inc. v. City of Moreno Valley, 103 F.3d 814, 819 (9th Cir. 1996).

[128] *See* Norton Outdoor Adver., Inc. v. Vill. of Arlington Heights, 433 N.W.2d 198 (Ohio 1982).

[129] *See* Nat'l Adver. Co. v. Town of Niagara, 942 F.2d 145 (2d Cir. 1991).

[130] 18 F.3d 1043 (3d Cir. 1994).

[131] Although concurring in the panel's result, then-Judge Alito said that if sitting alone he would employ a different analysis, 18 F.3d at 1079. The third member of the panel, Judge Garth, dissented, accusing the majority of departing from the instructions of *Metromedia* without justification, 18 F.3d at 1080, and of fashioning the new test from the whole cloth, 18 F.3d at 1083.

[132] 878 F.2d 513 (1st Cir. 1989).

off-site commercial advertising. Signs that had carried noncommercial messages, regardless of location, and other signs displaying on-site commercial messages could remain in operation. The net effect was to subject most billboards to an amortization scheme. The First Circuit agreed with the city that its ordinance did not suffer from the same flaws as *Metromedia* but agreed with the billboard company that the city's law still violated the First Amendment because

> [T]he issue is whether a severe penalty—a prohibition against future speech—may be imposed on a speaker because he in the past engaged in a certain kind of lawful but less favored speech. We conclude that the First Amendment does not permit this particular discrimination.[133]

The First Circuit subsequently decided a similar case, *Ackerley Communications of Massachusetts v. City of Cambridge.*[134] This problem of "punishing past speech" can be avoided by drafting sign rules that do not exempt signs from amortization based on past use.

F. Regulation of Physical Characteristics of Signs

Courts rarely have trouble sustaining sign regulations that concern only structural and location factors such as size, height, setback, illumination method, and so forth, as long as such factors do not turn on or regulate the message content. Such regulations seem to be limited only by a rule of reasonableness.[135] Several cases have approved bans on portable or movable

---

[133] *Id.* at 518.

[134] 88 F.3d 33 (1st Cir. 1996).

[135] *See, e.g.,* Harp Adver. Ill., Inc. v. Vill. of Chicago Ridge, 9 F.3d 1290 (7th Cir. 1993) (finding billboard company lacked standing to challenge city's sign ordinance "because it could not put up its sign even if it achieved total victory in this litigation" because its proposed sign would measure 1,200 square feet and village's law limited billboards to 200 square feet); Rzadkowolski v. Vill. of Lake Orion, 845 F.2d 653 (6th Cir. 1988); Barber v. Muni. of Anchorage, 776 P.2d 1035 (Alaska 1989) (upholding ban on rooftop signs, off-premise advertising signs, and portable signs was sufficiently tailored to serve city's legitimate interests in community aesthetics); Hilton v. City of Toledo, 405 N.E.2d 1047 (Ohio 1980) (upholding Uniform Sign Code, which controls standards for fabrication, erection, and use of signs, including a ban on flashing and portable signs); *but see* Nat'l Adver. Co. v. City of Rolling Meadows, 789 F.2d 571 (7th Cir. 1986) (finding that under state law, city could regulate billboard supports and total height of the structure but could not impose sign face size limits that prohibited "customary use," *i.e.,* industry standard format billboard ads).

signs.[136] However, see *Dills v. Cobb County*, where a setback requirement for portable signs was found not to serve the asserted governmental interests in aesthetics and traffic safety.[137]

Occasionally there is a question about whether a given display qualifies as a sign or is exempted from the local code as an artistic mural.[138] These distinctions are suspect after *Reed*[139] and are discussed at greater length in chapter 4.

VII. Political and Protest Signs

Before the Supreme Court's decision in *Reed*, special rules for political signs—generally defined as signs advocating a vote on an upcoming election—were found in many, if not most, local sign codes. After *Reed*, special political sign rules are highly problematic because they are content based, within the broad category of noncommercial speech, and subject to strict scrutiny. Indeed, the cases that have reviewed special rules applied to political signs following *Reed* have uniformly found that such rules are invalid.[140]

Generally speaking, the courts are at least as keen to protect the speech rights of "lonely pamphleteers" and people expressing personal grudges or disputes with "city hall" as they are to protect the free speech rights of the major political parties and their candidates.[141]

---

[136] *See, e.g.,* Lone Star Sec. & Video, Inc. v. City of Los Angeles, 827 F.3d 1192 (9th Cir. 2016); Harnish v. Manatee Cnty., 783 F.2d 1535 (11th Cir. 1986); Don's Portasigns v. City of Clearwater, 829 F.2d 1051 (11th Cir. 1987); Lindsay v. City of San Antonio, 821 F.2d 1103 (5th Cir. 1985); Dills v. Cobb Cnty., 755 F.2d 1473 (11th Cir. 1985); Showing Animals Respect and Kindness v. City of W. Hollywood, 166 Cal. App. 4th 816 (2008).

[137] 755 F.2d 1473 (11th Cir. 1985).

[138] *See* Wag More Dogs, L.L.C. v. Cozart, 680 F.3d 359 (4th Cir. 2012); Complete Angler, LLC v. City of Clearwater, 607 F. Supp. 2d 1326 (M.D. Fla. 2009); City of Indio v. Arroyo, 143 Cal. App. 3d 151 (1983), *rehearing denied* (finding mural on exterior of store depicted Mexican heritage themes; mural was clearly ideological, not commercial); City of Corpus Christi v. Azoulay, No. 13-04-592-CV, 2006 WL 1172330 (Tex. Ct. App. 2006) (finding proposed three-dimensional shark structure would not be a sign).

[139] *See* Cent. Radio Co., Inc. v. City of Norfolk, 811 F.3d 625, 634 (4th Cir. 2016).

[140] *See, e.g.,* Marin v. Town of Southeast, 136 F. Supp. 3d 548 (S.D.N.Y. 2015).

[141] Knoeffler v. Town of Mamakating, 87 F. Supp. 2d 322 (S.D.N.Y. 2000) (addressing yard signs reading "Warning: Town Justice Allows Neighbor's Biting Dog to Run Loose!!"; "Tie Up Your Biting Dog"; "Poison Your Own Air, Not Ours!"; "Stop the Smoke Pollution"); Lawson v. City of Kankakee,

(footnote continued on next page)

The law of billboards, large and permanent structures with messages that change on a monthly basis, does not necessarily apply to election-oriented campaign posters, which are usually small and temporary in nature.[142] An alternative method for dealing with election-season signage is suggested by *G.K. Ltd. Travel v. City of Lake Oswego*,[143] where the allowable sign area was increased in a defined period before an election, but the increase applied to all signs, not just political signs.

A. Honoring Debate, Dissent, and the Political Sign

For an encomium to political free speech, its role in the proper functioning of a democratic society, and the judicial protection of it, see *McIntyre v. Ohio Elections Commission*, which found that a state law banning distribution of anonymous campaign literature violated the First Amendment.[144] And for paeans to signs as a crucial medium of political expression, see, *City of Ladue v. Gilleo*,[145] *Baldwin v. Redwood City*,[146] and *Collier v. City of Tacoma*.[147]

B. Total Bans on All Political Signs

Even before *Reed v. Gilbert*, courts routinely declared city-wide total bans on political signs to be unconstitutional, generally concluding that the freedoms of speech, press, and assembly, as well as interests in wide-open political debate and efficient operation of the democratic election process, outweigh the aesthetic interest. A leading case is the Ohio Supreme Court's decision in *Peltz v. City of South Euclid*.[148] The city enacted an ordinance that explicitly declared its purpose to "eliminate political signs," on the

---

(*footnote continued from previous page*)

81 F. Supp. 2d 930 (C.D. Ill. 2000) (reviewing sign reading "Mayor Don Green is unfair to landlords, his City sign is an attack on free speech in the 1st Amendment. Call the Mayor at home: 939-2897 and tell him to take down his sign"); Goward v. City of Minneapolis, 456 N.W.2d 460 (Minn. 1990) (addressing yard sign that read, "Attention: Minneapolis Dept. of Inspections; City Attorneys Office; My dear neighbor: You have made my life a living hell for the last two years!"); Barber v. Dep't of Transp., 111 S.W.3d 86 (Tex. 2003) (addressing attorney's sign near freeway: "Just Say NO to Searches").

[142] Arlington Cnty. Republican Comm. v. Arlington Cnty., 983 F.2d 587, 593 (4th Cir. 1993).
[143] 436 F.3d 1064 (9th Cir. 2006).
[144] 514 U.S. 334 (1994).
[145] 512 U.S. 43 (1994).
[146] 540 F.2d 1360 (9th Cir. 1976).
[147] 854 P.2d 1046 (Wash. 1993).
[148] 228 N.E.2d 320 (Ohio 1967).

finding that such signs "were often unattractive even when freshly erected and unspoiled." The court found the ordinance unconstitutional under both the state and federal constitutions, explaining:

> The ordinance is not saved by its purpose to eliminate traffic hazards on main thoroughfares and at street intersections. The proscription is against *all* political signs, irrespective of location. Even the regulation of traffic may not be attempted by means which invade explicit constitutional liberties.[149]

In *Matthews v. Town of Needham*, the First Circuit invalidated a town bylaw that banned all political signs but allowed certain other signs, both commercial and noncommercial, as unconstitutional under *Metromedia*.[150] Other cases include *Ross v. Goshi*, finding that an amended version of an ordinance, featuring selective prohibition of political signs while allowing most other types of temporary signs, violated candidates' constitutional rights of free speech and equal protection; the court's invalidation of the amended version automatically restored the original version, which regulated political signs on the same basis as other signs and gave special privileges to political signs sixty days before and ten days after a general election.[151]

C. Political and Protest Signs in Residential Neighborhoods

In *City of Ladue v. Gilleo*,[152] the U.S. Supreme Court invalidated a city ordinance that prohibited all signs in residential areas, with certain exceptions that did not include political signs. The court rejected the time, place, and manner defense, noting that under that doctrine, the government must leave open adequate alternatives for expressing the same message. Because residential signs are unusually cheap and convenient, the Court was not persuaded that the adequate substitutes requirement could be met.[153]

---

[149] *Id.* at 324.
[150] 764 F.2d 58, 60 (1st Cir. 1985).
[151] 351 F. Supp. 949 (D. Haw. 1972), *see also* People v. Middlemark, 420 N.Y.S.2d 151 (N.Y. Sup. Ct. 1979) (complete ban on freestanding political signs is unconstitutional).
[152] 512 U.S. 43 (1994).
[153] *Id.* at 57.

The Court also noted the long history of special respect for individual liberty in the home, both in the law and culture:

> Most Americans would be understandably dismayed, given that tradition, to learn that it was illegal to display from their window an 8-by-11 inch sign expressing their political views. . . . It bears mentioning that individual residents themselves have strong incentives to keep their own property values up and to prevent "visual clutter" in their own yards and neighborhoods—incentives markedly different from those of persons who erect signs on others' land, in others' neighborhoods, or on public property. Residents' self-interest diminishes the danger of the "unlimited" proliferation of residential signs that concerns the City of Ladue.[154]

Although the Court struck down the total ban, it also hinted that "more temperate measures" might be sustained.[155] Since *Ladue*, "more temperate" cases have been rare, but in *Kroll v. Steere*, the court upheld size limits applied to residential sign protesting the killing of deer.[156]

D. Government as Employer Restricting Political Speech of Employees

The rights of a government acting as an employer can overcome the free expression rights of its employees, despite the principles expressed in *Ladue*. For example, in *Horstkoetter v. Department of Public Safety*,[157] the Tenth Circuit upheld a highway patrol policy order forbidding state troopers from displaying political signs on their residences, even if the signs were placed by their spouses who were not employees. The court said the officers' free speech rights were outweighed by the state's interests, which included (1) assuring persons aspiring to careers in law enforcement that they are not obliged to make public display of political affiliation or defer to the wishes of political dignitaries in order to guarantee retention and

---

[154] *Id.* at 58.
[155] *Id.*
[156] 759 A.2d 541 (Conn. Ct. App. 2000).
[157] 159 F.3d 1265 (10th Cir. 1995).

promotion; (2) promoting efficiency and harmony among law enforcement personnel by avoiding controversy within police departments; and (3) proclaiming that police protection will be available to the public, free from political overtones, and that the police will deal impartially with all who give them concern. However, in *International Association of Firefighters v. City of Ferguson*,[158] the court invalidated such a ban when it applied to spouses of public employees.

E. Durational Limits on Political Signs in Residential Neighborhoods

One federal district court has interpreted *Ladue* to mean that limitations on display time for political signs in residential neighborhoods are per se unconstitutional. In *Curry v. Prince George's County*, the court commented that the most reasonable construction to put upon the Supreme Court's reference to "mere regulations short of a ban" is that although they may include size, shape, and location restrictions for campaign signs, they may not include durational ones.[159] Most other courts considering the question have reached the same conclusion.[160]

F. Durational Limits on Political Signs—All Areas

Many local codes limit the display time for political signs to a certain period before and after an election. All such rules are highly questionable in the aftermath of *Reed*. Even before *Reed*, most courts tended to invalidate such display limits on both equal protection and First Amendment grounds. Virtually all the reported decisions note that if the durational limit applies only to political signs, then it is content based, and strict scrutiny applies.[161]

---

[158] 283 F.3d 969 (8th Cir. 2002).

[159] 33 F. Supp. 2d 447 (D. Md. 1999).

[160] *See, e.g.*, Dimas v. City of Warren, 939 F. Supp. 554 (E.D. Mich. 1996); City of Euclid v. Mabel, 484 N.E.2d 249 (Ohio Ct. App. 1984); *see also* Tauber v. Town of Longmeadow, 695 F. Supp. 1358 (D. Mass. 1988) (stating in dicta that "[t]his Court is not convinced that a thirty or sixty day durational limit is per se unconstitutional (although upon consideration of the issue, the Court believes that a thirty day limit would be less likely to survive review).").

[161] *See, e.g.*, Outdoor Sys., Inc. v. City of Lenexa, 67 F. Supp. 2d 1231 (D. Kan. 1999); Collier v. City of Tacoma, 854 P.2d 1046 (Wash. 1993).

In *Whitton v. Gladstone*, the Eighth Circuit invalidated a city ordinance with a display limit of thirty days before an election and a seven-day postelection removal requirement.[162] Impermissible favoring of commercial signs over noncommercial signs was shown by the ninety-day display limit for temporary construction signs and the thirty-day limit for political signs. The law was content based because the display limits were triggered by the political content of the signs; it was not enough that the regulation was viewpoint neutral within the category of political speech.[163]

In *Collier v. City of Tacoma*,[164] the Washington Supreme Court applied the free speech provision of the state constitution to invalidate a sixty-day pre-election durational limit, principally because it was not narrowly tailored to serve the city's interests in aesthetics and traffic safety. Similarly, in *City of Painesville v. Dworken & Bernstein Co.*, the Ohio Supreme Court struck down a city law limiting display time to seventeen days before an election, saying:

> a narrowly drawn municipal ordinance imposing reasonable time, place, and manner restrictions on the display of temporary signs, including political yard signs posted on private property, could constitutionally be enacted. [The law under review], however, is not such an ordinance, and is unconstitutional when applied to prohibit the owner of private property from posting a single political sign on that property outside the durational period set by the ordinance.[165]

In *Donnelly v. Campbell*, the First Circuit found a statewide ban on freeway billboards valid as to commercial messages but invalid because the exceptions for noncommercial speech did not go far enough. The court explained:

> We doubt that three weeks is enough time to publicize a campaign, particularly for the little-known or unpopular candidate, or cause, with

---

[162] 54 F.3d 1400 (8th Cir. 1995).
[163] *Id.* at 1404–05.
[164] 854 P.2d 1046 (Wash. 1993).
[165] 733 N.E.2d 1152, 1154 (Ohio 2000).

the greatest need for exposure. Moreover, no exception is available for signs on important public issues as to which no referendum is pending.[166]

However, pre-election durational limits have been approved when they were interpreted as allowing a short-term increase in political signage, against a backdrop that allowed some political signs at all times.[167]

One relatively old case approved durational time limits.[168] And in *Arlington County Republican Committee v. Arlington County*, the Fourth Circuit listed "durational limits" as among the "less restrictive means" the county could use to serve its interests;[169] however, this statement was characterized as dicta in *Curry v. Prince George's County*.[170]

G. Limits on Size of Political Signs

In *Baldwin v. Redwood City*, the city limited the size of temporary signs on both per parcel and city-wide cumulative bases. The per parcel limit was sixteen square feet for an individual sign and eighty square feet for all signs combined. The Ninth Circuit found these size limits valid, stating:

> There is nothing in the record to suggest that the numbers of parcels in separate ownership in Redwood City is so limited that the [eighty] square foot per parcel limit imposes any significant restriction on the total exposure a candidate can obtain.[171]

The size limits for individual signs were justified as reducing the accumulation of clutter and minimizing traffic hazards. However, the city-wide cumulative limit—sixty-four square feet for all temporary signs advertising a particular candidate, in a city of fifty-five thousand people—restricted the quantity of campaign speech by candidates and partisans, limiting expression at the

---

[166] 639 F.2d 6, 15 (1st Cir. 1980).
[167] *See, e.g.,* Ross v. Goshi, 351 F. Supp. 949 (D. Haw. 1972); Brayton v. City of New Brighton, 519 N.W.2d 243 (Minn. Ct. App. 1994).
[168] *See* Town of Huntington v. Estate of Schwartz, 313 N.Y.S.2d 918 (N.Y. Sup. Ct. 1970).
[169] 983 F.2d 587, 594 (4th Cir. 1993).
[170] 33 F. Supp. 2d 447, 455 n. 9 (D. Md. 1999).
[171] 540 F.2d 1360, 1369 (9th Cir. 1976).

core of First Amendment protection, and was thus unconstitutional. A size limit of eleven inches high for individual temporary signs was upheld in *Candidates' Outdoor Graphic Service v. San Francisco.*[172]

VIII. Signs In Residential Neighborhoods

A. Tranquility Versus Freedom of Expression

Residential neighborhoods present a dilemma for sign regulation. On the one hand, most people want their neighborhood to be free of the crowds, traffic, noise, and visual distractions of typical commercial districts, and almost always the local government is eager to help them protect this special residential character through restrictive zoning laws. On the other hand, our culture still honors the tradition that a "man's home is his castle"; an aspect of that value is that residents should be free to fly flags and post signs expressing political, religious, and other messages in their own yards. Most people will tolerate a certain number of signs in their neighbor's yard but demand action by the city, or the homeowners' association, when things "get out of hand."

B. Real Estate "For Sale" Signs

The first U.S. Supreme Court case addressing signage rights in residential neighborhoods was *Linmark Associates, Inc. v. Township of Willingboro.*[173] In an effort to stem "white flight"—panic selling by whites in neighborhoods undergoing racial integration—the city banned on-site real estate "for sale" signs. The Court's unanimous decision first reviewed the reasons that First Amendment protection had been extended to commercial speech in the previous two terms, then held that the ordinance violated the First Amendment. Justice Marshall condemned the paternalistic motivation of the Township Council, which he said had acted to prevent its residents from obtaining certain information.

---

[172] 574 F. Supp. 1240 (N.D. Cal. 1983).
[173] 431 U.S. 85 (1977).

That information, which pertains to sales activity in Willingboro, is of vital interest to Willingboro residents, since it may bear on one of the most important decisions they have a right to make: where to live and raise their families. The Council has sought to restrict the free flow of these data because it fears that otherwise homeowners will make decisions inimical to what the Council views as the homeowners' self-interest and the corporate interest of the township: they will choose to leave town. The Council's concern, then, was not with any commercial aspect of "For Sale" signs—with offerors communicating offers to offerees—but with the substance of the information communicated to Willingboro citizens. If dissemination of this information can be restricted, then every locality in the country can suppress any facts that reflect poorly on the locality, so long as a plausible claim can be made that disclosure would cause the recipients of the information to act "irrationally."[174]

Even though *Linmark* struck down a total ban on real estate "for sale" signs, in *South Suburban Housing Center v. Greater South Suburban Board of Realtors*, the Seventh Circuit approved the laws of several cities that limited the size, number, and placement of such signs, which the cities said they had enacted to serve the aesthetic interest.[175] The court found no evidence to contradict this statement of purpose and motivation. In addition, the court also approved a special permit fee for such signs that one city had imposed.

In *Cleveland Board of Realtors v. City of Euclid*, the city adopted a law banning "for sale" signs in residential yards but allowed them, with a maximum size of three square feet (or four feet if the setback was greater than seventy-five feet) in home windows.[176] In the recitals for the law, the city council said: "real estate and other commercial graphics are an unneeded commercial intrusion into non commercial residential neighborhoods; and . . . this Council finds and determines that real estate signs, in particular, can damage the image and perception about the viability and desirability of

[174] *Id.* at 96.
[175] 935 F.2d 868 (7th Cir. 1991).
[176] 88 F.3d 382 (6th Cir. 1995).

a neighborhood as a good place to live and invest for persons of all races." The trial judge conducted a driving tour of the city and concluded that the window signs were ineffective and amounted to a de facto ban on "for sale" signs; he also found considerable evidence that the real motivation was to combat the practice of realtors "steering" buyers and that it was "more likely than not" that the ordinance was enacted to ameliorate any negative messages that a proliferation of "for sale" signs might convey.

The Sixth Circuit said the trial judge erred by rejecting the city's claim of a motivation to serve the aesthetic interest but agreed that "the wholesale ban on lawn signs in the name of aesthetics in this case is, simply, not sufficiently narrowly tailored to withstand constitutional scrutiny. Indeed, it appears that the regulation is not 'tailored' at all."[177] Finally, the "alternative" methods left open—window signs—were not adequate.

Several other cases have struck down bans on real estate "for sale" signs.[178]

C. Commercial Message Signs in Residential Neighborhoods

Even though the courts have found a constitutional right to display on-site real estate "for sale" and political and protest yard signs, most have upheld restrictions on other sorts of commercial speech in residential zones.[179] The well-drafted local sign code will thus either avoid any content rules for residential yard signs or allow residential and yard signs to display any variety and combination of noncommercial messages, as well as real estate "for sale" signs.

---

[177] *Id.* at 387.

[178] *See, e.g.,* Citizens United for Free Speech II v. Long Beach Twp. Bd. of Comm'rs, 802 F. Supp. 1223 (D.N.J. 1992); E. Bergen Cnty. Bd. of Realtors, Inc. v. Borough of Fort Lee, 720 F. Supp. 51 (D.N.J. 1989); Greater Baltimore Bd. of Realtors v. Hughes, 596 F. Supp. 906 (D. Md. 1984); Prus v. City of Chicago, 711 F. Supp. 469 (N.D. Ill. 1989), *but see* Kennedy v. Avondale Estates, 414 F. Supp. 2d 1184 (N.D. Ga. 2005).

[179] *See, e.g.,* Jim Gall Auctioneers v. City of Coral Gables, 210 F.3d 1331 (11th Cir. 2000) (upholding city ordinance prohibiting auctions of nonhomeowner goods at private residences and the advertising of them, even though "yard sale" signs were allowed); City of Rochester Hills v. Schultz, 592 N.W.2d 69 (Mich. 1999) (upholding municipal ordinance prohibiting the erection of a sign advertising a home business in a residential area—although several types of signs, including some commercial messages, were allowed in residential neighborhoods, they were all compatible with the character).

IX. Conclusion: Practical Applications

The drafting or updating of a local sign code is a major project, requiring input and teamwork from knowledgeable legal counsel and professional land use planners. Serious consideration should be given to a citizens advisory committee, which will meet a few times to discuss policy choices and then prepare a recommendation report. Such a committee should include representatives of scenic and historic preservation groups in addition to the obvious groups, such as business owners, realtors, car dealers, stores, and sign shops. One key to success is a detailed agenda for the entire process, listing the date and time that each topic will be discussed. The first meeting should include an orientation and legal overview from counsel, including the lessons from *Reed v. Town of Gilbert* and any peculiarities arising from state statutory law.

One practical lesson from *Reed* is to "treat all varieties of non commercial speech on signs exactly the same way." Every local sign code should include message substitution; focus primarily on time, place, and manner rules; and avoid rules based on message content or category.

The inevitable call for "political sign rules" should be answered with "rules for temporary signs displaying noncommercial messages." Such signs should be allowed at all times, even if the signage display allowance is greater in the pre-election period. Consideration should be given to a two-chapter approach, one for regulation of signs on private property and another for rules and policies regarding private signs on city-owned property. This approval will give the city maximum flexibility for managing its own property under the governmental speech and public forum doctrines.

3

Electronic Signs
A First Amendment Perspective

Christopher Lake Brown
Deputy Law Director
City of Mansfield
Mansfield, Ohio

I. Introduction

With the proliferation of electronic signs in recent years, the editor of this book thought it important to dedicate a short commentary to the growing jurisprudence of their regulation. Because the foundations of First Amendment law relating to signs differ little between electronic and nonelectronic signs, this commentary focuses on the differences between electronic signs and their traditional counterparts. Due to the nature of electronic signs, time, place, and manner considerations such as size and brightness play a larger role in the regulation of electronic signs as compared with traditional signage.

 The reader is encouraged to read this commentary only after reviewing the basic law of sign regulation contained in chapter 2. Chapter 2 discusses some of the key distinctions in the law of sign regulation: commercial and noncommercial speech, on-premises and off-premises signage, and content neutrality versus content based regulation. All of these doctrines apply equally to electronic and nonelectronic signage. This commentary simply applies the traditional First Amendment doctrines associated with sign regulation to the regulation of electronic signs.

II. The Electronic Explosion

In the middle of the nineteenth century, the first illuminated signs appeared in front of businesses across America, but they were not lit by electricity: they were gas-lit. At the end of the nineteenth century, Thomas Edison invented the electric light bulb, and it wasn't long before it found its way into signage. The first known electric sign in the United States was erected in New York City in 1892; it read, "MANHATTAN BEACH—SWEPT BY OCEAN BREEZES."[1] These incandescent-bulb signs were eventually joined by neon and fluorescent tubes, and those were followed by the internally illuminated plastic signs that are ubiquitous today.

Typically, the primary distinction between electronic and nonelectronic signs is based on the source of the light: a traditional sign with lights shining on it is different from a sign that is lit from within. For regulatory purposes, this is one major determining factor for whether a sign is considered electronic or not. This classification is that of "luminance" versus "illuminance," where *luminance* refers to a measure of the perceived brightness of a surface from which light originates, and *illuminance* refers to light that falls upon (and thereby "illuminates") the sign. Another key distinction between electronic signs and nonelectronic signs is that the former are "variable" and the latter are "static," but there are exceptions to this broad dichotomy, including the variable billboard that does not generate its own luminance, such as a tri-face changeable copy sign.[2] Local governments may desire to regulate each type of sign differently based on its specific characteristics, and yet they all can be considered a group that is regulated in a different manner than a traditional static billboard or sign.

Today, there are many types of electronic signs, but increasingly common are those referred to as *digital signs*. The most common nomenclature may

---

[1] American Sign Museum, *Through the Years*, http://www.americansignmuseum.org/through-the-years/.
[2] *See* CBS Outdoor, Inc. v. Bd. of Zoning Appeals, No. 98141, 2013 WL 1279684 (Ohio Ct. App. Mar. 28, 2013). The City of Cleveland claimed that a changeable tri-face billboard violated the "automatic changeable copy signs" portion of its billboard ordinance. The sign owner, CBS, said the sign did not. Cleveland's Board of Zoning Appeals and the Cuyahoga County Court of Common Pleas found that the sign did violate Cleveland's sign ordinance, but the case was overturned by the appellate court on procedural grounds.

be *digital signs*, but local governments and their ordinances use a plethora of names: *electronic message displays, electronic variable message signs, LED signs, digital signage, electronic billboards, dynamic signage, constantly variable signage*, and others. For the purposes of this commentary, I use the term *digital signs* to refer to electronic signs backlit by light-emitting diodes (LEDs), liquid crystal display (LCD), or plasma that are capable of automatically changing displays, including scrolling text and animation. When drafting an ordinance regulating digital signage, local governments should endeavor to use terms and definitions that cover a broad range of electronic signage and that respond to the specific circumstances for which the local government is regulating.

III. Basics of Electronic Sign Regulation

Any consideration of electronic sign regulation must begin with the same First Amendment principles governing nonelectronic signs.[3] Courts analyze regulations of noncommercial signage based on how the ordinances regulate the signs: content based restrictions must withstand strict scrutiny[4] from the courts and often fail constitutional analysis.[5] Conversely, content neutral regulations, also known as "time, place, and manner" regulations, face an intermediate level of scrutiny from the courts. Content neutral regulations are much more likely to survive judicial review; the Supreme Court has "often noted that restrictions of this kind are valid provided that they are justified without reference to the content of the regulated speech, that they are narrowly tailored to serve a significant governmental interest, and that they leave open ample alternative channels for communication of the information."[6] As a result, the determination of a sign ordinance's constitutionality almost always depends on the court's determination of whether the ordinance is content based or not. To determine if the ordinance

---

[3] *See* City of Ladue v. Gilleo, 512 U.S. 43, 48 (1994).
[4] *See, e.g.,* Simon & Schuster, Inc. v. Members of N.Y. State Crime Victims Bd., 502 U.S. 105 (1991).
[5] *See* Burson v. Freeman, 504 U.S. 191, 200 (1992) ("[W]e readily acknowledge that a law rarely survives such scrutiny . . . .").
[6] Clark v. Cmty. for Creative Non Violence, 468 U.S. 288, 293 (1984).

is content based, courts must ask whether the "law applies to particular speech because of the topic discussed or the idea or message expressed."[7] Although these determinations may be based on the subject matter of the speech, some regulations may be considered content based laws because they regulate speech by the speech's function or purpose.[8]

Noncommercial speech is afforded more protection than commercial speech,[9] and although commercial speech regulations are permitted to have some element of content bias, commercial speech regulations must still satisfy an intermediate scrutiny analysis. Commercial speech regulations are analyzed under the familiar *Central Hudson* test, an intermediate form of scrutiny similar to, but distinct from, the time, place, and manner test.[10] The *Central Hudson* test and commercial sign regulation are discussed in greater detail in chapter 2.

For regulations of both commercial and noncommercial speech, two common "significant governmental interests" frequently appear, and they are very important to the regulation of electronic signs: traffic safety and aesthetics. Of these two, aesthetics is more often at the center of legal disputes. Local governments' ability to regulate aesthetics began with *Berman v. Parker*, when the Supreme Court of the United States held that:

> The concept of the public welfare is broad and inclusive. The values it represents are spiritual as well as physical, aesthetic as well as monetary. It is within the power of the legislature to determine that the community should be beautiful as well as healthy, spacious as well as clean, well-balanced as well as carefully patrolled.[11]

Metromedia followed, where seven justices concluded that aesthetics alone was a justifiable reason for regulating billboards.[12] However, the Court

---

[7] Reed v. Town of Gilbert, 135 S. Ct. 2218, 2227 (2015).

[8] *Id.*

[9] *See* Metromedia, Inc. v. City of San Diego, 453 U.S. 490, 513 (1981); Cent. Hudson Gas & Elec. Corp. v. Public Serv. Comm'n, 447 U.S. 557, 562–63 (1980).

[10] *See Central Hudson*, 447 U.S. at 566.

[11] 348 U.S. 26, 28 (1954) (internal citations omitted).

[12] *See* 453 U.S. at 507–08, 530, 570.

decided that case on different grounds, and the substantiality of aesthetics as a governmental interest was not yet binding law. The issue was put to rest with *Members of City Council v. Taxpayers for Vincent*, when the Court decided aesthetic concerns were "sufficiently substantial to provide an acceptable justification for a content-neutral prohibition against the use of billboards."[13]

Since *Vincent*, courts have repeatedly found that safety and aesthetic concerns are justifiable reasons to restrict the use of electronic signage.[14] Furthermore, some courts have found that aesthetics alone is justification enough to ban electronic signage, including internally lit static signage.[15] Initially, *electric signs* referred to signs that were internally illuminated, as opposed to signs that are illuminated by an external source such as a spotlight. Although these signs may seem quaint or less obtrusive than the increasingly common digital signs, courts have found that these signs may be regulated, and even banned, in the same manner as digital signs, and for the same safety and aesthetic reasons.

In *Asselin v. Town of Conway*,[16] a small New Hampshire community banned all signs "illuminated from within." However, signs illuminated by external lights were allowed. Conway was historically a tourist town drawing outdoor enthusiasts from the nearby White Mountain National Forest; its restriction on internally lit signs was enacted with the stated purpose of preserving the aesthetic charms of the town. Because the ban was content neutral, the court applied the intermediate scrutiny test and found that the community's goals of "preserving scenic vistas" and "promoting community character" were significant and legitimate.[17] Importantly, when deciding that the ban was rationally related to the legitimate aesthetic concerns of the town, the court relied on an expert witness who testified that internally lit signs appear as "disconnected squares of light," whereas externally lit signs are less obtrusive because the light is softer and dissipates more naturally.[18]

---

[13] 466 U.S. 789, 807 (1984).
[14] *See, e.g.,* Naser Jewelers, Inc. v. City of Concord, 513 F.3d 27 (1st Cir. 2008); La Tour v. City of Fayetteville, 442 F.3d 1094 (8th Cir. 2006); Carlson's Chrysler v. City of Concord, 938 A.2d 69 (N.H. 2007).
[15] *See, e.g.,* Asselin v. Town of Conway, 628 A.2d 247 (N.H. 1993).
[16] *Id.*
[17] *Id.* at 250.
[18] *Id.*

Furthermore, the court held that the ban on internally lit signs promoted those goals without being oppressive to free speech. In the words of the intermediate test, the ban left ample alternative channels for communication by allowing billboards and signs that were illuminated by external lights.[19]

Similarly, in *Naser Jewelers, Inc. v. City of Concord*, Concord, New Hampshire, enacted a total ban on "electronic messaging centers."[20] Because it was a complete ban on a physical type of sign, the court analyzed the ordinance as content neutral.[21] The court of appeals upheld the city's ordinance using an analysis very similar to that of the state court in the *Asselin* case, finding the city passed the ordinance for the legitimate reasons of safety and aesthetics; furthermore, the ordinance was a narrowly tailored, content neutral ordinance that left open alternative channels of communication. Some may question how courts interpret an ordinance that completely bans electronic signs to be "narrowly tailored" under the intermediate scrutiny test. In *Naser Jewelers*, the court relied on established precedent from *Vincent* and held that "[w]hen the medium itself is the 'evil the city [seeks] to address,' then a ban of that entire medium is narrowly tailored."[22]

A routine form of content based restriction that frequently appears in electronic sign regulations involves signs that display only date, time, and temperature. These are typically smaller signs that are relatively ubiquitous. In *Carlson's Chrysler v. City of Concord*, the city's sign ordinance banned all electronic signs with the exception of signs that "solely indicate date, time, or temperature."[23] The New Hampshire Supreme Court analyzed the ordinance using the *Central Hudson* test, as the plaintiff considered the ban an unconstitutional restriction on commercial speech. Under *Central Hudson*, courts

---

[19] *See id.* at 251.
[20] 513 F.3d 27 (1st Cir. 2008).
[21] *See id.* at 32.
[22] *Id.* at 36. The Second Circuit Court of Appeals recently found that the City of New York's ban on lighted signs more than forty feet above the sidewalk was content neutral, using an analysis similar to that of the court in *Naser Jewelers*. *See* Vosse v. City of New York, 666 Fed. App'x 11 (2d Cir. Oct. 14, 2016).
[23] 938 A.2d 69 (N.H. 2007).

must determine whether the expression is protected by the First Amendment. For commercial speech to come within that provision, it at least must concern lawful activity and not be misleading. Next, we ask whether the asserted governmental interest is substantial. If both inquiries yield positive answers, we must determine whether the regulation directly advances the governmental interest asserted, and whether it is not more extensive than is necessary to serve that interest.[24]

Under this analysis, the court found that the government's stated interests of safety and aesthetics were substantial and that given the potential distractions and aesthetic damages posed by numerous scrolling or varying commercial advertisements, the ban on everything except date, time, and temperature was no more extensive than necessary to achieve the city's goals.[25] In a separately concurring opinion, one justice wrote: "Because a message displaying time, date and temperature is short and rudimentary, the City could have reasonably found that such a message is less distracting and thus poses less of a traffic hazard than other messages."[26]

In a federal case with a similar legal issue, *La Tour v. City of Fayetteville*,[27] the plaintiff had a small electric sign with moving text. The city's ordinance banned any "sign which flashes, blinks, or is animated."[28] The city's ordinance was not a complete ban on electronic signs and would have allowed the plaintiff's sign if the sign's electronic message were static. Furthermore, the city did not enforce its ordinance against variable signs that displayed date, time, and temperature. Although the ordinance was content neutral as written, the plaintiff argued it was content based as applied. In determining that the ordinance was content neutral, the court held that "the City's desire to promote traffic safety is in no way tied to the content of the flashing signs it seeks to regulate."[29] Just like the *Carlson's Chrysler* court, the Eighth Circuit held that because a sign displaying date, time, and temperature was so rudimentary,

---

[24] *Central Hudson*, 447 U.S. at 557, 566.
[25] *See Carlson's Chrysler*, 938 A.2d at 72–74.
[26] *Id.* at 75 (Duggan, J., concurring).
[27] 442 F.3d 1094 (8th Cir. 2006)
[28] *Id.* at 1095.
[29] *Id.* at 1097.

it would not significantly affect safety as much as other signs with animated text or flashing lights. Under the intermediate scrutiny standard, the court agreed that a sign displaying only the date, time, and temperature would not cause the level of distraction caused by other signs and held that the ordinance was narrowly tailored to meet the city's stated goals of safety and aesthetics.[30] However, these types of "time, date, and temperature" exceptions are of questionable constitutionality in the wake of *Reed v. Town of Gilbert*, where the Supreme Court held that the "commonsense meaning of the phrase 'content based' requires a court to consider whether a regulation of speech 'on its face' draws distinctions based on the message a speaker conveys."[31]

Notwithstanding *Reed*'s implications, exceptions for date, time, and temperature signs are not always constitutional. San Diego, California's ordinance in *Metromedia* gave preference to commercial signs and restricted noncommercial signs, with exceptions including signs displaying date, time, and temperature. The plurality in *Metromedia* wrote, "[a]lthough the city may distinguish between the relative value of different categories of commercial speech, the city does not have the same range of choice in the area of noncommercial speech to evaluate the strength of, or distinguish between, various communicative interests."[32] In other words, courts have allowed ordinances that ban all electronic signs with the exception of date, time, and temperature signs, but a court would likely strike down an ordinance that sought to restrict electronic noncommercial signs with an exception for date, time, and temperature signs.

Perhaps most importantly, when seeking to justify its regulation of electronic signage, a local government must be specific about the purposes of its regulation and equally specific when tailoring the restriction to meet the stated goals of the regulation. Local governments have been tripped up by poorly written ordinances. In *Outdoor Systems, Inc. v. City of Clawson*, the city's ordinance banned signs "on which a display can be posted, painted or otherwise affixed in a manner which is readily changed."[33] In analyzing the

---

[30] *See id.* at 1100.
[31] 135 S. Ct. 2218, 2227 (2015).
[32] 453 U.S. at 514.
[33] 686 N.W.2d 815 (Mich. Ct. App. 2004).

ordinance and whether the city's stated reasons for the ban were significantly justifiable, the court found that safety and aesthetics were justifiable goals. However, the court held that the ordinance was not narrowly tailored to achieve those goals: "Whether a sign is readily changeable or not, it presents the same sort of traffic distraction or aesthetic problem."[34] Indeed, the *City of Clawson* case is interesting in light of the several cases that have found complete bans of all billboards constitutional.

Similarly, when drafting sign ordinances, local governments must consider various types of changeable signage. In *CBS Outdoor v. Cleveland Board of Zoning Appeals*,[35] Cleveland's sign ordinance banned "automatic changeable copy signs (i.e., electronic message centers)"[36] and defined automatic changeable copy signs as any "sign or portion thereof on which the copy changes automatically or animation is displayed through electrical or electronic means" as opposed to manually changeable signs, which were defined as any "sign or portion thereof on which copy is changed manually through placement of letters or symbols on a sign panel."[37] A billboard company erected a "tri-face" billboard, which was comprised of multiple three-sided slats that rotated by means of an electronic motor to display up to three different billboards at different times. The billboard company argued that the sign was not banned by the ordinance because it was not a digital billboard but was illuminated by an external light source like a traditional billboard. The city argued that because the sign could display three distinct messages, and those messages changed "automatically," the sign was prohibited by the ordinance. Although the case was ultimately decided on procedural issues, the fact remains that Cleveland's ambiguously drafted code gave the plaintiffs an opportunity to challenge the sign regulations.

The 2016 New Jersey case *E & J Equities, LLC v. Board of Adjustment of the Township of Franklin*,[38] provides a cautionary tale regarding the narrow tailoring analysis for local governments seeking to use safety and aesthetics

---

[34] *Id.* at 821.
[35] No. 98141, 2013 WL 1279684 (Ohio Ct. App. Mar. 28, 2013).
[36] CLEVELAND, OHIO CODIFIED ORDINANCE § 350.10(j) (2012).
[37] CLEVELAND, OHIO CODIFIED ORDINANCE § 350.03(f) (2012).
[38] 146 A.3d 623 (N.J. 2016).

as government interests motivating electronic sign bans. In that case, a township council adopted an ordinance[39] that amounted to a complete ban on electronic billboards in the township. A billboard company challenged the ordinance on First Amendment grounds. The trial court found the ordinance unconstitutional under immediate scrutiny requirements of commercial speech regulation. The intermediate appellate court overturned that decision after finding the ordinance to be constitutional under the time, place, and manner test of *Clark* and *Ward*.

The New Jersey Supreme Court also analyzed the ordinance as being content neutral and similarly analyzed the ordinance with the time, place, and manner test of *Clark* and *Ward*. However, the state's high court overturned the appellate court and found the ordinance to violate the First Amendment. Although the Court acknowledged that aesthetics and safety have long been recognized as substantial and legitimate government interests, the Court held that the township failed to provide any support for how the ordinance furthered those interests, stating in part:

> The record provides no basis to discern how three static billboards are more aesthetically palatable than a single digital billboard . . . . The record is also bereft of any examination of the safety impact of the installation of three static billboards [compared to a single digital billboard] . . . . [A] governing body seeking to restrict expression cannot simply invoke those interests with scant factual support informing its decision-making and expect to withstand a constitutional challenge.[40]

As a result of the lack of case-specific evidence, the Court found the ordinance to be unconstitutional. The case is noteworthy in that it seems to conflict with very similar cases addressing electronic billboard bans. Commentators have said the case serves to illustrate a trend—notably, beginning with the

---

[39] "No billboard or billboard display area or portion thereof shall rotate, move, produce noise or smoke, give the illusion of movement, display video or other changing imagery, automatically change, or be animated or blinking, nor shall any billboard or portion thereof have any electronic, digital, tri-vision or other animated characteristics resulting in an automatically changing depiction." *Id.* at 630.
[40] *Id.* at 643, 644.

U.S. Supreme Court's decision in *McCullen v. Coakley*[41]—in which courts are increasingly requiring local governments to provide greater evidence to support their claims of government interests and narrowly tailored restrictions;[42] however, the New Jersey Supreme Court does not explicitly mention that line of cases as support for its analysis in this case. Ultimately, local governments must ensure that they have sufficient evidentiary support for their stated government interests when drafting ordinances.

IV. Highway Billboard Regulation

The Highway Beautification Act (HBA) is a 1965 federal statute with the purpose of encouraging the maintenance of the scenic nature of the federal highway system through limitations on outdoor advertising along highways.[43] The HBA restricts federal highway funding to any state that does not regulate highway advertising in accordance with the federal law. All fifty states have negotiated a federal–state agreement with the Secretary of Transportation under the HBA.[44] In 1978, language was added to include signs "which may be changed at reasonable intervals by electronic process or by remote control."[45] The HBA sets a minimum level of regulation for federally funded highways to which state and local governments may add. Other than broad language requiring states to adopt regulations for certain signs within 660 feet of the highway, the law does not provide any specific regulations for electronic signs. That task is left to the state and local governments.

In *Hucul Advertising, LLC v. Charter Township of Gaines*,[46] a Michigan township's zoning ordinance required at least four thousand feet between digital billboards adjacent to a highway. The plaintiff argued that the

---

[41] 134 S. Ct. 2518 (2014).

[42] *See* Brian J. Connolly, *New Jersey Supreme Court: Digital Billboard Ban Unconstitutional*, Rocky Mountain Sign Law Blog (Sept. 29, 2016), http://www.rockymountainsignlaw.com/2016/09/2097/#more-2097.

[43] *See* 23 U.S.C. § 131(a): "The Congress hereby finds and declares that the erection and maintenance of outdoor advertising signs, displays, and devices in areas adjacent to the Interstate System and the primary system should be controlled in order to protect the public investment in such highways, to promote the safety and recreational value of public travel, and to preserve natural beauty."

[44] *See, e.g.*, Scenic Am., Inc. v. Dep't of Transp., 983 F. Supp. 2d 170 (D.D.C. 2013).

[45] 23 U.S.C. § 131(c), (j).

[46] 748 F.3d 273 (6th Cir. 2014).

restriction unconstitutionally restricted its commercial speech. Although the plaintiff argued that the restriction was content based, the court found that the spacing regulation was a time, place, and manner restriction. In arguing that the township's ordinance was not narrowly tailored to advancing its stated goals, part of the plaintiff's argument relied on the fact that the state's highway billboard law only required one thousand feet between digital billboards. The court held that the standard established by the state law was a minimum that local governments could exceed if they wished. The plaintiff also argued that the ordinance was unconstitutional because it did not demand the same amount of spacing for traditional, static billboards. The court held that the township did not need to provide an "exact justification" for its specific space restrictions because doing so would be burdensome to local governments and would not improve the courts' ability to review the law.[47] *Hucul Advertising* provides another example of the great level of discretion local governments are given when regulating electronic billboards, provided the regulations are content neutral and the reasons for the regulation are legitimate. In the words of the Sixth Circuit, "[t]he fact that different townships may exercise their discretion differently and reach different judgments does not render the restrictions imposed by any one township unreasonable and not 'narrowly tailored' to a township's goals."[48]

In addition, state laws regulating highway advertising can prohibit otherwise constitutional ordinances. In *Lamar Advertising v. City of Rapid City*, the city's billboard ordinance prohibited all off-premises signs "with internal illumination or which display electronic variable messages."[49] Much like the other cases mentioned in this chapter, the court analyzed whether a ban that treated off-premises signs differently than on-premises signs was content based. The court found that such a distinction was not content based and that the ordinance did not violate the First Amendment. Despite that holding, the ordinance was found invalid as a matter of South

---

[47] *Id.* at 279.

[48] *Id.*

[49] Lamar Adver. of S.D., Inc. v. City of Rapid City, No. Civ. 11-5068-JLV, 2014 WL 692956, *4 (D.S.D. Feb. 21, 2014).

Dakota state law. South Dakota's Highway Beautification and Regulation of Advertising statutes regulate outdoor advertising, including electronic signs and billboards, and expressly permit changeable off-premises signs, "regardless of the technology used, if the message is changed not more than once every six seconds and if the message is not continuously scrolled."[50] The court found that Rapid City's complete ban on off-premises digital signs directly conflicted with South Dakota's outdoor advertising law and, as a result, could not be enforced.

V. Important Differences From Nonelectronic Sign Regulation

Many content neutral regulations that apply to nonelectronic signs also apply to electronic signage, without much difference in the legal analysis. However, as is evident in cases like the aforementioned *Hucul Advertising,* restrictions on the size and placement, including dispersal, may be more severe because of safety and aesthetic concerns. Regulation of electronic signs based on characteristics such as message change rates, size, brightness, and other functional aspects of signs constitute content neutral restrictions. With electronic signage, generally, it is the way the signs *present* their messages rather than the contents of those messages that finds them at odds with local ordinances. Many studies have been published regarding the effects that electronic signs, especially digital signs, have on driver distraction and safety.

A. Safety and Aesthetics Concerns Magnified

Litigation over sign regulation frequently involves experts weighing in on the aesthetic and traffic safety goals of sign regulations. Whereas aesthetics may be harder to quantify with data, there is substantial literature on safety issues.[51] The most significant of these studies relate to two concerns: the

---

[50] S.D. CODIFIED LAWS § 31-29-66(4).

[51] Perhaps the most comprehensive of these reports is a 2009 report by Jerry Wachtel that analyzed over forty safety studies, among other electronic sign issues such as proposed regulations and new technologies. *See* JERRY WACHTEL, SAFETY IMPACTS OF THE EMERGING DIGITAL DISPLAY TECHNOLOGY FOR OUTDOOR ADVERTISING SIGNS (2009), *available at* http://apps.trb.org/cmsfeed/TRBNetProject-Display.asp?ProjectID=2334.

reflexive tendency for a driver's gaze to be unconsciously drawn to bright objects in an otherwise dark visual field[52] and the likelihood that drivers will look away from the road for longer periods of time at digital billboards with changing messages, especially when the signs include animation.[53] Experts argue that each of these factors results in less attention to the road and a higher probability of traffic accidents.[54] Of course, many opponents of digital billboards are quick to point out that manufacturers advertise their products as being able to draw the gaze of every person around: "[n]othing's as eye-catching as an electronic LED display. The brightly lit text and graphics can be seen from hundreds of feet away, drawing the attention of everyone within view."[55]

The outdoor advertising industry has responded that this eye-catching ability does not distract drivers but, to the contrary, keeps drivers more focused on the road: "In some situations, the use of electronic operations had a beneficial effect on traffic safety, by creating a more visually-stimulating environment along an otherwise mind-numbing segment of highway, helping

---

[52] *Id.* at 22, *citing* Jan Theeuwes et al., *Our Eyes Do Not Always Go Where We Want Them To Go: Capture of the Eyes by New Objects*, 9 PSYCHOLOGICAL SCIENCE 5, 370 (1998) *and* Jan Theeuwes et al., *Influence of Attentional Capture on Oculomotor Control*, 25 J. EXPERIMENTAL PSYCHOLOGY: HUMAN PERCEPTION AND PERFORMANCE 6, 1595 (1999) ("When we add the results of these recent, applied research studies, to the earlier theoretical work by Theeuwes and his colleagues (1998, 1999), in which they demonstrated that our attention and our eye gaze is reflexively drawn to an object of different luminance in the visual field, that this occurs even when we are engaged in a primary task, and regardless of whether we have any interest in this irrelevant stimulus, and that we may have no recollection of having been attracted to it, we have a growing, and consistent picture of the adverse impact of irrelevant, outside-the-vehicle distracters such as DBBs on driver performance.").

[53] WACHTEL, *supra* note 46, at 181, *citing* S. E. LEE ET AL., DRIVER PERFORMANCE AND DIGITAL BILLBOARDS (2007) ("We also have data to show, despite a lack of analysis by the researchers, that an on-road study (Lee et al., 2007) using an instrumented vehicle found many more such long glances made to DBBs and similar "comparison sites" consisting of (among other things) on-premise digital signs, than there were to sites containing traditional, static billboards, or sites with no obvious visual elements.").

[54] *Id.* ("From the same study, we have evidence expressed by the researchers that if we were to conduct our research at night we would find that all measures of eye glance behavior would demonstrate significantly greater amounts of distraction to digital advertisements than to fixed billboards or to the natural roadside environment, and that driver vehicle control behaviors such as lane-keeping and speed maintenance would also suffer in the presence of these digital signs.")

[55] Trans-Lux company promotional video, quoted in Scenic America, Billboards in the Digital Age (2007); http://keepwashingtonbeautiful.org/public/resources/unsafe_and_unsightly.pdf; Scenic Kentucky, Scenic Kentucky Newsletter (2010), http://www.kapa.org/documents/Scenic%20Kentucky%20Newsletter.pdf.

to re-focus and sharpen the driver's attention to his or her surroundings."[56] Reviews of the advertising industry's reports have alleged bias, misleading reporting, and inconsistent treatment of statistics in the reports.[57]

B. Brightness of Signs and White Area

The source of light and its brightness are two of the key factors on which regulations of electronic signs focus. When regulating electronic signage, measurements of luminance and illuminance are very important for regulation and enforcement purposes. Luminance is the brightness created by the sign and is measured at the source of light. Illuminance is the perceived brightness at a particular position the light falls upon. The two are inherently tied together, as a brighter light source (with a high luminance reading) will ultimately result in more ambient light being scattered (i.e., more illuminance). And yet, the light is different enough that each type is measured in different metrics, and each requires a different type of light meter. "Luminance meters are single element detectors that measure photometric brightness . . . in lumens,"[58] whereas "[i]lluminance meter products are single element detectors that measure photometric brightness falling upon a surface . . . in footcandles or in lux."[59]

A luminance meter measures the light's output at the source, whereas an illuminance meter measures ambient light. Thus, the two types of meters offer different ways of gauging the brightness of an electronic sign: using a luminance meter, one may measure the output of the light directly; using an illuminance meter, one must measure the ambient light around the sign when the sign is on, then measure the ambient light when the sign is off, and determine the difference as the contribution of the sign's illuminance to the ambient light in the area around the sign. As the time of day and amount of other surrounding lights can greatly affect the ambient light

---

[56] Electronic Display Educational Resource Association, a branch of the Electronic Display Manufacturers Association, Regulation of Electronic Message Display Signs (2004), http://landuselaw.wustl.edu/articles/electronicsign4_07.pdf

[57] WACHTEL, *supra* note 46, at 89–101.

[58] Konica Minolta, *Luminance Meters*, http://sensing.konicaminolta.us/technologies/luminance-meters/.

[59] *Id.*

measurement, reading digital signs with illuminance meters can be a complex and inconsistent exercise. For this reason, some proponents of luminance meters claim that using an illuminance meter is less accurate for regulating the brightness of a sign.[60]

Because the two types of light are distinguishable, it is important for regulators to understand how treating the two types of light differently can help them achieve their goals. In other words, regulations benefit from basing their restrictions on the different types of light readings, luminance or illuminance. Consider a local jurisdiction that wants to cut down on bright digital billboards because it feels that brighter billboards create greater distractions to drivers. This jurisdiction should probably draft a regulation that restricts the brightness of billboards as measured by the luminance the signs produce. Similarly, if a local government wants to reduce ambient light—sometimes called light trespass or light pollution—in a mixed-use zone to protect residential properties from the bright lights of electronic signage, the local government would probably elect to measure the amount of light falling upon a particular property, most likely adjacent properties, with an illuminance meter.

Because the two types of light measurement are distinct and serve different purposes, ordinance drafters would be wise to tailor their ordinances directly to the type of light they wish to regulate. Not only will such tailoring increase the likelihood of prevailing in a challenge to the eventual ordinance, but it will also ultimately result in more effective achievement of regulatory goals. Whereas a high luminance reading may help prove that a billboard is very distracting, a high illuminance reading would provide a stronger argument against light trespass.

C. Complete Ban on Electronic Signs in Certain Districts

Some local governments have responded to electronic signs by banning them in certain zoning districts, such as residential districts, or conversely, only allowing them in certain districts, such as downtown entertainment districts.[61]

---

[60] Illinois Coalition for Responsible Outdoor Lighting, *Digital Billboards: New Regulations for New Technology* (2010), http://www.illinoislighting.org/billboards.html.
[61] *See* MINNEAPOLIS, MINN. CITY CODE § 544.20 (2016).

In New York City, each district has separate limits on illuminated signs to preserve the aesthetic character of each neighborhood. In *Vosse v. City of New York*, a resident had an illuminated peace sign in her high-rise apartment window. She was fined under a New York City zoning law that prohibited displaying illuminated signs higher than forty feet above the street in her district. She claimed that the restriction was an unreasonable time, place, and manner restriction; however, the court agreed with the city's argument that the prohibition was "narrowly tailored to serving the City's significant interests in maintaining an aesthetically pleasing cityscape and preserving neighborhood character."[62]

D. Off-Premises Versus On-Premises Bans of Electronic Signs

The impact of *Reed* on whether on-premises/off-premises distinctions are considered content neutral remains unclear. However, limiting electronic signs to either on- or off-premises signs may be considered content neutral. Cobb County, Georgia, passed an ordinance that prohibited off-premises electronic signs, which ultimately was redundant because the county also prohibited all off-premises signs.[63]

Granite State Outdoor Advertising, Inc. challenged a number of Cobb County's ordinances in federal court, including both the total ban of off-premises signs and the electronic-specific ban. In analyzing the total ban on off-premises signs under the *Central Hudson* test, the court held that the ordinance did not violate the First Amendment because "Cobb County's asserted purposes of aesthetics and traffic safety were 'substantial government interests' that were 'no more extensive than necessary.'"[64] However, the district court—and later, the appellate court—held that Granite State did not have standing to challenge the ordinance specifically relating to electronic signs.[65]

---

[62] Vosse v. City of New York, 144 F. Supp. 3d 627, 631 (S.D.N.Y. 2015).
[63] Cobb County, Ga. Sign Ordinance § 134-313(o) ("Electronic signs may only be used to advertise activities actually conducted on the property").
[64] Granite State Outdoor Adver., Inc. v. Cobb Cnty., 193 F. App'x 900, at *3 (11th Cir. 2006)
[65] *See id.*

Electronic signs are not new, but as technology develops, signs will likely continue to get larger, brighter, and cheaper, making them increasingly attractive to advertisers. Many aspects of electronic signs are analyzed using the same legal tests developed for traditional signs, whereas the law regarding the more technical aspects of electronic signs remains to be developed. Although the specter of *Reed* now hangs over most sign regulations, Justice Alito specifically noted in his concurrence that distinguishing between signs with fixed messages and electronic signs with messages that change remains a form of content neutral regulation.[66] However, challenges to off- and on-premises distinctions and how they affect electronic signage are already being brought in light of *Reed*.[67] Although it may be a short while before we see high courts conclusively decide these issues, there will be no shortage of litigation to develop the questions raised by *Reed*. As with any regulation of speech, a narrowly tailored, content neutral law bolstered by legitimate government concerns will be more likely to withstand challenge.

IV. Suggestions for Practice

There are several ways for local governments to protect themselves from first Amendment litigation pertaining to electronic signs, including the following:

- Keep ordinances and regulations content neutral;
- Use language that encompasses a broad range of electronic signs; however, any regulation should be specific and narrowly tailored to advance the stated purpose of the regulation;
- Complete bans are permissible, provided the reasons for the ban provide clear justification; and
- Ordinances should be severable in the case that portions are found to be unconstitutional.

---

[66] *See* Reed v. Town of Gilbert, 134 S. Ct. 2218, 2233 (2015) (Alito, J., concurring).

[67] *See, e.g.*, Geft Outdoor LLC v. Consolidated City of Indianapolis, 187 F. Supp. 3d 1002 (S.D. Ind. 2016).

4

Government Regulation of Art and Architecture

Brian J. Connolly

Otten Johnson Robinson Neff + Ragonetti, P.C.
Denver, Colorado

I. Introduction: Defining "Aesthetics"

This chapter addresses local government control and regulation of two broad categories of aesthetic interest: art and architecture. This chapter will address some nonphysical artistic media, such as music, however, for purposes of this chapter, *art* or *artwork* primarily means any form of physical artistic media, including, for example, print media such as painting or photography, or sculpture, carpentry, and other three-dimensional forms of artwork.

Local government control of art arises frequently—for example, in the regulation of murals as a form of outdoor signage or advertising, in the abatement of nuisances such as graffiti, or in the government's selection of artwork for display in public parks or public buildings. Furthermore, local architectural controls are evident in building design requirements, design review programs, and basic zoning and building code requirements. Yet local control of artwork and architecture may give rise to First Amendment concerns. If, say, Alexander Calder, the notable modernist sculptor, designed a sculpture for placement in the front yard of a wealthy suburban landowner, but the local government's zoning code prohibited any such structure

77

within the front yard setback, would Calder have a First Amendment claim? Or what if Frank Gehry, known for his unique postmodern building designs, designed a home for construction in an otherwise neocolonial neighborhood, only to be rejected by a publicly appointed design review board, would the local government be liable under the First Amendment? This chapter addresses these concerns.

Chapter 2 addresses aesthetics as a governmental regulatory interest in the context of First Amendment litigation, particularly in the area of sign regulation. In the course of that discussion, the author addressed the primacy of aesthetics as a governmental interest in the regulation of speech. For example, local governments are empowered to control the size, location, and placement of signs in part based on aesthetic interests. Local regulation of artwork, particularly with respect to private property, presents many First Amendment concerns similar to those regarding the regulation of signs and other forms of speech. For example, because art has been characterized by the courts as a form of speech protected by the First Amendment, regulations pertaining to artwork must be content neutral, contain adequate procedural safeguards, and may not be unconstitutionally vague.

Conversely, however, artwork differs from other forms of speech, particularly signage, in one critical respect: in the case of artwork, the medium is commonly the message. Whereas a written message on a sign could theoretically be conveyed regardless of the height, size, location, color, materials, or brightness of the sign structure—although many sign owners would beg to differ—artwork is different. In many cases, the size, orientation, color, or materials comprising the work of art are of critical importance to the piece's communicative intent. Thus, although local government aesthetic regulatory interests are implicated in the regulation or control of art, the appropriateness of aesthetic interests in regulating artwork may be more debatable as a result of First Amendment limitations.

Similarly, issues of governmental control of artwork, and the government's ability to communicate an artistic message, arise in cases where a governmental authority is acquiring artwork or dictating the placement of artwork on public property. As this chapter will discuss, governments generally have broader freedom to control the artwork that is placed on government property, although governmental authority in this arena is not unlimited.

Although the First Amendment has been widely applied by the courts to artistic media, First Amendment concerns regarding the regulation of architecture are still in an antenatal state. Few court cases have considered First Amendment challenges to local design review requirements, building design mandates, or ordinances that restrict the extent to which buildings may look similar or different from one another. Yet as First Amendment protections have gradually expanded since the Constitution was ratified, this author predicts that First Amendment challenges to architectural controls may increase in the coming years, and this chapter therefore provides some background on this issue.

This chapter discusses the ways in which local governments most commonly regulate artwork and architecture, and then proceeds to provide an overview of the authority of local governments to regulate on the basis of aesthetics. The chapter then goes on to discuss the protections afforded artwork by the First Amendment, and the limitations on governmental regulation and control of artwork on both private and public property. In conclusion, the chapter contains a brief discussion of some of the issues associated with architectural regulation. Because many of the other chapters of this book address in detail some of the particular First Amendment doctrines applicable to regulations of all forms of speech, such as content neutrality, this chapter avoids any lengthy restatement of these principles. The reader is thus encouraged to review other chapters of this book for more complete discussion of these topics.

In addition, it is important for the reader to understand that the case law pertaining to local government control of artwork and architecture is actually quite sparse. Although many cases have addressed issues of copyright, ownership of artwork, and other such matters, very few have delved into local government regulation and control of artwork, particularly as a land use or zoning issue. Although most of the reported cases in this area are discussed in this chapter, the reader is again encouraged to review cases generally applicable to speech regulation and, as discussed further herein, the government speech doctrine and public forum law, for additional guidance in this area.

II. Forms of Local Government Regulation of Art and Architecture

Local governments regulate or control artwork in myriad ways. This section reviews some of the ways in which local governments exercise control over artwork and generally divides these controls according to whether the artwork is occurring or existing on private property or government-owned property. Although this section provides several zoning and municipal code citations to give the reader some examples of these regulations, these code citations have not been thoroughly vetted for compliance with the First Amendment and are for the purpose of example only.

On private property, art regulation frequently arises via zoning codes, sign regulations, and general police power nuisance-abatement controls. Murals, paintings, and other works of art located on private property and that may be affixed to building walls, on signposts, or elsewhere may be regulated specially as "murals" or other forms of artwork, or as signs under local sign regulations.[1]

Three-dimensional works of art located on private property, including sculptures or statuary, may be regulated by zoning regulations that restrict the placement or size of structures[2] or by building or fire codes. Additionally, artwork may be regulated by local governments pursuant to their general authority to regulate nuisances; for example, many local governments prohibit graffiti and other nontraditional forms of artwork under their nuisance-control codes.[3] In some circumstances, nuisance regulations, such

---

[1] *See, e.g.,* HANFORD, CALIF. ZONING CODE § 17.44.122 (2003); INDIANAPOLIS, IND. SIGN REGULATIONS § 734-201 (2015); LINCOLN, NEB. MUNICIPAL CODE § 27.69.190 (2015); LOS ANGELES, CALIF. MUNICIPAL CODE § 14.4.20 (2014); PORTLAND, ORE. CITY CHARTER, TIT. 4 (2015); WYANDOTTE, MICH. ZONING ORD. § 2201 (2012).

[2] *But see* INDIANAPOLIS, IND. SIGN REGULATIONS § 734-201 (2015) (exempting sculptures from regulation).

[3] *See, e.g.,* SALEM, ORE. REV. CODE § 95.600 *et seq.*; BINGHAMTON, N.Y. CODE § 256-1 *et seq.* (2007); LARIMER COUNTY, COLO. ORD. No. 12042006001 (2007); SEATTLE, WASH. MUNICIPAL CODE § 10.07 (1996); MONROE, N.C. CODE OF ORDINANCES § 93.20 *et seq.* (2008).

as those prohibiting the location of trash or junk cars on private property, may limit displays of artwork.

On public property, local governments exercise other forms of artwork regulation. Local governments with control over public property such as public streets, sidewalks, and parks may have ordinances or other laws controlling private individuals' use and placement of objects—including works of art—within public property.[4] Additionally, local governments may exercise control over artwork on public property through procurement and selection processes for art displays.[5] For example, many local governments select artwork for placement in public buildings.[6]

In addition to imposing restrictions on art displays, some local jurisdictions have initiated programs that *require* public art, or cash payments into public art funds, in connection with private development applications.[7] Some of these ordinances require that the public art installed in connection with private development be reviewed by local art committees. Additionally, in recognition of the benefits of publicly accessible art, many local governments have adopted "percent-for-art" ordinances requiring that governmental expenditures on public works include public art.[8] Additionally, some local governments may totally exempt works of art on private property from regulation under zoning or sign codes.[9]

---

[4] *See, e.g.*, DENVER, COLO. REV. MUNICIPAL CODE §§ 39-221 (procedures for acceptance of donated property in parks) and 49-246 (2015) (requiring removal of any encumbrances in public right-of-way).
[5] *See, e.g.*, CITY OF BERKELEY, CALIF. MUNICIPAL CODE CH. 6.14 (2015).
[6] *See, e.g.* DALLAS, TEX. PUBLIC ART PROGRAM, *available at* http://www.dallasculture.org/publicArt. asp (last viewed Jun. 14, 2015); HONOLULU, HAW. ART IN THE CITY BUILDINGS PROGRAM, *available at* http://www.honolulu.gov/moca/moca-artincitybuildings.html (last viewed Jun. 14, 2015); PALM BEACH COUNTY, FLA. ART IN PUBLIC PLACES PROGRAM, *available at* http://www.co.palm-beach.fl.us /fdo/art/ (last viewed Jun. 14, 2015).
[7] *See, e.g.*, BURBANK, CALIF. CODE OF ORDINANCES § 10-1-1114 (2012); SANTA ROSA, CALIF. CITY CODE §§ 21-08.010-21-08.090 (2006); SEDONA, ARIZ. LAND DEV. CODE §§ 1801-1803; SARASOTA, FLA. ZONING CODE DIV. 7 (2011).
[8] *See, e.g.*, CHICAGO, ILL. MUNICIPAL CODE §§ 2-92-080 to 2-92-180 (2007); SEATTLE, WASH. MUNICIPAL CODE § 20.32.010. Similar "percent-for-art" ordinances have been adopted in Chicago, Ill., Denver, Colo., and St. Paul, Minn., as well as other cities.
[9] *See, e.g.*, DENVER, COLO. ZONING CODE § 13.3.

III. Local Government Authority To Regulate Aesthetics

Before proceeding to discuss the limitations applicable to local governments in the regulation of artwork, it is necessary to provide some background on government regulation of aesthetics and the role of aesthetics as a regulatory interest in areas of First Amendment concern.

Local governments today have the ability to regulate land uses, including land uses with First Amendment implications, on the basis of aesthetic interests.[10] In the early twentieth century, the majority of state courts did not recognize aesthetic justifications for police power regulation, or at least held that aesthetic interests were permissible only as secondary bases for regulation.[11] This trend reversed course beginning in the 1950s. In 1954, in the case of *Berman v. Parker*,[12] a unanimous U.S. Supreme Court stated that aesthetic regulation was appropriately within the scope of the public welfare:

> The concept of the public welfare is broad and inclusive. The values it represents are spiritual as well as physical, aesthetic as well as monetary. It is within the power of the legislature to determine that the community should be beautiful as well as healthy, spacious as well as clean, well-balanced as well as carefully patrolled.[13]

---

[10] *See* Members of City Council v. Taxpayers for Vincent, 466 U.S. 789, 805 (1984) ("It is well settled that the state may legitimately exercise its police powers to advance esthetic values.").

[11] *See, e.g.*, Thille v. Bd. of Public Works of City of Los Angeles, 255 P. 294, 296 (Cal. 1927); City of Chicago v. Gunning Sys., 73 N.E. 1035 (Ill. 1905); Opinion of the Justices to the Senate, 128 N.E.2d 557, 561 (Mass. 1955); Wolverine Sign Works v. City of Bloomfield Hills, 271 N.W. 823, 825 (Mich. 1937); City of Passaic v. Paterson Bill Posting Adver. & Sign Painting Co., 62 A. 267, 268 (N.J. 1905) ("Aesthetic [considerations] are a matter of luxury and indulgence rather than of necessity, and it is necessity alone which justifies the exercise of the police power to take private property without compensation."); People ex rel. M. Wineburgh Adver. Co. v. Murphy, 88 N.E. 17, 20 (N.Y. 1909); City of Youngstown v. Kahn Bros. Bldg. Co., 148 N.E.2d 842, 843 (Ohio 1925). *See also* St. Louis Poster Adver. Co. v. City of St. Louis, 249 U.S. 269, 274 (1919) (rejecting due process challenge to billboard regulations where aesthetic interests were not the principal regulatory concern).

[12] 348 U.S. 26 (1954).

[13] *Id.* at 33.

Although this statement was made in the context of an eminent domain decision, *Berman's* reach became expansive. Most state courts have since adopted the rationale that the government has the authority to regulate land use in the interest of protecting community aesthetics.[14]

The U.S. Supreme Court has conclusively determined that aesthetic concerns are sufficiently significant so as to meet the "significant governmental purpose" requirement of the First Amendment intermediate scrutiny analysis.[15] A clearly articulated aesthetic interest, combined with narrow tailoring and ample alternative channels, will generally support a content neutral regulation of speech or a regulation of commercial speech.[16] Conversely, federal appellate courts have generally held that aesthetic interests are not *compelling*,[17] and thus content or viewpoint based regulation

---

[14] *See, e.g.,* Veterans of Foreign Wars, Post 4264 v. City of Steamboat Springs, 575 P.2d 835, 840–41 (Colo. 1978); John Donnelley & Sons, Inc. v. Outdoor Adver. Bd., 339 N.E.2d 709 (Mass. 1975); Temple Baptist Church v. City of Albuquerque, 646 P.2d 565, 571 (N.M. 1982); Westfield Motor Sales Co. v. Town of Westfield, 324 A.2d 113 (N.J. Super. 1974); People v. Stover, 12 N.Y.2d 462, 467 (1963); Oregon City v. Hartke, 400 P.2d 255, 262 (Ore. 1965); Markham Adver. Co. v. State, 439 P.2d 248, 259 (Wash. 1968); State ex rel. Saveland Park Holding Corp. v. Wieland, 69 N.W.2d 217, 222-23 (Wis. 1955). Some states still hold that aesthetic considerations are proper only as a secondary consideration in exercising the police power. *See, e.g.,* USCOC of Va. RSC#3, Inc. v. Montgomery Cnty. Bd. of Supers., 343 F.3d 262, 269 (4th Cir. 2003); Coscan Washington, Inc. v. Maryland-Nat'l Capital Park & Plan. Comm'n, 590 A.2d 1080 (Md. App. 1991). *See also generally* Kenneth Pearlman et al., *Beyond the Eye of the Beholder Once Again: A New Review of Aesthetic Regulation,* 38 URB. LAW. 1119 (2006).

[15] *See Taxpayers for Vincent,* 466 U.S. at 807; Metromedia, Inc. v. City of San Diego, 453 U.S. 490, 507-08 (1981) (finding aesthetics to be a substantial goal for purposes of commercial speech regulation). Generally speaking, speech regulation on the basis of content is subject to "strict scrutiny," requiring the demonstration of a compelling interest and narrow tailoring. Turner Broad. Sys., Inc. v. FCC, 512 U.S. 622, 642 (1994). Content neutral regulations of speech are subject to "intermediate scrutiny," requiring such regulations to be narrowly tailored to serve a significant governmental interest and to leave open ample alternatives channels for communication. McCullen v. Coakley, 134 S. Ct. 2518, 2534 (2014); Ward v. Rock Against Racism, 491 U.S. 781, 791 (1989). Regulations of commercial speech must directly advance a substantial governmental interest, and not reach further than necessary to accomplish the interest. *Metromedia,* 453 U.S. at 507, citing Cent. Hudson Gas & Elec. Corp. v. Public Serv. Comm'n of N.Y., 447 U.S. 557, 564 (1980).

[16] *See, e.g.,* Hucul Adver., LLC v. Charter Twp. of Gaines, 748 F.3d 273, 277–78 (6th Cir. 2014); Interstate Outdoor Adver., L.P. v. Zoning Bd. of Twp. of Mt. Laurel, 706 F.3d 527, 534–35 (3d Cir. 2013); Brown v. Town of Cary, 706 F.3d 294, 305 (4th Cir. 2013); Outdoor Sys., Inc. v. City of Mesa, 997 F.2d 604, 612 (9th Cir. 1993). *But see* E & J Equities, LLC v. Bd. of Adjustment, 146 A.3d 623, 644 (N.J. 2016) (finding that governmental interest in aesthetics and ban on digital billboards had only "scant factual support" and was therefore unconstitutional).

[17] *See, e.g.,* Neighborhood Enters., Inc. v. City of St. Louis, 644 F.3d 728, 737–38 (8th Cir. 2011).

of speech—issues that are discussed in the next section—cannot survive strict scrutiny on the basis of aesthetic justifications for such regulation.[18]

IV. First Amendment Application To and Protections for Art

As a general rule, artwork is considered protected speech under First Amendment doctrine. Of course, defining art in any objective sense is a nearly impossible task, and courts have historically been disinclined to make attempts at doing so in the First Amendment context.[19] One court has referred to art as "a famously malleable concept the contours of which are best defined not by courts, but in the proverbial 'eye of the beholder.'"[20] Instead of defining artwork, the courts have more frequently opted to draw distinctions between forms of art that receive First Amendment protection and those that do not. This section discusses the general protection for artwork under the First Amendment and then provides an overview of some limitations on protection for artwork. Some of these limitations should be familiar from other chapters of this book.

Despite the inherent tension between artists' and viewers' assignment of expressive value to particular works of art, the courts frequently err in favor of affording artists' subjective viewpoints significant latitude in determining the First Amendment's application to artwork.[21] Therefore, the First Amendment's protections extend to a broad range of visual and other forms of artwork. Courts have conclusively found music, theater, film, and visual art—including paintings, prints, photographs, and

---

[18] *See, e.g.,* Metromedia, 453 U.S. at 516–17.

[19] *See, e.g.,* Mazer v. Stein, 347 U.S. 201, 214 (1954) ("Individual perception of the beautiful is too varied a power to permit a narrow or rigid concept of art."); Bleistein v. Donaldson Lithographing Co., 188 U.S. 239, 251 (1903); Hoepker v. Kruger, 200 F. Supp. 2d 340, 352 (S.D.N.Y. 2002) ("Courts should not be asked to draw arbitrary lines between what may be art and what may be prosaic as the touchstone of First Amendment protection."). *See also* Margaret L. Mettler, Note, *Graffiti Museum: A First Amendment Argument for Protecting Uncommissioned Art on Private Property*, 111 MICH. L. REV. 249, 254 (2012).

[20] Mastrovincenzo v. City of New York, 435 F. 3d 78, 90 (2d Cir. 2006).

[21] *See, e.g.,* Cohen v. California, 403 U.S. 15, 25 (1971) ("[O]ne man's vulgarity is another's lyric. Indeed, we think it is largely because governmental officials cannot make principled distinctions in this area that the Constitution leaves matters of taste and style so largely to the individual.").

sculpture—as well as several other forms of expressive conduct, including tattooing, to merit First Amendment protection.[22] In *Bery v. City of New York*, the Second Circuit Court of Appeals observed that "[v]isual art is as wide ranging in its depiction of ideas, concepts and emotions as any book, treatise, pamphlet or other writing, and is similarly entitled to full First Amendment protection."[23] Whereas it is clearly discernible that written or spoken word receives First Amendment protection, a particular work of art need not be immediately and obviously identifiable as a work of art (i.e., the artwork could be fairly abstract) in order for that work to receive First Amendment protection.[24]

Although the scope of First Amendment protection for artwork is expansive, it is not boundless. The same carve-outs from First Amendment protection applicable to other media of speech, including carve-outs for obscenity, fighting words, and incitement, exist with respect to artwork. It is well established that the First Amendment does not protect obscenity.[25] The U.S. Supreme Court has defined obscenity as "works which, taken as a whole, appeal to the prurient interest in sex, which portray sexual conduct in a patently offensive way, and which, taken as a whole, do not have serious literary, artistic, political, or scientific value," as determined by an "average person, applying contemporary community standards."[26] Applications of the foregoing test do not provide bright-line clarity as to what types of artwork are obscene for constitutional purposes. For example, the Supreme

---

[22] *See, e.g.*, Ward v. Rock Against Racism, 491 U.S. 781, 790 (1989) (music); Se. Promotions, Ltd. v. Conrad, 420 U.S. 546, 557–58 (1975) (theater); Joseph Burstyn, Inc. v. Wilson, 343 U.S. 495, 501-02 (1952) (film); Anderson v. City of Hermosa Beach, 621 F.3d 1051, 1060 (9th Cir. 2010) (tattooing); White v. City of Sparks, 500 F.3d 953, 956 (9th Cir. 2007) (paintings); Bery v. City of New York, 97 F.3d 689, 695 (2d Cir. 1995) (finding visual art to be entitled to First Amendment protection on par with written or spoken words).

[23] *Id.*

[24] *See* Hurley v. Irish-American Gay, Lesbian and Bisexual Grp. of Boston, 515 U.S. 557, 569 (1995) ("[A] narrow, succinctly articulable message is not a condition of constitutional protection, which if confined to expressions conveying a 'particularized message,' would never reach the unquestionably shielded painting of Jackson Pollock, music of Arnold Schoenberg, or Jabberwocky verse of Lewis Carroll." (internal citations omitted)).

[25] Roth v. United States, 354 U.S. 476, 485 (1957).

[26] Miller v. California, 413 U.S. 15, 24 (1973).

Court has found "hardcore" pornography[27] and child pornography[28] to be outside of the scope of First Amendment protection; however, courts have struck down legislative limitations on speech and expressive conduct as they related to poetry with a sexual content,[29] pornography that may be understood as degrading toward women,[30] depictions of animal cruelty,[31] virtual depictions of child pornography,[32] films or artwork where obscene images are paired with nonobscene material, and parody material.[33] Thus, artwork that depicts nudity, violence, or thought-provoking portrayals that might be cast as having sexual content is not likely to fall outside the scope of First Amendment protection. However, to the extent art exhibits material of a vulgar, pornographic nature, it may not enjoy First Amendment protections and may properly be limited by local codes or ordinances.

As with artwork of an obscene nature, artwork that contains elements of "fighting words," incitement, or defamation may also fall outside of the umbrella of First Amendment protection. So-called fighting words, including words that "by their very utterance inflict injury or tend to incite an immediate breach of the peace," fall outside the scope of First Amendment protection;[34] however, the exception from First Amendment protection for fighting words has been generally very limited.[35] Similarly, First Amendment protection is also unavailable in the limited context where advocative speech "is directed to inciting or producing imminent lawless action and is likely to incite or produce such action."[36] Under this principle,

---

[27] *Id.* at 36.

[28] New York v. Ferber, 458 U.S. 747, 764 (1982); *see also* Osborne v. Ohio, 495 U.S. 103, 111 (1990) (upholding ban on possession and viewing of child pornography).

[29] *See* Kois v. Wisconsin, 408 U.S. 229, 231–32 (1972).

[30] *See* Am. Booksellers Ass'n v. Hudnut, 771 F.2d 323, 331–32 (7th Cir. 1985).

[31] *See* United States v. Stevens, 559 U.S. 460, 472 (2010).

[32] *See* Ashcroft v. Free Speech Coal., 535 U.S. 234, 236 (2002).

[33] *See* Baker v. Glover, 776 F. Supp. 1511, 1515 (M.D. Ala. 1991).

[34] Chaplinsky v. New Hampshire, 315 U.S. 568, 572 (1942).

[35] *See, e.g.,* Am. Freedom Defense Initiative v. Washington Metro. Area Transit Auth., 898 F. Supp. 2d 73, 79–80 (D.D.C. 2012); State v. Dugan, 303 P.3d 755, 762–63 (Mont. 2013) (noting that the U.S. Supreme Court has never upheld a conviction on "fighting words" grounds since the 1942 *Chaplinsky* decision); State v. Drahota, 788 N.W.2d 796, 802–03 (Neb. 2010).

[36] Brandenburg v. Ohio, 395 U.S. 444, 447 (1969).

criminal aiding and abetting lacks First Amendment protection,[37] yet mere endorsements or encouragement of violent or unlawful action receive First Amendment protection.[38] Thus, where a work of art is intended to counsel viewers toward criminal violence, it may lack First Amendment protection. For example, where an artist does not intend for his work to provoke unlawful action, and where the risk of such unlawful action is not great, the work would presumably be entitled to First Amendment protection.[39]

An artist's First Amendment right to free speech may additionally be limited by state common law limitations on "verbal torts," including defamation—slander or libel—as well as torts such as intentional infliction of emotional distress.[40] Specifically, where defamatory speech is a matter of private concern and involves private individuals, the First Amendment generally does not protect the defendant speaker.[41] Conversely, where speech critical of another relates to a matter of public concern—meaning, in essence, that the speech relates to "any matter of political, social, or other concern to the community," is a subject of news or other general interest, or occurs in a public place[42]—or where such speech involves a public figure,[43] the speaker may have a First Amendment defense against a claim sounding in tort. For example, when the host of a nationally syndicated television program challenged a magazine's parody portrayal of him, the challenger was found to be a public figure such that the publisher of the portrayal could successfully raise a First Amendment defense to an intentional infliction of emotional distress claim.[44] Thus, artwork that criticizes a public figure or

[37] *See, e.g.*, Rice v. Paladin Enters., Inc., 128 F.3d 233 (4th Cir. 1997) (publisher of an instructional work on how to commit murder, complete with photographs and diagrams, was not entitled to First Amendment protection); United States v. Kelley, 769 F.2d 215, 217 (4th Cir. 1985) (speaker instructing listeners on how to commit tax fraud was not entitled to First Amendment protection); United States v. Barnett, 667 F.2d 835 (9th Cir. 1982) (publisher of instructions on how to fabricate illegal drugs was not entitled to First Amendment protection).
[38] *See Brandenburg*, 395 U.S. at 448; NAACP v. Claiborne Hardware Co., 458 U.S. 886, 929 (1982).
[39] *See* Nelson v. Streeter, 16 F.3d 145, 150 (7th Cir. 1994).
[40] *See, e.g.*, New York Times Co. v. Sullivan, 376 U.S. 254, 269 (1964).
[41] *See, e.g.*, Dun & Bradstreet, Inc. v. Greenmoss Builders, Inc., 472 U.S. 749, 760–61 (1985).
[42] Snyder v. Phelps, 562 U.S. 443, 453, 458 (2011).
[43] *See* Hustler Magazine, Inc. v. Falwell, 485 U.S. 46, 56 (1988).
[44] *Id.* at 57.

addresses a matter of public concern would likely carry First Amendment protections that would be unavailable if the work criticized or parodied a private individual on a matter of private concern.

Although the foregoing exceptions to First Amendment protection are generally applicable to speech, another exception to First Amendment protection pertains specifically to artwork. In recent decades, courts have been called upon to establish the boundary between art meriting First Amendment protection and commercial merchandise that is not protected speech.[45] Many of these cases arise in the context of street vendors of clothing or other souvenir-like products who claim that efforts by local governments to enforce licensing requirements interfere with protected speech. Artwork does not lose its First Amendment protection by virtue of the fact that it is bought or sold in a commercial transaction, and speech does not lose First Amendment protection when it relates to commercial matters. However, commercial merchandise lacking "a political, religious, philosophical or ideological message" falls outside the scope of the First Amendment's protections.[46]

To determine whether a product is artwork protected by the First Amendment, the Second Circuit Court of Appeals adopted a five-factor analysis that looks at whether the product was individually created, the maker's motivation for producing the work, the maker's artistic bona fides, whether the product conveys a personal message of the maker, and, if the product has expressive elements, whether it has "a common non expressive purpose or utility" that dominates the expressive elements of the product.[47] In contrast, the Ninth Circuit has adopted an alternative approach whereby sales of commercial products are protected when the products are "inherently expressive," or alternatively, where the sale of a product is "inextricably intertwined" with a statement carrying a message protected by

---

[45] See, e.g., Hunt v. City of Los Angeles, 638 F.3d 703 (9th Cir. 2011); White v. City of Sparks, 500 F.3d 953 (9th Cir. 2007); Mastrovincenzo v. City of New York, 435 F. 3d 78, 90 (2d Cir. 2006).

[46] White v. City of Sparks, 341 F. Supp. 2d 1129, 1139 (D. Nev. 2004) (quoting Am. Civil Liberties Union of Nev. v. City of Las Vegas, 333 F.3d 1092, 1107 (9th Cir. 2003)).

[47] Mastrovincenzo, 435 F. 3d at 94–95. For additional commentary, see also Genevieve Blake, Comment, Expressive Merchandise and the First Amendment in Public Fora, 34 FORDHAM URB. L.J. 1049, 1065–66 (2007).

the First Amendment.[48] For example, political buttons, paintings, clothing displaying graffiti-like artwork, and tattoos—and the sale of such items—are considered protected expression.[49] Conversely, products such as generic clothing, shea butter, incense, and oils are not protected speech, and neither is the sale thereof.[50] In 2010, the Fifth Circuit held that a junked car used as both a planter and novelty shop advertisement, that contained the words "Make Love Not War" was not protected speech.[51] But the federal Southern District of New York has held that graffiti painted as part of an art exhibition constituted protected noncommercial speech.[52]

Although cases have identified a distinction between artwork meriting First Amendment protection and commercial merchandise, it is important to note that artwork does not lose its First Amendment protection simply because such artwork is commercial in nature.[53] As discussed in depth in chapter 2, commercial speech receives First Amendment protection[54]—albeit less than noncommercial speech.[55] Commercial speech has been defined by the Supreme Court as "expression related solely to the economic interests of the speaker and its audience,"[56] or speech which otherwise proposes a commercial transaction.[57] Art in the form of commercial advertising, which bears the logo or trademark of a particular business or firm or otherwise proposes a commercial transaction, retains First Amendment

---

[48] *White,* 500 F.3d at 955. *See also* Blake, *supra* note 47, at 1074–75.
[49] *See Bery,* 97 F.3d at 696; *White,* 341 F. Supp. 2d at 1140; Coleman v. City of Mesa, 284 P.3d 863, 870 (Ariz. 2012) (holding tattoos to be protected by the Arizona Constitution's First Amendment equivalent).
[50] Hunt v. City of Los Angeles, 601 F. Supp. 2d 1158, 1179 (C.D. Cal. 2009), *aff'd* 638 F.3d 703 (9th Cir. 2011); Al-Amin v. City of New York, 979 F. Supp. 168 (E.D.N.Y. 1997) (finding that, even when paired with dissemination of information regarding the vendors' religious beliefs, the sale of such products was not protected speech); People v. Lam, 21 N.Y.3d 958, 960 (2013).
[51] Kleinman v. City of San Marcos, 597 F.3d 323, 327–28 (5th Cir. 2010).
[52] Ecko. Complex LLC v. Bloomberg, 382 F. Supp. 2d 627, 629 (S.D.N.Y. 2005).
[53] *See* 44 Liquormart, Inc. v. Rhode Island, 517 U.S. 484, 496-98 (1996).
[54] *See, e.g.,* Cent. Hudson Gas & Elec. Corp. v. Pub. Serv. Comm'n of N.Y., 447 U.S. 557, 561–62 (1980); Va. State Bd. of Pharmacy v. Va. Citizens Consumer Council, Inc., 425 U.S. 748, 770 (1975).
[55] *See* Metromedia, Inc. v. City of San Diego, 453 U.S. 490, 506 (1981).
[56] *Cent. Hudson,* 447 U.S. at 561.
[57] *See* Bd. of Trustees of State Univ. of N.Y. v. Fox, 492 U.S.469, 473–74 (1989); *Va. Pharmacy Bd.,* 425 U.S. at 762.

protection. The limits on protection for commercial artwork are further addressed in this chapter.

V. First Amendment Limits on Regulation of Art

This section specifically addresses limitations on local governments' regulation and control of artwork. Because the First Amendment's application to specific situations is based in large part on the ownership of the underlying property where the artwork is being displayed, this section is organized according to the type of property where the artwork may be displayed.

Regardless of the whether artwork is displayed on public or private property, developing code definitions that meet First Amendment limitations is perhaps the most important and difficult task in regulating artwork because the way in which artwork is defined frequently dictates how it is regulated and thus whether such regulation raises First Amendment concerns. Many local regulations, particularly regulations of signage that also address murals and other forms of two-dimensional artwork, contain regulatory distinctions between signage and artwork. Because it is almost impossible to distinguish between signage and artwork without reference to the content of the message, the vast majority of existing code definitions defining artwork are likely content based and may therefore be legally questionable following the U.S. Supreme Court's 2015 decision in *Reed v. Town of Gilbert*.[58] Ensuring that code definitions meet the First Amendment standards discussed in this section is critical to ensuring that local regulations survive First Amendment challenges.

A. Art on Private Property

As noted earlier, artwork on private property typically falls into the categories of two-dimensional artwork, such as wall murals or signage displaying murals or paintings, and three-dimensional artwork, such as sculpture or statuary. Graffiti is another form of artwork that frequently occurs on private property and is discussed in this section.

---

[58] 135 S. Ct. 2218 (2015).

The First Amendment doctrine relating to regulation of artwork located on private property closely mirrors the doctrine associated more generally with signage occurring on private property. Chapter 2 provides a detailed overview of these First Amendment doctrines, such as content neutrality, prior restraint, vagueness, and overbreadth, that apply to sign regulation and that similarly apply to regulation of artwork. In reviewing local regulations applicable to art, courts will generally look first to whether a regulation of noncommercial artwork on private property is content and viewpoint neutral,[59] and if so, whether the regulation is tailored to serve a substantial governmental interest and whether ample alternative channels of communication are available.[60] If the regulation is content based, strict scrutiny applies, requiring a showing of a compelling governmental interest and least restrictive means of achieving that interest.[61] For commercial artwork, courts apply the *Central Hudson* test requiring such regulations to assert a substantial governmental interest, directly advance that regulatory purpose, and not restrict more speech than is necessary.[62]

Other concerns that might arise in the regulation of artwork on private property include whether the regulation acts as an unconstitutional prior restraint[63] and whether the regulation is vague[64] or overbroad.[65] If a local regulation is content based, the government has failed to establish a substantial regulatory interest, or the regulation is not appropriately tailored to the regulatory interest, it will likely be found unconstitutional.[66] Similarly, if the regulation does not provide adequate procedural safeguards, such as a

---

[59] *See, e.g., Reed*, 135 S. Ct. at 2226–27; Lone Star Sec. & Video, Inc. v. City of Los Angeles, 827 F.3d 1192, 1197 (9th Cir. 2016); Norton v. City of Springfield, 806 F.3d 411, 412 (7th Cir. 2015); Cahaly v. LaRosa, 796 F.3d 399, 404 (4th Cir. 2015); Neighborhood Enters., Inc. v. City of St. Louis, 644 F.3d 728, 736 (8th Cir. 2011).

[60] *See* Ward v. Rock Against Racism, 491 U.S. 781, 789 (1989); Peterson v. Vill. of Downers Grove, 150 F. Supp. 3d 910, 921 (N.D. Ill. 2015).

[61] *See Reed*, 135 S. Ct. at 2231; *Lone Star*, 827 F.3d at 1197.

[62] *Cent. Hudson*, 447 U.S. at 564.

[63] *See* FW/PBS, Inc. v. City of Dallas, 493 U.S. 215, 223-24 (1990); Advocates for Arts v. Thomson, 532 F.2d 792, 795 (1st Cir. 1976); City of Indio v. Arroyo, 143 Cal. App. 3d 151, 157 (1983); Mahaney v. City of Englewood, 226 P.3d 1214, 1219 (Colo. App. 2009).

[64] *See* Buckley v. Valeo, 424 U.S. 1, 40–41 (1976).

[65] *See* Virginia v. Hicks, 539 U.S. 113, 118–19 (2003).

[66] *Reed*, 135 S. Ct. at 2226–27; E & J Equities, LLC v. Bd. of Adjustment, 146 A.3d 623, 644 (N.J. 2016).

concrete review timeframe, or if the regulation leaves administrative officers with unbridled discretion to approve or deny the display of certain artwork, the regulation may be an unconstitutional prior restraint.[67] Moreover, if the regulation is vague or overbroad,[68] or if the result of the regulation is the suppression of too much speech,[69] it may also be found unconstitutional. To avoid repetition, this chapter focuses on these doctrines as applied in the context of artwork and, in doing so, reviews several specific cases.

B. Avoiding Content Bias: Definitions and Other Problems

Content concerns arise in many areas of art regulation, but the most common problems relate to definitions of *sign, mural, art,* or *artwork.* Recent case law from federal appellate courts has called into question several common definitions of these terms, and such case law should caution local governments away from any definitions that are content based in nature and that distinguish between artwork and other forms of noncommercial speech.

In *Neighborhood Enterprises, Inc. v. City of St. Louis,*[70] the owner of a mural protesting alleged eminent domain abuses by St. Louis, Missouri, challenged the city's enforcement of its sign ordinance against the mural. The Eighth Circuit Court of Appeals held that the city's definition of "sign," which rested on whether an object was used to "advertise, identify, display, direct or attract attention to an object, person, institution, organization, business product, service, event, or location by any means including words, letters, figures, designs, symbols, fixtures, colors, motion illumination or projected images," but that exempted from this definition all flags, civic crests, and similar objects, was content based because the code's application to the mural rested on the message of the mural.[71] The court reasoned that enforcement of the city's sign code against the mural required the

---

[67] *See FW/PBS,* 493 U.S. at 223–24; *Mahaney,* 226 P.3d at 1219.
[68] *See* Grayned v. City of Rockford, 408 U.S. 104, 108–109, 114–15 (1972).
[69] *See, e.g.,* City of Ladue v. Gilleo, 512 U.S. 43, 58 (1994).
[70] 644 F.3d 728 (8th Cir. 2011). A good overview of the facts of the case and procedural background can be found in the district court opinion, memorandum and order granting summary judgment to the city. *See* Neighborhood Enters., Inc. v. City of St. Louis, 718 F. Supp. 2d 1025, 1029–32 (E.D. Mo. 2010).
[71] *Id.* at 1036.

code enforcement officer to review the content of the mural to determine whether it was subject to the code.[72]

A similar problem existed in the 2016 case of *Central Radio Co., Inc., v. City of Norfolk*.[73] There, the Fourth Circuit Court of Appeals considered a City of Norfolk, Virginia, sign ordinance that exempted from regulation "works of art which in no way identify or specifically relate to a product or service."[74] The Fourth Circuit, on remand from the Supreme Court following its decision in *Reed*, found, in part because of the provisions relating to works of art, "[o]n its face, the former sign code was content based because it applied or did not apply as a result of content, that is, 'the topic discussed or the idea or message expressed.'"[75] The court went on to find that the city's differential regulation of works of art was not narrowly tailored because artwork could have the same detrimental impact on community aesthetics or traffic safety that garish signage might have.[76]

In a 2009 case originating in Florida, *Complete Angler, LLC v. City of Clearwater*,[77] an ordinance that required the local code enforcement officer to determine whether a mural was noncommercial "art work" based on the material displayed on the object was also found to be content based.[78] The code defined "[a]rt work and/or architectural detail" as "drawings, pictures, symbols, paintings or sculpture which do not identify a product or business and which are not displayed in conjunction with a commercial, for profit or nonprofit enterprise."[79] As with *Neighborhood Enterprises*, the court in *Complete Angler* found that the code necessarily required a code enforcement officer to review the mural's content to determine whether it was subject to enforcement and regulation.[80]

---

[72] *Neighborhood Enters.*, 644 F.3d at 736–37. The approach adopted by the Eighth Circuit has often been termed the "need to read" approach to determining whether a speech regulation is content neutral.
[73] 811 F.3d 625 (4th Cir. 2016).
[74] *Id.* at 629.
[75] *Id.* at 633 (quoting *Reed*, 135 S. Ct. at 2227).
[76] *Id.* at 634.
[77] 607 F. Supp. 2d 1326 (M.D. Fla. 2009).
[78] *Id.* at 1333.
[79] *Id.* at 1331.
[80] *Id.* at 1333.

Central Radio, *Neighborhood Enterprises*, and *Complete Angler* reflect the narrow view of content neutrality that was adopted by the U.S. Supreme Court in *Reed* and that requires speech regulation to be content neutral on both the face of the regulation and in the regulation's purpose.[81] Although this view of content neutrality is a mechanical approach to determining whether a regulation is content based—if a code enforcement officer is required to review the content of a mural in order to enforce the code, the code is automatically content based—these decisions make defining artwork or murals in a content neutral manner a difficult, or perhaps even impossible, task. Because of the risks that such distinctions might be found content based, local governments are therefore advised to avoid distinctions between noncommercial murals and other two-dimensional forms of artwork and noncommercial signage, and it may even be advisable to remove special definitions of and treatment for "mural" or other categories of artwork from local codes.

However, in *Peterson v. Village of Downers Grove*,[82] a federal district court in Illinois upheld a local government's ban on "painted wall signs." The court found that the ban was content neutral because it did not contain any references to the message on a given sign.[83] *Peterson* is instructive for local governments regarding the need to establish code definitions that do not create content based distinctions, particularly in the arena of regulating artwork on private property. After *Reed*, it will be a vexing challenge for a local government to distinguish between, say, a "mural" and a "sign," or between a "sculpture" and a "structure," in a content neutral manner, although it may be possible to identify specific media of artwork in the same manner as was done in *Peterson*.

As with sign regulation, content neutral regulations of artwork should focus on the noncommunicative aspects of the artwork. Examples

---

[81] Reed v. Town of Gilbert, 135 S. Ct. 2218, 2227 (2015).

[82] 150 F. Supp. 3d 910 (N.D. Ill. 2015).

[83] *Id.* at 920. Note, however, that in *Clear Channel Outdoor, Inc. v. City of Portland*, 262 P.3d 782 (Or. Ct. App. 2011) the Oregon Court of Appeals held that Portland's sign code definition of "painted wall decorations" as "[d]isplays painted directly on a wall which are designed and intended as a decorative or ornamental feature" and "[p]ainted wall decorations do not contain text, numbers, registered trademarks, or registered logos" was content based.

of content neutral regulation of art include regulating the size, height, placement, or lighting of works of art.[84] Unlike with signage, however, regulating some of the locational aspects of art may give rise to claims of content discrimination, particularly where a particular work of art is alleged to be context or location specific.[85] Similarly, regulation of materials or color may be problematic because the materials and colors used in the creation of a work of art are often central to the message of the particular work.[86] Moreover, regulating noncommercial artwork differently from other forms of noncommercial speech may violate the First Amendment. For example, where a local sign code contains different size, height, or other display limitations on murals as compared with political signage, that code is at risk of being found to be content based.[87]

C. Analysis of Content Neutral Regulations of Artwork

Content neutral regulations must be supported by a substantial or significant regulatory interest, and the regulation must be narrowly tailored to that interest.[88] When applied to matters of artistic expression, this analysis raises fewer answers than questions. As discussed previously, in the context of sign and visual display cases, the U.S. Supreme Court has conclusively determined that both aesthetic and traffic safety interests are significant or substantial as they relate to sign regulation.[89]

There is scant case law to inform local governments of the interests that may support regulation of artwork. Whereas traffic safety may suffice

---

[84] *See Reed*, 135 S. Ct. at 2232; *Id.* at 2233 (Alito, J., concurring).

[85] *See, e.g.*, Serra v. Gen. Svcs. Admin., 847 F.2d 1045, 1047 (2d Cir. 1988) (describing the concept of "site-specific" artwork, in which the locational aspects of the work are part of the expressive content); Phillips v. Pembroke Real Estate, Inc., 288 F. Supp. 2d 89 (D. Mass 2003).

[86] *See, e.g.*, Tinker v. Des Moines Indep. Cmty. Sch. Dist., 393 U.S. 503, 508–509 (1969) (rejecting school district's prohibition on students' wearing of black armbands to protest the Vietnam War); *but see* Tipp City v. Dakin, 929 N.E.2d 484, 502 (Ohio Ct. App. 2010) (finding five-color limitation on murals to be content neutral). The notion that government control of materials or colors might infringe upon First Amendment rights of expression is paralleled by the statutory prohibition against state and local government-directed alteration of registered trademarks under federal trademark protection law. *See* 15 U.S.C. § 1121(b).

[87] *See, e.g.*, Cent. Radio Co., Inc. v. City of Norfolk, 811 F.3d 625, 633 (4th Cir. 2016).

[88] *See, e.g.*, McCullen v. Coakley, 134 S. Ct. 2518, 2529 (2014).

[89] Members of City Council v. Taxpayers for Vincent, 466 U.S. 789, 806–807 (1984); Metromedia, Inc. v. City of San Diego, 453 U.S. 490, 507–508 (1981).

as a governmental interest for purposes of regulating works of art, aesthetics is less sound given that the aesthetic concerns of a local government may be at odds with the message of a particular work of art. If the government is in the business of making the community beautiful,[90] can the government prohibit "ugly" artwork whose ugliness is a critical part of its message?[91] For example, a local government's restriction on the size, height, or color of murals for aesthetic purposes may directly conflict with the central message of a muralist's work.[92] Similarly, whereas many sign codes regulate the placement of signs within property and with respect to street right-of-ways in order to preserve a particular community character, an artist's placement of a sculpture or mural—if the artwork is site-specific—may be driven in large part by the message that the artist wishes to convey with his or her work.[93] In essence, the government's aesthetic preferences may directly contradict the message that an artist wishes to convey. However, no reported cases have closely reviewed aesthetics as a government interest in the regulation of artwork.

In addition, the author is aware of no reported case that has addressed the application of building and zoning codes to three-dimensional artwork such as statuary or sculpture, and thus building safety, nuisance control, and other purposes for zoning and building restrictions have not been widely reviewed for whether they constitute significant governmental interests. In *Kleinman v. City of San Marcos*,[94] the City of San Marcos, Texas, had an ordinance prohibiting property owners from keeping junked vehicles on their properties. A novelty store placed a wrecked Oldsmobile 88 in its front

---

[90] *See, e.g.,* Berman v. Parker, 348 U.S. 26, 33 (1954).

[91] In the case of *State ex rel. Stoyanoff v. Berkeley*, 458 S.W.2d 305 (Mo. 1970), the Missouri Supreme Court upheld a local design review board's decision to prohibit a pyramidal house from a neighborhood that otherwise included only Colonial, French Provincial, and Tudor residential styles in the face of a Due Process Clause challenge. The local legislative determination that the community should include only traditional architectural style was reviewed on an arbitrary and capricious standard. *Id.* at 310. There's no telling how a court would review that legislative determination under the intermediate scrutiny or strict scrutiny analysis applicable in First Amendment review.

[92] *See generally* Darrel C. Menthe, *Aesthetic Regulation and the Development of First Amendment Jurisprudence,* 19 B.U. Pub. Int. L.J. 225 (2010).

[93] *See, e.g.,* Serra v. Gen. Servs. Admin., 847 F.2d 1045, 1047 (2d Cir. 1988) (describing artist's view of sculpture as being "site-specific," i.e., the message was intended for a specific location).

[94] 597 F.3d 323 (5th Cir. 2010), *cert den.*, 562 U.S. 837 (2010).

lawn, which was planted with vegetation and painted colorfully with the message "Make Love Not War." The city ticketed the property owner for a violation of the junked vehicle ordinance. Even after the city stipulated to the fact that the car-planter had some artistic expressive value, the Fifth Circuit found that the car's expressive value was secondary to its utility as a junked vehicle: "When the 'expressive' component of an object, considered objectively in light of its function and utility, is at best secondary, the public display of the object is conduct subject to reasonable state regulation, [and w]e therefore pretermit 'recourse to principles of aesthetics.'"[95] The court then applied the intermediate scrutiny test as articulated in *United States v. O'Brien*[96] for expressive conduct, found that the junked vehicle ordinance was content neutral in purpose,[97] and found that the junked vehicle ordinance was narrowly tailored to serve the government's interest in prevention of attractive nuisances to children, prevention of rodents and other pests, and reduction in urban blight, vandalism, and depressed property values.[98] Although San Marcos's recitation of governmental interests in blight prevention and preserving property values may have had some aesthetic component, the Fifth Circuit did not analyze whether purely aesthetic interests could support a prohibition of the creative car-planter form of artwork.

Narrow tailoring requires that the regulation in question directly advance the interest(s) asserted by the government. In the context of artwork, problems may arise where local codes treat murals differently from other forms of noncommercial speech, and where the regulatory interests at stake are not directly served by the differential treatment. Readers are encouraged to review other chapters in the book that address narrow tailoring in greater detail.

---

[95] *Id.* at 327–28.

[96] 391 U.S. 367 (1968).

[97] *Kleinman*, 597 F.3d at 328. Of course, *Kleinman* was decided five years before *Reed v. Town of Gilbert*, so the Fifth Circuit's failure to conduct a content neutrality analysis "skips the crucial first step in the content-neutrality analysis: determining whether the law is content neutral on its face." Reed v. Town of Gilbert, 135 S. Ct. 2218, 2228 (2015).

[98] *Kleinman*, 597 F.3d at 328.

D. Distinguishing Between Noncommercial and Commercial Artwork

Perhaps more than with other forms of speech, the distinction between noncommercial and commercial artwork is difficult. When a municipal code requires a property owner to obtain a permit for a commercial wall sign but does not require a permit for a noncommercial mural, how does one address artwork displayed on the wall of a building that contains images of products sold inside the building? Business owners are often inclined to utilize blank wall space on the side of a building to advertise products sold inside the building, beautify the premises, or convey noncommercial or political messages. Determining whether such images constitute commercial or noncommercial speech is rarely simple,[99] and courts have arrived at opposite conclusions on this point.

Case law provides several illustrations of this problem. When a California city attempted to regulate a fuel station owner's mural depicting "the geography, indigenous plants, and archaeology of Mexico, [the] social advancements of the Mexican people in contemporary society as well as reflections upon a colonial period of Mexican history," placed ostensibly in an effort to beautify the property and presumably in part to attract customers to the station, the California Court of Appeals found the mural to be noncommercial speech.[100] The court stated, "[a]lthough the [station owners'] mural appears on the wall of a commercial establishment, it is clearly ideological expression, not commercial speech."[101]

And when a Clearwater, Florida, shop that sold fishing equipment, including bait and tackle, displayed a painted wall mural depicting fish and other aquatic plant and animal species, the mural was determined to be noncommercial speech: "[A]s the evidence demonstrate[d] . . . it reflects a

---

[99] For a good discussion of the troublesome nature of the distinction and some insight as to how courts go about making the distinction between commercial and noncommercial speech, see the California Supreme Court's discussion in *Kasky v. Nike, Inc.*, 45 P.3d 243, 253–55 (Cal. 2002).

[100] City of Indio v. Arroyo, 143 Cal. App. 3d 151, 154 (1983).

[101] *Id.* at 158.

local artist's impression of the natural habitat and waterways surrounding [the subject shop], and also alerts viewers to threatened species of fish."[102]

Conversely, a mural in Tipp City, Ohio, depicting a "mad scientist" on the outside of a shop that sold nitrous oxide for racing cars was found to constitute commercial speech.[103] In arriving at that conclusion, the Ohio Court of Appeals stated, "the crucial inquiry is whether the expression depicted in the appellants' mural either extends beyond proposing a commercial transaction or relates to something more than the economic interests of the appellants and their customers."[104] The court found that "[t]he sign plainly is intended to attract attention to [the racing shop], which directly relates to that company's economic interests."[105]

In another case, *Wag More Dogs, LLC v. Cozart*,[106] a Virginia pet daycare owner displayed a mural depicting dogs playing on the side of the building, in plain view of a dog park. The Fourth Circuit Court of Appeals, relying on the Supreme Court's multiple-factor analysis in *Bolger v. Youngs Drug Products Corp.*,[107] concluded that the mural was commercial speech because the mural was intended to attract attention of potential customers, it depicted images relating to services provided on the premises, and the owner had an economic motivation for displaying the mural.[108]

These cases are only somewhat instructive for local governments that wish to regulate commercial artwork differently from noncommercial artwork. The courts recognize distinctions between commercial and noncommercial speech, and local governments are thus entitled to regulate these forms of speech differently.[109] As demonstrated by the cases just de-

---

[102] Complete Angler, LLC v. City of Clearwater, 607 F. Supp. 2d 1326, 1328 (M.D. Fla. 2009).

[103] Tipp City v. Dakin, 929 N.E.2d 484, 494 (Ohio Ct. App. 2010).

[104] *Id.*

[105] *Id.*

[106] 680 F.3d 359 (4th Cir. 2012).

[107] 463 U.S. 60, 66–67 (1983).

[108] *Wag More Dogs*, 680 F.3d at 370.

[109] The judicial distinction between commercial and noncommercial speech may be closing as a result of the U.S. Supreme Court's decision in *Sorrell v. IMS Health*, 564 U.S. 552 (2011), where the Court analyzed a regulation of commercial speech in part under the approach typically applied to noncommercial speech, reviewing the regulation for content bias. *Id.* at 571. This analysis in *Sorrell*, combined with *Reed v. Town of Gilbert*'s failure to even mention the commercial speech doctrine, potentially portends a slow death for the commercial speech doctrine and the courts' differential treatment of

(footnote continued on next page)

scribed, courts are generally more deferential to governmental regulations of commercial speech as compared with regulations of noncommercial speech, in part because the commercial speech doctrine does not require an initial determination regarding the content neutrality of the regulation in question. However, local governments should take care to define the boundary between commercial and noncommercial speech. Where they distinguish between commercial and noncommercial speech, the regulations should utilize distinctions found in case law, preferably in a jurisdiction applicable to the local government.

E. Other First Amendment Issues

Aside from issues of content neutrality, other First Amendment doctrines may limit or restrict local government regulation of artwork on private property. Prior restraint issues arise where local codes leave administrative or elected officials with too much discretion in the approval of permits for artwork. For example, a Colorado city's failure to provide a timeframe for review of a permit application to display a mural was found to constitute an unconstitutional prior restraint.[110] Similarly, local codes without sufficiently clear approval standards can also create unconstitutional prior restraints. In a 1983 California case, a city code that required the planning director to assess murals for "architectural compatibility," "sign effectiveness," and

---

(footnote continued from previous page)

commercial speech under the First Amendment. However, in recent post-*Reed* sign cases, the lower courts have observed that the Supreme Court has not yet directly overruled the commercial speech doctrine, and most courts have thus opted to maintain the distinction. *See, e.g.,* Contest Promotions, LLC v. City and Cnty. of San Francisco, No. 15-CV-00093, 2015WL4571564 ("*Reed* does not concern commercial speech, and therefore does not disturb the framework which holds that commercial speech is subject only to intermediate scrutiny as defined by the Central Hudson test."); Lamar Cent. Outdoor, LLC v. City of Los Angeles, 199 Cal. Rptr. 3d 620 (Cal. Ct. App. 2016); *but see* Thomas v. Schroer, 116 F. Supp. 3d 869 (W.D. Tenn. 2015) (finding the Tennessee highway advertising control law to be content based in violation of the First Amendment); Auspro Enters., L.P. v. Dep't of Transp., 506 S.W.3d 688 (Tex. Ct. App. 2016) (finding the Texas Highway Beautification Act to be a content based law in violation of the First Amendment).

[110] Mahaney v. City of Englewood, 226 P.3d 1214 (Colo. App. 2009).

"indecent or immoral matter" prior to approval was found to constitute an unlawful prior restraint.[111]

F. Special Considerations

An area that has been mostly unexplored in case law relates to local anti-graffiti ordinances. Many local governments have taken measures to prevent graffiti, based primarily on aesthetic concerns and an interest in preventing vandalism and property-related crime.[112] In the 2007 case of *Vincenty v. Bloomberg*,[113] a group of graffiti artists challenged New York City's prohibitions on the sale of aerosol paint cans and broad-tipped markers to persons under twenty-one years of age and the possession of such objects in public places by persons under twenty-one, which were intended to control unwanted graffiti in the city. The Second Circuit Court of Appeals agreed with the district court's determination that regulation was content neutral,[114] but the court also agreed with the conclusion that the ordinance provisions burdened more speech than was necessary to achieve the city's goals.[115] Earlier cases found similar restrictions to pass constitutional muster, although not necessarily on First Amendment grounds.[116]

To the extent anti-graffiti ordinances regulate in a content neutral manner and do not burden more speech than necessary, they are likely to be upheld by courts. However, local governments should beware that many current anti-graffiti ordinances likely contain content based definitions of

---

[111] City of Indio v. Arroyo, 143 Cal. App. 3d 151 (1983).

[112] *See, e.g.*, ANSONIA, CONN. CODE OF ORDINANCES § 17-39 (2014); INDIANAPOLIS–MARION CNTY. CODE § 575-201 *et seq.* (2013).

[113] 476 F.3d 74 (2d Cir. 2007).

[114] *Id.* at 84.

[115] *Id.* at 87 ("We see no error in the district court's finding that '[i]t appears . . . at this stage of the litigation' that subsection (c–1)'s prohibition against young adults' possession of spray paint and markers in public places—because it applies 'even where the individuals have a legitimate purpose for their use"—imposes a substantial burden on innocent expression.' (internal citations omitted)).

[116] *See, e.g.*, Nat'l Paint & Coatings Ass'n v. City of Chicago, 45 F.3d 1124, 1127–28 (7th Cir. 1995) (reviewing legislative prohibition on sale of certain paint devices under rational basis standard of review); Sherwin-Williams Co. v. City and Cnty. of San Francisco, 857 F. Supp. 1355, 1371 (N.D. Cal. 1994).

the term *graffiti*. An example of a definition of *graffiti* that likely passes muster is one that references graffiti based on its unauthorized nature.[117]

Another area that has received little judicial attention relates to public art programs in private development projects. Some local governments require that private development projects include public art, require dedications of money or artwork in connection with private development projects, or undergo design review of artwork. The constitutionality of these arrangements has not been fully vetted; however, there are some corollary examples of judicial treatment of these arrangements. In a case originating in Leavenworth, Washington,[118] a federal district court found that the city's requirement that signs be of a Bavarian style was not content based,[119] did not constitute forced speech,[120] and it further found that a design review board charged with reviewing signs and architecture in the community did not constitute an unlawful prior restraint despite having "somewhat elastic" criteria for review.[121] Similarly, the Oregon Court of Appeals held that the City of Portland's design review process as applied to billboards did not constitute an overbroad regulation or unconstitutional prior restraint due to the narrow construction of the design review board's purview.[122] To the author's knowledge, no case has analyzed whether design review as applied to works of art would be an unconstitutional prior restraint or unconstitutionally vague, or whether a mandate that a private development project contain or dedicate some form of public art constitutes forced speech contradictory to the First Amendment.

---

[117] *See, e.g.*, Indianapolis, Indiana's definition: "Graffiti means any *unauthorized* inscription, word, figure, design, painting, writing, drawing or carving that is written, marked, etched, scratched, sprayed, drawn, painted, or engraved on or otherwise affixed on a component of any building, structure, or other facility by any graffiti implement, visible from any public property, the public right-of-way, or from any private property other than the property on which it exists. There shall be a rebuttable presumption that such inscription, word, figure, painting, or other defacement is unauthorized. This article does not apply to easily removable chalk markings on the public sidewalks and streets." Indianapolis–Marion Cnty. Code § 575-202 (2013) (emphasis added).

[118] Demarest v. City of Leavenworth, 876 F. Supp. 2d 1186 (E.D. Wash. 2012).

[119] *Id.* at 1195.

[120] *Id.* at 1196-97.

[121] *Id.* at 1202-03.

[122] Clear Channel Outdoor, Inc. v. City of Portland, 262 P.3d 782, 165–66 (Or. Ct. App. 2011).

VI. Private Art on Public Property

The regulation of artwork on public property carries different considerations than artwork on private property. On public property, the manner and degree to which artwork can be regulated are largely dependent on the *type* of government property in question, that is, where the property falls within the public forum analysis. Because chapters 9 through 11 contain extensive discussion of the public forum doctrine, that discussion is not restated here. The reader is instead directed to review the discussion contained in chapters 9 through 11. This section addresses two specific problems that arise in the regulation of artwork on public property: the sale or display of artwork on public property, such as parks, sidewalks, or streets, and government selection of artwork for public property, including government buildings, plazas, and parks.

A. Sale or Display of Private Artwork by Private Individuals on Public Property

Many local codes prohibit the sale of commercial products or the solicitation of business on public property. Some of these code provisions create express exemptions for nonprofit organizations or other forms of noncommercial speech.[123] This chapter has already addressed First Amendment protection for artwork as differentiated from commercial merchandise, which lacks the protection of the First Amendment; however, there are some cases in which materials displayed or sold on public property have been found to merit First Amendment protection.

In these cases, courts first review where the property falls within the public forum doctrine—that is, whether the property is a traditional, designated, limited, or nonpublic forum.[124] If the property is a traditional or

---

[123] *See, e.g.,* ST. AUGUSTINE, FLA. CODE OF ORDINANCES § 22-6 (2000) ("It shall be unlawful for any person or organization to use or occupy any public square, park, street, sidewalk or other public property within the city for the purpose of selling, displaying, offering for sale or peddling any goods, wares or merchandise, except any nonprofit organization, religious, literary, scientific, charitable, educational purpose who shall have obtained a permit from the city manager or his designee.").

[124] *See generally* Perry Educ. Ass'n v. Perry Local Educ. Ass'n, 460 U.S. 37, 44 (1983) ("The existence of a right of access to public property and the standard by which limitations upon such a right must be evaluated differ depending on the character of the property at issue.").

designated public forum, restrictions must be content neutral and narrowly tailored to serve significant governmental interests, and these restrictions may regulate only the time, place, and manner of speech.[125] If the property is a limited public forum or a nonpublic forum, the restrictions must only be viewpoint neutral and reasonable, a far more deferential standard than that applied in traditional and designated public fora.[126]

In a 2000 case involving St. Augustine, Florida, the city attempted to enforce its ordinance prohibiting "selling, displaying, offering for sale or peddling any goods, wares or merchandise" on public property, including streets and sidewalks, against a street artist displaying and selling newspapers and art that contained political messages.[127] The code provision exempted nonprofit and religious organizations, but it did not contain any exemption for political speech. In a fairly cursory analysis, the court found that the artist's visual art and newspapers were protected by the First Amendment[128] and found that the public property regulated by the ordinance was a traditional public forum, thus requiring the regulation to be content neutral and narrowly tailored to a significant governmental interest.[129] Because the ordinance favored nonprofit and religious organizations over other forms of noncommercial speech, the court held the restriction to be content based.[130]

Similarly, a New York City law requiring street vendors to obtain a city license—with exceptions for vendors of newspapers, books, or other written matter—for the sale of items on city sidewalks was found not to be narrowly tailored or to provide sufficient alternative channels for communication.[131] The restriction capped the total number of licenses available to sidewalk vendors citywide.[132] After finding that the works being sold by sidewalk vendors were subject to First Amendment protection[133] and that the

---

[125] See id. at 45–46.
[126] See Cornelius v. NAACP Legal Defense & Ed. Fund, Inc., 473 U.S. 788, 808 (1985).
[127] Celli v. City of St. Augustine, 214 F. Supp. 2d 1255 (M.D. Fla. 2000).
[128] Id. at 1258–59.
[129] Id. at 1260.
[130] Id.
[131] Bery v. City of New York, 97 F.3d 689 (2d Cir. 1996).
[132] Id. at 692.
[133] Id. at 696.

traditional public forum analysis applied to the case,[134] the Second Circuit Court of Appeals found that the license requirement, and the cap on the total number of licenses that could be issued, was not narrowly tailored to the city's goals of reducing congestion and ensuring clear passage on the sidewalks.[135] The court reasoned that the city could have employed time, place, and manner restrictions to ensure clear passage on the sidewalks while still offering vendors the opportunity to obtain a license and that exceptions to the licensing cap called into question the rule's tailoring.[136] The court also found that the restriction did not provide ample alternatives and that the sale of artwork on the street was more accessible than sales in galleries or elsewhere.[137]

In both of the foregoing cases, the restrictions at issue had serious defects: one impermissibly distinguished between forms of noncommercial speech, and the other had gaping exceptions to a generally strict licensing requirement. To the extent local governments prohibit the sale or display of commercial products on sidewalks or other public properties, exceptions made for noncommercial speech, including noncommercial artwork, should not distinguish among forms of noncommercial speech. Moreover, an outright ban or severe limitations on the display of noncommercial artwork in traditional public fora, such as streets or sidewalks, is likely to fail the narrow tailoring part of the intermediate scrutiny test. Time, place, and manner restrictions are permissible, for example, where necessary to ensure safe passage for pedestrians along public sidewalks or to limit traffic congestion along public streets. Additionally, where the regulation of artwork is taking place in a limited or nonpublic forum, restrictions and prohibitions can be much broader, so long as they are viewpoint neutral.

B. Government Selection of Artwork for Public Property

Another circumstance where possible First Amendment concerns arise with respect to public property is when governments select artwork for

---

[134] *See id.* at 696–97.
[135] *Id.* at 698.
[136] *Id.*
[137] *Id.*

temporary or permanent placement in public buildings or other public properties. Government agencies, from federal agencies to local governments, routinely seek to beautify public properties through the use of artwork, including murals, sculpture, and other works of art. In some cases, these works of art are commissioned by the government, and in other cases, they are selected through an artwork selection process.

In general, the government has wide latitude to engage in the selection of artwork for government properties and to relocate or remove that artwork in the event the government chooses to redevelop or otherwise modify government properties. This principle is best enshrined in the case of *National Endowment for the Arts v. Finley*,[138] in which the U.S. Supreme Court held that the federal government could "allocate competitive funding [for the arts] according to criteria that would be impermissible were direct regulation of speech or a criminal penalty at stake."[139] The Court found that, in the allocation of funding, the government has broad discretion to fund "one activity to the exclusion of the other" and that the government's selection of works of art to patronize—even where the criteria are somewhat imprecise—does not give rise to a First Amendment violation.[140] Even prior to *Finley*, however, the courts gave significant deference to the government in its decisions regarding the funding, selection, display, and relocation of privately produced artwork.[141]

Cases addressing questions of government acquisition and placement of artwork have generally held that artwork acquired by the government for display on public property becomes the property and expression of the government[142] or, alternatively, that the government's acquisition and display of artwork creates a nonpublic forum, where the acquisition process need only be viewpoint neutral and reasonable.[143] In *Serra v. General Services Administration*, the court stated that a sculpture located on the grounds of a

---

[138] 524 U.S. 569 (1998).

[139] *Id.* at 587–88.

[140] *Id.* at 588, 589–90 (internal citations omitted).

[141] *See* Serra v. U.S. Gen. Svcs. Admin., 847 F.2d 1045, 1049–50 (2d Cir. 1988); Advocates for Arts v. Thompson, 532 F.2d 792, 795–96 (1st Cir. 1976).

[142] *See Serra*, 847 F.2d at 1049.

[143] *See* Sefick v. Gardner, 164 F.3d 370 (7th Cir. 1998).

federal government building constituted the expression of the government and could be relocated freely without the consent of the artist.[144] The *Serra* court additionally found that even if the sculpture's location had been a public forum, the sculpture's relocation was a time, place, and manner restriction because the government's purpose in relocating the sculpture was related to free passage of pedestrians in the plaza where the sculpture was located.[145] Other cases have held that government acquisition of artwork for display in public buildings or galleries creates a nonpublic forum, and government decisions to reject or remove artwork that could be offensive or critical are permissible where the purposes of the forum are undermined by the artwork's offensive or critical nature.[146]

The foregoing judicial approach to government control of artwork on government property was recently reaffirmed by the First Circuit Court of Appeals in the case of *Newton v. LePage*.[147] There, the Maine Department of Labor sought to remove a mural from a waiting room within its offices on the grounds that the mural did not depict evenhanded treatment of issues associated with labor. According to the court:

> The mural contained panels which depicted a shoemaker teaching an apprentice, child laborers, women textile workers, workers casting secret ballots, the first Labor Day, woods workers, the 1937 shoe strike in Lewiston and Auburn, labor reformers, women workers during World War II, the 1987 strike at the International Paper Mill in Jay, and the future of Maine labor.[148]

In analyzing *Newton*, the court did not rely on the public forum doctrine but rather on the government speech doctrine, which had been articulated by the Supreme Court just three years earlier.[149] Although the

---

[144] *Serra*, 847 F.2d at 1049.
[145] *Id.* at 1049–50.
[146] *See Sefick*, 164 F.3d at 372–73; Piarowski v. Ill. Cmty. Coll. Dist. 515, 759 F.2d 625, 629–30 (7th Cir. 1985).
[147] 700 F.3d 595 (1st Cir. 2012).
[148] *Id.* at 598.
[149] *Id.* at 602 (citing Pleasant Grove City v. Summum, 555 U.S. 460, 469–70 (2009)).

court did not conclude whether the mural was government speech, it nonetheless provided great deference to the government's choice to remove the mural and concluded that there was no First Amendment violation in so doing.[150]

The rise of the government speech doctrine, which is discussed in greater detail in Chapter 9, lends additional support to local governments engaged in the selection and ownership of artwork on public property. Even before the U.S. Supreme Court adopted the government speech doctrine—which carves out from First Amendment application any speech promulgated by the government—federal appeals courts had used the concept of "government speech" to reject First Amendment claims of message or viewpoint discrimination, or prior restraint, by artists.[151] With the adoption and expansion of the government speech doctrine by the U.S. Supreme Court, it can be expected that government decisions regarding the acquisition, display, relocation, and removal of works of art will be subject to even lesser scrutiny than before.[152] Although fairly recent and still in its infancy, the Supreme Court's government speech jurisprudence holds that government speech occurs where the government seeks to convey a message, members of the public routinely and reasonably understand the message to be that of the government, and where the government effectively controls the message.[153] The Supreme Court has found that donated monuments in a public park constitute government speech,[154] as do specialty license plates.[155] Given this recent case law, artwork selected by the government

---

[150] *Id.* at 602–03.
[151] Serra v. U.S. Gen. Svcs. Admin., 847 F.2d 1045, 1049 (2d Cir. 1988).
[152] *See* Walker v. Texas Div., Sons of Confederate Veterans, Inc., 135 S. Ct. 2239, 2245 (2015) ("When government speaks, it is not barred by the Free Speech Clause from determining the content of what it says.").
[153] *Walker,* 135 S. Ct. at 2247; Pleasant Grove City v. Summum, 555 U.S. 460, 470–73 (2009).
[154] *Summum,* 555 U.S. at 470–72.
[155] *Walker,* 135 S. Ct. at 2249.

for display on public property is likely to be considered by a court to be government speech.[156]

Still, local governments that select artwork for display on government property should carefully consider the parameters of the government speech doctrine to ensure that their art programs are classified as government speech. Following the *Serra* and *Newton* line of cases, for example, the government should ensure that it controls the artwork by taking ownership of the artwork and negotiating with the artist for complete control over the artwork's placement, care, and eventual removal or relocation.

VII. Regulation of Architecture

The First Amendment issues relating to the regulation of architecture require more discussion than is possible or even wise in a chapter devoted to practical considerations for local governments. Local governments exercise control over architectural design in many ways, including through local building code requirements; height, setback, and building separation limitations imposed via zoning restrictions; and the prescriptive design requirements of form-based codes, design review procedures, historic building and district designations, and even sign codes. In all of these cases, architectural creativity is regulated and limited. If, for example, Richard Meier wanted to design one of his signature white structures within a historic district containing red-brick structures, the historic district regulations might prohibit him from doing so. And if Frank Gehry's design for the Walt Disney Concert Hall in Los Angeles had been developed under a form-based code requiring a certain amount of fenestration, the sweeping stainless-steel design may have turned out radically different.

---

[156] In a 2012 decision, the First Circuit Court of Appeals declined to extend the government speech doctrine to murals located in a public administration building, in part because the government defendant argued that the murals did not constitute government speech; that court still found that the government could effectively control the relocation of such murals because the murals were government property. Newton v. LePage, 700 F.3d 595, 604 (1st Cir. 2012).

In the past several decades, authors of scholarly works have vigorously debated whether the First Amendment considerations relating to speech and subsets thereof, including artwork, should be applicable to architecture.[157] Starting with the premise that architecture is or could be considered a form of speech, scholars have suggested that, just as regulations that control the color or design of artwork such as murals would likely be found to be content based, regulations controlling the form, transparency, or materials of buildings could be considered content based under a First Amendment analysis.[158] Moreover, it is not clear that a local government's aesthetic preferences for particular architectural styles, colors, materials, or building activation would be considered sufficiently significant or compelling if tested under a First Amendment challenge. For example, where a pyramid-shaped house in a predominantly neocolonial neighborhood is intended to serve as a statement of rebellion against architectural—or even cultural—uniformity,[159] the First Amendment considerations may be of equal prominence as those for an individual carrying a political protest sign along a city street. And certainly, "corporate architecture" similar to that used by McDonald's restaurants, AutoZone automotive parts stores, Wal-Mart, and other commercial establishments is an effective means of conveying an advertising message by the business owner.

To this author's knowledge, no First Amendment challenge has been brought against a form-based code, design guidelines, or architectural review board relating to local control of architectural design. Generally speaking, architectural controls have been upheld against challenges under other constitutional and state law provisions, including the Due Process

---

[157] *See generally* Kevin G. Gill, *Freedom of Speech and the Language of Architecture*, 30 Hastings Const. L.Q. 395 (2003); Janet Elizabeth Haws, Comment, *Architecture as Art? Not in My Neocolonial Neighborhood: A Case for Providing First Amendment Protection to Expressive Residential Architecture*, 2005 B.Y.U. L. Rev. 1625 (2005); Menthe, *supra* note 92; Thomas Pak, *Free Exercise, Free Expression, and Landmarks Preservation*, 91 Colum. L. Rev. 1813 (1991); Samuel E. Poole III, *Architectural Appearance Review Regulations and the First Amendment: The Good, the Bad, and the Consensus Ugly*, 19 Urb. Law. 287 (1987); Shawn G. Rice, Comment, *Zoning Law: Architectural Appearance Ordinances and the First Amendment*, 76 Marq. L. Rev. 439 (1993).

[158] *See, e.g.,* Poole, *supra* note 158, at 307–11.

[159] *See generally* State ex rel. Stoyanoff v. Berkeley, 458 S.W.2d 305 (Mo. 1970).

Clause.[160] In the First Amendment context, architectural controls have been found valid where historic district regulations prohibited the placement of news racks on streets within the historic district[161] and where they provided five arguably subjective criteria for the review of signs.[162]

Conversely, whereas the Ohio Supreme Court upheld architectural controls as a valid exercise in legislative discretion in 1984, a dissenting justice observed possible First Amendment concerns associated with architectural regulation.[163] There are also examples of cases where local historic district regulations controlling architectural matters have been found to violate the rights of religious organizations. Of note, in *First Covenant Church of Seattle v. City of Seattle*,[164] the Washington Supreme Court found that a church's exterior architecture constituted an "architectural 'proclamation' of religious belief" and was "religious speech,"[165] and in applying the *Sherbert* test[166] for Free Exercise claims, the court invalidated the city's historic preservation ordinance as it applied to the church.[167]

As the foregoing cases begin to illustrate, there are more questions than answers in the realm of the First Amendment's applicability to architecture. Until a court is charged with the difficult task of addressing a First Amendment challenge to architectural design limitations, there is no telling how such a challenge would play out. Local governments are therefore encouraged to carefully consider the First Amendment implications

---

[160] *See Stoyanoff*, 458 S.W.2d at 310–12; State ex rel. Saveland Park Holding Corp. v. Wieland, 69 N.W.2d 217 (Wis. 1955); Reid v. Architectural Review Bd. of Cleveland Heights, 162 N.E.32d 74 (Ohio 1963); City of New Orleans v. Levy, 64 So. 2d 798 (La. 1953).

[161] Globe Newspaper Co. v. Beacon Hill Architectural Comm'n, 100 F.3d 175, 188 (1st Cir. 1996) (finding prohibition on newsstands to be content neutral and narrowly tailored to interest in preserving aesthetic character of district); Hop Publications, Inc. v. City of Boston, 334 F. Supp. 2d 35, 49 (D. Mass. 2004).

[162] Lusk v. Vill. of Cold Spring, 475 F.3d 480, 494–95 (2d Cir. 2007). The court in *Lusk* did, however, find that the code in question constituted an unconstitutional prior restraint on speech because it failed to provide a short timeframe for review of temporary signs. *See id.* at 491–92.

[163] *See* Albrecht v. Vill. of Hudson, 458 N.E.2d 852, 858 (Ohio 1984) ("This zoning case has now placed us in the era of Orwell's '1984' where Big Brother tells us what to do and think in a realm that is protected by the constitutional right of privacy under the First Amendment to the United States Constitution.").

[164] 840 P.2d 174 (Wash. 1992).

[165] *Id.* at 182 (stating also that "[t]he relationship between theological doctrine and architectural design is well recognized.").

[166] *See* Sherbert v. Verner, 374 U.S. 398, 403 (1963).

[167] *First Covenant*, 840 P.2d at 185.

of their architectural and design review ordinances and to ensure that such ordinances avoid obvious content bias; reduce or eliminate, where possible, any effective prior restraints that might delay permitting; and apply sufficiently definite standards so as to direct applicants.

VIII. Conclusion

This chapter's review of artwork and architecture through a First Amendment lens is largely dealing in the frontier of constitutional jurisprudence. Yet as First Amendment protections expand as a result of the broadened content neutrality doctrine arising out of *Reed v. Town of Gilbert* and the heightened evidentiary standards applicable in the narrow tailoring analysis as a result of *McCullen v. Coakley*, we may very well be witnessing an expansion of First Amendment applicability that may sweep up previously unchecked governmental controls on artwork and architecture. Local governments are therefore advised to carefully consider how their zoning codes and other regulations affect the ability of artists and architects to speak through their work and to ensure that local efforts to make regulations content neutral and otherwise consistent with the First Amendment preserve the free speech rights of all speakers.

Regulating Religious Land Uses Under the First Amendment

A Practical Approach for Local Governments

Evan J. Seeman

Robinson & Cole LLP
Hartford, Connecticut

I. Introduction

This chapter examines religious land use disputes brought under the First Amendment's Free Exercise and Establishment Clauses (known collectively as the religion clauses). Regulating religious land uses is one of the most personal, intensely contested, and divisive of all land use disputes. As noted by one federal judge deciding a religious land use dispute: "[f]ew principles are more venerable or more passionately held in American society than those of local control over land use and the right to assemble and worship where one chooses."[1] Not only is this area of the law emotionally charged, often with sensitive allegations of discrimination, but there are also high stakes associated with challenging the constitutionality of a local government's

---

[1] Vineyard Christian Fellowship of Evanston, Inc. v. City of Evanston, 250 F. Supp. 2d 961, 963 (N.D. Ill. 2003).

zoning code or its actions in enforcing the code. There is the risk of the government's potential exposure to substantial attorneys' fees in the event of a loss. There is also the risk that a challenge to the zoning code itself could decimate a local government's comprehensive planning scheme. These disputes can be and often are confusing, substantively and procedurally, even for the most seasoned government practitioner. This confusion is largely due in part to (a) the hectic pace at which this area of the law has evolved, and (b) the competing philosophies of the religion clauses.

The confusion began in 1990 with the U.S. Supreme Court's decision in *Employment Division v. Smith*,[2] when Justice Scalia's majority opinion changed decades' worth of free exercise jurisprudence. *Smith* reduced constitutional protection under the Free Exercise Clause by establishing that neutral laws of general applicability (meaning those that are not specifically directed at religious practice) are per se constitutional no matter their effect on religion.[3] Before *Smith*, the opposite was true—any law, even if neutral and generally applicable, could violate the Free Exercise Clause if it burdened religious exercise and warranted constitutional protection. Three years later, the Supreme Court limited the reach of *Smith* to some extent in *Church of the Lukumi Babalu Aye, Inc. v. City of Hialeah*[4] by ruling that *Smith* did *not* apply to laws that were not neutral or not generally applicable.[5] Still, *Lukumi* did not undo the drastic change of course marked by *Smith*.

Congress responded to *Smith* the same year as *Lukumi* by "restoring" religious protection that had existed prior to *Smith* through the enactment of the Religious Freedom Restoration Act (RFRA).[6] Restoration was short-lived when, in 1997, the Supreme Court invalidated RFRA as it applied to the states after finding that the statute was so broadly applicable that Congress had exceeded its constitutional enforcement powers.[7] Since

---

[2] 494 U.S. 872 (1990).
[3] *Id.* at 893.
[4] 508 U.S. 520 (1993).
[5] *Id.* at 546.
[6] 42 U.S.C. § 2000bb (1996).
[7] City of Boerne v. Flores, 521 U.S. 507, 516 (1997).

Boerne, several states have enacted their own laws modeled after RFRA.[8] Three years after *Boerne* was decided, Congress enacted the Religious Land Use and Institutionalized Persons Act (RLUIPA)[9] in yet another attempt to restore religious protections in two areas that it believed were especially susceptible to discrimination: land use regulation and institutional settings. Since then, courts across the nation have applied First Amendment and statutory protection in the land use context in varying ways, and without any guidance from the Supreme Court, which has yet to review and adjudicate the merits of a religious land use case. Chapter 6 provides a more detailed discussion of RLUIPA and its implications for local governments, whereas this chapter reviews religious land use matters under the First Amendment.

Further confusion results from what appears to be the diametrically opposed "guarantees" of the religion clauses, applicable to states and local governments through the Fourteenth Amendment.[10] The First Amendment guarantees freedom of religion in two distinct areas. First, the government cannot take action that would constitute an "establishment" or "advancement" of religion. This is known as the Establishment Clause. Second, the government cannot prohibit or burden the "free exercise" of religion. This is known as the Free Exercise Clause.

To ensure religious freedom, the Free Exercise Clause mandates that accommodation of religion is sometimes necessary "because, without it, government would find itself effectively and unconstitutionally promoting the absence of religion over its practice."[11] At the same time, the Establishment Clause prohibits the advancement of religion over nonreligion.[12] But "advancing" religion sounds a lot like the accommodation of religion required under the Free Exercise Clause, and this has troubled some governments seeking to regulate religious uses. Consider a local government

---

[8] As of September 3, 2015, twenty-one states had enacted state religious freedom legislation. *See* NATIONAL CONFERENCE OF STATE LEGISLATURES, 2015 STATE RELIGIOUS FREEDOM RESTORATION LEGISLATION, *available at* http://www.ncsl.org/research/civil-and-criminal-justice/2015-state-rfra-legislation.aspx (last visited Dec. 22, 2016).

[9] 42 U.S.C. § 2000cc (2016).

[10] *See, e.g.,* Cantwell v. Connecticut, 310 U.S. 296, 303 (1940).

[11] Ehlers-Renzi v. Connelly Sch. of the Holy Child, 224 F. 3d 283, 287 (4th Cir. 2000).

[12] *See, e.g.,* Lemon v. Kurtzman, 403 U.S. 602, 612 (1971).

that exempts religious uses from certain zoning requirements; would such action illegally advance religion in violation of the Establishment Clause? And if government does not exempt or accommodate religious uses in some way, when acting on an application for a zoning permit or through the zoning code itself, does it risk violating the Free Exercise Clause by burdening religious exercise?

Despite this lack of clarity, local government lawyers and officials must understand that they *can* regulate religious uses,[13] and they may rest assured knowing that there are some basic principles that can mitigate the risk of liability under the religion clauses. This chapter will explore these principles, as well as the development of the law in these areas, the types of claims that governments may face under the religion clauses, and the differences between claims under the Free Exercise Clause and RLUIPA. The chapter will conclude by providing some "practice tips" for governments to avoid such claims in the first instance and, if unsuccessful, to defend against such claims.

II. The Establishment Clause

The Establishment Clause prohibits governmental action that "aid[s] one religion, aid[s] all religions, or prefer[s] one religion over another."[14] The Supreme Court first considered an Establishment Clause challenge in *Everson v. Board of Education*, in which it upheld a New Jersey statute authorizing the government to reimburse parents for the cost of sending their children to school, including parochial Catholic schools, using public transportation. The Supreme Court ruled that there was no violation of the Establishment Clause because the statute merely allowed parents to send their

---

[13] *See* Emp't Div. v. Smith, 494 U.S. 872, 879 (1990) (noting that the "right of free exercise does not relieve an individual of the obligation to comply with a valid and neutral law of general applicability on the ground that the law proscribes (or prescribes) conduct that his religion proscribes (or prescribes)"); Congregation Rabbinical College of Tartikov, Inc. v. Vill. of Pomona, 915 F. Supp. 2d 574, 631 (S.D.N.Y. 2013) ("Indeed, to exempt religious institutions from the normal permit/variance process would result in favoring these institutions, something which RLUIPA (or the Free Exercise Clause) does not require (and which the Establishment Clause might prohibit)").

[14] Everson v. Board of Ed. of Ewing, 330 U.S. 1, 15 (1947).

children to school regardless of religion, with the government contributing no money to the schools.[15] Although *Everson* did not establish a test to assess Establishment Clause claims, it noted examples of governmental limitations with respect to religion that still apply today:

> Neither a state nor the Federal Government can set up a church. Neither can it pass laws which aid one religion, aid all religions, or prefer one religion over another. Neither can force nor influence a person to go to or to remain away from church against his will or force him to profess a belief or disbelief in any religion. No person can be punished for entertaining or professing religious beliefs or disbeliefs, for church attendance or non attendance. No tax in any amount, large or small, can be levied to support any religious activities or institutions, whatever they may be called, or whatever form they may adopt to teach or practice religion. Neither a state nor the Federal Government can, openly or secretly, participate in the affairs of any religious organizations or groups and vice versa. In the words of Jefferson, the clause against establishment of religion by law was intended to erect "a wall of separation between church and State."[16]

More than two decades later, in *Lemon v. Kurtzman*,[17] the Supreme Court developed a three-part test to evaluate Establishment Clause claims. To avoid liability under the *Lemon* test, a government's law or action must: (1) have a secular purpose, (2) have a primary effect that neither advances nor inhibits religion, and (3) not foster excessive government entanglement with religion.[18] Failure to satisfy any one of these prongs is a constitutional violation. Although the application of the *Lemon* test continues, some courts have expressed dissatisfaction with its use but have not gone so far as to overrule it.[19]

---

[15] *See id.* at 15–18.

[16] *Id.* at 15–16 (citation omitted).

[17] 403 U.S. 602 (1971).

[18] *Id.* at 614.

[19] *See, e.g.*, Justice O'Connor's "endorsement" test analysis in *Cnty. of Allegheny v. Am. Civil Liberties Union*, 492 U.S. 573, 625–26 (1989) (O'Connor, J., concurring). Another test was developed by the Supreme Court in *Marsh v. Chambers*, 463 U.S. 783 (1983), and used in *Town of Greece v. Galloway*, 134 S. Ct. 1811 (2014).

(footnote continued on next page)

Establishment Clause claims usually do not involve land use regulation. Local government practitioners, especially those focusing on land use regulation, may not be aware of the several types of Establishment Clause claims that can be raised in the zoning context. Instead, such claims are frequently brought to challenge public or private religious displays, including, for example, Ten Commandments monuments, nativity scenes, or other holiday displays;[20] religion in public schools (e.g., prayer at high school graduation);[21] and prayer before government meetings.[22]

Public religious displays have been the subject of extensive litigation. The Establishment Clause not only limits the religious content of the government's own communications but "also prohibits the government's support and promotion of religious communications by religious organizations."[23] This means that an Establishment Clause violation may exist if the government exhibits its own public display or allows a religious group to exhibit a private display on public property. In either scenario, these cases are fact-intensive, and the outcomes are difficult to predict.

(footnote continued from previous page)

The *Town of Greece/Marsh* test "teaches that the Establishment Clause must be interpreted 'by reference to historical practices and understandings.'" *Town of Greece*, 134 S. Ct. at 1819 (2014) (citing *Cnty. of Allegheny*, 492 U.S. at 670). In *Town of Greece*, the Supreme Court found that prayers given prior to government meetings did not violate the Establishment Clause based in part on an analysis of ceremonial prayers "[f]rom the earliest days of the Nation," even examining the first prayer delivered to the Continental Congress by a reverend in 1774. 134 S. Ct. at 1823. The Supreme Court reasoned that the history of ceremonial prayers shows that "adult citizens, firm in their own beliefs, can tolerate and perhaps appreciate a ceremonial prayer delivered by a person of a different faith." *Id.* at 1823–34; *see also Marsh*, 463 U.S. at 792 (stating that the "practice of opening legislative sessions with prayer has become part of the fabric of our society," it is sustained without need to subject it to formal tests customarily used to determine First Amendment challenges). The Supreme Court developed a third test in *Lee v. Weisman*, 505 U.S. 577, 587 (1992), which examines whether the government has coerced anyone to support or participate in religion or religious exercise. But just because religious speech may be offensive and cause a nonbeliever to feel disrespected or excluded does not equate to coercion. *See id.* Some courts have applied each of these tests seriatim when analyzing an Establishment Clause claim. *See, e.g.*, Devaney v. Kilmartin, 88 F. Supp. 3d 34 (D.R.I. 2015); Freedom from Religion Found. v. Hanover Sch. Dist., 626 F.3d 1, 7 (1st Cir. 2010).

[20] *See, e.g.*, McCreary Cnty. v. Am. Civil Liberties Union of Ky., 544 U.S. 844 (2005); Felix v. City of Bloomfield, 841 F.3d 848 (10th Cir. 2016); Am. Atheists, Inc. v. Port Auth. of N.Y. &N.J., 760 F.3d 227 (2d Cir. 2014).

[21] *See, e.g.*, Lee v. Weisman, 505 U.S. 577 (1992).

[22] *See, e.g., Town of Greece*, 134 S. Ct. 1811; *Marsh*, 463 U.S. 783.

[23] Cnty. of Allegheny v. Am. Civil Liberties Union, 492 U.S. 573, 600 (1989) (citation omitted).

For example, in *County of Allegheny v. American Civil Liberties Union*,[24] the Supreme Court found that a crèche owned by a Roman Catholic group displayed in a county courthouse was an illegal endorsement of religion, but it ruled in the same case that the public display in a government building of a menorah owned by a Jewish group was constitutionally permissible.[25] The context of these holiday displays was deemed the critical determining factor by the Supreme Court. The crèche included figures of baby Jesus, Mary, Joseph, farm animals, shepherds, and wise men, each placed in or in front of a wooden representation of a manger, with an angel hovering at the apex of the crèche and proclaiming "Gloria in Excelsis Deo!"[26] The crèche, which stood alone, occupied a substantial amount of space on the courthouse's Grand Staircase—"the 'main' and 'most beautiful part' of the building that is the seat of county government."[27] Although the Court noted that government may celebrate Christmas in some manner, Allegheny County had transgressed the line because "[i]t has chosen to celebrate Christmas in a way that has the effect of endorsing a patently Christian message: Glory to God for the birth of Jesus Christ."[28] Unlike the crèche, the eighteen-foot menorah did not stand alone but was next to a forty-five-foot Christmas tree and a sign entitled "Salute to Liberty."[29] The Court found that the menorah did not impermissibly endorse religion but instead was part of a winter festival display.[30] The Court based this conclusion on the fact that the Christmas tree, which is a secular, not a religious, symbol occupied the central position of the overall display,

---

[24] *Id.*

[25] *Id.* at 600–02, 620–21.

[26] *Id.* at 580. The phrase "Gloria in Excelsis Deo" comes from Luke, "who tells of an angel appearing to the shepherds to announce the birth of the Messiah. After the angel told the shepherds that they would find the baby lying in a manger, 'suddenly there was with the angel a multitude of the heavenly host praising God, and saying, Glory to God in the highest, and on earth peace, good will towards men." *Id.* at note 5 (citing Luke 2:13–14, King James Version).

[27] *Id.* at 599.

[28] *Id.* at 601.

[29] *Id.* at 582. The "Salute to Liberty" sign stated: "During the holiday season, the city of Pittsburgh salutes liberty. Let these festive lights remind us that we are the keepers of the flame of liberty and our legacy of freedom." *Id.*

[30] *Id.* at 620–21.

meaning that a reasonable observer would similarly view the menorah as a secular celebration.[31]

One of the more common Establishment Clause challenges has concerned Ten Commandments monuments on public grounds. *Perry v. Van Orden* involved a challenge to a six-foot Ten Commandments monument placed on twenty-two acres surrounding the Texas State Capitol with seventeen other monuments and historical markers commemorating the "people, ideals, and events that compose Texan identity."[32] The monument did not violate the Establishment Clause because its inclusion with the other monuments and historical markers that reflected several strands of Texas' political and legal history had a "dual significance partaking of both religion and government."[33] But in *Felix v. City of Bloomfield*, the U.S. District Court for the District of New Mexico found that a Ten Commandments monument standing on the lawn in front of the City of Bloomfield, New Mexico, municipal complex building violated the Establishment Clause.[34] Although the monument stood next to three other historical monuments—a Declaration of Independence monument, a Gettysburg Address monument, and a Bill of Rights monument—the Ten Commandments monument appeared to be the most prominent of all.[35] Further, although the City of Bloomfield had adopted a forum policy, it had only done so *after* approval of the monument, and even though it adopted such a policy, it had "not actually opened the City Hall Lawn to 'many different historical viewpoints.'"[36]

---

[31] *Id.* at 617–18. The Court noted that "the menorah's message is not exclusively religious. The menorah is the primary visual symbol for a holiday that, like Christmas, has both religious and secular dimensions." *Id.* at 613–14. Based on the context of the menorah display with the Christmas tree and "Salute to Liberty" sign, the Court determined that the menorah's message was secular. *Id.* at 617–18.

[32] 454 U.S. 677, 681 (2005).

[33] *Id.* at 691–92.

[34] 36 F. Supp. 3d 1233 (2014).

[35] *Id.* at 1251.

[36] *Id.* at 1249, 1254. In addition, the monument's sponsor, a former city councilmember, "had acted in such a way that a reasonable person would conclude his primary reason for erecting and maintaining the Ten Commandments monuments is religious." *Id.* at 1249. At a dedication ceremony, the monument's sponsor stated:

> Some would believe that this monument is a new thing. They have been so busy trying to remove God from every aspect of our lives that they have overlooked our history. Well, I've got news for you, it's been here all along. . . . You and I are average citizens who believe just like most of our fellow Americans. We want the government to leave us alone and to keep

(footnote continued on next page)

The Second Circuit considered an Establishment Clause claim in *American Atheists v. Port Authority of New York and New Jersey* involving the National September 11 Museum's display of a seventeen-foot-high column and cross beam retrieved from World Trade Center debris that gave many the impression of a Latin Cross.[37] American Atheists, Inc. argued that the display of the cross impermissibly promoted Christianity in violation of the Establishment Clause because the museum did not display items acknowledging atheists who were among the September 11 victims.[38] The Second Circuit rejected the claim, reasoning in part that "an objective observer would not view the display as endorsing religion generally, or Christianity specifically, because it is part of an exhibit entitled 'Finding Meaning at Ground Zero;' the exhibit includes various nonreligious as well as religious artifacts that people at Ground Zero used for solace; and the textual displays accompanying the cross communicates its historical significance within this larger context."[39]

A. Land Use Claims Under the Establishment Clause

Local government practitioners, officials, and planners should also be aware that Establishment Clause claims may arise in land use regulation. Both religious groups and opponents of proposed religious uses raise such claims to further their respective interests. Most frequent are claims brought by religious groups challenging zoning application denials on the ground that a government's laws or actions have inhibited religion or advanced some other religion (or nonreligion) over their religion.[40] Religious groups have

---

(footnote continued from previous page)

> our—their hands off our money, our religion, our Ten Commandments, our guns, our private property, and our lives . . . God and his Ten Commandments continue to protect us from our evil. . . . May God bless us and protect this monument.

Id. at 1250. Also, "[f]rom the beginning, [the sponsor] signaled to the public the connection in his mind between the Ten Commandments monument project and the Christian community by fundraising through local churches exclusively, rather than through a variety of local civic organizations." *Id.* at 1249.

[37] 760 F.3d 227 (2d Cir. 2014).

[38] *Id.* at 233.

[39] *Id.* at 247.

[40] *See, e.g.* Ehlers-Renzi v. Connelly Sch. of the Holy Child, Inc., 224 F.3d 283 (4th Cir. 2000) (advancement of religion over nonreligion); Prater v. City of Burnside, 289 F.3d 417 (6th Cir. 2002) (advancement of one religion over another).

also sued to challenge governmental actions or laws becoming excessively entangled with religion.[41] Other claims are brought by opponents to proposed religious uses that have been approved by the government (usually by contending that a government has advanced religion over nonreligion). Fortunately for local governments, these claims are defensible, so long as there is a clear and identifiable secular purpose behind the governmental law or action—even if that purpose is to avoid entanglement with religion or to comply with the Free Exercise Clause.[42] However, any secular purpose asserted in defense of an Establishment Clause claim must be "sincere."[43] In other words, a justification manufactured only after litigation has commenced will not be viewed favorably by the courts. Instead, any justification, such as comprehensive planning principles or government interests, should be made clear and supported from the outset. Generally, there are three types of Establishment Clause claims in the zoning context.

1. Advancement of Religion over Nonreligion

The first situation in which Establishment Clause claims are brought in the zoning context is where a government is alleged to advance religion over nonreligion, either by exempting religious uses from land use regulation or subjecting religious uses to less stringent standards than secular uses. *Ehlers-Renzi v. Connelly School of the Holy Child* involved the first scenario. There, the Fourth Circuit considered a zoning ordinance that required private educational institutions and other nonresidential uses to obtain a special exception permit for improvements and additions but exempted parochial schools from this requirement.[44] The case involved a religious school that sought to improve its property by replacing two buildings with a thirty thousand square-foot facility. After neighboring landowners learned that the religious group was not required to, and would not, seek special exception approval, they sued, alleging that the ordinance illegally favored parochial schools over private secular schools and other

---

[41] *E.g.,* Lucas Valley Homeowners Ass'n, Inc. v. Cnty. of Marin, 233 Cal. App. 3d 130 (1991).
[42] Tenafly Eruv Ass'n, Inc. v. Borough of Tenafly, 309 F.3d 144 (3d Cir. 2002).
[43] Vision Church, United Methodist v. Vill. of Long Grove, 468 F.3d 975, 991 (7th Cir. 2006).
[44] 224 F.3d 283 (4th Cir. 2000).

secular uses. The Fourth Circuit upheld the ordinance because it had the secular purpose of avoiding entanglement with the church's execution of its religious mission to educate its youth through the exemption and was therefore a permissible accommodation of religion consistent with the Free Exercise Clause.[45]

The Seventh Circuit addressed a similar issue in *Cohen v. City of Des Plaines* and reached the same outcome.[46] There, a zoning ordinance allowed as-of-right "[c]hurches, temples, religious reading rooms and parish houses, including nursery schools operated in any of such buildings" in the city's residence zone but required that daycare centers obtain a special use permit to locate in the same zone.[47] The plaintiff, whose application for a special permit to operate a daycare center in the subject zone was denied, claimed that the ordinance illegally promoted religious uses over secular uses because nursery schools operating in various types of religious buildings were allegedly treated better than secular daycare centers in the same zone. The Seventh Circuit found that the ordinance had the secular purpose of "minimizing governmental meddling in religious affairs" through the differential treatment and concluded that the ordinance was consistent with the Establishment Clause.[48] To reach this conclusion, the court noted that the religious component of child care and education for nursery schools operated in religious buildings would come from religious members rather than government officials.[49] Still, the Seventh Circuit cautioned that the

---

[45] *See id.* at 288–92. The Fourth Circuit also found that exempting religious uses from regulation did not have the principal or primary effect of advancing or inhibiting religion because the school's religious education would come from church leaders and not government officials. Nor did exempting religious uses from regulation create governmental entanglement with religion; in fact, exemption had the opposite effect. *See id.* at 291–92. The court concluded by observing that governments will not violate the Establishment Clause when exempting religious uses from land use regulations, because "such an exemption removes the State from forums in which religious conflict might otherwise require improper State action," again, because this is consistent with principles of religious accommodation. *Id.* at 288–92. *But see* Congregation of Jehovah's Witnesses, Inc. v. City of Lakewood, 699 F.2d 303, 304 n.1 (6th Cir. 1983) (observing in dicta that treating religious uses better than secular uses by exempting the former from land use regulation may violate the Establishment Clause).

[46] 8 F.3d 484 (7th Cir. 1993).

[47] *Id.* at 487.

[48] *Id.* at 491.

[49] *See id.* at 490–91. The court noted that "[h]istory and common sense teach that the care and education of young children fall within the mission of most, if not all, religious organizations." *Id.* at 491–92.

zoning ordinance conferred some benefits upon churches not available to others seeking to operate daycare centers in residential zones and, for this reason, interpreted the zoning ordinance to require that church nursery schools and daycare centers be not-for-profit.[50]

The California Court of Appeals also rejected an establishment of religion claim, in *Foothill Communities Coalition v. County of Orange*,[51] after finding that approval of an application to rezone a church's 7.25-acre parcel from single-family residential to senior residential housing to allow the church to develop the site with a living community for senior citizens had a secular purpose of addressing specific housing needs for the elderly. An entity opposing this group's housing facility claimed that the rezoning was an impermissible endorsement of religion based on the religious character of the applicant, but the California court determined that the primary effect of the rezoning was to provide needed housing alternatives for senior citizens, not to advance religion.[52] And the court rejected the claim that the religious nature of the applicant meant there was excessive governmental entanglement with religion because to rule otherwise on this point would mean that any approval of a religious use would impermissibly advance religion and would contradict the Supreme Court precedent that "[i]t has never been thought either possible or desirable to enforce a regime of total separation between religion and government."[53]

---

[50] *See id.* at 492–93. The court was "mindful of the well settled principle that statutes should be interpreted to avoid constitutional difficulties." *Id.* (citing Gomez v. United States, 490 U.S. 858, 864 (1989); Frisby v. Schultz, 487 U.S. 474, 482-83 (1988); United States v. Witkovich, 353 U.S. 194, 202, (1957)). The Seventh Circuit concluded that the ordinance did not constitute excessive governmental entanglement with religion because it, in fact, effectuated a separation between government and church. *Cohen*, 8 F.3d at 492–93. The Seventh Circuit also found the zoning ordinance to comply with Equal Protection Clause of the Fourteenth Amendment because it was "rationally related to the legitimate purpose of 'alleviating significant governmental interference with the ability of religious organizations to define and carry out their religious missions.'" *Id.* at 494. The ordinance was also rationally related to serving "the larger goals of residential zoning," including "protect[ing] residents from the ill effects of urbanization, such as crowding, encroachment of commercial businesses or industries, traffic congestion and noise." *Id.* (citations omitted).

[51] 222 Cal. App. 4th 1302, 1320 (2014).

[52] *Id.*

[53] Comm. for Pub. Educ. & Religious Liberty v. Nyquist, 413 U.S. 756, 760 (1973).

2. Denominational Discrimination

Establishment Clause claims may also be brought to allege that a government has discriminated between different religious denominations. "[T]he clearest command of the Establishment Clause is that one religious denomination cannot be officially preferred over another."[54] Commentators have noted that such a violation will exist where government action or law discriminates between denominations, regardless of the *Lemon* test.[55] Indeed, the Supreme Court has found the *Lemon* test inapplicable in the presence of denominational discrimination, instead subjecting the government's laws or actions to strict scrutiny review.[56] A zoning agency that routinely grants zoning relief to one denomination while denying the same relief to another denomination is an example of potential denominational discrimination.[57]

Other examples may appear in zoning codes that distinguish between religious denominations, oftentimes without the government even realizing, much less intending, it. For example, consider a zoning ordinance that allows "churches" but is silent as to other houses of worship, such as temples, synagogues, or mosques. Also consider a zoning ordinance that imposes a height limitation on all uses in a particular zone, excepts steeples from the height limit, but does not provide a similar exception for other nonhabitable architectural elements traditional to religious architecture of non Christian denominations, such as minarets on a mosque. Finally, consider a zoning code that permits religious uses but with some qualification—such as mandating that religious uses be "duly incorporated," not generally open to the public, or consisting of members who "regularly" congregate for religious exercise—which might exclude some religious uses that do not meet such qualifications. Each of these could prove problematic for a government insofar as it may give rise to a colorable claim under the Establishment Clause.

The Sixth Circuit has held that evidence of *religious animus* is required to establish denominational discrimination even if there is differential

---

[54] Larson v. Valente, 456 U.S. 228, 244 (1982).
[55] *See* BRIAN W. BLAESSER & ALAN C. WEINSTEIN, FEDERAL LAND USE LITIGATION, § 7.2, 669–70 (2014 ed.).
[56] *See Larson*, 456 U.S. at 246–47, 251–52.
[57] *See* BLAESSER & WEINSTEIN, *supra*, note 38, § 7.2 at 669–70.

treatment. In *Prater v. City of Burnside*,[58] a Baptist church claimed that its religious beliefs obligated it to develop two lots it owned as well as a dedicated public roadway allowing it to access its land.[59] The city denied the church's proposal and instead decided to construct the roadway to allow access to a separate lot operated by another religious group. The Baptist church complained that the city's action to construct the roadway was denominational discrimination because the city chose to allow a different religious group to benefit from use of the roadway. Because there was no evidence of religious animus, the Sixth Circuit rejected the claim.[60] Although the requirement of religious animus makes such claims more difficult to establish, in some situations, discrimination may be inferred by the effect of a government law or action because governments sometimes attempt to mask their true motives.[61] Also, although *Prater* required religious animus for an Establishment Clause violation, the Supreme Court applied strict scrutiny review in the absence of such evidence in *Larson v. Valente*.[62] The different evidentiary requirements in *Prater* and *Larson* appear inconsistent but might be explained by the nature of the facts before the two courts (facial challenge to state statute in *Larson* that explicitly subjected certain religious denominations to different requirements versus challenge to a government's action in enforcing a zoning ordinance to deny a zoning application in *Prater*).

The Seventh Circuit considered an interesting denominational discrimination claim in *Vision Church, United Methodist v. Village of Long Grove*.[63] There, a church applied for, but was denied, a special permit to erect a ninety nine thousand square-foot church facility consisting of five main buildings and a 1,000-seat sanctuary. The church alleged that the village's newly enacted "public assembly" ordinance, which encompassed religious uses and had inhibited its religion by imposing restrictions on

---

[58] 289 F.3d 417 (6th Cir. 2002).
[59] *See id.* at 422, 427.
[60] *See id.* at 431.
[61] *See, e.g.*, Church of the Lukumi Babalu Aye, Inc. v. City of Hialeah, 508 U.S. 520, 538 (1993) ("It is not unreasonable to infer, at least when there are no persuasive indications to the contrary, that a law which visits 'gratuitous restrictions' on religious conduct . . . seeks not to effectuate the stated governmental interests, but to suppress the conduct because of its religious motivation.") (citation omitted).
[62] 456 U.S. 228, 244 (1982).
[63] 468 F.3d 975 (7th Cir. 2006).

the size and capacity of buildings to be put to religious use, discriminated against new religious uses compared with existing religious uses. Unlike new religious uses, which would have to comply with the new ordinance, existing religious uses were grandfathered and would not have to do so. The court concluded that the restrictions were not aimed at religion; they advanced the secular purposes of minimizing development and maximizing open space.[64] Perhaps more important, however, the court rejected the church's claim that the government had discriminated against new uses in favor of existing uses because accepting the church's contention would mean that a government could never amend its zoning code with respect to religious uses, which the court was unwilling to accept.[65]

3. Entanglement with Religion

The third type of claim is that a governmental law or action is excessively entangled with religion in violation of the Establishment Clause. As a general rule, "to constitute excessive entanglement, the government's action must 'involve intrusive government participation in, supervision of, or inquiry into religious affairs.'"[66] Approval of an application for zoning relief of a religious organization does not create an entanglement between government and religion just based on the religious nature of the applicant.[67] But if the government is called upon to define religious conduct, a violation may exist.

In *Lucas Valley Homeowners Association, Inc. v. County of Marin*, the California Court of Appeals rejected an Orthodox Jewish congregation's claim that conditions imposed by the government in approving the Jewish group's conversion of a home to a synagogue was an entanglement with religion because the government delved into defining the religious affairs of the congregation.[68] Most of the conditions were characterized by the court as "mundane" because they pertained to numbers, hours, location, and noise restrictions.[69] Although one condition stating that "only events

---

[64] *Id.* at 992.
[65] *Id.* at 994.
[66] *Id.* at 995 (internal citation omitted).
[67] *See, e.g.,* Foothill Communities Coal. v. Cnty. of Orange, 222 Cal. App. 4th 1302, 1320 (2014).
[68] 233 Cal. App. 3d 130, 149–52 (1991).
[69] *Id.* at 151.

or functions with specific religious content" were permitted on site could constitute excessive entanglement, by calling on the government to define religion, there was no excessive entanglement based on the facts of the case; because all "religious events and functions" had been approved by the county, no excessive entanglement was found.[70]

Religious groups have also used entanglement claims to challenge dispersal requirements for disfavored uses, such as liquor stores or adult-oriented uses. In *People Tags, Inc. v. Jackson County*, a federal court ruled that a zoning ordinance requiring that adult bookstore, theater, or mini-motion picture uses be at least 1,500 feet from any church or school was not an excessive entanglement with religion.[71] However, if a religious group has some unbridled authority to act in government affairs, excessive entanglement will be found. Such was the case in *Larkin v. Grendel's Den, Inc.*, where the Supreme Court found that a Massachusetts statute giving churches discretionary veto power over any use seeking a liquor permit license within five hundred feet of a church violated the Establishment Clause because it "enmeshes churches in the exercise of substantial governmental powers" under *Lemon's* third prong.[72]

---

[70] *Id.* at 151–52. One such claim was brought in the Second Circuit by a church that claimed that New York City's actions in reviewing the church's application for a certificate of appropriateness to convert a "community house" used for religious and social activities into an office tower. *See* Rectors, Wardens v. City of New York, 914 F.2d 348, 351–52 (2d Cir. 1990). The church alleged that the city had excessively entangled itself in religious affairs when reviewing the application, but the Second Circuit was not persuaded, stating that "the matters scrutinized were exclusively financial and architectural." *Id.* at 356, n.4. The Second Circuit noted in *Rectors* that the Supreme Court, in *Jimmy Swaggart Ministries v. Bd. of Equalization*, 493 U.S. 378 (1990), found no entanglement where a regulation taxing the sale of religious materials by a religious organization "imposed only routine administrative and recordkeeping obligations, involved no continuing surveillance of the organization, and did not inquire into the religious doctrine or motives of the organization." *Rectors*, 914 F.3d at 356 n.4.

[71] 636 F. Supp. 1345, 1355 (W.D. Mo. 1986).

[72] 459 U.S. 116, 126 (1982). The Supreme Court also found that the Massachusetts statute had the principal and primary effect of advancing religion by providing standardless authority to churches, allowing churches to veto liquor permits being issued to establishments within five hundred feet "for no reasons, or reasoned conclusions." *Id.* at 125. Further, the statute did not mandate that churches use their veto power in any religiously neutral way, leaving open the possibility that churches could promote goals beyond insulating themselves from undesirable neighbors, such as favoring liquor licenses for members of their faith. *Id.*

B. Practice Tips to Avoid or Defend Against Establishment Clause Claims

Local officials should take care to adhere to the following practice tips to avoid zoning issues under the Establishment Clause:

- Identify clear and sincere secular purposes in advance of rendering a zoning decision or text amendment that can be used to defend an Establishment Clause challenge. Build secular purposes into the text of the zoning code.
- When deciding a religious group's application for zoning relief or taking some other action against a religious use, state the secular purpose to be advanced either on the record or through a resolution.
- Do not define religious use. To this end, assume the use is religious in nature. If imposing conditions of approval on a zoning permit for a religious use, make sure the conditions do not call for the government to determine whether a particular use or act is or is not religious (e.g., "only events or functions with religious content will be permitted").
- To avoid denominational discrimination, regulate religious uses broadly. Do not single out churches, temples, synagogues, mosques, or other particular houses of worship or religions. Instead, regulate "religious" uses generally to ensure that all faiths are treated equally.
- To the extent possible, regulate all assembly uses (secular and religious) in the same manner in an effort to avoid an advancement of religion claim.
- Understand that in many situations, treating religious uses more favorably than secular uses is a permissible accommodation of religion under the Free Exercise Clause and has been recognized as a valid secular purpose.
- Do not permit only certain religious uses with some qualification (e.g., religious uses that are "duly incorporated") because this runs the risk of discriminating against denominations that do not meet such qualifications.

III. Free Exercise Clause

The Free Exercise Clause "means, first and foremost, the right to believe and profess whatever religious doctrine one desires."[73] In land use, free exercise claims arise in two situations. First, a government's laws, usually its zoning code, are said to target religion and substantially burden religious exercise. This type of claim, known as a "facial" challenge, can be made even without submitting an application for zoning relief because it challenges the text of the ordinance itself. An example of this is found in *Church of the Lukumi Babalu Aye, Inc. v. City of Hialeah*, discussed *infra*. And, second, free exercise claims are made to contest a government's actions in enforcing its laws as substantially burdening religious conduct. This is known as an "as-applied" challenge. Although the Supreme Court has never decided a Free Exercise Clause case pertaining to zoning, the Free Exercise cases it has decided provide important guidance for governments, practitioners, and courts. What follows is a brief history of the evolution of free exercise claims over the years based on Supreme Court jurisprudence and legislative action. But even before that, the first question that should be asked by local governments attempting to avoid free exercise claims is "what constitutes religious exercise?"

A. What Is Religious Exercise?

Religious exercise under the First Amendment is "the observation of a central religious belief or practice."[74] What is and is not religious exercise is not always clear and can be an area of confusion, especially for local government officials. Some religious uses may appear secular in nature, that is, not inherently religious, but for the religious character of the landowner or user. Consider eleemosynary uses, such as soup kitchens, food pantries, or homeless shelters. On the one hand, many secular organizations perform acts of charity without any religious purpose. On the other

---

[73] Cent. Rabbinical Coll. of the U.S. v. N.Y. City Dep't of Health & Mental Hygiene, 763 F.3d 183, 193 (2d Cir. 2014).

[74] Hernandez v. Comm'r, 490 U.S. 680, 699 (1989); *see also* Sherbert v. Verner, 374 U.S. 398, 404 (1963) (religious exercise as adherence to the central precepts of a religion).

hand, acts of charity may also be religious exercise, and one federal court has observed "acts of charity as an essential part of religious worship is a central tenet of all major religions."[75] The Second Circuit, in *Fifth Avenue Presbyterian Church v. City of New York*, found "religious exercise" to be a vast concept under the First Amendment and ruled that providing shelter to the homeless on a church's steps "effectuates a sincerely held religious belief."[76] Therefore, when considering whether a use or activity is religious exercise, it is irrelevant whether the same type of use or activity can also be secular in nature. All that matters, as explained later in this discussion, is that the religious individual or entity asserts a "sincerely held" belief that the act or use is religious in nature and central to religious beliefs.[77]

Although religious exercise is a broad concept under the First Amendment, the act or use for which constitutional protection is sought must be "central" to the religious beliefs. If the act or use is not central to the religion, the free exercise claim will fail.[78] Courts have rejected free exercise claims involving the proposed construction of houses of worship based on the conclusion that the houses of worship were not central to the groups' religious beliefs.[79] The courts' reasoning in these cases suggests that if the religious groups had claimed that the houses of worship were central to their religions, the analyses would at least have proceeded to the next phase: whether there were substantial burdens on religious exercise.

It is important to note that religious exercise under the First Amendment is narrower than RLUIPA's definition of religious exercise: "any exercise of

---

[75] W. Presbyterian Church v. Bd. of Zoning Adjustment, 862 F. Supp. 538, 545 (D.D.C. 1994) (citation omitted; internal quotation marks omitted).

[76] 293 F.3d 570, 575 (2d Cir. 2002).

[77] *See* Emp't Div. v. Smith, 494 U.S. 872, 893 (1990).

[78] *See, e.g.*, Wisconsin v. Yoder, 406 U.S. 205, 218 (1972).

[79] *See* Congregation of Jehovah's Witnesses, Inc. v. City of Lakewood, 699 F.2d 303, 306–307 (6th Cir. 1983) ("The Congregation's 'religious observance' is the construction of a church building in a residential district. In contrast to prior cases, the activity has no religious or ritualistic significance for the Jehovah's Witnesses. There is no evidence that the construction of Kingdom Hall is a ritual, a 'fundamental tenet,' or a 'cardinal principle' of its faith. At most the Congregation can claim that its freedom to worship is tangentially related to worshipping in its own structure. However, building and owning a church is a desirable accessory of worship, not a fundamental tenet of the Congregation's religious beliefs."); *see also* Love Church v. City of Evanston, 671 F. Supp. 508 (N.D. Ill. 1987) ("Plaintiffs' freedom to worship is at best tangentially related to worshipping in their own building. While convenient and desirable, leasing property is not a fundamental tenet or cardinal principle of the religion.").

religion *whether or not compelled by, or central to*, a system of religious beliefs," including "the use, building, or conversion of real property for the purpose of religious exercise."[80] Although the differences in these definitions may appear significant, generally, in practice, they are not. This is because the validity of religious beliefs cannot be called into question by the legislature or the courts.[81] In other words, local officials and the courts cannot question the truth or falsity of religious beliefs, but must instead take the religious entity at its word, including whether a use or activity is central to religious exercise.[82] Local officials who question whether a group's use or activity is religious exercise run the risk of defining religion, prohibited by the Establishment Clause. Consistent with this logic, the Supreme Court has noted that "religious beliefs need not be acceptable, logical, consistent, or comprehensible to others in order to merit First Amendment protection."[83] The consumption of sacramental tea containing hallucinogens,[84] animal sacrifice,[85] smoking marijuana for broad-based healing missions,[86] and conjugal visits to consummate marriage and procreate[87] have all been found to be sincere religious beliefs.

---

[80] 42 U.S.C. § 2000cc-5(7) (emphasis added); *see* Civil Liberties for Urban Believers v. City of Chicago, 342 F.3d 752, 670-61 (7th Cir. 2003) (noting difference of "religious exercise" under First Amendment and RLUIPA).

[81] *See* Int'l Church of the Foursquare Gospel v. City of San Leandro, 673 F.3d 1059, 1169 (9th Cir. 2011) (citing United States v. Ballard, 322 U.S. 78, 86-87 (1944)) (noting "the Supreme Court's admonition that while a court can arbiter the sincerity of an individual's religious beliefs, courts should not inquire into the truth or falsity of stated religious beliefs"); Cohen v. City of Des Plaines, 8 F.3d 484, 490 (7th Cir. 1993) ("[I]t is not up to legislatures (or to courts for that matter) to say what activities are sufficiently 'religious.'").

[82] The Second Circuit has reasoned that "[b]ecause '[t]he free exercise of religion means, first and foremost, the right to believe and profess whatever religious doctrine one desires,' courts are not permitted to inquire into the centrality of a professed belief to the adherent's religion or to question its validity in determining whether a religious practice exists." Fifth Ave. Presbyterian Church v. City of New York, 293 F.3d 570, 574 (2d Cir. 2002) (quoting Emp't Div. v. Smith, 494 U.S. 872, 886-87 (1990)); *see also* United States v. Lee, 455 U.S. 707, 714 (1981) (Stevens, J., concurring) (noting that judging the centrality of religious practice is akin to the unacceptable "business of evaluating the relative merits of differing religious claims").

[83] Thomas v. Review Bd. of the Ind. Emp. Sec. Div., 450 U.S. 707, 714 (1981).

[84] *See* Gonzalez v. O Centro Espirita Beneficente Uniao do Vegetal, 546 U.S. 418, 422 (2006).

[85] *See* Church of the Lukumi Babalu Aye, Inc. v. City of Hialeah, 508 U.S. 520, 524-25 (1993).

[86] *See* Multi Denominational Ministry of Cannabis and Rastafari, Inc. v. Mukasey, No. C 06-4264, 2008 WL 914448 (N.D. Cal. Mar. 21, 2008) (finding as potentially credible plaintiffs' religious belief of distributing cannabis to heal the sick).

[87] *See* Pouncil v. Tilton, 704 F.3d 568 (9th Cir. 2012).

Although religious beliefs themselves cannot be called into question, they must be "sincerely held" to receive First Amendment protection.[88] Governments and courts may therefore legitimately question whether a religious group's religious beliefs are, in fact, sincerely held. The sincerity analysis typically focuses on whether a religious group or individual attempts to use religion as a guise to conduct some use that would otherwise be prohibited. This issue was addressed in *Church of Universal Love & Music v. Fayette County*[89] in the context of a RLUIPA substantial burden claim in which a religious group sought to use a 150-foot tract of land zoned for agricultural use to host music events in a pavilion and canopy to accommodate "members' religious beliefs relating to music."[90] The Court declined to enter summary judgment in favor of the group because there was an open question as to whether the group's religious beliefs were sincerely held; there was evidence suggesting that one of the bases for formation of the group was to "circumvent zoning regulations."[91]

Lastly, in some rare circumstances, the courts have distinguished between a "way of life" compared with religious beliefs. An individual or entity will not receive First Amendment protection if the uses or activities at issue amount to a "way of life" instead of religious exercise.[92] Beliefs comprise a way of life as opposed to religion if they fail to offer some "organizing principle or authority other than" the individual prescribing

---

[88] *See* United States v. Seeger, 380 U.S. 163, 185 (1965).

[89] No. 06-872, 2008 WL 4006690 (W.D. PA. Aug. 26, 2008).

[90] Plaintiffs asserted that the Church of Universal Love and Music's religious mission was to "advance religion through music and to provide a spiritual resource for all . . . [and] to create an environment to improve communities and the world by espousing a message of unity, love and appreciation for music, spirituality and our place in it." *Id.*

[91] In 2006, a group of Georgetown college students attempted to circumvent Washington, D.C.'s zoning regulations' prohibition against more than six unrelated persons living together. The students did so by claiming they were a religious order calling themselves the Apostles of Peace and Unity. Washington's Zoning Administrator, however, issued a cease and desist order, finding that the students' use constituted a "fraternity house" requiring a variance and additional parking, apparently seeing through their attempt to circumvent zoning. Michelle Boorstein, 'Apostles' Ordered to Abide by Zoning Laws, WASHINGTON POST (November 23, 2006), *available at* http://www.washingtonpost.com/wp-dyn/content/article/2006/11/22/AR2006112201924.html. See also Tony Gonzalez, *Tenn. Swingers Club to Open As Church Instead*, THE TENNESSEAN (April 24, 2015), for a Tennessee swinger's club repurposing itself as a church.

[92] *See, e.g.*, Wisconsin v. Yoder, 406 U.S. 205, 215–16 (1972).

religious convictions because to allow otherwise would threaten "the very concept of ordered liberty."[93] The Supreme Court has found that the Amish's seclusion from modern society is a way of life "but one of deep religious conviction, shared by an organized group, and intimately related to daily living" that thus warrants constitutional protection.[94] The Fourth Circuit, however, rejected a psychic's claim that her beliefs were religious and declined to afford her First Amendment protection because rather than following any particular religion, the psychic declared that she instead "pretty much goes with [her] inner flow, and that seems to work best."[95]

B. History of Free Exercise Claims

Much of the confusion about free exercise claims involves the level of review to be applied by the courts to determine whether there has been a constitutional violation. There are two types of review applied: (a) rational basis review and (b) the more exacting strict scrutiny review. Rational basis review is more deferential to local governments and easier to satisfy. "Under the rational basis test, a [law] will be upheld 'if there is a rational relationship between the disparity in treatment and some legitimate governmental purpose.'"[96] The law will be upheld "even if the law seems unwise or works to the disadvantage of a particular group, or if the rationale for it seems tenuous."[97] Strict scrutiny is a more demanding standard for local governments to meet. To survive strict scrutiny, local governments must establish that their actions were taken to serve "compelling" interests (as opposed to "legitimate" interests) and that their actions are narrowly tailored to serve those interests.[98] According to the Supreme Court, a law

---

[93] Moore-King v. Cnty. of Chesterfield, 708 F.3d 560, 571 (4th Cir. 2013).

[94] *Yoder*, 406 U.S. at 216.

[95] *Moore-King*, 708 F.3d at 571 (4th Cir. 2013). The Fourth Circuit reasoned: "That a wide variety of sources—the New Age movement, the teachings of Jesus, natural healing, the study of metaphysics, etc.—inform and shape Moore-King's 'inner-flow' does not transform her personal philosophical beliefs into a religion any more than did Thoreau's commitment to Transcendentalism and idealist philosophy render his view religious." *Id.*

[96] Roman Catholic Diocese of Rockville Ctr. v. Vill. of Old Westbury, 128 F.Supp.3d 566, 584 (E.D.N.Y. 2015) (citation omitted).

[97] *Id.* (citation omitted).

[98] *See, e.g.,* Church of the Lukumi Babalu Aye, Inc. v. City of Hialeah, 508 U.S. 520, 533 (1993).

cannot be narrowly tailored to serve compelling interests "when it leaves appreciable damage to that supposedly vital interest[s] unprohibited."[99]

As explained later in this chapter, the level of review to be applied depends on a couple of factors. First, in as-applied challenges, strict scrutiny is imposed only if there is a substantial burden on religious exercise. If a religious group establishes a substantial burden on religious exercise, the government must then justify its actions with a compelling interest that is narrowly tailored to advance that interest. But if there is no substantial burden at all, the free exercise claim likely fails, and the government action is upheld so long as the government did not act arbitrarily or capriciously. Second, in facial challenges, strict scrutiny review applies only if a law is found to be either not neutral or not generally applicable, as discussed in *Church of the Lukumi Babalu Aye*. Otherwise, rational basis review applies.

The modern era of free exercise jurisprudence began with the 1961 case of *Braunfeld v. Brown*.[100] Orthodox Jewish merchants challenged a criminal statute prohibiting retail sales on Sundays as a violation of the Free Exercise Clause. The Supreme Court upheld the statute and distinguished between direct and indirect burdens on religious exercise: "if the State regulates conduct by enacting a general law within its power, the purpose and effect of which is to advance the State's secular goals, the statute is valid despite its indirect burden on religious observance unless the State may accomplish its purpose by means which do not impose such a burden."[101] Although direct burdens were forbidden, the effect of the criminal statute was deemed indirect because it only made religious exercise more expensive but not impossible and had the secular goal of establishing a uniform day of rest.[102] The Court considered whether exemptions from the law might be available to accommodate the Orthodox Jewish merchants' religious beliefs but concluded they were not because they would prevent effective enforcement and could lead to fraudulent claims.[103] *Braunfeld* is important

---

[99] *Id.* at 547.
[100] 366 U.S. 599 (1961).
[101] *Id.* at 607.
[102] *Id.* at 606–07.
[103] *Id.* at 608–09.

for two reasons. First, it employed a balancing test of sorts that has been further refined over time and is used today. Second, the principle that financial burdens cannot be burdens on religious exercise is an important one relied on by governments to defend against free exercise claims where financial considerations come into play.

Two years later, in *Sherbert v. Verner*,[104] the Supreme Court used a three-part balancing test to evaluate free exercise claims under strict scrutiny. The case involved a state unemployment compensation benefit law requiring employees to be available for work any day of the week to be eligible for compensation. The Court found that even though the law was neutral (not religious specific) and generally applicable (equally applied to everyone, regardless of religion), it burdened the religious exercise of a member of the Seventh-Day Adventist Church who refused to work on Saturday (the day of her Sabbath) and was therefore denied unemployment benefits. The Court first concluded that there was such a burden because the law "forces her to choose between following the precepts of her religion and forfeiting benefits on the one hand, and abandoning one of the precepts of her religion in order to accept work on the other hand."[105] *Sherbert* next proceeded to consider the second part of the balancing test, often referred to as "strict scrutiny" review, in which it applied strict scrutiny to examine whether there was a "compelling state interest" to justify the burden on religious exercise. Concluding there was no state interest sufficient to justify the burden, the Court did not move to the third part of the balancing test: whether there were alternative forms of regulation available to the state that would be less burdensome to religion.[106] *Sherbert* is difficult to reconcile with *Braunfeld* because both cases involved the choice of forfeiting benefits to adhere to religious beliefs or violate those beliefs, with each case reaching opposite conclusions.

---

[104] 374 U.S. 398 (1963).

[105] *Id.* at 404.

[106] *Id.* at 407–08. The state claimed that it had a compelling interest in preventing the possibility that fraudulent claims for unemployment benefits would be filed. Even though there was no evidence in the record to support such a fear, the Supreme Court nevertheless stated that "it is highly doubtful whether such evidence would be sufficient to warrant a substantial infringement of religious liberties." *Id.* at 407.

Strict scrutiny review was also applied by the Supreme Court in *Wisconsin v. Yoder*, in 1972, to find that Wisconsin's compulsory attendance education law burdened the Amish's free exercise of religion, even though the law was neutral and generally applicable.[107] The Amish believe that sending their children to high school, as required by the compulsory attendance law, would "expose themselves to the danger and censure of the church community" and "also endanger their own salvation and that of their children."[108] The compulsory attendance law burdened the Amish's religious exercise because, like *Sherbert*, it "compel[led] them, under threat of criminal sanction, to perform acts undeniably at odds with fundamental tenets of their religious beliefs."[109] The Court next considered whether the government had an interest sufficient to justify the burden and found that it did not. Specifically, the state's argument that it had an interest "of sufficient magnitude" to ensure that children who choose to leave the Amish community are well equipped for life was rejected by the Court as highly speculative.[110] Had there been specific evidence of Amish children leaving the community only to be ill-equipped for life, perhaps the Court would have found otherwise.

Eighteen years later, in *Employment Division v. Smith*, Justice Scalia, writing for the majority, abandoned the strict scrutiny standard of *Sherbert* and *Yoder* and concluded that laws that were neutral and generally applicable would not violate the Free Exercise Clause because any burden on religion would be incidental.[111] In *Smith*, a member of the Native American Church was fired from his job as a drug counselor after ingesting peyote for sacramental purposes, a controlled substance under Oregon's drug laws. Because the employee was fired for his "misconduct," he was denied unemployment benefits. Rather than proceeding under the balancing test utilized in *Sherbert* and *Yoder*, the Court instead ruled that denying

---

[107] 406 U.S. 205, 220 (1972) ("A regulation neutral on its face may, in its application, nonetheless offend the constitutional requirement for governmental neutrality if it unduly burdens the free exercise of religion.").
[108] *Id.* at 209.
[109] *Id.* at 218.
[110] *Id.* at 224.
[111] 494 U.S. 872 (1990).

unemployment compensation was permissible under the Free Exercise Clause because the law at issue was neutral and generally applicable. In other words, no matter the burden on religion, there would be no constitutional violation if the law was neutral and generally applicable. Justice Scalia wrote that the Court has "never held that an individual's religious beliefs excuse him from compliance with an otherwise valid law prohibiting conduct that the State is free to regulate."[112] Thus, the *Smith* decision directly contrasts with *Sherbert* and *Yoder*, both of which determined that even laws that were neutral and of general applicability could violate the Free Exercise Clause.

In 1993, the Supreme Court addressed the scope of *Smith* in *Church of the Lukumi Babalu Aye, Inc. v. City of Hialeah.*[113] It found that laws that are not neutral or not generally applicable and that target religious exercise are subject to strict scrutiny. Members of the Santeria religion, whose religious practice includes animal sacrifice, leased space in Hialeah, Florida, to establish a house of worship, school, cultural center, and museum. Because these practices were distressing to some members of the community, the city held an emergency meeting, and subsequent meetings, in which it passed three ordinances to prevent the killing of animals in religious ceremonies. The Court found that the ordinances were not neutral for several reasons. First, the text of the ordinances expressly singled out religious uses by including the terms "sacrifice" and "ritual."[114] The circumstances surrounding the ordinances' enactment, including discriminatory statements made by government officials, also showed that their purpose was to target the Santeria religion.[115] Beyond this, the Court observed that the Free Exercise Clause protects against governmental hostility that is masked (known as a "religious gerrymander") in addition to overt hostility. Here, the effect of the ordinances was a religious gerrymander because "few if any killing of animals are prohibited other than Santeria sacrifice."[116]

---

[112] *Id.* at 879.
[113] 508 U.S. 520 (1993).
[114] *Id.* at 533–34.
[115] *Id.* at 541–42.
[116] *Id.* at 536.

For this same reason, the ordinances were not generally applicable, but were "drafted with care to forbid few killings but those occasioned by religious sacrifice."[117] For example, although the ordinances prohibited animal sacrifice, the city permitted fishing, euthanasia of stray animals, extermination of mice and rats in homes, disposal of animal carcasses, and consumption of uninspected meat.[118] In this regard, the ordinances were underinclusive because other forms of animal killing that were allowed were at odds with the city's stated secular purposes of protecting public health and preventing animal cruelty.

Because the ordinances were neither neutral nor generally applicable, the Supreme Court applied strict scrutiny review. Although public health and cruelty to animals could under ordinary circumstances be compelling governmental interests, they were not so here because "[w]here government restricts only conduct protected by the First Amendment and fails to enact feasible measures to restrict other conduct producing substantial harm or alleged harm of the same sort, the interest given in justification of the restriction is not compelling."[119] As has been noted, *Lukumi's* importance is based on its "strong signal to the lower courts that the *Smith* decision should not be read to permit the targeting of religious practices under the guise of a purportedly general and religiously neutral ordinance."[120]

Although the Supreme Court has never considered the merits of a free exercise case relating particularly to zoning, other federal courts have done so. These federal cases reflect the divergent approaches taken by the Supreme Court with respect to free exercise claims before and after *Smith*. The Eleventh Circuit, in a pre-*Smith* decision, for example, employed a balancing test to determine whether the City of Miami Beach's application of a zoning ordinance burdened an Orthodox Jewish group's exercise of religion, in *Grosz v. City of Miami Beach*.[121] The Jewish group sought to conduct religious services from the home of its rabbi, but the city's zoning

---

[117] *Id.* at 543.
[118] *Id.* at 543–44.
[119] *Id.* at 546–47.
[120] *See* BLAESSER & WEINSTEIN, *supra,* note 38, § 7.4, at 684.
[121] 721 F.2d 729 (11th Cir. 1983); *see also* Christian Gospel Church, Inc. v. City. and Cnty. of San Francisco, 896 F.2d 1221 (9th Cir. 1990) (applying pre-*Smith* balancing test to find free exercise violation).

code prohibited religious uses in the zone district where the home was located while permitting religious uses in every other zone district. Relying on the Supreme Court's pre-*Smith* cases, the Eleventh Circuit performed a balancing test in which it considered both the burden on government and the burden on religion.[122] First, the court found substantial the government's interest in enforcing its zoning laws so as to preserve the residential quality of its RS-4 zones, particularly by protecting the zoning district's inhabitants from problems of traffic, noise and litter, spot zoning, and preserving a coherent land use plan.[123] Next, *Grosz* examined the burden on religion, which it found to be minimal because the zoning code allows religious uses in every other zone, the nearest of which was only four blocks from the subject property.[124] Further, unlike the cases where the Supreme Court found free exercise violations, the plaintiffs did "not confront the limited choice of ceasing their conduct or incurring criminal liability," especially because the Jewish group could "conduct the required services in suitably zoned areas, either by securing another site away from their current house or by making their home elsewhere in the city."[125]

Federal courts deciding free exercise land use cases abandoned this balancing test in favor of the neutral and generally applicable inquiry in the years following *Smith*. The Second Circuit employed the *Smith* analysis in *St. Bartholomew's Church v. City of New York*,[126] where a church sought to convert one of its religious buildings into a commercial office building to

---

[122] The Eleventh Circuit noted that the balancing test applied if two components were met. First, relying on *Braunfeld v. Brown*, 366 U.S. 599 (1961), the Eleventh Circuit noted that it had to consider whether the zoning ordinance regulated religious beliefs because "[t]he government may never regulate religious beliefs; but, the Constitution does not prohibit absolutely government regulation of religious conduct." *Grosz*, 721 F.2d at 733. In *Grosz*, the zoning ordinance focused on conduct, not belief. *Id.* The Eleventh Circuit, therefore, proceeded to consider the second threshold principle—whether the law has a secular purpose and a secular effect. Deciding that the law also met this requirement, the Eleventh Circuit found that application of the balancing test was appropriate. *Id.* at 733–34.

[123] *Grosz* also relied on *Village of Euclid v. Ambler Realty Co.*, 272 U.S. 365 (1926), to note the importance of zoning objectives, stating that segregation of residential from nonresidential neighborhoods "will increase the safety and security of home life, greatly tend to prevent street accidents, especially to children by reducing traffic and resulting confusion, . . . decrease noise . . . [and] preserve a more favorable environment in which to raise children." *Id.* at 394.

[124] *Id.* at 739.

[125] *Id.*

[126] 914 F.2d 348 (2d Cir. 1990).

raise funds to support its religious mission. After being denied by the city on three separate occasions, the church sued, alleging that the landmark law substantially burdened its religion by preventing it from carrying on and expanding the ministerial and charitable activities central to its religion.[127] Although the landmark law "drastically restricted the Church's ability to raise revenues to carry out its various charitable and ministerial programs," the Second Circuit deemed it constitutional because it was neutral and generally applicable.[128] And in another case,[129] a religious group sued Collier County, Florida, after a county official charged the group with violating several zoning ordinances by converting its church facility into a homeless shelter, the operation of which the group claimed was an essential aspect of its religion. Because the ordinances were neutral and generally applicable, the court found that any effect on the group's religious exercise was only incidental, and the claim failed.[130]

IV. Congress' Response to *Smith*

A. The Religious Freedom Restoration Act

Religious and political groups were not pleased with *Smith's* undoing of strict scrutiny, under which no free exercise violation would exist so long as a law did not target religious uses explicitly or in effect. These groups lobbied for Congress to "restore" religious protection as it had existed prior to *Smith*, in the form of a balancing test.[131] In 1993, the same year that *Lukumi* was decided, Congress responded directly by enacting RFRA

---

[127] The landmarking law, codified at NEW YORK CITY ADMINISTRATIVE CODE §§ 25-301 to 25-321 (1986), allowed the city to designate as landmarks buildings that "have a special character, special historical and aesthetic interest and value as part of the development, heritage and cultural aspects of New York City." *St. Bartholomew's*, 914 F.2d at 351. Such a designation would prohibit the building from being altered or demolished without approval from New York City's Landmarks Preservation Commission. *Id.*
[128] *Id.* at 355. Although the Court chose not to employ any balancing test, it did observe that there was no proof of "discriminatory motive, coercion in religious practice or the Church's inability to carry out its religious mission in its existing facilities." *Id.*
[129] First Assembly of God, Naples, Florida, Inc. v. Collier Cnty., 20 F.3d 419 (11th Cir. 1994).
[130] *Id.* at 423-24; *see also* Islamic Ctr. of Miss., Inc. v. City of Starkville, 840 F.2d 293, 300–303 (5th Cir. 1988) (applying pre-*Smith* balancing test to find free exercise violation).
[131] Marci Hamilton, *The Case for Evidence-Based Free Exercise Accommodation: Why the Religious Freedom Restoration Act Is Bad Public Policy*, 9 HARV. L. & POL'Y REV. 129, 135–36 (2015).

to restore religious protection, which can be seen in the text of the statute itself: "in . . . *Smith* . . . the Supreme Court virtually eliminated the requirement that the government justify burdens on religious exercise imposed by laws neutral toward religion."[132] RFRA further provides that it is meant to "restore the compelling interest test as set forth in *Sherbert v. Verner* . . . and *Wisconsin v. Yoder* . . . and to guarantee its application in all cases where free exercise of religion is substantially burdened."[133] Finally, RFRA adds that "laws 'neutral' toward religion may burden religious exercise as surely as laws intended to interfere with religious exercise."[134]

Under RFRA's strict scrutiny mandate, a government may substantially burden religious exercise *only if* the law or action "is in furtherance of a compelling governmental interest" and "is the least restrictive means of furthering that compelling governmental interest."[135] The religious entity must first establish a substantial burden on religious exercise. If a substantial burden on religious exercise is found, the government must then justify its actions with a compelling interest. Finally, if the government establishes a valid compelling interest, it must also show that its laws or actions are the least restrictive means possible to achieve their purposes to avoid liability.

When first enacted, RFRA applied to *any* governmental law or action—federal or state—no matter the context.[136] However, RFRA's application to the states and local governments was short-lived, as it was struck down by the Supreme Court in *City of Boerne v. Flores*.[137] In *Boerne*, St. Peter Catholic Church wished to expand its house of worship to accommodate additional parishioners at Sunday masses. A few months after the Archbishop of San Antonio gave permission to St. Peter Catholic Church to enlarge its house of worship, the city passed an ordinance requiring that any historic landmarks or buildings within a historic district, such as

---

[132] 42 U.S.C. § 2000bb(a)(4).

[133] 42 U.S.C. § 2000bb(b)(1).

[134] 42 U.S.C. § 2000bb(a)(2). The statute also says that "Government shall not substantially burden a person's exercise of religion even if the burden results from a *rule of general applicability* . . ." 42 U.S.C. § 2000bb-1(a).

[135] 42 U.S.C. § 2000bb-1(b).

[136] *See* City of Boerne v. Flores, 521 U.S. 507, 516 (1997).

[137] *Id.*

St. Peter Catholic Church, obtain Historic Landmark Commission approval. Relying on the ordinance, the city denied the application, and the Archbishop of San Antonio, P. F. Flores, sued in federal court, alleging a violation of RFRA. The Supreme Court ruled that RFRA was unconstitutional as applied to the states because it exceeded the powers that Congress had been granted under the Fourteenth Amendment's Enforcement Clause. The statute still applies to the federal government.[138] Although a comprehensive analysis of RFRA is beyond the scope of this chapter, in the wake of *Boerne*, several states have responded by enacting their own religious freedom restoration acts.[139]

B. The Religious Land Use and Institutionalized Persons Act

After *Boerne*, public interest and religious organizations lobbied Congress for a new law in response to *Smith* that would be applicable to both state and federal government, aimed at protecting religious exercise, and able to pass constitutional muster.[140] After a bill similar in scope to RFRA, known as the Religious Liberty Protection Act,[141] failed to pass, the following year, RLUIPA was signed into law by President Clinton. Unlike RFRA, which applied to *any* federal, state, or local law, RLUIPA applies in two very specific contexts: land use regulation and the religious rights of institutionalized persons. In effect, RLUIPA imposes the same test as RFRA.[142] Yet, RLUIPA provides additional protections by requiring that government treat religious and secular assemblies and institutions equally,[143] not discriminate against any religious assembly or institution on the basis of religion or religious denomination,[144] not totally exclude religious assemblies,[145]

---

[138] *See, e.g.*, Burwell v. Hobby Lobby Stores, Inc., 134 S. Ct. 2751, 2759 (2014).
[139] For more about RFRA, see Chapter 6.
[140] Roman P. Storzer & Anthony R. Picarello, *The Religious Land Use and Institutionalized Persons Act of 2000: A Constitutional Response to Unconstitutional Zoning Practices*, 9 Geo. Mason L. Rev. 929, 943–44 (2001).
[141] H.R. 1691, 106th Cong. (1999).
[142] 42 U.S.C. § 2000cc(a)(1).
[143] 42 U.S.C. § 2000cc(b)(1).
[144] 42 U.S.C. § 2000cc(b)(2).
[145] 42 U.S.C. § 2000cc(b)(3)(A).

and not unreasonably limit religious assemblies or institutions.[146] For an in-depth discussion of RLUIPA, see chapter 6.

V. Free Exercise Claims Following RLUIPA

Since RLUIPA was signed into law, free exercise claims arise in several situations. A religious group that seeks zoning relief to develop property and use it for some religious purpose but is denied outright,[147] not permitted to develop or use the property for religious purposes to the extent desired,[148] or obtains approval subject to conditions that are onerous and overly burdensome may bring a free exercise claim under the Free Exercise Clause.[149] Issuance of an order, such as a cease and desist order, to a religious group can also give rise to a free exercise claim.[150] These are all examples of "as-applied" challenges because they involve the government's application of zoning laws to specific religious groups. If the religious group proves that its religious exercise has been substantially burdened by some governmental act or law, the burden of proof then shifts to the government to justify its actions with a compelling interest, as with RFRA and RLUIPA. If the government has a compelling interest, it must also establish that its laws or actions are narrowly tailored to serve that interest to avoid liability.

Other free exercise challenges may appear in the form of a "facial" challenge. An example of this is where a religious group wants to develop property for a religious use in a zoning district, but such uses are prohibited in the zone.[151] An ordinance that prohibits certain actions central to a group's religious beliefs, as with animal sacrifice in *Lukumi*, will also give rise to a facial challenge. If the law is not neutral or not generally applicable, it must withstand strict scrutiny.

---

[146] 42 U.S.C. § 2000cc(b)(3)(B).

[147] *See, e.g.,* Eagle Cove Camp & Conference Ctr., Inc. v. Town of Woodboro, 734 F.3d 673 (7th Cir. 2013).

[148] *See, e.g.,* Living Water Church of God v. Charter Twp. of Meridian, 258 Fed. App'x. 729 (6th Cir. 2007).

[149] *See, e.g.,* Roman Catholic Diocese of Rockville Ctr. v. Inc. Vill. of Old Westbury, 2012 WL 1392365 (E.D.N.Y., April 23, 2012).

[150] *See, e.g.,* Murphy v. New Milford Zoning Comm'n, 402 F.3d 342 (2d Cir. 2005).

[151] *See, e.g.,* Lakewood, Ohio Congregation of Jehovah's Witnesses, Inc. v. City of Lakewood, 699 F.2d 303 (6th Cir. 1983).

VI. As-Applied Free Exercise Challenges

In recent years, free exercise claims based on governmental action enforcing and implementing zoning codes have been subject, in large part, to the same analysis as claims brought under RLUIPA's substantial burden provision.[152] As explained by the Seventh Circuit: "Given the similarities between § 2(a)(1) of RLUIPA and First Amendment jurisprudence, we collapse [appellant's] claims for the purpose of this analysis; this approach seems most consistent with post-RLUIPA case law."[153] This raises the obvious question—what does a free exercise claim add, if anything, to a lawsuit already invoking RLUIPA's substantial burden? Substantively, very little. There is the possibility that bringing a free exercise claim in addition to a RLUIPA claim could mean increased attorneys' fees for prevailing plaintiffs because finding success in one will very likely mean the same result for the other. And the more counts pled against the government, perhaps the greater the financial cost on the government to defend such claims throughout the life of the case, especially in discovery. These tactical approaches might cause governments to be more apt to settle rather than litigate.

Beyond these considerations, there are some differences to note between RLUIPA and free exercise claims. On the one hand, free exercise

---

[152] *See* Chabad Lubavitch of Litchfield Cnty., Inc. v. Borough of Litchfield, 768 F.3d 183, 198 (2d Cir. 2014) (noting that RLUIPA "codified 'existing Free Exercise, Establishment Clause[,] and Equal Protection rights against states and municipalities' that discriminated against religious use") (citing Midrash Sephardi, Inc. v. Town of Surfside, 366 F.3d 1214, 1239 (11th Cir. 2004)); Moore-King v. Cnty. of Chesterfield, 708 F.3d 560, 570–72 (4th Cir. 2013) (same analysis for RLUIPA substantial burden and free exercise claims and rejecting both on basis of no religious exercise at issue); Eagle Cove Camp & Conference Ctr., Inc. v. Town of Woodboro, 734 F.3d 673, 681–82 (7th Cir. 2013); Guatay Christian Fellowship v. Cnty. of San Diego, 670 F.3d 957, 978 (9th Cir. 2011) (noting that "Congress endeavored to codify existing Free Exercise jurisprudence" when it enacted RLUIPA . . ."); Church of Scientology v. City of Sandy Springs, 843 F. Supp. 2d 1328, 1349–50 n.19 (N.D. Ga. 2012); Calvary Temple Assembly of God v. City of Marinette, 2008 WL 2837774 (E.D. Wis. July 18, 2008) (noting similarities between RLUIPA substantial burden and free exercise claims, and collapsing analysis); Murphy v. Zoning Comm'n of the Town of New Milford, 289 F. Supp. 2d 87, 113 (D. Conn. 2003) ("Because the elements of a RLUIPA claim are virtually identical to a free exercise claim . . . the court holds based on the reasoning already articulated, that plaintiffs are entitled to summary judgment on their RLUIPA claim"), vacated on other grounds, 402 F.3d 342 (2d. Cir. 2005); *see also* Daniel P. Dalton, LITIGATING RELIGIOUS LAND USE CASES, 57–58 (2014) (explaining that "RLUIPA's legislative history reveals that Congress deliberately did not define 'substantial burden' in the statutory language, but rather intended that courts utilize the definition developed through Supreme Court jurisprudence") (citations omitted).

[153] Vision Church v. Vill. of Long Grove, 468 F.3d 975, 996 (7th Cir. 2007); *see* John Infranca, *Institutional Free Exercise and Religious Land Use*, 34 CARDOZO L. REV. 1694, 1695 n. 4 (2012) (noting that "[p]arties often bring claims under both RLUIPA and the Free Exercise Clause of the First Amendment, but RLUIPA tends to govern the analysis").

claims may be slightly more difficult to establish than RLUIPA substantial burden claims insofar as religious exercise must be "central" to religious beliefs, although this is largely a distinction without a difference given the deference afforded to religious groups' characterizations of religious beliefs. However, there is one important area where free exercise claims are more favorable to governments. Under the Free Exercise Clause, a government must only prove that its compelling interest is *narrowly tailored,* whereas RLUIPA obligates the government to establish that any compelling interest has been advanced in the *least restrictive means* possible.

The degree of the burden on religious exercise necessary to establish such a claim varies among the courts. For example, some courts require that the burden directly coerce the religious group to change its behavior,[154] put substantial pressure on the religious group to modify its behavior,[155] be oppressive to a significantly great extent,[156] place substantial pressure on a religious group to cause it to violate its religious beliefs or effectively bar it from using its property for religious exercise,[157] or cause religious exercise to become effectively impracticable.[158] And, as discussed in chapter 6, different courts examine different factors to assess the claims under RLUIPA, which also are applicable to free exercise claims. In *Chabad Lubavitch of Litchfield County, Inc. v. Borough of Litchfield,* the Second Circuit notes several factors that have been used by the courts to assess these claims, including the following:

- Whether the agency's decision is arbitrary and unlawful or supported by the record;
- Whether denial of an application for zoning relief was an absolute denial or left open the possibility for reapplication;

---

[154] *See, e.g.,* Westchester Day Sch. v. Vill of Mamaroneck, 504 F.3d 338, 349 (2d Cir. 2007).

[155] *See, e.g.,* Bethel World Outreach Ministries v. Montgomery Cnty. Council, 706 F.3d 548, 556 (4th Cir.2013).

[156] *See, e.g.,* San Jose Christian Coll. v. City of Morgan Hill, 360 F.3d 1024, 1034 (9th Cir.2004).

[157] *See, e.g.,* Living Water Church of God v. Charter Twp. of Meridian, 258 Fed. App'x 729, 737 (6th Cir. 2007).

[158] Civil Liberties for Urban Believers v. City of Chicago, 342 F.3d 752, 761 (7th Cir. 2003); *but see* Schlemm v. Wall, 784 F.3d 362, 364 (7th Cir. 2015) (noting that the Seventh Circuit's substantial burden standard was made easier to satisfy following Holt v. Hobbs, 135 S. Ct. 853 (2015) and Burwell v. Hobby Lobby Stores, Inc., 134 S. Ct. 2751 (2014)).

- Whether there are ready and feasible alternatives for the religious group, including alternative sites;
- Whether the religious group can adequately exercise its religion in light of governmental action;
- Whether the religious group had a "reasonable expectation" of obtaining approval when it purchased property;
- Whether the zoning relief sought is a matter of preference and convenience or truly central to the group's religious beliefs; and
- Whether the religious group has changed its religious behavior as a result of governmental action.[159]

This list is by no means exhaustive, and other courts may consider additional factors. Nonetheless, it provides important guidance for local governments and lawyers when faced with or bringing such claims.

Savvy government lawyers will attempt to recast the issues as financial burdens, matters of personal preference, or convenience for the religious group, as opposed to a burden on the exercise of religion. This is because federal courts have repeatedly rejected claims of "financial cost and inconvenience, as well as the frustration of not getting what one wants" as constituting a substantial burden on religious exercise.[160]

VII. Facial Free Exercise Challenges

Facial challenges to zoning ordinances are still regularly brought under the Free Exercise Clause.[161] If the law is neutral and generally applicable, the forgiving rational basis standard of review will apply. If, however, the law is either not neutral or not generally applicable, courts will apply strict scrutiny. Some courts have imposed an additional requirement on plaintiffs bringing a facial challenge by requiring plaintiffs to "explain why the inability to locate

---

[159] 768 F.3d at 195-96 (citations and quotation marks omitted).
[160] Castle Hills First Baptist Church v. City of Castle Hills, No. SA-01-CA-1149-RF, 2004 WL 546792, at *11 (W.D. TX March 17, 2004).
[161] See, e.g., Alger Bible Baptist Church v. Twp. of Moffat, 2014 WL 462354 (E.D. Mich. 2014) (zoning ordinance that permits only structures promoting commercial retail and generate revenue in highway commercial district was neutral, generally applicable, and in line with constitutional requirements).

in the specific area affects its religious exercise."[162] Without some evidence to
show why developing a specific parcel is important to religious exercise and
when the area from which the religious use is excluded is not large, there will
be no constitutionally cognizable burden on religious exercise.[163] The Third
Circuit, in *Lighthouse Institute for Evangelism, Inc. v. City of Long Branch*,
considered a free exercise challenge to a redevelopment plan established
to attract and strengthen retail trade and generate city revenues. The plan
allowed nonreligious assemblies, such as theaters, cinemas, performing art
venues, restaurants, and bars and clubs, but prohibited religious uses. The
plan was neutral because, unlike *Lukumi*, it did not target religion, and there
was no evidence that it had been developed with the aim to infringe religious
exercise. It was also generally applicable because the government pursued
its redevelopment aims evenhandedly by prohibiting secular assembly uses,
in addition to religious uses, that would be at odds with the redevelopment
goals. For this reason, only rational basis review applied—which the government easily met.[164] In another case, the Seventh Circuit rejected the claim
that inclusion of "church" among various land uses allowed by special permit
indicates that it facially discriminates against churches under Free Exercise
Clause.[165] Another court held that a zoning ordinance that simply treated
small and large uses differently is not religious discrimination and did not
cause an ordinance to become nonneutral or nongenerally applicable.[166]

---

[162] Lighthouse Inst. for Evangelism, Inc. v. City of Long Branch, 510 F.3d 253, 274 (3d Cir. 2007).

[163] *See id.* (citing Grace United Methodist Church v. City of Cheyenne, 451 F.3d 643, 654 (10th Cir. 2006);
Messiah Baptist Church v. Cnty. of Jefferson, 859 F.2d 820, 824–25 (10th Cir. 1988); Lakewood, Ohio
Congregation of Jehovah's Witnesses, Inc. v. City of Lakewood, 699 F.2d 303, 306–307 (6th Cir. 1983)).

[164] *See Lighthouse Inst.*, 510 F.3d at 275–77; *see also* Riverside Church v. City of St. Michael, 2016 WL
4545310, at *18–19 (D. Minn. August 8, 2016) (finding as neutral and generally applicable an ordinance banning "assembly, religious institution, and house of worship" uses from zoning district and
moratorium applying to "assembly, theater or church purposes").

[165] Civil Liberties for Urban Believers v. City of Chicago, 342 F.3d 752, 763 (7th Cir. 2003) (rejecting
plaintiff's claim that inclusion of "church" among various land uses allowed by special permit indicates
that it facially discriminates against churches under Free Exercise Clause).

[166] Adhi Parasakthi v. Twp. of West Pikeland, 721 F. Supp. 2d 361, 378 (E.D. Pa. 2010); *see also* Castle
Hills First Baptist Church v. City of Castle Hills, 2004 U.S. Dist. LEXIS 4669, at *59 (W.D. TX March
17, 2004) ("Were there a cause of action for facilities size discrimination, then the Church might have
a claim. Rather, this record suggests no hostility or discrimination visited upon the Church that would
not also have greeted a Wal-Mart or large hospital or university, where an entity's proposed growth
threatened to outstrip the character and size of the city.").

VIII. Compelling Interest

No government wants to find itself in the position of having to justify a burden on religious exercise because it is very difficult to do so. To carry its burden, a government must identify compelling interests that are meant to be advanced through the government's burdening of religion. This is no easy task, as the Supreme Court has observed that in the free exercise context, compelling interests are "interests of the highest order" (think public health and safety).[167] In zoning, compelling interests may exist in the form of upholding zoning laws;[168] maintaining the integrity of a zoning district;[169] or restoring safety, securing and preventing crime.[170] Preserving property values,[171] revenue generation,[172] and, perhaps, concerns about traffic and parking,[173] do not constitute compelling interests. Whatever the compelling interest, it cannot be generalized or speculative but must be supported by evidence of particular harms likely to occur.[174] As an example, if a government denies a zoning permit to a religious group wishing to open a soup kitchen in a residential neighborhood on the ground that it would lead to increased crime in the area, the government must have specific evidence to support its concern. Without it, a court is not likely to find a compelling interest.[175]

IX. Narrow Tailoring

A difficult concept for many practitioners to comprehend is what is meant by "narrowly tailored." The final component of the strict scrutiny analysis requires the government to show that its laws or actions are narrowly tailored

---

[167] Wisconsin v. Yoder, 406 U.S. 205, 215, 220 (1972).

[168] *See, e.g.*, Bikur Cholim, Inc. v. Vill. of Suffern, 664 F. Supp. 2d 267, 291 (S.D.N.Y. 2009).

[169] *See, e.g.*, Eagle Cove Camp & Conf. Ctr. v. Town of Woodboro, 734 F.3d 673, 682 (7th Cir. 2013), *cert. denied*, 134 S. Ct. 2160 (2014).

[170] *See, e.g.*, Harbor Missionary Church v. City of San Buenaventura, 642 Fed. App'x 726, 728 (9th Cir. 2016).

[171] *See, e.g.*, Westchester Day Sch. v. Vill. of Mamaroneck, 417 F.Supp.2d 477, 553 (S.D.N.Y. Mar. 2, 2006), *aff'd*, 504 F.3d 338 (2d Cir. 2007).

[172] *See, e.g.*, Cottonwood Christian Ctr. v. City of Cypress, 218 F.Supp.2d 1203, 1228 (C.D. Cal. Aug. 6, 2002).

[173] *See Westchester Day Sch.*, 386 F.3d at 191.

[174] *See* Gonzales v. O Centro Espirita Beneficente Uniao do Vegetal, 546 U.S. 418, 432 (2006).

[175] *See, e.g.*, Wisconsin v. Yoder, 406 U.S. 205, 224–27 (1972) (rejecting state's interest as speculative).

to advance its compelling interests.[176] Take, for example, *Lukumi*. There, the Supreme Court concluded that the ordinances were not "drawn in narrow terms to accomplish" compelling interests because they were "overbroad or underinclusive in substantial respects."[177] As discussed, the proffered objectives of the ordinances (protecting public health and safety and preventing animal cruelty) were not pursued with respect to analogous nonreligious conduct. Therefore, for a government law or action to be narrowly tailored, the objectives it seeks to advance through regulating a religious use in some way must be equally pursued through the regulation of secular uses that cause the same concerns.

One area that has caused some confusion is whether there is any difference between this narrowly tailored requirement and RLUIPA's "least restrictive means" requirement. Although RFRA and RLUIPA were meant to "restore" religious protection as it existed before *Smith*, the Supreme Court has noted that free exercise jurisprudence never included the least restrictive means component.[178] Narrow tailoring "means the law is well-tailored to the government interests it is supposed to serve."[179] In contrast, least restrictive means requires the government to show significantly more, such as considering and rejecting all lesser restrictive alternatives.[180] In *Burwell v. Hobby Lobby Stores, Inc.*, the Supreme Court stated the following:

> In *City of Boerne v. Flores*, . . . we wrote that RFRA's least restrictive means requirement was not used in the pre-*Smith* jurisprudence RFRA purported to codify . . . On this understanding of our pre-*Smith*

---

[176] *See, e.g.*, Church of the Lukumi Babalu Aye, Inc. v. City of Hialeah, 508 U.S. 520, 546 (1993).

[177] *Id.*

[178] Hamilton, *supra* note 114, at 134–35.

[179] *Id.* at 135.

[180] *Id.* Cases interpreting the least restrictive means have also been less than clear in what is required for governments to satisfy this requirement. The Second Circuit found that the least restrictive means requirement was not met where the zoning board of appeals had the opportunity to approve the application subject to conditions that could be less restrictive than outright denial of a special permit, but refused to consider doing so. *See* Westchester Day Sch. v. Vill. of Mamaroneck, 504 F.3d 338, 353 (2d Cir. 2007). In *Holt v. Hobbs*, Justice Sotomayor states in her concurrence that "nothing in the Court's opinion suggests that prison officials must refute every conceivable option to satisfy RLUIPA's least restrictive means requirement." 135 S. Ct. 853, 868 (2015) (Sotomayor, J., concurring). Thus, the Second Circuit has said that government must do something more than nothing and the Supreme Court, according to Justice Sotomayor, has concluded that governments need not do everything, leaving much room in the middle to question what is sufficiently enough to be the least restrictive means.

cases, RFRA did more than merely restore the balancing test used in the *Sherbert* line of cases; it provided even broader protection for religious liberty than was available under those decisions.[181]

However, Justice Ginsburg notes in her dissent in *Hobby Lobby* that "[o]ur decision in *City of Boerne*, it is true, states that the least restrictive means requirement 'was not used in the pre-*Smith* jurisprudence RFRA purported to codify' . . . As just indicated, however, that statement does not accurately convey the Court's pre-*Smith* jurisprudence."[182] Whether the narrow tailoring requirement is something different than the least restrictive means requirement may still be an open issue.

X. Ripeness

Free exercise claims must be "ripe" to be adjudicated by a court. Most courts require that a religious group establish that the government has taken a final, definitive position as to how the group can and cannot use its property, including exhaustion of the variance process, under *Williamson County Regional Planning Commission v. Hamilton Bank*.[183] If a religious group sues without first submitting an application for zoning relief, including exhaustion of any administrative appeals process, a court may lack subject matter jurisdiction to consider the claim and dismiss the lawsuit. If the religious group has suffered an "immediate injury" that is adequately defined by the existing record, some courts may consider the merits of the claim.[184] Other courts rely on traditional notions of ripeness, considering both "the fitness of the issues for judicial decision and the hardship to the parties to withholding court consideration."[185] Facial challenges are ripe from the outset and need not go through these procedures for a court to consider the merits of such a claim.[186]

---

[181] 134 S. Ct. 2751, 2761 n.3 (2014).

[182] *Id.* at 2793 (Ginsburg, J. dissenting).

[183] 473 U.S. 172 (1985).

[184] *See, e.g.*, Dougherty v. Town of N. Hempstead Bd. of Zoning Appeals, 282 F.3d 83, 90 (2d Cir. 2002); Murphy v. New Milford Zoning Comm'n, 402 F.3d 342, 352 (2d Cir. 2005).

[185] Roman Catholic Bishop of Springfield v. City of Springfield, 724 F.3d 78, 89–93 (1st Cir. 2013).

[186] Suitum v. Tahoe Reg'l Planning Agency, 520 U.S. 725, 736 n.10 (1997).

XI. Practice Tips to Avoid or Defend Free Exercise Claims

- Assume that the use or activity is religious, and do not question the truth or falsity of religious beliefs. Instead, consider whether the religious beliefs have been conceived to circumvent zoning. If so, they may not be "sincerely held."
- Carefully scrutinize your zoning code to ensure that religion is not targeted and that the zoning ordinances are neutral and generally applicable. One way to do this is by regulating assembly uses, including religious uses, broadly and subjecting them to the same standards.
- Create a surplus of land zoned for religious use. The more land available for religious use, the greater the possibility there will be ready and feasible alternatives (a factor under the substantial burden analysis) for a religious group suing under the First Amendment.
- If denying an application for zoning relief, encourage the religious group to modify its proposal and submit a new application (another factor under the substantial burden analysis).
- Identify and plan around compelling interests. Sit down with your planner and other government officials in advance to build these interests into the zoning code. Courts will not look favorably upon an after-the-fact justification of government actions.
- Hire consultants to study and produce reports about likely impacts of a proposed religious use, particularly as it relates to compelling interests, so that the government will have evidence to support a potential denial.
- If during a public hearing, an agency member makes a comment that may be discriminatory, immediately cleanse the record, renounce the statement, have the member recuse him- or herself, and ask the applicant if it has any other suggestions to cleanse the record. Repeat the same process if discriminatory comments are made by members of the public when given the opportunity to speak.

- Consider whether the religious group's claim is "ripe" for review or has been prematurely brought. If it appears that the claim is premature, move to dismiss.
- Educate local officials now; do not wait for an application or, worse, a lawsuit. Religious land use and constitutional considerations are difficult to comprehend even for experienced lawyers.

XII. Conclusion

With proper planning and education of local officials, religion clause disputes may be avoided. Leaders must understand that religious uses are not exempt from zoning and can be regulated like any other use. However, at the same time, the religion clauses afford real protections that can sometimes surmount governmental interests. Because these claims, particularly free exercise claims, can quickly spiral out of control, the best approach may be to engage religious groups early on in an to attempt to reach an amicable solution. Typically, the alternative is long, protracted, hostile litigation, with legal fees quickly mounting, and with much to lose. No government should willingly accept such an alternative, unless the adverse party is so unwilling to compromise that there is no other reasonable option available.

As in any governmental matter, politics often come into play, with hard lines taken and little, if any, room for compromise. Given the significant risks associated with religious land use litigation, local officials must not be blinded by politics to the detriment of their respective communities. They should understand and anticipate opposition to any controversial religious land use proposal. If accommodating a religious use will avoid costly litigation but upset a group of neighbors or contradict the zoning scheme to some manageable extent, that is a decision that a government must be prepared to make, stand by, and, if necessary, defend in court.

6

Religious Land Use Regulation Under the Religious Land Use and Institutionalized Persons Act

Alan C. Weinstein

Professor and Director
Maxine Goodman Levin College of Urban Affairs
Cleveland-Marshall College of Law
Cleveland State University
Cleveland, Ohio

I. Introduction

The Religious Land Use and Institutionalized Persons Act of 2000 (RLUIPA)[1] is the second effort by Congress to respond to *Employment Division v. Smith*,[2] a 1990 Supreme Court ruling that dramatically altered free exercise jurisprudence. Prior to *Smith*, Court decisions over the previous three decades had established that government action that placed a "substantial burden" on the exercise of religion would be upheld only if it could survive strict scrutiny. But in *Smith*, the Court

---

[1] Codified at 42 U.S.C. §§ 2000cc to 2000cc-5.
[2] 494 U.S. 872 (1990).

unexpectedly abandoned the strict scrutiny standard and held that a religiously neutral law of general applicability should be reviewed under the rational basis test.

The *Smith* ruling led to a concerted effort by a broad spectrum of religious and political groups to seek to "restore" through congressional action the religious protections that *Smith* had removed. That effort succeeded when the Religious Freedom Restoration Act of 1993[3] (RFRA) was enacted and signed into law by President Clinton. RFRA legislatively mandated the restoration of strict scrutiny by imposing that standard when government at any level imposed a substantial burden on a person's exercise of religion, even if the burden resulted from a religiously neutral law of general applicability. There was no doubt that the constitutionality of a law of such broad scope would be challenged. In 1997, just four years after RFRA was enacted, the Court ruled in *City of Boerne v. Flores* that RFRA was unconstitutional as applied to states and local governments.[4]

After RFRA was struck down, the same groups that had advocated for RFRA, and their congressional supporters, began advocating for a new religious freedom measure, albeit in a form better suited to withstand judicial scrutiny. After a failed effort in 1999 to enact a bill that was similar in scope to RFRA,[5] a more limited statute, the Religious Land Use and Institutionalized Persons Act of 2000 (RLUIPA), focusing solely on land use and the religious rights of prisoners, gained broad support, unanimously passed both houses of Congress in July of 2000, and was signed into law by President Clinton on September 22, 2000.[6]

---

[3] Pub. L. No. 103-141, 107 Stat. 1488, 42 U.S.C. § 2000bb. *See generally*, Douglas Laycock, *Free Exercise and the Religious Freedom Restoration Act*, 62 FORDHAM L. REV. 883 (1994).

[4] 521 U.S. 507, 532 (1997) (holding that RFRA was unconstitutional because Congress had exceeded its enforcement power granted under Section 5 of the Fourteenth Amendment by seeking to enforce a constitutional right by changing what the right is).

[5] Religious Liberty Protection Act, H.R. 1691, 106th Cong. (1999). *See* Legislative Hearing on H.R. 1691, Religious Liberty Protection Act of 1999, Before the Subcomm. On the Constitution of the House Committee on the Judiciary, 106th Cong. 4 (1999).

[6] Pub. L. No. 106-274, 114 Stat. 803 to 807, codified at 42 U.S.C. §§ 2000cc to 2000cc-5. *See generally*, Marci A. Hamilton, *Federalism and the Public Good: The True Story Behind the Religious Land Use and Institutionalized Persons Act*, 78 IND. L. J. 311 (2003).

RLUIPA was intended by its supporters to confirm and enforce the religious exercise protections of the First Amendment in the implementation of state and local land use regulations, as well as in the programs for institutionalized persons. This chapter deals only with the land use regulation provisions of RLUIPA.

Under RLUIPA, *land use regulation* is defined as follows:

> [A] zoning or landmarking law . . . that limits or restricts a claimant's use or development of land (including a structure affixed to land), if the claimant has an ownership, leasehold, easement, servitude or other property interest in the regulated land or a contract or option to acquire such an interest.[7]

Although some religious institutions have used RLUIPA to challenge governmental efforts to acquire property through eminent domain, almost every court that has considered the issue has ruled that an exercise of eminent domain is *not* a land use regulation and thus not governed by RLUIPA.[8] Other regulatory actions that are clearly outside RLUIPA's jurisdiction include building or fire safety permits, permits for utility connections, and other types of ministerial permits that are outside of zoning or historical preservation codes. The Second Circuit, however, has ruled that RLUIPA is triggered when an application for land use approval is reviewed under New York's State Environmental Quality Review Act (SEQRA),[9] and a federal district court in Alabama recently ruled that an

---

[7] 42 U.S.C.A. § 2000cc-5(5).

[8] *See* St. John's United Church of Christ v. City of Chicago, 502 F.3d 616 (7th Cir. 2007) (holding that eminent domain was not a land use regulation, listing other cases in accord, and noting that the only exception was dicta in an early RLUIPA case, *Cottonwood Christian Center v. Cypress Redevelopment Agency*, 218 F. Supp. 2d 1203, 1222 (C.D. Cal. 2002)). *But see* Albanian Associated Fund v. Twp. of Wayne, No. 06-CV-3217, 2007 WL 2904194 (D.N.J. Oct. 1, 2007) (arguing that RLUIPA could apply to an eminent domain action if the condemnation is a mechanism to implement a land use regulation). *See generally*, Christopher Serkin & Nelson Tebbe, *Condemning Religion: RLUIPA and the Politics of Eminent Domain*, 85 NOTRE DAME L. REV. 1 (2009); Daniel N. Lerman, *Taking the Temple: Eminent Domain and the Limits of RLUIPA*, 96 GEO. L.J. 2057 (2008).

[9] Fortress Bible Church v. Feiner, 694 F.3d 208, 217 (2d Cir. 2012). *But see* Bernstein v. Vill. of Wesley Hills, 95 F. Supp. 3d 547 (S.D.N.Y. 2015) (holding that local government's lawsuit challenging adequacy

(footnote continued on next page)

Alabama sex offender registry statute was a land use regulation to which RLUIPA applies.[10]

RLUIPA affects land use regulations by setting forth a general rule prohibiting government from imposing or implementing a land use regulation in a manner that imposes a substantial burden on the religious exercise of a person, including a religious assembly or institution,[11] unless the government can demonstrate that imposition of the burden is in furtherance of a compelling governmental interest and is the least restrictive means of furthering that compelling governmental interest.[12] RLUIPA provides that this general rule applies in any case in which the substantial burden is imposed from a program or activity that is federally funded; the substantial burden, or its removal, affects interstate commerce; or the substantial burden is imposed as a result of land use regulations that permit the government to make individualized decisions regarding the use of the affected property.[13] In short, RLUIPA requires that government demonstrate both that it has a compelling governmental interest to justify

---

(footnote continued from previous page)

of another local government's compliance with SEQRA did not "impose or implement" a land use regulation under RLUIPA).

[10] Martin v. Houston, 176 F. Supp. 3d 1286 (M.D. Ala. 2016) (finding that the plaintiff adequately pleaded that the sex offender registry statute is a land use regulation because the allegations in the complaint supported the reasonable inference that the statute divides the state of Alabama into territories and prescribes permissible uses of land within those territories).

[11] RLUIPA does not define the term "religious assembly or institution." RLUIPA's "Exclusion and Limits" provision, 42 U.S.C. § 2000cc (b)(3), prohibits government from imposing or implementing a land use regulation that: "(A) totally excludes religious assemblies from a jurisdiction; or (B) unreasonably limits religious assemblies, institutions or structures within a jurisdiction." The greater protection for "religious assemblies" suggests that it is a broader category than "religious institution," encompassing religious exercise in homes or other settings outside of buildings regularly dedicated to religious use.

[12] 42 U.S.C. § 2000cc(a)(1) provides: "No government shall impose or implement a land use regulation in a manner that imposes a substantial burden on the religious exercise of a person, including a religious assembly or institution, unless the government demonstrates that imposition of the burden on that person, assembly, or institution—(A) is in furtherance of a compelling governmental interest; and (B) is the least restrictive means of furthering that compelling governmental interest."

[13] 42 U.S.C. § 2000cc(a)(2) provides that the compelling interest test is applied in any case in which: "(A) the substantial burden is imposed in a program or activity that receives Federal financial assistance, even if the burden results from a rule of general applicability; (B) the substantial burden affects, or removal of that substantial burden would affect, commerce with foreign nations, among the several States, or with Indian tribes, even if the burden results from a rule of general applicability; or (C) the substantial burden is imposed in the implementation of a land use regulation or system of land use regulations, under which a government makes, or has in place formal or informal procedures or practices that permit the government to make, individualized assessments of the proposed uses for the property involved."

any land use regulation that substantially burdens free exercise and that it has used the least restrictive means to advance that interest.

As regards this general rule, RLUIPA mirrors RFRA. Thus, land use cases decided under RFRA could arguably be controlling in RLUIPA litigation that meets one of the act's jurisdictional requirements.[14] RLUIPA also mirrors RFRA in declining to define the term *substantial burden*. The legislative history of both statutes clearly shows that Congress intended that courts look to pre-*Smith* case law for the meaning of "substantial burden."[15] In contrast, it defines the "religious exercise" to which a substantial burden must apply in two ways, labeled "In general" and "Rule." The "In general" definition includes "any exercise of religion whether or not compelled by or central to a system of religious belief."[16] The "Rule" definition states: "[t]he use, building, or conversion of real property for the purpose of religious exercise shall be considered to be religious exercise of the person or entity that uses or intends to use the property for that purpose."[17] RLUIPA also expressly states that it must be construed broadly to protect religious exercise "to the maximum extent permitted by the terms of the Act and the Constitution,"[18] and the Supreme Court has confirmed that RLUIPA's religious freedom guarantees must be construed broadly.[19]

The broad definitions of *religious exercise* combined with construing RLUIPA's guarantees generally have led courts to apply RLUIPA to a wide scope of activities beyond approvals for houses of worship or religious schools. These have included, for example, worship and

---

[14] *Id.*

[15] RLUIPA's legislative history shows that the failure to define "substantial burden" was intentional. RLUIPA was not intended to create a new standard for the term, but rather the term was to be interpreted by reference to "Supreme Court jurisprudence." 146 CONG. REC. S7774, 7776 (daily ed. Jul. 27, 2000) (joint statement of Sens. Hatch and Kennedy). The legislative history for RFRA is similar; *see Senate Comm. on the Judiciary, Religious Freedom Restoration Act of 1993*, S. REP. NO. 111, 103RD CONG., 1ST SESS., AT 8–9 (1993); *House Comm. On the Judiciary, Religious Freedom Restoration Act of 1993*, H. REP. NO. 88, 103D CONG., 1ST SESS. AT 6 (1993). *See generally*, Jonathan Knapp, *Making Snow in the Desert: Defining A Substantial Burden Under RFRA*, 36 ECOLOGY L.Q. 259, 309 (2009).

[16] 42 U.S.C. § 2000cc-5(7)(A).

[17] 42 U.S.C. § 2000cc-5(7)(B).

[18] 42 U.S.C. § 2000cc-3(g).

[19] Holt v. Hobbs, 135 S. Ct. 853, 859 (2015) (speaking generally about RLUIPA in a case involving its institutionalized persons provisions).

religious study in private homes,[20] religiously sponsored residential drug and alcohol rehabilitation programs,[21] establishment of a guesthouse at a hospital for Sabbath-observant Jews,[22] and a commercial wedding business.[23]

There are, of course, limits to how far courts are willing to go to find "religious exercise." In one case, the Tenth Circuit Court of Appeals upheld a federal jury's determination that a church should be permanently enjoined from operating a daycare center because operation of the center was not a "sincere" exercise of its religious beliefs and thus was not "religious exercise" under RLUIPA.[24] In another case, the Michigan Supreme Court ruled against a church's claim that building an apartment complex constitutes religious exercise under RLUIPA.[25]

In addition to the provisions governing substantial burdens on religious exercise, RLUIPA contains provisions mandating that land use regulations must grant "equal treatment" to a religious assembly or institution as compared with secular assemblies or institutions;[26] not discriminate against any assembly or institution on the basis of religion or religious denomination;[27] and not impose or implement a land use regulation that totally excludes religious assemblies from a jurisdiction or unreasonably limits religious

---

[20] *See, e.g.,* Dilaura v. Ann Arbor Charter Twp., 30 Fed. App'x. 501 (6th Cir. 2002) (unpublished); Murphy v. Zoning Comm'n of Town of New Milford, 289 F. Supp. 2d 87 (D. Conn. 2003), *judgment vacated on other grounds,* 402 F.3d 342 (2d Cir. 2005).

[21] *See, e.g.,* Men of Destiny Ministries v. Osceola Cnty., No. 6:06-CV-624-ORL-31DAB, 2006 WL 3219321 (M.D. Fla. Nov. 6, 2006). *But see* Glenside Ctr., Inc. v. Abington Twp. Zoning Hearing Bd., 973 A.2d 10 (Pa. Commw. Ct. 2009) (finding that Alcoholics Anonymous meetings are not protected as a religious use under RLUIPA).

[22] *See, e.g.,* Bikur Cholim, Inc. v. Vill. of Suffern, 664 F. Supp. 2d 267 (S.D.N.Y. 2009).

[23] *See, e.g.,* Kaahumanu v. Cnty. of Maui, 315 F.3d 1215 (9th Cir. 2003)

[24] *See* Grace United Methodist Church v. City of Cheyenne, 235 F. Supp. 2d 1196 (D. Wyo. 2002), *aff'd,* 427 F.3d 775 (10th Cir. 2005), *opinion vacated on reh'g,* 451 F.3d 643 (10th Cir. 2006).

[25] Greater Bible Way Temple of Jackson v. City of Jackson, 733 N.W.2d 734, 746 (Mich. 2007). *See also,* Calif.-Nev. Annual Conf. of the Methodist Church v. City and Cnty. of San Francisco, 74 F. Supp. 3d 1144 (N.D. Cal. 2014) (finding that religious organization's commercial endeavors, such as the sale of property for a secular use, do not constitute "religious exercise" protected by RLUIPA, even if undertaken in order to fund the organization's religious mission).

[26] 42 U.S.C. § 2000cc (b)(1) provides: "No government shall impose or implement a land use regulation in a manner that treats a religious assembly or institution on less than equal terms with a nonreligious assembly or institution."

[27] 42 U.S.C. § 2000cc(b)(2) provides: "No government shall impose or implement a land use regulation that discriminates against any assembly or institution on the basis of religion or religious denomination."

assemblies, institutions, or structures within a jurisdiction.[28] RLUIPA also prescribes rules for legal claims brought under the statute,[29] including shifting the burden of persuasion to government once a plaintiff produces prima facie evidence of a violation—excepting that the plaintiff retains the burden of persuasion on whether the challenged land use regulation "or government practice" substantially burdens the plaintiff's exercise of religion[30]—and the statute amended 42 U.S.C. § 1988 to provide for the recovery of attorneys' fees by successful RLUIPA litigants.[31]

II. Substantial Burden Claims

A. What Is a Substantial Burden?

As noted previously, RLUIPA did not define the term *substantial burden* but instead left courts to interpret that term in line with "Supreme Court jurisprudence."[32] Unfortunately, that provides limited guidance because the Supreme Court has never addressed the substantial burden question in the context of land use regulation. Lower courts thus must try to apply to land use regulation Court rulings on substantial burden that derive largely from the very different context of denials of an employee's claim to unemployment compensation.[33] The Second Circuit discussed the problem in a 2007 case,

---

[28] 42 U.S.C. § 2000cc(b)(3) provides: "No government shall impose or implement a land use regulation that —(A) totally excludes religious assemblies from a jurisdiction; or (B) unreasonably limits religious assemblies, institutions, or structures within a jurisdiction."

[29] 42 U.S.C. § 2000cc-2 is titled "Judicial relief."

[30] 42 U.S.C. § 2000cc-2(b).

[31] 42 U.S.C. § 1988(b).

[32] *See* 146 CONG. REC. S7774-01, Ex. 1, S7776 (daily ed. July 27, 2000) (Joint Statement of Sen. Hatch & Sen. Kennedy on the Religious Land Use and Institutionalized Persons Act of 2000) ("The Act does not include a definition of the term 'substantial burden' because it is not the intent of this Act to create a new standard for the definition of 'substantial burden' or religious exercise. Instead, that term as used in the Act should be interpreted in reference to Supreme Court jurisprudence. Nothing in this Act, including the requirement in Section 5(g) that its terms be broadly construed, is intended to change that principle. The term 'substantial burden' as used in the Act is not intended to be given any broader interpretation than the Supreme Court's articulation of the concept of substantial burden or religious exercise.").

[33] *See* Hobbie v. Unemp't Appeals Comm'n, 480 U.S. 136 (1987); Thomas v. Review Bd. of Ind. Emp't Sec. Div., 450 U.S. 707 (1981); Sherbert v. Verner, 374 U.S. 398 (1963). The general formulation of when government action constitutes a substantial burden that derives from these unemployment compensation cases is that a substantial burden is one that places "[s]ubstantial pressure on an adherent to modify his behavior and to violate his beliefs . . . ." *Thomas* 450 U.S. at 717.

noting that although substantial burden had to be interpreted in light of the Supreme Court's free exercise jurisprudence, the Court's precedents are expressed in terms that do not fit precisely into the context of land use regulation.[34] The Court's precedents focus on government action that forces an individual to choose between following religious precepts or violating those precepts to gain a government benefit such as unemployment compensation. In the land use context, however, the Second Circuit observed that it is more appropriate to "speak of government action that directly coerces the religious institution to change its behavior, rather than government action that forces the religious entity to choose between religious precepts and government benefits."[35]

Not unsurprisingly, attempting to apply such a general formulation of what constitutes a substantial burden under RLUIPA in the context of land use regulation has resulted in the federal circuit courts of appeals expressing that formulation in various ways.[36] Further, some circuits have articulated the substantial burden test differently depending on the effect of the land use regulation at issue or the manner in which it was applied. The Seventh Circuit provides a good example.

The Seventh Circuit first explained its view of the substantial burden test in *C.L.U.B. v. City of Chicago,*[37] a 2003 case in which the court held that a substantial burden under RLUIPA should be viewed narrowly: "land-use regulation that imposes a substantial burden on religious exercise is one that necessarily bears direct, primary, and fundamental responsibility for rendering religious exercise—including the use of real property for the purpose thereof within the regulated jurisdiction generally—effectively impracticable . . . ."[38] In this view, the normal barriers facing any entity

---

[34] Westchester Day School v. Village of Mamaroneck, 504 F.3d 338, 349 (2d Cir. 2007).

[35] *Id.*

[36] *See, e.g.,* Roman Catholic Bishop of Springfield v. City of Springfield, 724 F.3d 78, 95–96 (1st Cir. 2013) (finding the tests for determining what constitutes a substantial burden used by the Fourth, Sixth, Seventh, Ninth and Eleventh Circuits to be "abstract formulations" that lacked consistency). *But see* Robert M. Bernstein, Note, *Abandoning the Use of Abstract Formulations in Interpreting RLU-IPA's Substantial Burden Provision in Religious Land Use Cases,* 36 COLUM. J. L. & ARTS, 283, 305–10 (2013) (explaining common factors that courts have considered in assessing substantial burden under RLUIPA regardless of how standard has been formulated).

[37] 342 F.3d 752 (7th Cir. 2003).

[38] *Id.* at 761.

seeking to acquire or develop property in an urban environment—"scarcity of affordable land . . . along with the costs, procedural requirements, and inherent political aspects of [regulatory] approval processes"—"do not amount to a substantial burden on religious exercise."[39]

In 2005, the Seventh Circuit revisited its interpretation of the substantial burden test in *Sts. Constantine & Helen Greek Orthodox Church, Inc. v. City of New Berlin*.[40] The church in question had applied to rezone part of its recently acquired property in a residential district from residential to institutional in order to build a new church. To address the city's concern that some other use might be developed on the rezoned parcel if the church did not build a house of worship, the church agreed that the city would promulgate a planned unit development ordinance limiting the parcel to church-related uses as a condition of the rezoning. The city council, however, still denied the rezoning, based on concerns the court found to be mistaken, and proposed alternatives that the court deemed unrealistic. Because the court found the church willing to bind itself by any means necessary not to sell the land for a nonreligious institutional use, a factor that would eliminate the city's only expressed concern, the court concluded that the church was substantially burdened.[41]

Judge Posner argued that the church had suffered a substantial burden because "[t]he [c]hurch could have searched around for other parcels of land (though a lot more effort would have been involved in such a search than, as the [planning commission] would have it, calling up some real estate agents), or it could have continued filing applications with the

---

[39] *Id.* In *San Jose Christian Coll. v. City of Morgan Hill*, 360 F.3d 1024 (9th Cir. 2004), the Ninth Circuit adopted a version of the substantial burden test that it saw as "entirely consistent" with that of the Seventh Circuit in *C.L.U.B. Id.* at 1035. *San Jose Christian College* involved a challenge to the city's denial of an application for a zoning variance that would have allowed an educational facility in an area zoned for hospitals. The application's estimates of the number of students that would use the facility were inconsistent, and the city requested additional information. The college did not provide the requested information, and the city denied the college's application. The court determined that the city's requirement did not impose a substantial burden because the city's action "merely require[d the] College to submit a *complete* application, as is required of all applicants." *Id.* (emphasis in original). *See also*, Mesquite Grove Chapel v. DeBonis, 633 Fed. App'x 906 (9th Cir. 2015) (finding no substantial burden where the primary burdens presented—relocating or submitting a modified application—were not substantial and inspector's decision was not arbitrary or made in bad faith).
[40] 396 F.3d 895 (7th Cir. 2005).
[41] *Id.* at 901.

[commission], *but in either case there would have been delay, uncertainty, and expense* [emphasis added]. That the burden would not be insuperable would not make it insubstantial."[42]

In 2006 and 2007, the Seventh Circuit decided two RLUIPA cases that provided guidance on how its previous rulings in *C.L.U.B.* and *Sts. Constantine* could be reconciled: *Vision Church v. Village of Long Grove*[43] and *Petra Presbyterian Church v. Village of Northbrook*.[44] In *Vision Church*, the village denied an annexation the church had sought so that the sanctuary it was planning to build would be in the village rather than in an unincorporated portion of the county. After a subsequent annexation resulted in the church's land being surrounded on all sides by property within the village's corporate boundaries, the village became authorized by statute to annex the church's land without the church's consent, and it did so. After the annexation, the church applied for a special use permit to construct a complex of almost one hundred thousand square feet. While that application was pending, the village amended its zoning regulations to restrict the size of "public assembly" uses, including religious institutions, depending on the acreage of the parcel where the building(s) would be located and other factors. The village then denied the church's permit application on the ground that it far exceeded the fifty-five thousand square-foot maximum allowed under the zoning amendment.[45]

The church claimed that the involuntary annexation, the conditions imposed upon the church at annexation, and the enactment of the zoning amendment substantially burdened its religious exercise.[46] The Seventh Circuit found that the conditions the village imposed on the annexation and on the grant of a special permit (*e.g.*, restrictions on size, activities and

---

[42] *Id.* Judge Posner, noting that "[a] separate provision of the Act forbids government to 'impose or implement a land use regulation in a manner that treats a religious assembly or institution on less than equal terms with a nonreligious assembly or institution,'" argued that RLUIPA's "substantial burden" provision must mean something different from "greater burden than imposed on secular institutions." *Id.* at 900.

[43] 468 F.3d 975 (7th Cir. 2006).

[44] 489 F.3d 846 (7th Cir. 2007).

[45] *Vision Church*, 468 F.3d at 981–84.

[46] The Seventh Circuit summarily rejected the involuntary annexation claim for failure to state a valid cause of action under RLUIPA because annexation is not a land use regulation as defined by the statute. *Id.* at 997–98.

hours of operation), although inconvenient, did not constitute a substantial burden and, further, ruled that the zoning amendment did not impose a substantial burden because it still allowed the church to construct a facility on the property it currently owned that would be of sufficient size to accommodate the immediate and future needs of the congregation, even if it was not of a size that the church would have preferred.[47]

In *Petra Presbyterian*, the church had made informal requests to the village concerning the rezoning of an industrially zoned warehouse property, where churches were then prohibited, so as to allow its use as a church. After receiving preliminary indications that the village viewed the rezoning favorably, the church contracted to purchase the property, but it made the sale contingent on its being permitted to use the warehouse as a church. The church then submitted formal requests for rezoning and a use permit. When the village planning commission indicated an unfavorable view, the church withdrew its application to avoid a formal denial but inexplicably went ahead and bought the warehouse and began using it as a church. When the village sought to enjoin the church from using the warehouse for worship services, the church brought a RLUIPA challenge.[48]

The court of appeals rejected the church's claim that barring them from the industrial zone was a substantial burden under RLUIPA, arguing as follows: "Religious organizations would be better off if they could build churches anywhere, but denying them so unusual a privilege could not reasonably be thought to impose a substantial burden on them."[49] The court emphasized, "[u]nless the requirement of substantial burden is taken seriously, the difficulty of proving a compelling governmental interest will free religious organizations from zoning restrictions of any kind."[50]

---

[47] *Id.* at 999–1000.
[48] *Petra Presbyterian*, 489 F.3d 846, 847–48 (7th Cir. 2007).
[49] *Id.* at 851.
[50] *Id.* The court also noted that where a church is denied the right to build in a particular zoning district, but "there is plenty of land" available elsewhere for churches to build a new church or convert an existing structure to use as a church, there is no substantial burden under RLUIPA. It distinguished the situation in *Sts. Constantine* because there, the church had brought property reasonably expecting to obtain a permit, but the village had subsequently denied the application without grounds for the denial. *Id.*

Taken together, these two rulings significantly clarified the Seventh Circuit's prior statements on the substantial burden issue. In *C.L.U.B.*, the Seventh Circuit indicated that denying a church its preferred site was not a substantial burden provided that other sites were available. At first blush, *Sts. Constantine* appeared to contradict that: the church was denied its preferred site, and other sites were available, but the Seventh Circuit found a substantial burden. *Vision Church* and *Petra Presbyterian* show that these rulings are not in conflict. In *Sts. Constantine*, the church owned property and had every reasonable expectation its application would be approved, but then was denied for no reason. In that circumstance, forcing the church to look again for a site was found to be a substantial burden. In *Petra*, the church owned the property but had acquired it *without* any reasonable expectation an application would be approved. In that circumstance, requiring it to seek another property where many were available would *not* be a substantial burden.[51] In *Vision Church*, the church owned the property but, after passage of the zoning amendment, had no reasonable expectation it could build a church of the size it wanted. Thus, when the village denied the application but arguably would allow the church a permit for a complex that would be large enough to serve the congregation's needs, there was no substantial burden under RLUIPA.

Other appellate courts, after reviewing the varying formulations adopted by different circuits, have foregone "abstract formulations" or standards and have turned to "relevant factors" or a "helpful consideration" to determine when a regulation substantially burdens religious exercise. For example, in a 2013 ruling, the First Circuit noted that it had not yet offered its own interpretation of what constituted a substantial burden under RLUIPA and then examined the tests adopted by other circuits, which it labeled as "abstract formulations" and remarked on their lack of consistency.[52] Rejecting that approach, the court declined to adopt any

---

[51] *See also* Calvary Temple Assembly of God v. City of Marinette, No. 06-C-1148, 2008 WL 2837774 (E.D. Wis. Jul. 21, 2008) (finding no substantial burden from permit denial where alternate sites where available and church could not demonstrate any financial burden resulted from its inability to use its preferred site).

[52] *See* Roman Catholic Bishop of Springfield v. City of Springfield, 724 F.3d 78, 95–96 (1st Cir. 2013). The First Circuit examined rulings from the Second, Fourth, Sixth, Seventh, Ninth, and Eleventh

(*footnote continued on next page*)

abstract test and instead identified some relevant factors that could be used in a "functional approach to the facts of a particular case," noting that it "recognize[d] different types of burdens and that such burdens may cumulate to become substantial."[53] The court then identified some factors that courts have considered relevant when determining whether a particular land use regulation constitutes a substantial burden under RLUIPA. The list, which the court stated was not intended to be exhaustive, included the following: (1) whether the regulation "appears to target a religion, religious practice, or members of a religious organization because of hostility to that religion itself"; (2) "whether local regulators have subjected the religious organization to a process that may appear neutral on its face but in practice is designed to reach a predetermined outcome contrary to the group's request"; and (3) "whether the land use restriction was 'imposed on the religious institution arbitrarily, capriciously or unlawfully.'"[54]

(footnote continued from previous page)

Circuits, including *Westchester Day School v. Vill. of Mamaroneck*, 504 F.3d 338, 349 (2d Cir. 2007) (formulating the question as whether "government action . . . directly coerces the religious institution to change its behavior" (emphasis omitted)); *Bethel World Outreach Ministries v. Montgomery Cnty. Council*, 706 F.3d 548, 566 (4th Cir. 2013) ("[A] plaintiff can succeed on a [RLUIPA] substantial burden claim by establishing that a government regulation puts substantial pressure on it to modify its behavior."); *Living Water Church of God v. Charter Twp. of Meridian*, 258 Fed. Appx. 729, 737 (6th Cir. 2007) (asking whether, "though the government action may make religious exercise more expensive or difficult, does the government action place substantial pressure on a religious institution to violate its religious beliefs or effectively bar a religious institution from using its property in the exercise of its religion?"); *C.L.U.B. v. City of Chicago*, 342 F.3d 752, 761 (7th Cir. 2003) ("[I]n the context of RLU-IPA's broad definition of religious exercise, a land use regulation that imposes a substantial burden on religious exercise is one that necessarily bears direct, primary, and fundamental responsibility for rendering religious exercise . . . effectively impracticable."); *San Jose Christian Coll. v. City of Morgan Hill*, 360 F.3d 1024, 1034 (9th Cir. 2004) ("[F]or a land use regulation to impose a 'substantial burden,' it must be 'oppressive' to a 'significantly great' extent."); *Midrash Sephardi, Inc. v. Town of Surfside*, 366 F.3d 1214, 1127 (11th Cir. 2004) (holding that substantial burden is one that "place[s] more than an inconvenience on religious exercise" and is "akin to significant pressure which directly coerces the religious adherent to conform his or her behavior accordingly").

[53] *Roman Catholic Bishop of Springfield*, 724 F.3d at 96.

[54] *Id.* at 96–97. The court noted that an arbitrary, capricious or unlawful application of a land use regulation could occur when "local regulators disregard objective criteria and instead act adversely to a religious organization based on the objections of a 'small but influential group in the community'" or where "local regulators base their decisions on misunderstandings of legal principles." *Id.* at 97 (citations omitted).

B. "Compelling Governmental Interest" and "Least Restrictive Means" Tests

Under RLUIPA, once a plaintiff demonstrates that government has imposed a substantial burden on its free exercise of religion, the burden of proof shifts to the government to justify its action by demonstrating that "imposition of the burden on that person, assembly or institution: (A) is in furtherance of a compelling interest; and (B) is the least restrictive means of furthering that compelling governmental interest."[55] This is, of course, the strict scrutiny standard for judicial review that RFRA sought to restore before it was struck down in *City of Boerne* and that RLUIPA revived. Strict scrutiny is the most demanding standard of judicial review,[56] and so legislation, including land use regulations, subjected to the strict scrutiny standard survives "only in rare cases."[57]

RLUIPA cases, and others involving challenges to land use regulations, have been decidedly mixed on the issue of what may be considered a "compelling interest." For example, in one case,[58] after the federal district court stated that traffic and parking issues "have never been deemed compelling government interests,"[59] the Second Circuit opinion vacating and remanding that decision explicitly rejected the claim that traffic concerns could never be deemed a compelling government interest.[60]

A number of courts have found that enforcing zoning regulations to protect the health and safety of a community is a compelling governmental

---

[55] 42 U.S.C. § 2000cc (a)(1).

[56] City of Boerne v. Flores, 521 U.S. 507, 534 (1997) ("Requiring a State to demonstrate a compelling interest and show that it has adopted the least restrictive means of achieving that interest is the most demanding test known to constitutional law.").

[57] Church of the Lukumi Babalu Aye, Inc. v. City of Hialeah, 508 U.S. 520, 546 (1993).

[58] Westchester Day Sch. v. Vill. of Mamaroneck, 280 F. Supp. 2d 230 (S.D.N.Y. 2003), *judgment vacated*, 386 F.3d 183 (2d Cir. 2004).

[59] *Id.* at 242 (citing Transportation Alternatives, Inc. v. City of New York, 218 F. Supp. 2d 423, 438 (S.D.N.Y. 2002) (holding that a municipality's asserted interests in traffic safety and aesthetics, while significant, have never been found compelling)); *see also* Love Church v. City of Evanston, 671 F. Supp. 515, 519 (N.D. Ill. 1987) ("While traffic concerns are legitimate, we could hardly call them compelling.").

[60] Westchester Day Sch. v. Vill. of Mamaroneck, 386 F.3d 183, 191 (2d Cir. 2004). On remand, the district court chose to assume, without determining, "that traffic constitutes a compelling interest in this instance," but then ruled that the village's denial of a special permit was not the least restrictive means of addressing that interest. 417 F. Supp. 2d 477, 551 (S.D.N.Y. 2006), *judgment aff'd*, 504 F.3d 338 (2d Cir. 2007).

interest.[61] For example, a Connecticut federal district court found that a zoning commission had established a compelling interest in enforcing the town's zoning regulations and ensuring the safety of residential neighborhoods[62] and the Ninth Circuit, in an unpublished opinion, found that promoting public safety and preventing crime was a compelling government interest.[63] In contrast, tax generation and avoiding blight were held to be less-than-compelling governmental interests,[64] as has preserving land for industrial use as required by a city's general plan.[65] It is also unlikely that aesthetics would be found to be a compelling interest under RLUIPA because that claim has been rejected in the context of content based sign regulations subjected to strict scrutiny.[66]

---

[61] *See, e.g.*, Konikov v. Orange Cnty., 302 F. Supp. 2d 1328, 1343 (M.D. Fla. 2004), *aff'd in part, rev'd in part and remanded*, 410 F.3d 1317 (11th Cir. 2005) (county had compelling interest in upholding its zoning regulations); Libolt v. Town of Irondequoit Zoning Bd. of Appeals, 885 N.Y.S.2d 806 (N.Y. App. Div. 2009) (finding that maintaining the community's single-family zoning was a compelling state interest justifying the denial of a permit to a religious order to operate a halfway house, which charged a per diem fee, in a single-family district); Greater Bible Way Temple of Jackson v. City of Jackson, 733 N.W.2d 734, 751 (Mich. 2007) (stating "[i]t has long been recognized that local governments have a compelling interest in protecting the health and safety of their communities through the enforcement of the local zoning regulations. All property is held subject to the right of the government to regulate its use in the exercise of the police power so that it shall not be injurious to the rights of the community or so that it may promote its health, morals, safety and welfare. Therefore, a municipal body clearly has a compelling interest in enacting and enforcing fair and reasonable zoning regulations") (internal quotation marks and citations omitted). *See also* Eagle Cove Camp & Conf. Ctr., Inc. v. Town of Woodboro, 734 F.3d 673 (7th Cir. 2013) (finding, in RLUIPA litigation, that a state constitutional claim was precluded because a Wisconsin jurisdiction had a compelling state interest in preserving the rural nature of property surrounding a lake). *But see* Congregation Rabbinical Coll. of Tartikov Inc. v. Vill. of Pomona, 138 F. Supp. 3d 352 (S.D.N.Y. 2015) (ruling that zoning and wetland laws that allegedly discriminated against religious congregation did not address a compelling state interest).

[62] Murphy v. Zoning Comm'n of Town of New Milford, 289 F. Supp. 2d 87 (D. Conn. 2003), *judgment vacated*, 402 F.3d 342 (2d Cir. 2005), citing Murphy v. Zoning Comm'n of Town of New Milford, 148 F. Supp. 2d 173, 191 (D. Conn. 2001).

[63] Harbor Missionary Church Corp. v. City of San Buenaventura, 642 Fed. App'x 726 (9th Cir. 2016).

[64] Cottonwood Christian Ctr. v. Cypress Redev. Agency, 218 F. Supp. 2d 1203 (C.D. Cal. 2002).

[65] Int'l Church of the Foursquare Gospel v. City of San Leandro, 632 F. Supp. 2d 925 (N.D. Cal. 2008), *rev'd*, 634 F.3d 1037 (9th Cir. 2011), *amended and superseded on denial of rehearing en banc*, 673 F.3d 1059 (9th Cir. 2011) (noting that if cities could cite reserving areas for industrial or other forms of development for purposes of revenue generation as a compelling interest, then churches, because they are tax exempt, could be excluded from any area).

[66] *See* City of Ladue v. Gilleo, 512 U.S. 43, 49 (1994); *see also* North Olmsted Chamber of Commerce v. City of North Olmsted, 86 F. Supp. 2d 755, 767 (N.D. Ohio 2000) (explaining that while traffic safety and aesthetics are substantial interests they are not compelling ones).

Even if a RLUIPA defendant can establish that it had a compelling governmental interest for its regulatory action, it still must demonstrate that the action was the least restrictive means of achieving that interest.[67] Although the outright denial of an application for land use approval poses the greatest challenge to passing the least restrictive means test,[68] the denial of an application may meet the least restrictive means test under appropriate circumstances. For example, where an applicant refused to negotiate with the county or accept any compromise to its preferred plan, a federal district court found that denial of the application met the standard.[69]

III. Equal Terms Requirement

RLUIPA provides that "[n]o government shall impose or implement a land use regulation in a manner that treats a religious assembly or institution on less than equal terms with a nonreligious assembly or institution."[70] The appellate courts' Equal Terms cases have differed as to the proper test to employ in evaluating such a challenge. A Seventh Circuit *en banc* ruling, *River of Life Kingdom Ministries v. Village of Hazel Crest*,[71] provided both an overview of the question and announced a new test for Equal Terms

---

[67] *See, e.g.*, Murphy v. Zoning Comm'n of Town of New Milford, 289 F. Supp. 2d 87 (D. Conn. 2003), *judgment vacated*, 402 F.3d 342 (2d Cir. 2005) (ruling that limiting the number of persons allowed to attend religious worship in a private home was not the least restrictive means of addressing concerns about traffic and parking because the Town could have directly addressed traffic and parking issues by restricting the number of cars and/or where they could be parked rather than limiting the number of persons who could attend). *See also* Int'l Church of the Foursquare Gospel v. City of San Leandro, 632 F. Supp. 2d 925 (N.D. Cal. 2008), *rev'd*, 634 F.3d 1037 (9th Cir. 2011), *amended and superseded on denial of rehearing en banc*, 673 F.3d 1059, 1071 (9th Cir. 2011) (ruling that seeking to reserve property desired by church for industrial purposes did not meet least restrictive means test where the city presented no evidence that it could not achieve its goals by using other property in the jurisdiction for that purpose) *and* Harbor Missionary Church Corp. v. City of San Buenaventura, 642 Fed. App'x 726 (9th Cir. 2016) (ruling that denial of a conditions use permit was not the least restrictive means when city failed to analyze whether proposed conditions could address public safety concerns).

[68] *See, e.g.*, Westchester Day Sch. v. Vill. of Mamaroneck, 417 F. Supp. 2d 477, 551 (S.D.N.Y. 2006), *judgment aff'd*, 504 F.3d 338 (2d Cir. 2007) (listing various ways traffic concerns could have been mitigated short of an outright denial of an application for a special permit).

[69] Redwood Christian Sch. v. Cnty. of Alameda, No. C-01-4282 SC, 2007 WL 2022030 (N.D. Cal. 2007) at *3.

[70] 42 U.S.C. § 2000cc (b)(1).

[71] 611 F.3d 367 (7th Cir. 2010).

challenges in a majority opinion by Judge Richard Posner that was critiqued in concurring and dissenting opinions.

Judge Posner's review of the other circuits' rulings on this question began by noting that the Eleventh Circuit, the first court to adopt an explicit test for an Equal Terms challenge,[72] had not only interpreted the language of RLUIPA's Equal Terms provision literally[73] but was unique in reading the strict scrutiny standard from the substantial burden subsection into the separate Equal Terms subsection.[74] In Posner's view, this approach, if "[p]ressed too hard . . . would give religious land uses favored treatment" because a "seemingly unequal treatment of religious uses that nevertheless is consistent with the 'strict scrutiny' standard for determining the propriety of a regulation affecting religion" would not be seen as violating the Equal Terms provision.[75]

Posner next noted that, in contrast to the Eleventh Circuit, the Third Circuit had ruled that "a regulation will violate the Equal Terms provision only if it treats religious assemblies or institutions less well than secular

---

[72] *See* Midrash Sephardi, Inc. v. Town of Surfside, 366 F.3d 1214 (11th Cir. 2004).

[73] The *Midrash Sephardi* court wrote: "a zoning ordinance that permits any 'assembly,' as defined by dictionaries, to locate in a district must permit a church to locate there as well even if the only secular assemblies permitted are hospital operating theaters, bus terminals, air raid shelters, restaurants that have private dining rooms in which a book club or professional association might meet, and sports stadiums." *Id.* at 1230–31. Subsequent Eleventh Circuit decisions followed the *Midrash Sephardi* approach; *see* Konikov v. Orange Cnty. 410 F.3d 1317, 1324–29 (11th Cir. 2005) and Primera Iglesia Bautista Hispana of Boca Raton, Inc. v. Broward Cnty., 450 F.3d 1295, 1308–10 (11th Cir. 2006).

[74] According to the Eleventh Circuit, once a RLUIPA plaintiff produces prima facie evidence of an Equal Terms violation, the government defendant bears the burden of showing that the challenged land use regulation passes strict scrutiny. *See, e.g.*, Primera Iglesia Bautista Hispana of Boca Raton, Inc. v. Broward Cnty., 450 F.3d 1295, 1308 (11th Cir. 2006). *See also* Covenant Christian Ministries, Inc. v. City of Marietta, 654 F.3d 1231 (11th Cir. 2011) (ruling that ordinance did not survive strict scrutiny under RLUIPA's Equal Terms provision).

[75] River of Life Kingdom Ministries v. Vill. of Hazel Crest, 611 F.3d at 369. Other circuits have also declined to apply strict scrutiny to Equal Terms challenges; *see, e.g.*, Centro Familiar Cristiano Buenas Nuevas v. City of Yuma, 651 F.3d 1163 (9th Cir. 2011), 1172, n.37 (declining to follow the Eleventh Circuit in reading the strict scrutiny provisions from the substantial burden subsection into the separate Equal Terms subsection). Although the federal circuits have disagreed on whether strict scrutiny applies to equal treatment claims and the nature of the inquiry they should make on such claims, they do agree that a less than Equal Terms claimant need not prove that the unequal treatment imposes a substantial burden. *See, e.g.*, Lighthouse Inst. for Evangelism, Inc. v. City of Long Branch, 510 F.3d 253 (3d Cir. 2007); Digrugilliers v. Consolidated City of Indianapolis, 506 F.3d 612 (7th Cir. 2007); Konikov v. Orange Cnty., 410 F.3d 1317 (11th Cir. 2005) (per curiam); Midrash Sephardi, Inc. v. Town of Surfside, 366 F.3d 1214 (11th Cir. 2004).

assemblies or institutions that are similarly situated as to the regulatory purpose."[76] Judge Posner argued that under the Third Circuit's approach, the court must first identify the goals of the zoning ordinance and then determine what types of secular assemblies are comparable to the religious plaintiff's assembly use "in the sense of having roughly the same relation to those goals."[77] If a religious assembly is being excluded for the same zoning reasons that apply to comparable secular assemblies, then the ordinance does not violate the Equal Terms provision. But if a religious assembly and a secular assembly don't differ in terms of their relation to the regulatory purpose in the ordinance, and the secular assembly is allowed when the religious assembly is not, then "neutrality has been violated and equality denied."[78]

Posner found neither of these tests to be satisfactory. He took issue with three aspects of the Eleventh Circuit test: (1) the definition of assembly is so broad that it encompasses many secular land uses, "even though most of them have different effects on the municipality and its residents from a church";[79] (2) "it may be too friendly to religious land uses, unduly limiting municipal regulation and maybe even violating the First Amendment's prohibition against establishment of religion by discriminating in favor of religious land uses";[80] and (3) "equality" in the land use context "signifies not equivalence or identity but proper relation to relevant concerns," then "[i]f a church and a community center, though different in many respects, do not differ with respect to any accepted zoning criterion, . . . an ordinance that allows one and forbids the other denies equality and violates the equal-terms provision."[81]

Posner also criticized the Third Circuit test, arguing that the court's "use of 'regulatory purpose' as a guide to interpretation invites speculation

---

[76] *River of Life*, 611 F.3d at 368 (quoting *Lighthouse Inst.*, 510 F.3d at 266).

[77] *River of Life*, 611 F.3d at 367, 368.

[78] *Id.* at 369.

[79] *Id.* at 370, noting: "We are troubled by the Eleventh Circuit's rule that mere 'differential treatment' between a church and some other 'company of persons collected together in one place . . . usually for some common purpose' (the court's preferred dictionary definition of 'assembly') violated the equal-terms provision" (citing *Midrash Sephardi*, 366 F.3d at 1230–31).

[80] *Id.*

[81] *Id.* at 371.

concerning the reason behind exclusion of churches; invites self-serving testimony by zoning officials and hired expert witnesses; facilitates zoning classifications thinly disguised as neutral but actually systematically unfavorable to churches (as by favoring public reading rooms over other forms of nonprofit assembly); and makes the meaning of 'Equal Terms' in a federal statute depend on the intentions of local government officials."[82] Posner then argued that the problems he identified with the Third Circuit's test "can be solved by a shift of focus from regulatory purpose to 'accepted zoning criteria'"; arguing that "'Purpose' is subjective and manipulable, so asking about 'regulatory purpose' might result in giving local officials a free hand in answering the question 'equal with respect to what?,'" whereas "'Regulatory criteria' are objective—and it is federal judges who will apply the criteria to resolve the issue."[83] But other judges on the Seventh Circuit *en banc* panel took issue with Judge Posner's view, with several concurring judges viewing the Third Circuit's "regulatory purpose" test as "equally valid"[84] or "most appropriate"[85] and one dissenting judge supporting the Eleventh Circuit's test.[86]

A subsequent Second Circuit case acknowledged the split among the circuits and noted that it was unable to define "the precise outlines of what it takes to be a valid comparator under RLUIPA's [E]qual [T]erms provision."[87] In recognition of that fact, the court shifted its focus from

---

[82] *Id.*

[83] *Id.* at 372. Applying that test to the case at hand, where the action challenged was the exclusion of a church—along with other new noncommercial uses—from an area close to the town's train station designated for revitalization as a commercial center, Judge Posner found that the designation of exclusively commercial districts was an accepted zoning criterion, noting that the village "really was applying conventional criteria for commercial zoning in banning noncommercial land uses from a part of the village suitable for a commercial district because of proximity to the train station." *Id.* at 373–74. Judge Posner readily acknowledged that the facts of this case did not pose much of a challenge to application of the "regulatory criteria" test and that the court is "likely to have cases in the future challenging zoning ordinances that are harder to classify." *Id.* at 374.

[84] *Id.* at 374. Arguing that "the 'accepted regulatory criteria test' . . . presents a risk of self-serving testimony just as the majority believes the 'regulatory purpose' approach would," *Id.* at 376–77.

[85] *Id.* at 376. Arguing that "the search by the different circuits for an entirely objective test is probably in vain." *Id.* at 374–75.

[86] *Id.* at 377–92 (finding a violation under that test). *See also* Rocky Mountain Christian Church v. Bd. of Cnty. Comm'rs of Boulder Cnty., 612 F. Supp. 2d 1163 (D. Colo. 2009), *aff'd*, 613 F.3d 1229 (10th Cir. 2010) (applying the Eleventh Circuit test and finding a violation of RLUIPA's Equal Terms provision).

[87] Third Church of Christ, Scientist of N.Y. City v. City of New York, 626 F.3d 667, 669 (2d Cir. 2010).

the "formal" differences between the religious and secular uses that were being compared—catering services at a church versus catering services at two hotels—to the question of "whether, in practical terms, secular and religious institutions are treated equally."[88] Applying that practical standard, the Second Circuit upheld the trial court's finding that the city had violated RLUIPA's Equal Terms provision when it sought to prohibit the catering services at the church.[89] But a later Fifth Circuit decision argued that the Second Circuit's ruling had, even if unintentionally, "created a fourth test—somewhat combining the Third and Seventh Circuits' tests—which identifies a comparator that is similarly situated for all 'functional intents and purposes' of the regulation."[90]

As the discussion in this section shows, there is significant disagreement as to the proper standard for evaluating an Equal Terms claim under RLUIPA both among several circuits and, occasionally, within a single circuit. Although this disagreement has provided fodder for numerous law review articles,[91] it leaves both local governments and religious institutions guessing as to what the test might be in circuits that have yet to address the issue as well as circuits such as the Seventh, where *en banc* rulings have revealed divisions among the judges on the issue, and the Second, with its undefined "practical" standard.

IV. Anti-Discrimination Requirement

RLUIPA prohibits land use regulations from being imposed or implemented "that discriminate against any assembly or institution on the basis of religion or religious denomination."[92] To state a prima facie case under this provision, a religious claimant must present evidence that a

---

[88] *Id.* at 671.

[89] *Id.* at 672–73.

[90] Elijah Group, Inc. v. City of Leon Valley, 643 F.3d 419, 423 (5th Cir. 2011).

[91] *See, e.g.,* Brian K. Mosley, Note, *Zoning Religion Out of the Public Square: Constitutional Avoidance and Conflicting Interpretations of RLUIPA's Equal Terms Provision,* 55 Ariz. L. Rev. 465 (2013); Peter T. Reed, Note, *What Are Equal Terms Anyway?* 87 Notre Dame L. Rev. 1313 (2012); Sarah Keeton Campbell, Note, *Restoring RLUIPA's Equal Terms Provision,* 58 Duke L.J. 1071 (2009).

[92] 42 U.S.C. § 2000cc (b)(2).

government engaged in intentional or purposeful discrimination either because of the claimant's denomination or merely because the claimant's activity or land use is religious rather than secular.[93] There have been relatively few RLUIPA cases involving this provision, with even fewer successful claims.[94]

A recent Second Circuit case, *Chabad Lubavitch of Litchfield County,* discussed RLUIPA's nondiscrimination provision. The court noted that "the plain text of the provision makes clear that, unlike the substantial burden and [E]qual [T]erms provisions, evidence of discriminatory *intent* is required to establish a claim."[95] Thus the nondiscrimination provision "enshrine[s]' principles announced in *Church of the Lukumi Babalu Aye, Inc. v. City of Hialeah*, which casts a jaundiced eye on laws that target religion."[96] Because *Lukumi* examined equal protection principles to determine whether a law was discriminatory, courts have looked to equal protection cases in analyzing nondiscrimination claims.[97]

The court next described the three types of equal protection violations it generally recognized: "(1) a facially discriminatory law; (2) a facially neutral statute that was adopted with a discriminatory intent and applied with a discriminatory effect (i.e., a 'gerrymandered' law); and (3) a facially neutral law that is enforced in a discriminatory manner."[98] Because the claim before it involved selective enforcement of a facially neutral statute,

---

[93] Chabad Lubavitch of Litchfield Cnty., Inc. v. Borough of Litchfield, 768 F.3d 183 (2nd Cir. 2014). *See* Church of Scientology of Georgia, Inc. v. City of Sandy Springs, 843 F. Supp. 2d 1328, 1370 (N.D. Ga. 2012) (listing cases).

[94] *Chabad Lubavitch*, 768 F.3d at 199-200 (remanding for consideration of whether claimant established a prima facie nondiscrimination claim); Muslim Cmty. Ass'n of Ann Arbor and Vicinity v. Pittsfield Charter Tp., 947 F. Supp. 2d 752 (E.D. Mich. 2013) (finding plaintiff pled sufficient facts to establish a prima facie RLUIPA discrimination claim); Irshad Learning Ctr. v. Cnty. of Dupage, 937 F. Supp. 2d 910 (N.D. Ill. 2013) (finding evidence not sufficient to support an inference that conditional-use permit was denied on the basis of religion or religious denomination); *Church of Scientology of Georgia*, 843 F. Supp. 2d 1328 (finding sufficient evidence of discrimination to support a prima facie case); Adhi Parasakthi Charitable, Medical, Educational, and Cultural Soc'y of N. Am. v. Twp. of West Pikeland, 721 F. Supp. 2d 361 (E.D. Pa. 2010) (finding claimant established a genuine issue of material fact as to whether the ordinance was discriminatorily applied).

[95] 768 F.3d at 198.

[96] *Id.* (citations omitted).

[97] *See id.* (citing Midrash Sephardi, Inc. v. Town of Surfside, 366 F.3d 1214, 1231–32).

[98] *Id.* at 199.

the court noted that Supreme Court precedents taught that courts should look "to both direct and circumstantial evidence of discriminatory intent" in such cases.[99] The court then further noted that "courts assessing discriminatory intent under RLUIPA's nondiscrimination provision have considered a multitude of factors, including a series of events leading up to a land use decision, the context in which the decision was made, whether the decision or decision-making process departed from established norms, statements made by the decision-making body and community members, reports issued by the decision-making body, whether a discriminatory impact was foreseeable, and whether less discriminatory avenues were available."[100]

Other recent decisions have also clarified that a religious claimant need not identify similarly situated comparators that have been treated more favorably in order to make a successful prima facie claim.[101]

V. Total Exclusion and Unreasonable Regulation

RLUIPA provides: "No government shall impose or implement a land use regulation that: A) totally excludes religious assemblies from a jurisdiction; or (B) unreasonably limits religious assemblies, institutions, or structures within a jurisdiction."[102] Very few cases have been decided involving RLUIPA's exclusions and limits provision.[103] The Tenth Circuit found a violation of the unreasonable limitations provision where sufficient evidence had been presented to allow a jury to conclude that a county's land use regulations had effectively deprived the plaintiff church and other religious institutions of reasonable opportunities to practice

---

[99] *Id.* (citing Vill. of Arlington Heights v. Metro. Hous. Dev. Corp., 429 U.S. 252, 266 (1977)).

[100] *Id.* (citations omitted).

[101] *See* Muslim Cmty. Ass'n of Ann Arbor and Vicinity v. Pittsfield Charter Twp., 947 F. Supp. 2d 752 (E.D. Mich. 2013) (rejecting requirement that claimant is required to identify a similarly situated comparator that received more favorable treatment to adequately plead a RLUIPA discrimination claim).

[102] 42 U.S.C. § 2000cc (b)(3).

[103] *See generally*, Comment, *The Religious Land Use and Institutionalized Persons Act: A Perspective on the Unreasonable Limitations Provision*, 78 TENN. L. REV. 531 (2011).

their religion.[104] In contrast, the Third and Seventh Circuits, among other courts, have rejected unreasonable limitation or total exclusion claims.[105]

VI. RLUIPA Procedure: Ripeness and Other Issues

Religious claimants frequently combine their RLUIPA claim(s) with any appropriate federal constitutional claims under 42 U.S.C. § 1983 for First Amendment, takings, due process, or equal protection violations, as well as any pertinent state statutory or constitutional claims.[106] Complaints typically also seek appropriate injunctive and declaratory relief, attorney's fees, and, in some cases, money damages. The federal courts of appeal have issued varying decisions on when a RLUIPA claim is ripe. The circuits that addressed the issue have applied the final decision ripeness requirement of *Williamson County Regional Planning Commission v. Hamilton Bank of Johnson City*[107] to "as-applied" RLUIPA claims,[108] but they have also

---

[104] Rocky Mountain Christian Church v. Bd. of Cnty. Comm'rs of Boulder Cnty., 605 F.3d 1081 (10th Cir. 2010). *See also*, Chabad of Nova, Inc. v. City of Cooper City, 575 F. Supp. 2d 1280 (S.D. Fla. 2008) (finding that the city's ordinances prohibiting religious assemblies from locating in business and certain other districts imposed unreasonable limitations on the ability of the assemblies either to rent or buy property for religious use).

[105] *See* Lighthouse Inst. for Evangelism Inc. v. City of Long Branch, 100 Fed. App'x 70 (3d Cir. 2004) (upholding denial of motion for preliminary injunction based on finding that city had not excluded religious uses as of right from central business district). In subsequent litigation, a split panel of the Third Circuit ruled that the ordinance in question, which had later been superseded by a district plan, did not violate RLUIPA's Equal Treatment provision. Lighthouse Inst. for Evangelism, Inc. v. City of Long Branch, 510 F.3d 253 (3d Cir. 2007). *See also* Eagle Cove Camp & Conference Ctr., Inc. v. Town of Woodboro, 734 F.3d 673 (7th Cir. 2013) (rejecting unreasonable limitations claim where ample land was available in jurisdiction for proposed use); Petra Presbyterian Church v. Vill. of Northbrook, 409 F. Supp. 2d 1001 (N.D. Ill. 2006) (denying claim of total exclusion where religious institutions, although prohibited at a church's preferred location, were allowed in district's comprising 70 percent of the land in the jurisdiction); Redwood Christian Sch. v. Cnty. of Alameda, No. C-01-4282 SC, WL 781794 (N.D. Cal. 2007) (rejecting unreasonable limitation claim where county denied plaintiff right to build a school on its preferred site but had allowed expansion of the school at its existing site, and numerous other sites for a school were available).

[106] *See* discussion of state Religious Freedom Restoration Acts, *infra* at nn. 123–146.

[107] 473 U.S. 172 (1985).

[108] *See* Guatay Christian Fellowship v. Cnty. of San Diego, 670 F.3d 957, 979 (9th Cir. 2011). Note, however, that in Yee v. City of Escondido, 503 U.S. 519, 533–34 (1992), the Court held that *Williamson Cnty.* does not apply to facial challenges. Further, exhaustion of administrative remedies is not required under *Williamson Cnty. See Guatay Christian Fellowship*, 670 F.3d at 979 (collecting cases).

held that a RLUIPA claim was ripe where plaintiffs argued that the mere enactment of a historic preservation ordinance or designation of a religious structure as historic violated the act.[109]

Although the subject is generally beyond the scope of this chapter, it is important to note that if a state agency or state employee acting in his or her official capacity is a RLUIPA defendant, RLUIPA does not of itself abrogate sovereign immunity, and therefore, money damages against a state agency or state employee acting in his or her official capacity are generally not available.[110] Municipalities, of course, are liable for damages under RLUIPA,[111] and courts have awarded significant damages to successful claimants.[112] The usual rules for lawyers regarding good litigation and professional judgment apply under RLUIPA concerning whether you should seek money damages against governmental actors in their personal capacities. Attorneys' fees are available under RLUIPA and are regularly awarded to successful claimants.[113]

VII. RLUIPA and the U.S. Department of Justice

The Department of Justice has played a significant role in the enforcement of RLUIPA.[114] A Justice Department Report issued in September 2010

---

[109] Temple B'Nai Zion, Inc. v. City of Sunny Isles Beach, 727 F.3d 1349 (11th Cir. 2013) (finding claim challenging landmark designation ripe for review); Roman Catholic Bishop of Springfield v. City of Springfield, 724 F.3d 78 (1st Cir. 2013) (finding claim challenging enactment of landmark ordinance ripe for review). *See generally,* Ryan M. Budd, *Apples to Apples: Yes, There Is (Or Can Be!) a Unified Approach to RLUIPA Ripeness,* 46 Urb. Law. 783 (2014).

[110] Sossamon v. Texas, 131 S. Ct. 1651 (2011) (holding, in a case brought under the institutionalized persons provisions of RLUIPA, that states, in accepting federal funding, do not consent to waive their sovereign immunity to private suits for money damages under RLUIPA).

[111] Centro Familiar Cristiano Buenas Nuevas v. City of Yuma, 651 F.3d 1163 (9th Cir. 2011) (holding that municipality could be liable for monetary damages under RLUIPA because the line of authority under the Eleventh Amendment which formed the basis for the Court's ruling in *Sossamon* does not apply to municipalities).

[112] *See, e.g.,* Reaching Hearts Int'l, Inc. v. Prince George's Cnty., 584 F. Supp. 2d 766 (D. Md. 2008), *judgment aff'd,* 368 Fed. App'x 370 (4th Cir. 2010) (upholding award of $3,714,822.36 in damages).

[113] *See generally* Bram Alden, Comment, *Reconsidering RLUIPA: Do Religious Land Use Protections Really Benefit Religious Land Users?* 57 UCLA L. Rev. 1779, 1810–11 (2010) (discussing awards of attorneys' fees and costs).

[114] *See generally* the department's Religious Freedom in Focus Newsletters, http://www.justice.gov/crt/spec—topics/religiousdiscrimination/newsletters.php.

stated: "The Department of Justice has used the full array of available enforcement tools to ensure the protection of religious freedom."[115] In 2016,
the Department of Justice issued a report that updated its RLUIPA land use
activities since September 2010.[116] The report noted that the department
has become involved in an increasing number of cases: since September
2010, the department has opened forty-five RLUIPA land use investigations,
compared with a total of fifty-one from 2000 to 2010, amounting to a 47%
increase in the average number of annual investigations. During that same
time, the department has filed eight RLUIPA land use lawsuits and has filed
amicus briefs in eight RLUIPA land use cases brought by private parties.[117]

VIII. Constitutional Challenges

RLUIPA has been held constitutional in the land use context in several
federal appellate cases[118] and numerous federal district court cases.[119] One

---

[115] U.S. DEP'T OF JUSTICE, CIVIL RIGHTS DIV., REPORT ON THE TENTH ANNIVERSARY OF THE RELIGIOUS
LAND USE AND INSTITUTIONALIZED PERSONS ACT, at 5 (2010), *available at* http://www.justice.gov/
crt/rluipa_report_092210.pdf. The report noted that since the enactment of RLUIPA, the department
had opened fifty-one RLUIPA investigations, filed seven RLUIPA lawsuits involving land use, filed ten
amicus briefs in private cases to inform the court about its interpretation of the law's provisions, and
intervened in private lawsuits to defend the constitutionality of RLUIPA in thirty land use cases. *Id.* at 5–6.
[116] U.S. DEP'T OF JUSTICE, UPDATE ON THE JUSTICE DEPARTMENT'S ENFORCEMENT OF THE RELIGIOUS
LAND USE AND INSTITUTIONALIZED PERSONS ACT: 2010–2016 (July 2016), *available at* https://www.
justice.gov/crt/file/877931/download. *See also* U.S. DEP'T OF JUSTICE, COMBATING RELIGIOUS DIS-
CRIMINATION TODAY: FINAL REPORT (July 2016), *available at* https://www.justice.gov/crt/file/877936/
download
[117] DEP'T OF JUSTICE, *supra* note 116, at 4. The report also noted that the department's experience in its
investigations since 2010 has reinforced the conclusion that minority groups have faced a disproportionate level of discrimination in zoning matters, reflected in the disproportionate number of suits and
investigations involving minority groups undertaken by the department. In particular, the percentage
of department RLUIPA investigations involving mosques or Islamic schools has risen dramatically in
the time since the 2010 report was issued—from 15 percent in the period from 2000 to August 2010 to
38 percent during the period from September 2010 to July 2016. Investigations involving Jewish institutions also remain disproportionate to the percentage of the overall U.S. population that is Jewish. *Id.*
[118] Westchester Day Sch. v. Vill. of Mamaroneck, 504 F.3d 338 (2d Cir. 2007); Guru Nanak Sikh Soc'y
of Yuba City v. Cnty. of Sutter, 456 F.3d 978 (9th Cir. 2006). Midrash Sephardi, Inc. v. Town of Surfside,
366 F.3d 1214 (11th Cir. 2004).
[119] Chabad Lubavitch v. Borough of Litchfield, 796 F. Supp. 2d 333 (D. Conn. 2011); Guru Nanak Sikh
Society of Yuba City v. Cnty. of Sutter, 326 F. Supp. 2d 1140 (E.D. Cal. 2003), *aff'd*, 456 F.3d 978 (9th Cir.
2006); United States v. Maui Cnty., 298 F. Supp. 2d 1010 (D. Haw. 2003); Westchester Day Sch. v. Vill.
of Mamaroneck, 280 F. Supp. 2d 230 (S.D.N.Y. 2003), *judgment vacated on other grounds*, 386 F.3d 183
(2d Cir. 2004); Murphy v. Zoning Com'n of Town of New Milford, 289 F. Supp. 2d 87 (D. Conn. 2003),

(footnote continued on next page)

federal district court declared RLUIPA to be unconstitutional in the land use context,[120] but that ruling was reversed and remanded by the Ninth Circuit in light of the court of appeals' previous holding that RLUIPA was constitutional.[121] In the land use context, no reported decision to date has found that RLUIPA violates the Establishment Clause, while in the institutionalized persons context, the Supreme Court's 2005 decision in *Cutter v. Wilkinson* upheld RLUIPA against an Establishment Clause challenge.[122]

IX. A Note on State Religious Freedom Legislation

As a result of the U.S. Supreme Court's declaration in *City of Boerne*[123] that RFRA was unconstitutional, a number of states have enacted religious freedom statutes modeled closely on that federal statute. These include the following: Arizona,[124] Arkansas,[125] Connecticut,[126] Florida,[127] Idaho,[128]

(footnote continued from previous page)

judgment vacated on other grounds, 402 F.3d 342 (2d Cir. 2005); Freedom Baptist Church of Delaware Cnty. v. Twp. of Middletown, 204 F. Supp. 2d 857 (E.D. Pa. 2002).

[120] Elsinore Christian Ctr. v. City of Lake Elsinore, 291 F. Supp. 2d 1083 (C.D. Cal. 2003), *rev'd*, 197 Fed. App'x 718 (9th Cir. 2006).

[121] Guru Nanak Sikh Soc. of Yuba City v. Cnty. of Sutter, 456 F.3d 978 (9th Cir. 2006).

[122] 544 U.S. 709 (2005).

[123] City of Boerne v. Flores, 521 U.S. 507 (1997).

[124] ARIZ. REV. STAT. § 41-1493.03 (2010). *See* Centro Familiar Cristiano Buenas Nuevas v. City of Yuma, 615 F. Supp. 2d 980 (D. Ariz. 2009) (finding that the denial of a conditional-use permit to use a building located within the city's recently redeveloped historic district did not constitute a substantial burden under RLUIPA or the Arizona Religious Freedom Restoration Act, especially because other viable locations were available).

[125] ARK. CODE § 16-123-401–407 (2015).

[126] CONN. GEN. STAT. § 52-571b (2000).

[127] FLA. STAT. ch. 761.01 to .05 (2003). *See* First Vagabonds Church of God v. City of Orlando, 578 F. Supp. 2d 1353 (M.D. Fla. 2008), *aff'd in part, rev'd in part and injunction vacated*, 610 F.3d 1274 (11th Cir. 2010), *vacated and hearing en banc granted*, 616 F.3d 1229 (11th Cir. 2010) (finding that although an ordinance may not violate the Florida RFRA, it may still be held unconstitutional in violation of First Amendment); Westgate Tabernacle, Inc. v. Palm Beach Cnty., 14 So. 3d 1027 (Fla. Ct. App. 2009), *review den.*, 22 So. 3d 539 (Fla. 2009) (holding that application of county land development code requiring that church obtain a conditional-use permit to operate homeless shelter did not violate Florida RFRA or RLUIPA); Christian Romany Church Ministries, Inc. v. Broward Cnty, 980 So. 2d 1164 (Fla. Ct. App. 2008) (holding that condemnation of church property does not violate Florida's Religious Freedom Restoration Act despite fact that church would have to find a new location for worship services).

[128] IDAHO CODE §§ 73-401 to 73-404 (2003).

Illinois,[129] Indiana,[130] Kansas,[131] Kentucky,[132] Louisiana,[133] Mississippi,[134] Missouri,[135] New Mexico,[136] Oklahoma,[137] Pennsylvania,[138] Rhode Island,[139] South Carolina,[140] Tennessee,[141] Texas,[142] Utah,[143] and Virginia.[144] In addition, Alabama amended its state constitution to require strict judicial scrutiny of religious freedom claims.[145] Although an examination of these various state statutory schemes is beyond the scope of this chapter, attorneys in states that have such statutes must consider claims under these statutes in addition to RLUIPA and/or federal or state constitutional claims.[146]

---

[129] 775 ILL. COMP. STAT. 35/1-99 (2002). *See* Irshad Learning Ctr. v. Cnty. of Dupage, 937 F. Supp. 2d 910 (N.D. Ill. 2013) (finding violation of substantial burden provisions of both RLUIPA and Illinois Religious Freedom Restoration Act); Christian Assembly Rios de Agua Viva v. City of Burbank, 948 N.E.2d 251 (Ill. Ct. App. 2011) (finding no violation of the Equal Protection Clause of the Illinois Constitution or the Illinois Religious Freedom Restoration Act where local zoning ordinance prohibited churches in an industrial zone where only uses that produce taxable income are permitted).

[130] Indiana Religious Freedom Restoration Act, SB 101, effective July 1, 2015.

[131] KAN. STAT. ANN. §§ 60-5301-60-5305 (2013).

[132] KY. REV. STAT. § 446.350 (2013).

[133] LA. REV. STAT. ANN. §§ 13:5231-13:5242 (2012).

[134] MISS. CODE § 11-16-1.

[135] MO. REV. STAT. ANN. §§ 1.302, 1.307 2004). *See also* Hanson, *Missouri's Religious Freedom Restoration Act: A New Approach to the Cause of Conscience*, 69 MO. L. REV. 853 (2004).

[136] N.M. STAT. ANN. §§ 28-22-1 to 28-22-5 (2000).

[137] OKLA. STAT. tit. 51, §§ 251 to 58 (2003).

[138] 71 PENN. STAT. § 2401 (2007). *See also* Chosen 300 Ministries, Inc. v. City of Philadelphia, No. 12–3159, 2012 WL 3235317 (E.D. Pa. 2012) (finding ban on distribution of free food to homeless within city park constituted a substantial burden under the act and that city failed to demonstrate that ban was the least restrictive means of furthering the governmental objectives sought by the city).

[139] R.I. GEN. LAWS § 42-80.1-3 (2011). *See also* New Life Worship Center v. Town of Smithfield Zoning Bd. of Review, No. 09-0924, 2010 WL 2729280 (R.I. Super. Ct. 2010) (finding no violation of the act where board denied special use permits to operate fitness facility and dance studio at private religiously affiliated high school).

[140] S.C. CODE ANN. §§ 1-32-10 to 1-32-60 (2002).

[141] TENN. CODE ANN. § 4-1-407.

[142] TEX. CIV. PRAC. & REM. CODE ANN. §§ 110.001 to 110.012 (2005). *See also* Barr v. City of Sinton, 295 S.W.3d 287 (Tex. 2009) (finding that a zoning ordinance that effectively prohibited the existence of religiously motivated halfway houses violated the Texas Religious Freedom Restoration Act).

[143] U.C.A. 1953 T. 63, Ch. 90b, UT ST T. 63, Ch. 90b (2007).

[144] VA. CODE ANN. § 57-2.02 (2013).

[145] ALA. CONST. Art. 1, § 3.01 (2004), *see* Thomas C. Berg & Frank Myers, *The Alabama Religious Freedom Amendment: An Interpretive Guide*, 31 CUMB. L. REV. 47 (2000-01).

[146] *See generally* Douglas Laycock, *State RFRAs and Land Use Regulation*, 32 U.C. DAVIS L. REV. 755 (1999). *See also* Christopher C. Lund, *Religious Liberty After Gonzalez: A Look at State RFRAs*, 55 S.D. L. REV. (2010).

X. Meeting the Challenge of RLUIPA

Each potential RLUIPA claim arises within the context of a particular site and the implementation of a specific land use code. Further, similar situations that might give rise to a RLUIPA claim can yield very different outcomes depending on the attitudes and knowledge of the parties involved. Local government reactions to potential RLUIPA claims have run the gamut from immediate, unconditional surrender at a church's mere mention of RLUIPA, to good-faith efforts at compromise, to willingness—perhaps even eagerness—to litigate the case all the way to the U.S. Supreme Court. These differing reactions are partly explained by the facts of particular RLUIPA disputes, but another critical factor is the attitude of the parties. If either or both of the parties is unwilling to acknowledge the legitimacy of, or minimizes, the other's concerns, conflict rather than compromise is the more likely outcome. Thus, for example, some religious leaders may believe that RLUIPA affords them almost *carte blanche* when it comes to complying with land use regulations. Similarly, some local officials may lack sensitivity to the legitimate needs of a particular religious group or, on rare occasion, actually view a particular religion or sect in a negative light. A final factor, as seen from the previous sections, is that the courts have differed in interpreting RLUIPA's provisions.

A. What Local Governments Can Do to Avoid a RLUIPA Claim

When facing an *actual* RLUIPA claim, local government officials need to understand that not all RLUIPA claims have merit. RLUIPA was enacted to address congressional concerns about unfair treatment of religious land uses, not to provide religious land uses with immunity from land use regulation. Local officials need to give serious consideration to any claim that a land use regulation violates RLUIPA, but if after such consideration, they decide that the claim lacks merit, they should not accede to a violation of a legitimate land use regulation merely to avoid possible litigation.

Local officials can avoid a potential RLUIPA claim both proactively and reactively. Proactively, local governments should examine their land use regulations affecting religious uses and how those regulations have been applied. At a minimum, zoning ordinances should provide reasonable locational options for new or expanding houses of worship and such accessory religious uses as schools. Although providing such options may not be particularly difficult in newer, less-developed communities, it can be a problem in older communities that are almost fully developed. Such communities may find that their current zoning effectively bans houses of worship from residential areas because no sites are available and also severely restricts their location in business and industrial areas, either because religious uses are seen as incompatible in such zones or out of concern for maintaining the city's tax base. Where locational options are effectively nonexistent or extremely limited, a local government should undertake a planning study that seeks to determine how it might accommodate the needs of religious uses without unduly harming surrounding property owners.

Local governments should also examine whether they are making adequate locational options for "social service" uses, such as shelters for the homeless or victims of domestic abuse and facilities to feed the homeless and indigent. The claims of religious institutions that a local government must allow them to "minister to the poor" at a location of their choosing are blunted when a zoning code designates reasonable locational options for both secular and religious groups to provide such services.

Historic preservation ordinances should also be reviewed. As a rule, such ordinances should not allow landmark designation of the interior of a sanctuary without the consent of the religious institution and should also contain a "hardship" exemption that could be applied to a designated structure if the church meets appropriate criteria. [147]

Local governments should also review the procedural requirements of their land use regulations to ensure that they are administered fairly and in a nondiscriminatory manner as applied to religious institutions. Officials need to make sure that land use procedures do not overtly or

---

[147] *See, e.g.*, Alan C. Weinstein, *The Myth of Ministry vs. Mortar: A Legal and Policy Analysis of Landmark Designation of Religious Institutions*, 65 TEMP. L. REV. 91, 104 (1992) (discussing issue and listing examples of hardship provisions).

inadvertently grant religious uses favorable or unfavorable treatment in the land use regulatory process and should also ensure that applications from religious uses are treated no differently than similar applications from secular uses.

Finally, local elected officials should also consider arranging for "sensitivity training" for themselves and other appropriate public employees to enhance their awareness of religious differences and the need to provide equal treatment to all religious adherents and institutions. It is far less costly to conduct such training before a lack of "sensitivity" to religious differences results in a RLUIPA claim than to do so afterward while defending such a claim.

Whereas providing specific substantive guidance on avoiding a potential claim is difficult, guidance on procedural matters is more straightforward. Local government officials and staff need to be aware that when dealing with an enforcement action or an application for a land use approval by a church, extra care is advisable, just as it is with other land uses—such as adult entertainment businesses, wireless communications towers, or signs and billboards—that have legal protection beyond the norm.

For example, when government employees and officials meet with principals or representatives of a church to discuss a land use application, they would be well advised to conclude the meeting by confirming with church officials, in writing, the points of agreement or disagreement in that discussion and then follow up with a letter or e-mail reiterating that understanding and requesting notification if there is any disagreement. This practice can help to avoid "we said/they said" disputes that could lead to litigation.

Another way of taking extra care is to establish some type of internal review process when enforcement actions target a religious use. The goal here is not to exempt churches from enforcement of land use regulations but rather to ensure that neither churches generally nor any particular church is being singled out for more frequent or severe enforcement, which could form the basis for a discriminatory treatment claim under RLUIPA. Cities should also be extremely cautious about departing from well-established precedents when handling a church's land use application. Such a departure can easily lead to a potential RLUIPA claim.[148]

The big question for local governments, of course, is how they should respond substantively when a church makes a land use application or challenges an enforcement action. The starting point for evaluating whether a potential RLUIPA claim can (or should) be avoided is to determine whether you need to be concerned about RLUIPA in the first place: Does the potential claim even fall within the protection of the statute? Remember that RLUIPA applies only to "land use regulations"—that is, zoning and historic preservation. As discussed previously, RLUIPA does not apply either to an exercise of eminent domain or to the issuance or enforcement of building or fire safety permits, permits for utility connections, and other types of "public health and safety" permits that are outside of either zoning or historical preservation codes.[149]

If a permit application or enforcement action is within the subject matter jurisdiction of RLUIPA, and a potential claimant asserts that the regulation or its implementation places a "substantial burden" on religious exercise, the next step in determining whether there could be a potential RLUIPA claim is to see whether it falls within one of RLUIPA's three jurisdictional elements: individualized assessments, affecting interstate commerce, or involving federal funding. Remember, however, that these jurisdictional elements apply only in the substantial burden section of RLUIPA and thus would not have to be satisfied if an enforcement action or denial of a permit application could be challenged as violating the Equal Terms, nondiscrimination, or exclusions and limits provisions of RLUIPA.

Most substantial burden claims under RLUIPA have relied on the "individualized assessments" element, which can easily be met when the

---

[148] For example, in *Hollywood Cmty. Synagogue, Inc. v. City of Hollywood*, 436 F. Supp. 2d 1325 (S.D. Fla. 2006), the plaintiff synagogue applied for a conditional-use permit that would allow it to use two houses on the edge of a residential district for religious worship and study. The city granted the permit but for a term of only one year, after which the application would have to be reconsidered. The city had considered many such applications in the past from both churches and secular uses and had never previously granted only a "temporary" permit. This different treatment of the plaintiff's application ultimately formed one aspect of a successful RLUIPA claim that led to a settlement in which the city paid the plaintiff $2 million in damages.

[149] *See* discussion in notes 8–10, *supra*.

church is applying for a conditional-use permit, variance, or some other form of approval where there is an opportunity for the exercise of discretion.[150] Courts have also proven to be relatively sympathetic to the claim that a substantial burden on religious exercise successfully invokes the "affects interstate commerce" jurisdictional element.[151] In short, meeting the jurisdictional element should not pose a significant problem for a religious institution as it considers a potential substantial burden RLUIPA claim.

On a substantive basis, what should local governments do—or refrain from doing—to avoid a potential RLUIPA claim when considering a permit application or an enforcement action? In very general terms, local governments have tended to prevail against RLUIPA challenges when they could demonstrate that the restrictions placed on a church do not target religious uses for discriminatory treatment, are necessary to achieve valid land use regulatory goals, and do not force the church to cease religious worship. Conversely, churches have tended to prevail when local government was unable to meet these same criteria.

Guidance becomes more difficult when we move away from those kinds of generalities. Substantial burden claims are particularly difficult in this regard. Recall that RLUIPA does not define "substantial burden." The drafters' intent was that courts define the term in line with prior precedent. That precedent strongly suggests that courts would be extremely unlikely to find that a land use regulation had imposed a substantial burden on a church. But that has not proven to be so. Although the majority of substantial burden claims have failed, courts have found in a number of cases that land use regulations indeed imposed a substantial burden on the exercise of religion.[152] As discussed previously, these differing outcomes

---

[150] *See, e.g.,* Guru Nanak Sikh Soc'y of Yuba City v. Sutter Cnty., 456 F.3d 978, 986 (9th Cir. 2006) (stating "RLUIPA applies when the government may take into account the particular details of an applicant's proposed use of land when deciding to permit or deny that use").

[151] *See, e.g.,* Cottonwood Christian Ctr. v. Cypress Redev. Agency, 218 F. Supp. 2d 1203, 1221 (C.D. Cal. 2002) ("Church activities have a significant impact on interstate commerce.").

[152] *See, e.g., Guru Nanak,* 456 F.3d 978; Elsinore Christian Ctr. v. City of Lake Elsinore, 197 F. App'x 718 (9th Cir. 2006), Sts. Constantine & Helen Greek Orthodox Church, Inc. v. City of New Berlin, 396 F.3d 895 (7th Cir. 2005); DiLaura v. Twp. of Ann Arbor, 112 F. App'x 445 (6th Cr. 2004); Living Water Church of God v. Charter Twp. of Meridian, 384 F. Supp. 2d 1123 (W.D. Mich. 2005), Castle Hills First Baptist Church v. City of Castle Hills, WL 546792 (W.D. Tex. 2004).

can be explained in part by the different ways that courts have articulated what constitutes a "substantial burden" combined with the unique factual settings of each case.

Providing guidance on avoiding a claim based on the other provisions of RLUIPA is somewhat easier. Local officials obviously need to avoid even the appearance of unequal treatment or discrimination—whether for or against—a particular church or sect and should avoid treating religious uses on less-than-equal terms with secular uses.

The best advice to local officials on how to avoid a potential RLUIPA claim may well be less legal and more just common sense: treat church representatives fairly and with respect, and try to engage in a good-faith effort to craft a reasonable compromise between the church's request and achieving the jurisdiction's land use policies. As a federal judge noted in one of the first reported RLUIPA cases, which involved a city's enforcement action to limit the number of attendees at prayer services held in a private home:

> Even absent a federal statute, one would expect that, before banning an ongoing private religious gathering, public officials in a free and tolerant society would enter into a dialogue with the participants to determine if the legitimate safety concerns of the neighbors could be voluntarily allayed. Particularly where the participants are enjoined by religious teachings to "do unto others" as they would have done unto them, it is not unreasonable to expect the parties to be able to agree on means of reducing the impact of weekly prayer meetings on this small cul-de-sac without undermining the benefit that participants seek to derive from the practice of their faith.[153]

XI. Conclusion

We are clearly in the midst of a dynamic environment socially, politically, and legally regarding the role of religion in our society. RLUIPA reflects this dynamism in the context of potential conflicts between churches and land use regulation. Congress has attempted to empower churches when they

---

[153] Murphy v. Zoning Comm'n of Town of New Milford, 148 F. Supp. 2d 173, 191 (D. Conn. 2001).

choose where and how they build a sanctuary or assemble for worship and to restrain local governments when they seek to apply zoning or landmark regulations to those churches. In this environment, local governments face a difficult task in seeking to avoid RLUIPA claims and in evaluating their likelihood of prevailing if challenged. Local officials can, however, take several steps to lessen the likelihood of a potential claim, including the following: undertaking a comprehensive review of the treatment of religious institutions in the city's land use codes, both substantively and procedurally; training officials and employees to be sensitive to religious differences; and recognizing that land use applications from and enforcement of regulations against religious institutions must be handled with special care.

7

Regulation of Sexually Oriented Businesses

Scott D. Bergthold

Law Office of Scott D. Bergthold, P.L.L.C.
Chattanooga, Tennessee

I. Introduction

It has been nearly forty years since the U.S. Supreme Court, in *Young v. American Mini-Theatres, Inc.*, first authorized cities to employ land use controls to address the "admittedly serious problems" caused by sexually oriented businesses.[1] Since then, hundreds of local governments have adopted zoning, licensing, and conduct regulations to address the negative secondary effects of adult businesses, including adverse impacts on surrounding properties and crimes such as prostitution, sexual trafficking, and illegal narcotics. The plethora of resulting case law has produced a detailed, if winding, roadmap for communities to follow in drafting and defending their ordinances. Communities that have followed that detailed roadmap have generally prevailed in court. This chapter is intended to help practitioners draft and defend regulations that successfully address secondary effects while satisfying constitutional standards. Whereas this chapter addresses the zoning and licensing of sexually oriented businesses broadly, chapter 8 deals with the particular problems of erotic dancing and entertainment.

---

[1] 427 U.S. 50, 71 (1976).

II. Legal Backdrop for Zoning Sexually Oriented Businesses

A. *Young*

In *Young*, the operators of two adult theaters in Detroit challenged the city's ordinances that required adult theaters—defined with reference to the content of films shown—to be licensed and to be located at least one thousand feet from any two other "regulated uses," including other adult theaters, taverns, pool halls, and similar commercial establishments. Based on the substantial justifications given by Detroit's Common Council,[2] the district court granted summary judgment for the city.[3] The Sixth Circuit reversed, holding that the ordinances were content based prior restraints on speech and were not justified by "establishing that they were designed to serve a compelling public interest."[4]

On certiorari, the Supreme Court reversed. Justice Stevens expressed the opinion of five members of the Court that (1) the ordinance was not vague for failing to specify exactly how much of a film must be sexual in nature before the film could be said to be "characterized by an emphasis" on sex (the plaintiff theaters regularly featured erotic films and thus fell within the core of the regulation); (2) the plaintiffs did not have standing to assert First Amendment rights of third parties because the threat of impermissible applications was not "real and substantial" and the ordinance could be narrowly construed by state courts, and (3) the licensing and zoning ordinances were not prior restraints on speech but valid means of protecting the quality of life in neighborhoods through proper planning.[5]

Four of the five justices voting to uphold the ordinances joined Part III of the opinion, in which they concluded that the content of sexually explicit adult films could, without violating equal protection principles,

---

[2] *Id.* at 55 ("In the opinion of urban planners and real estate experts who supported the ordinances, the location of several such businesses in the same neighborhood tends to attract an undesirable quantity and quality of transients, causes an increase in crime, especially prostitution, and encourages residents and businesses to move elsewhere.").

[3] *Id.* at 55–56.

[4] *Id.* at 57 (quoting Nortown Theater, Inc. v. Gribbs, 518 F.2d 1014, 1019–20 (6th Cir. 1975)).

[5] *Id.* at 52–63.

justify regulating adult theaters differently from other motion picture theaters. Noting that even nonobscene pornographic films are worthy of less protection than the untrammeled political debate at the core of the First Amendment, the plurality held that Detroit's interest in preserving the quality of life in neighborhoods was more than adequate justification for its zoning regulation.[6]

Justice Powell's important fifth vote rested not on the lower value of sexually explicit speech but rather on the straightforward application of *United States v. O'Brien*[7] to Detroit's attempt to curb the negative secondary effects of problematic businesses. He distinguished between true "speakers" and those who are simply exploiting the speech of others for profit. The free flow of ideas from speakers to their audiences is the First Amendment's central concern, and in Justice Powell's eyes, Detroit's ordinance had only an incidental impact on that. Justice Powell concluded that the regulation was properly subject to *O'Brien*'s four-part test,[8] which it easily satisfied.

According to Justice Powell, under the *O'Brien* analysis, the Court had "broadly sustained the power of local municipalities to utilize land use regulation[s]"[9] in order to protect citizens' quality of life. Moreover, the governmental interests supporting the ordinances were "both important and substantial. Without stable neighborhoods, both residential and commercial, large sections of a modern city quickly can turn into an urban jungle with tragic consequences to social, environmental, and economic values."[10] Detroit's content based classification of theaters was justified because only adult theaters tended to cause the deleterious effects. The government's interest in stable neighborhoods was unrelated to the suppression of any message.[11] Finally, per Justice Powell, the impact on expression was

---

[6] *Id.* at 71–72 (plurality opinion).

[7] 391 U.S. 367, 377 (1968) ("[A] government regulation is sufficiently justified if it is [1] within the constitutional power of the Government; [2] if it furthers an important or substantial governmental interest; [3] if the governmental interest is unrelated to the suppression of free expression; and [4] if the incidental restriction on alleged First Amendment freedoms is no greater than is essential to the furtherance of that interest.").

[8] *Young*, 427 U.S. at 80 (Powell, J., concurring).

[9] *Id.* at 73 (Powell, J., concurring).

[10] *Id.* at 80 (Powell, J., concurring).

[11] *Id.* at 81 (Powell, J., concurring).

incidental and no more than necessary to further the government's interest in protecting neighborhoods.[12]

B. *City of Renton*

Ten years after *Young*, a solid majority of the Supreme Court applied Justice Powell's analysis to uphold another adult business zoning ordinance against constitutional attack. In *City of Renton v. Playtime Theatres, Inc.*,[13] the Court concluded that Renton, Washington's adult theater zoning ordinance—although regulating based on the content of the films shown—targeted the negative land use impacts of adult theaters and thus "is completely consistent with our definition of 'content-neutral' speech regulations as those that 'are *justified* without reference to the content of the regulated speech."[14] The ordinance was analyzed as a content neutral time, place, and manner regulation and subjected to only intermediate scrutiny.[15]

Because Renton's stated purpose was to prevent the secondary effects of sexually oriented businesses on neighborhoods, the Court concluded that the ordinance served a substantial government interest. In doing so, the Court rejected the lower court's reasoning that Renton's failure to conduct a local study or demonstrate the impacts of adult theaters in Renton nullified the city's claim that substantial government interests justified the ordinance. The Supreme Court held that

> [t]he First Amendment does not require a city, before enacting such an ordinance, to conduct new studies or produce evidence independent of that already generated by other cities, so long as whatever evidence the city relies upon is *reasonably believed to be relevant* to the problem that the city addresses.[16]

---

[12] *Id.*

[13] 475 U.S. 41 (1986).

[14] *Id.* at 48 (quoting Va. Pharmacy Bd. v. Va. Citizens Consumer Council, Inc., 425 U.S. 748, 771 (1976)) (emphasis added).

[15] *Id.* at 49–50 ("The appropriate inquiry in this case, then, is whether the Renton ordinance is designed to serve a substantial government interest and allows for reasonable alternative avenues of communication."); *but see* Reed v. Town of Gilbert, 135 S. Ct. 2218 (2015) (applying strict scrutiny to town's content based sign code, regardless of sign code's allegedly benign purpose).

[16] *Id.* at 51–52 (emphasis added).

And although Renton had relied on nearby Seattle's experiences, the Court concluded that Renton's choice of a different kind of zoning regulation than Seattle chose was irrelevant because both regulations served the same substantial interest—limiting secondary effects.[17]

Finally, the Court turned to the question of whether the Renton ordinance allowed for "reasonable alternative avenues of communication."[18] The Court concluded that the ordinance easily met that standard because approximately 520 acres, more than 5 percent of Renton's land mass, was open to adult theaters. Although the theaters claimed that "practically none" of the land was for sale or lease and that none of the available sites were "commercially viable," the Court concluded that even if true, these circumstances would not prove the city's regulation defective.[19] Adult theaters "must fend for themselves in the real estate market, on an equal footing with other prospective purchasers and lessees . . . ."[20] According to the Court, market forces do not make a law unconstitutional because the First Amendment is concerned with legal, not economic, impact.[21]

C. *Alameda Books*

In *City of Los Angeles v. Alameda Books*, the Court dealt with a zoning regulation that prohibited an adult arcade use and an adult bookstore use from remaining under the same roof.[22] In that case, the sole study on which the City relied had reviewed only concentrations of separate adult businesses in a given neighborhood. The government *admitted* that the study did not address any secondary effects from a single adult business, whether a single adult use or a "combination" of adult uses.[23]

Because the city admitted that the study did not address harms from individual structures containing adult use(s), the case turned on whether the city could rely on an *inference* drawn from the study. Reversing the lower

---

[17] *Id.* at 52.
[18] *Id.* at 50.
[19] *Id.* at 53–54.
[20] *Id.* at 54.
[21] *Id.* at 54 (quoting Young v. American Mini-Theatres, Inc., 427 U.S. 50, 78 (Powell, J., concurring)).
[22] 535 U.S. 425 (2002).
[23] *Id.* at 437–39 (plurality opinion).

courts and reiterating the deferential *Renton* standard, the Court held that the government could rely on a reasonable inference drawn from the study.[24] It was in this context of relying on an inference—not evidence directly relevant to the targeted harm—that the plurality introduced a burden-shifting procedure to test whether the low *Renton* standard has been met:

> In *Renton*, we specifically refused to set such a high bar for municipalities that want to address merely the secondary effects of protected speech. We held that a municipality may rely on any evidence that is "reasonably believed to be relevant" for demonstrating a connection between speech and a substantial, independent government interest. This is not to say that a municipality can get away with shoddy data or reasoning. The municipality's evidence must fairly support the municipality's rationale for its ordinance. If plaintiffs fail to cast direct doubt on this rationale, either by demonstrating that the municipality's evidence does not support its rationale or by furnishing evidence that disputes the municipality's factual findings, the municipality meets the standard set forth in *Renton*. If plaintiffs succeed in casting doubt on a municipality's rationale in either manner, the burden shifts back to the municipality to supplement the record with evidence renewing support for a theory that justifies its ordinance.[25]

The explicit purpose of the plurality's burden-shifting procedure is to ensure that the government "meets the standard set forth in *Renton*," which may be met, as in *Renton* itself, by reliance on prior judicial decisions affirming the secondary effects basis for adult zoning regulations. The *Alameda Books* plurality also emphasized that *Renton* does not require "empirical data"[26] and that its procedure for testing inferences drawn from indirectly relevant information does not "raise the evidentiary bar"[27] above *Renton's* low standard of "any evidence reasonably believed to be relevant."

Justice Kennedy's concurrence in *Alameda Books* addressed two issues: (1) "what proposition does a city need to advance in order to sustain a

---

[24] *Id.* at 437–38.
[25] *Id.* at 438–39 (internal citations omitted).
[26] *Id.* at 439.
[27] *Id.* at 441.

secondary effects ordinance?" and (2) "how much evidence is required to support the proposition?"[28] He explicitly agreed with the plurality's answer to the second question—that the low *Renton* standard applies and that cities may rely on any evidence "reasonably believed to be relevant" when regulating to prevent the negative secondary effects of adult businesses.[29] With regard to the first issue, Justice Kennedy opined that a municipality's rationale need only advance "some basis" to show that its ordinance "may reduce the costs of secondary effects";[30] however, the rationale of possible secondary effects reduction cannot be *premised* upon the forced closure of adult businesses.[31]

Thus, the discussion by Justice Kennedy about seeking a reduction in secondary effects "while leaving the quantity and accessibility of speech substantially intact"[32] does not concern a new evidentiary standard or heightened narrow tailoring analysis. Rather, it concerns "the necessary rationale for applying intermediate scrutiny" instead of strict scrutiny, namely, "the promise that zoning ordinances like this one may reduce the costs of secondary effects without substantially reducing speech."[33]

D. Appellate Cases Since *Alameda Books*

The vast majority of appellate cases decided in the wake of *Alameda Books* have not viewed Justice Kennedy's fifth, and controlling, opinion as substantially changing the standard for regulating sexually oriented businesses, whether through zoning or other types of regulations. The Ninth Circuit explained that "[a]ll five Justices in the *Alameda Books* majority affirmed *Renton's* core principle that local governments are not required to conduct their own studies in order to justify an ordinance designed to combat the secondary effects of adult businesses."[34] In a case challenging

---

[28] *Id.* at 449 (Kennedy, J., concurring in judgment).
[29] *Id.* at 451.
[30] *Id.* at 450.
[31] *Id.* at 451.
[32] *Id.* at 449.
[33] *Id.* at 450.
[34] World Wide Video of Washington, Inc. v. City of Spokane, 368 F.3d 1186 (9th Cir. 2004).

restrictions on hours of operation for adult businesses, that same court observed that Justice Kennedy's "proportionality" language means only that a "city's rationale cannot be that when it requires businesses to disperse (or concentrate), it will force the closure of a number of those businesses, thereby reducing the quantity of protected speech."[35] In a nude dancing case, the Eighth Circuit noted that there is

> [n]othing to suggest that [Justice Kennedy] has retreated from his votes in *Barnes* [*v. Glen Theatre*] and *Pap's* [*A.M. v. City of Erie*]. In these circumstances, we conclude that the Court's holding in *Pap's* is still controlling regarding the deference to be afforded local governments that decide to ban live nude dancing.[36]

Indeed, "some courts have questioned whether Justice Kennedy's proportionality test has any logical application at all where, as here, the restrictions at issue do not relate to zoning but instead pertain to the clothing and activities within the business itself."[37] The Georgia Supreme Court emphasized that "this Court and the United States Supreme Court have explained that it is not necessary for a local government to prove that the negative secondary effects it reasonably fears, based on evidence of problems experienced elsewhere, have already been experienced locally."[38]

Thus, state and federal appellate courts have continued to apply the *Renton–Alameda Books* standard to afford substantial deference to local governments that rely on evidence "reasonably believed to be relevant" to their substantial government interest in preventing the negative secondary effects of sexually oriented businesses.[39]

---

[35] Ctr. for Fair Pub. Pol'y v. Maricopa Cnty., 336 F.3d 1153, 1163 (9th Cir. 2003).

[36] SOB, Inc. v. Cnty. of Benton, 317 F.3d 856, 863–64 (8th Cir. 2003) (citing Barnes v. Glen Theatre, Inc., 501 U.S. 560 (1991) and Pap's A.M. v. City of Erie, 529 U.S. 277 (2000)).

[37] *See* Ocello v. Koster, 354 S.W.3d 187, 213 (Mo. 2011) (citing Fantasy Ranch, Inc. v. City of Arlington, 459 F.3d 546, 562 (5th Cir. 2006); Ctr. for Fair Pub. Policy v. Maricopa Cnty., 336 F.3d 1153, 1162 (9th Cir. 2003)).

[38] Oasis Goodtime Emporium I, Inc. v. City of Doraville, 773 S.E.2d 728, 738 (Ga. 2015).

[39] Peek-A-Boo Lounge of Bradenton, Inc. v. Manatee Cnty., 630 F.3d 1346 (11th Cir. 2011); Sensations, Inc. v. City of Grand Rapids, 526 F.3d 291 (6th Cir. 2008); Trop, Inc. v. City of Brookhaven, 764 S.E.2d 398 (Ga. 2014); Ocello v. Koster, 354 S.W.3d 187 (Mo. 2011).

III. Types of Zoning Regulations for Sexually Oriented Businesses

By far, the most common form of adult business zoning regulation is the dispersal method approved by the Supreme Court in *Young*. This approach generally requires adult businesses to be separated by a certain distance from each other and from specified sensitive land uses, such as churches, schools, and residential neighborhoods. If—after objective zoning district and separation requirements are accounted for—the regulation provides for reasonable alternative sites for adult businesses, a court will usually uphold such a regulation as a valid exercise of the zoning power.[40]

Instead of dispersing sexually oriented businesses, some municipalities have sought to control adult uses by concentrating them in a particular area. In *Northend Cinema, Inc. v. City of Seattle*,[41] the Supreme Court of Washington upheld Seattle's zoning regulation that required adult uses to locate in particular downtown areas. A few years later, the City of Renton relied on this decision in defending its own adult use zoning ordinance. In upholding the Renton ordinance, the U.S. Supreme Court found it of little consequence that Renton decided to disperse, instead of concentrate, adult uses: "Seattle's choice of a different remedy to combat the secondary effects of adult theaters does not call into question either Seattle's identification of those secondary effects or the relevance of Seattle's experience to Renton."[42]

---

[40] *See, e.g.*, City of Renton v. Playtime Theatres, Inc., 475 U.S. 41 (1986) (requiring only separation from sensitive uses); Ambassador Books & Video, Inc. v. City of Little Rock, 20 F.3d 858 (8th Cir. 1994); Hart Bookstores, Inc. v. Edmistein, 612 F.2d 821 (4th Cir. 1979); SDJ, Inc. v. City of Houston, 636 F. Supp. 1359 (S.D. Tex. 1986), *aff'd*, 837 F.2d 1268 (5th Cir. 1988), *cert. denied*, 489 U.S. 1052 (1989); S & G News, Inc. v. City of Southgate, 638 F. Supp. 1060 (E.D. Mich. 1986), *aff'd*, 819 F.2d 1142 (6th Cir. 1987); Function Junction, Inc. v. Daytona Beach, 705 F. Supp. 544 (M.D. Fla. 1987); K. Hope Inc. v. Onslow Cnty., 911 F. Supp. 890 (E.D.N.C. 1995); Town of Islip v. Caviglia, 540 N.E.2d 215, 225–26 (N.Y. 1989); City of National City v. Wiener, 3 Cal. 4th 832, 838 P.2d 223 (Cal. 1992) (en banc); Stringfellow's of N.Y., Ltd. v. City of New York, 694 N.E.2d 407 (N.Y. 1998).
[41] 585 P.2d 1153 (1978).
[42] *City of Renton*, 475 U.S. at 52 (1986).

However, because the common opinion of land use planners is that concentrating adult uses tends to exacerbate, rather than ameliorate, their collective negative effects,[43] cities seldom employ this approach.[44]

IV. The Requirement of Allowing Reasonable Alternative Avenues of Communication

Generally, a city may not employ an adult use zoning ordinance that effectively precludes adult businesses from locating within the city.[45] In *Keego Harbor Co. v. City of Keego Harbor*,[46] the Sixth Circuit concluded that not all municipalities must provide an area for adult entertainment. Nevertheless, the court invalidated an ordinance passed by a city of three thousand people because it had the effect of totally prohibiting adult uses in the city and because the city had failed to establish a legislative record demonstrating a need for the ordinance.

The courts have not, however, gone so far as to require that every tiny town provide a zone in which adult businesses may locate.[47] The New Jersey Supreme Court, in *Township of Saddle Brook v. A.B. Family Center, Inc.*,[48] upheld a state statute[49] prohibiting sexually oriented businesses from locating within one thousand feet of another sexually oriented business or a predefined "sensitive" land use.[50] Although the effect of the statute was to

---

[43] *See Function Junction*, 705 F. Supp. at 547 ("[S]tudies show strong evidence that the central location of adult uses, like the 'Combat Zone' in Boston, causes the blighted area to grow and creates blight in fringe areas.").

[44] *But see* Alexander v. City of Minneapolis, 928 F.2d 278 (8th Cir. 1991) (upholding ordinance that restricted adult businesses to a single central district).

[45] *See* Schad v. Borough of Mount Ephraim, 452 U.S. 61 (1981).

[46] 657 F.2d 94 (6th Cir. 1981).

[47] *See* Peterson v. City of Florence, Minn., 727 F.3d 839 (8th Cir. 2013) (upholding prohibition on commercial uses, including adult uses, in tiny municipality where land in county provided reasonable alternative avenues of communication).

[48] 722 A.2d 530 (N.J. 1999).

[49] N.J. STAT. § 2C:34-7a. (2001) ("Except as provided in a municipal zoning ordinance adopted pursuant to N.J.S.2C:34-2, no person shall operate a sexually oriented business within 1,000 feet of any existing sexually oriented business, or any church. . . .").

[50] Sensitive uses generally include churches and other houses of worship, schools, residential neighborhoods, and so forth. Distance requirements designed to protect sensitive uses generally present no problems, provided that the requirement is reasonable *and* the sensitive use is defined. *See, e.g.*, Harris Books, Inc. v. City of Santa Fe, 647 P.2d 868 (1982) (invalidating zoning ordinance on the grounds that, as interpreted, "residential area" was unconstitutionally vague).

prohibit adult businesses from locating within the township's boundaries, the court determined that the relevant real estate market could include available sites for adult businesses in the surrounding vicinity and remanded the case for a determination of reasonableness. The same court more recently determined that the "relevant real estate market" could include land in an adjacent state.[51]

Issues concerning the quality and quantity of sites that must be legally available—and even how to define "available"—have been extensively litigated, and the decisions are as varied as the geographies of the municipalities involved in those cases.

A. Whether Sites Are "Available"

In *Renton*, the Supreme Court found that reasonable alternative avenues of communication were available because "the ordinance leaves some 520 acres, or more than five percent of the entire land area of Renton, open to use as adult theater sites."[52] It was constitutionally irrelevant to the Court that (1) much of the legally available land was already occupied, (2) almost none of the undeveloped land was for sale or lease, and (3) there were generally no sites that were commercially viable for adult theaters. The Court noted that these market conditions did not affect the constitutionality of the city's zoning ordinance:

> That respondents must fend for themselves in the real estate market, on an equal footing with other prospective purchasers and lessees, does not give rise to a First Amendment violation. And although we have cautioned against the enactment of zoning regulations that have the "effect of suppressing, or greatly restricting access to, lawful speech," we have never suggested that the First Amendment compels the Government to ensure that adult theaters, or any other kinds of speech-related businesses for that matter, will be able to obtain sites at bargain prices. "The inquiry for First Amendment purposes is not concerned with economic impact."[53]

---

[51] *See* Borough of Sayreville v. 35 Club LLC, 33 A.3d 1200 (N.J. 2012).
[52] City of Renton v. Playtime Theatres, Inc., 475 U.S. 41, 53 (1986).
[53] *Id.* at 54 (internal citations omitted).

The bottom line, the Court stated, is that the First Amendment requires only that the city refrain from denying adult businesses a reasonable opportunity to open and operate within the city—and Renton's ordinance clearly met that standard. Since *Renton,* many courts have upheld local ordinances over the objections of adult business owners who claimed that "commercial viability" analysis eliminated a number of the legally available sites, such that the remaining sites were insufficient under the *Renton* test.[54]

Nevertheless, a number of lower courts have struggled with defining the limits of *Renton's* deferential standard. In a series of cases entitled *Woodall v. City of El Paso,*[55] the plaintiffs challenged the city's position that the sites available for relocating all thirty-nine existing adult businesses were suitable locations. At trial, the jury—following an instruction that was lifted from the language of *Renton*—returned a verdict for the city. The Fifth Circuit reversed, holding that the jury should also have been instructed that although commercial viability is irrelevant, "land with physical characteristics that render it unavailable for *any* kind of development, or legal characteristics that exclude adult businesses, may not be considered 'available' for constitutional purposes under *Renton.*"[56] Specifically, the court drew a line between economic viability within a real estate market and the very existence of a commercial real estate market in the legally available areas:

> When *Renton* stated that the theater owners "must fend for themselves in the real estate market, on an equal footing with other prospective

[54] *See, e.g.,* Ambassador Books & Videos, Inc. v. City of Little Rock, 20 F.3d 858, 864–865 (8th Cir. 1994) (6.75 percent sufficient, despite relocation costs); Lakeland Lounge of Jackson v. City of Jackson, 973 F.2d 1255 (5th Cir. 1992) (upholding ordinance that allowed for 1.2 percent of the city's land for adult uses); Alexander v. City of Minneapolis, 928 F.2d 278, 284 (8th Cir. 1991); 3570 E. Foothill Blvd., Inc. v. City of Pasadena, 912 F. Supp. 1257 (C.D. Cal. 1995) (less than 1 percent, but containing twenty-six sites, sufficient where city had only one adult use); SDJ, Inc. v. City of Houston, 636 F. Supp. 1359, 1370–73 (S.D. Tex. 1986); S & G News, Inc. v. City of Southgate, 638 F. Supp. 1060 (E.D. Mich. 1986) (availability of 2.3 percent of county land sufficient); PA N.W. Distrib. v. Zoning Hearing Bd., 555 A.2d 1368, 1372 (Pa. Cmwlth. 1989); Town of Islip v. Caviglia, 540 N.E.2d 215, 220 (N.Y. 1989).
[55] Woodall v. City of El Paso, 49 F.3d 1120 (5th Cir. 1995) (*Woodall III*); Woodall v. City of El Paso, 959 F.2d 1305 (5th Cir. 1992) (*Woodall II*); Woodall v. City of El Paso, 950 F.2d 255 (5th Cir. 1992) (*Woodall I*).
[56] Woodall II, 959 F.2d at 1306 (emphasis added).

purchasers and lessees," the Court obviously contemplated that there was a "market" in which businesses could purchase or lease real property on which business could be conducted.[57]

On retrial, the adult businesses won a jury verdict, but the Fifth Circuit again reversed because the city had shown as a matter of law that it provided a sufficient number of sites. Specifically, the city had shown that *some* commercial business could locate on the proffered sites, but the jury had erroneously concluded that the fact that an *adult* business could not profit at those sites rendered the sites "unavailable."[58] The court defined physical availability in terms of "the cost of altering or developing the area to change its physical characteristics to make it suitable for some generic commercial enterprise."[59] As long as that cost is not an unreasonable obstacle for some generic commercial business to overcome, the site will be deemed available, even if the site would prove economically unfeasible for an *adult* business.[60] Some land that the court identified as truly unavailable included land under oceans, airstrips of airports, sports stadiums, areas not readily accessible to the public, and "areas developed in a manner unsuitable for any generic commercial business."[61]

Similarly, after surveying several cases decided under *Renton*, the Eleventh Circuit stated:

We can resolve this case with the aid of a few general rules. First, the economic feasibility of relocating to a site is not a First Amendment concern. Second, the fact that some development is required before a site can accommodate an adult business does not mean that the land

---

[57] *Id.* (citations omitted).
[58] *Woodall III*, 49 F.3d at 1123 ("In any event, the [a]dult [b]usinesses' evidence overwhelmingly concerned whether a topless bar could expect to make a reasonable profit at a particular site. It is plain after a thorough review of the record that the jury decided this case based on a misapprehension of the questions presented to it.").
[59] *Id.* at 1124.
[60] *Id.*
[61] *Id.* (citing Topanga Press, Inc. v. City of Los Angeles, 989 F.2d 1524 (9th Cir. 1993); *cf.* Playtime Theatres, Inc. v. City of Renton, 748 F.2d 527, 534 (9th Cir. 1984), *rev'd* 475 U.S. 41 (1986)) (noting that part of the 520 acres identified as available contained a sewage treatment facility, an oil tank farm, a group of industrial buildings, warehouses, and a fully developed shopping mall).

is, *per se*, unavailable for First Amendment purposes. The ideal lot is often not to be found. Examples of impediments to the relocation of an adult business that may not be of a constitutional magnitude include having to build a new facility instead of moving into an existing building; having to clean up waste or landscape a site; bearing the costs of generally applicable lighting, parking, or green space requirements; making due with less space than one desired; or having to purchase a larger lot than one needs. Third, the First Amendment is not concerned with restraints that are not imposed by the government itself or the physical characteristics of the sites designated for adult use by the zoning ordinance. It is of no import under *Renton* that the real estate market may be tight and sites currently unavailable for sale or lease, or that property owners may be reluctant to sell to an adult venue.[62]

Several courts are in accord, applying these or similar principles to uphold zoning restrictions for adult businesses.[63] This is because "[t]he proper enquiry looks to restrictions imposed by the government, not the market effects of other people's commerce or the economics of site clearance."[64]

B. Whether the Available Sites Are Sufficient

In determining whether a zoning scheme provides for reasonable alternative avenues of communication for adult businesses, courts will generally look at one of—or a combination of—three factors: (1) the number of adult businesses seeking sites versus the number of available sites under the zoning ordinance, (2) the percentage of commercial and industrial land zoned for adult businesses, and (3) the ratio between the number of adult use sites and the residential population of the relevant market. The first of these approaches is the dominant approach among the lower courts, followed by the second. The third approach is used only rarely.

---

[62] David Vincent, Inc. v. Broward Cnty., 200 F.3d 1325, 1334–35 (11th Cir. 2000).

[63] *See, e.g.,* Lund v. City of Fall River, 714 F.3d 65 (1st Cir. 2013); Allno Enterprises, Inc. v. Baltimore Cnty., 10 Fed. App'x 197 (4th Cir. 2001); Bronco's Entm't, Ltd. v. Charter Twp. of Van Buren, 421 F.3d 440, 452 (6th Cir. 2005); Blue Canary Corp. v. City of Milwaukee, 270 F.3d 1156, 1158 (11th Cir. 2001).

[64] *Lund,* 714 F.3d at 70; *but see* Lim v. City of Long Beach, 217 F.3d 1050, 1055 (9th Cir. 2000) (holding that currently occupied sites that are subject to *long-term* leases may not count because there may not be a "genuine possibility" of the sites becoming available, even though the long-term leases are created by private parties, not the government).

As one federal appellate court explained, under *Renton*, the question "is simply whether the ordinance denies '[plaintiff]s a reasonable opportunity to open and operate an adult [business] within the city[.]'"[65] This question, "by its terms, is fact-intensive."[66] Although "percentages or formulas can be relevant to the outcome," that "does not mean that the same percentage or formula governs in every case. The First Amendment does not prescribe a Uniform Zoning Code."[67]

In the *Woodall* trilogy and in subsequent cases, the trend has been to emphasize not the percentage of land available but, rather, the number of adult businesses seeking to locate (or relocate) and the number of spaces legally available for them.[68] If the number of sites available is greater than the number of adult businesses looking for sites, it would seem logical that the alternative avenues of communication are reasonable because no adult business is foreclosed from competing in the real estate market with other commercial enterprises.[69] The converse is also true: when a zoning ordinance provides fewer sites than the number of adult businesses needing sites, it will not satisfy *Renton*'s requirement of sufficient alternative sites.[70]

Courts have made "reasonableness" determinations under *Renton* according to a variety of standards.[71] As one court put it succinctly, there

---

[65] Big Dipper Entm't, LLC v. City of Warren, 641 F.3d 715, 718 (6th Cir. 2011) (quoting *Renton*, 475 U.S. at 54).

[66] *Id.* at 719.

[67] *Id.* at 718–19.

[68] *See, e.g., Big Dipper Entm't*, 641 F.3d at 720 ("So we are left with 27 as the number of sites available for Big Dipper's business. Meanwhile, it is undisputed that a total of two applications for adult businesses were filed in the city of Warren during the five years leading up to this lawsuit. That fact makes this case different from others on which Big Dipper relies. A supply of sites more than 13 times greater than the five-year demand is more than ample for constitutional purposes. The district court was correct to grant summary judgment on this claim.").

[69] *Woodall III*, 49 F.3d at 1127 ("However, even assuming that there was sufficient evidence to support findings that all the aforementioned areas were actually unavailable, the Ordinances still left a sufficient area physically and legally available for at least forty adult businesses to operate simultaneously in 1988, and for significantly more in 1992. When we compare this with the jury's findings that there were 39 adult businesses in operation in 1988 and only 22 in 1992, we see that, as a matter of arithmetic, there were at all relevant times more "reasonable" sites available than businesses with demands for them. The Ordinances therefore afforded the adult businesses adequate alternative means of communication.").

[70] Fly Fish, Inc. v. City of Cocoa Beach, 337 F.3d 1301, 1312 (11th Cir. 2003) ("As a result of these events, the City's 1999 zoning ordinance provided only three sites for four lawfully existing adult entertainment establishments. . . . Accordingly, we hold the zoning provisions of Ordinance 1204 unconstitutional.").

[71] Several courts in Florida have adopted an unusual method of determining whether an ordinance provides reasonable alternative avenues of communication. Under this approach, the court examines

(footnote continued on next page)

is no "bright-line rule" for determining whether a city has provided reasonable alternative avenues for adult businesses. "Rather, it appears from case law that a court must look to the facts of each case to determine the answer to this question."[72]

C. Burden of Identifying Sites

In general, where a plaintiff claims that the government has suppressed First Amendment speech rights, the plaintiff bears the initial burden of demonstrating that the ordinance, statute, or government action restricts speech.[73] Once this requirement is satisfied, the burden shifts to the government to prove the constitutionality of the regulation.[74] In adult business cases, courts have routinely held that the municipality bears this burden in the context of proving that reasonable alternative avenues of communication exist.[75]

The court in *Lim v. City of Long Beach* found that the city met this burden and that on remand, the burden would shift back to the plaintiffs to prove that the sites identified by the city were insufficient:

> According to the district court opinion, Long Beach provided pertinent, specific and detailed information about each site. . . . A city cannot merely point to a random assortment of properties and simply

---

(footnote continued from previous page)

the ratio of adult businesses to the population in the relevant geographic area. *See, e.g.* David Vincent, Inc. v. Broward Cnty., 200 F.3d 1325 (11th Cir. 2000) (following International Eateries of America, Inc. v. Broward Cnty., 941 F.2d 1157 (11th Cir. 1991); Centerfold Club, Inc. v. City of St. Petersburg, 969 F. Supp. 1288 (M.D. Fla. 1997); *but see* Lady J. Lingerie v. City of Jacksonville, 973 F. Supp. 1428, 1438 n. 7 (M.D. Fla. 1997); The Pack Shack, Inc. v. Howard Cnty., 770 A.2d 1028 (Md. Ct. Spec. App. April 24, 2001), *rev'd*, 832 A.2d 170 (Md. Ct. App. 2003) ("In determining whether reasonable alternative avenues of communication exist, it is appropriate to look at the physical and legal characteristics of alternative sites and assess their economic viability, but that assessment should be done in the context of considering the circumstances as a whole. A business operator of a speech-related business must compete in the market place and is not entitled to a preference.").

[72] 3570 E. Foothill Blvd., Inc. v. City of Pasadena, 912 F. Supp. 1257, 1264 (C.D. Cal. 1995).

[73] *See, e.g.*, Los Angeles Police Dep't v. United Reporting Publ'g Co., 528 U.S. 32, 38 (1999).

[74] *See, e.g.*, Greater New Orleans Broadcasting Ass'n. v. United States, 527 U.S. 173 (1999); Bolger v. Youngs Drug Products Corp., 463 U.S. 60, 71 n. 20 (1983) (commercial speech).

[75] *See* J & B Entertainment, Inc. v. City of Jackson, 152 F.3d 362, 370 (5th Cir. 1998); Phillips v. Borough of Keyport, 107 F.3d 164, 177 (3rd Cir. 1997); Acorn Invs. v. City of Seattle, 887 F.2d 219, 224 (9th Cir. 1989); Twp. of Saddle Brook v. A.B. Family Center, Inc., 722 A.2d 530, 536 (N.J. 1999); *but see* Centaur, Inc. v. Richland Cnty., 392 S.E.2d 165 (1990) (presumption of constitutionality of enactment does not shift even in First Amendment cases).

assert that they are reasonably available to adult businesses. The city's duty to demonstrate the availability of properties is defined, at a bare minimum, by reasonableness and good faith. . . . But where a city has provided a good faith and reasonable list of potentially available properties, it is for the plaintiffs to show that, in fact, certain sites would not reasonably become available.[76]

Depending upon the jurisdiction, a city may need to provide only the general areas where adult businesses may locate, along with proof that those areas contain available sites, in order to satisfy this burden.[77] Nevertheless, because the "availability" of particular sites is likely to become a focal point of litigation, city councils and planning professionals would do well to identify the specific parcels available to adult businesses.

D. Amortization of Nonconforming Adult Uses

Provided that a newly enacted zoning ordinance provides a reasonable amortization period, the Constitution does not require indefinite "grandfathering" for adult businesses that become nonconforming uses under the new ordinance.[78] Although the Supreme Court in *Young* did not have occasion to address this question,[79] many lower courts have considered the issue.

In *23 West Washington Street, Inc. v. City of Hagerstown,*[80] the city council decided not to enact "grandfather clauses" for existing adult businesses

---

[76] 217 F.3d 1050, 1055 (9th Cir. 2000).

[77] *See, e.g.*, Hickerson v. City of New York, 146 F.3d 99, 107 (2d Cir. 1998) ("We know of no federal case . . . that requires municipalities to identify the exact locations to which adult businesses may relocate, as opposed to identifying the general areas that remain available and proving that such areas contain enough potential relocation sites. . . .").

[78] *See* David Vincent, Inc. v. Broward Cnty., 200 F.3d 1325, 1332 (11th Cir. 2000) (upholding five-year amortization provision); Ambassador Books & Video v. City of Little Rock, 20 F.3d 858, 865 (8th Cir. 1994) (upholding three year amortization period); SDJ v. City of Houston, 636 F. Supp. 1359, 1370 (S.D. Tex. 1986), *aff'd*, 837 F.2d 1268, 1278 (5th Cir. 1988); Hart Book Stores, Inc. v. Edmisten, 612 F.2d 821 (4th Cir. 1979) (six months); Northend Cinema, Inc. v. City of Seattle, 585 P.2d 1153 (1978) (ninety days); Dumas v. City of Dallas, 648 F. Supp. 1061, 1171 (N.D. Tex. 1986), *aff'd* 837 F.2d 1298 (5th Cir. 1988) (three years); City of Vallejo v. Adult Books, 167 Cal. App. 3d 1169, 219 Cal. Rptr. 143 (1985) (one year plus additional year if extreme hardship); Town of Islip v. Caviglia, 540 N.E.2d 215 (N.Y. 1989) (1¼ to 5¼ years).

[79] *See* Young v. Am. Mini Theatres, Inc., 427 U.S. 50, 71 n. 35 (1976) (noting that the ordinances in question affected only the location of new adult businesses).

[80] 972 F.2d 342 (4th Cir. 1992).

that would be in violation of its new zoning law. The plaintiff argued that the failure to either grandfather or provide special exceptions for existing uses meant that the ordinance was not a narrowly tailored time, place, or manner regulation. The court rejected this contention and concluded that because the regulation was not substantially broader than necessary, the availability of a less restrictive regulation was irrelevant.[81] Furthermore, "To the extent either of the rejected alternatives would have permitted the unchanged operation of the existing adult bookstores to continue downtown, it would have severely undercut the purpose of the ordinance to reduce secondary effects of adult businesses in downtown Hagerstown."[82] Other courts have treated amortization provisions in a similar manner—as content neutral regulations valid under intermediate scrutiny.[83]

Although a majority of states allow the amortization of nonconforming uses, failure to grandfather pre-existing adult uses in states that do not permit amortization will result in the invalidation of the ordinance. In *J.L. Spoons, Inc. v. City of Brunswick*,[84] the city passed an ordinance that required a nonconforming use to terminate within one year. The federal court struck it down, citing state statutory and constitutional provisions that permit the indefinite continuation of nonconforming uses.[85] Similar provisions in the city's charter and in Tennessee state law led to the invalidation of the nonconforming use clause in a Memphis ordinance.[86]

Where state law does allow for termination of nonconforming uses, adult businesses have sometimes made Takings Clause attacks on zoning ordinances. These arguments typically fail because amortization of a nonconforming use does not generally render the property worthless.[87]

---

[81] *Id.* at *3 (citing Ward v. Rock Against Racism, 491 U.S. 781, 800 (1989)).

[82] *Id.*

[83] *See, e.g.*, Town of Islip v. Caviglia, 540 N.E.2d 215, 224 (N.Y. 1989) ("Since the ordinance is content-neutral under both the Federal and State Constitutions, the amortization provisions rest upon the same legal foundation as such provisions generally and, on the facts presented here, are valid.") (internal citations omitted).

[84] 49 F. Supp. 2d 1032 (N.D. Ohio 1999).

[85] *Id.* at 1040.

[86] E. Brooks Books, Inc. v. City of Memphis, 48 F.3d 220, 228 (6th Cir. 1995).

[87] *See, e.g.*, Ranch House, Inc. v. Amerson, 238 F.3d 1273 (11th Cir. 2001); 801 Conklin St. Ltd. v. Town of Babylon, 38 F. Supp. 2d 228 (E.D.N.Y. 1999); N.W. Enters. v. City of Houston, 27 F. Supp. 2d 754, 865 (S.D. Tex. 1998).

Finally, most decisions on amortization clauses turn on whether the amortization period is reasonable. Courts have upheld periods ranging from ninety days to five years,[88] with one-year and two-year periods being common.[89] If an exception procedure for hardships is allowed, however, the business will likely be obliged first to exhaust this administrative remedy before going to court.[90]

E. Moratoria

Moratoria are often used by local governments as a way to provide planners time to study a land use issue. But as applied to speech-related businesses, moratoria constitute a restraint on expressive activity and are therefore greatly disfavored by the courts.[91]

V. Legal Backdrop for Licensing Sexually Oriented Businesses

The Supreme Court has stated that cities can require periodic licensing of speech-related businesses "and may even have special licensing procedures for conduct commonly associated with expression."[92] When determining the constitutionality of licensing ordinances for speech-related activities, courts generally employ two tests—one for the procedural components

---

[88] *See* Northend Cinema, Inc. v. City of Seattle, 585 P.2d 1153 (1978) (upholding ninety-day amortization provision where plaintiffs' lease obligations were minimal, their improvements had been depreciated, and altering the use could mitigate losses); David Vincent, Inc. v. Broward Cnty., 200 F.3d 1325 (11th Cir. 2000) (upholding five-year amortization period).

[89] *See, e.g.*, Cook Cnty. v. Renaissance Arcade & Bookstore, 522 N.E.2d 73 (Ill. 1988) (upholding six-month amortization clause, which allowed an additional six-month extension to be obtained); Worldwide Video of Wash., Inc. v. City of Spokane, 368 F.3d 1186, 1199–1200 (9th Cir. 2004) (upholding one-year amortization period where adult bookstore operator obtained an additional six months administratively); Jake's, Ltd., Inc. v. City of Coates, 284 F.3d 884, 889 (8th Cir. 2002) (upholding two-year amortization period).

[90] Stringfellow's of New York, Ltd. v. City of New York, 694 N.E.2d 407, 420 (N.Y. 1998) ("Having failed to seek relief under this [hardship] provision, plaintiffs are not now in a position to complain that their constitutional due process rights have been violated.").

[91] *See e.g.* Schneider v. City of Ramsey, 800 F. Supp. 815, 817 (D. Minn. 1992), *aff'd sub nom.*, Holmberg v. City of Ramsey, 12 F.3d 140 (8th Cir. 1994) (invalidating moratorium passed to allow city time to draft zoning regulations for adult uses); ASF, Inc. v. City of Seattle, 408 F. Supp. 2d 1102 (W.D. Wash. 2005) (striking down moratorium as unconstitutional prior restraint).

[92] City of Lakewood v. Plain Dealer Publ'g Co., 486 U.S. 750, 760 (1988).

of the ordinance and the other for its substantive components. Of course, courts sometimes struggle with the question of which test they should apply to a particular requirement.[93] If the person seeking to engage in expressive conduct must first obtain some form of authorization from the government, a reviewing court will likely subject that requirement to the exacting procedural standards applicable to prior restraints. This is equally true where a city's zoning code treats adult businesses as subject to special conditional use permitting requirements because the operation of a speech-related business is subject to prior approval from the zoning authority.[94]

A. Procedural Safeguards: *Freedman, FW/PBS,* and *City of Littleton*

"The term 'prior restraint' is used 'to describe administrative and judicial orders *forbidding certain communications* when issued in advance of the time that such communications are to occur."[95] Historically, the purpose of the prior restraint doctrine has been to prevent government control of the content of expression—that is, censorship.[96] The primacy of the First Amendment free speech guarantee has led the courts to strictly scrutinize prior restraints and require them to overcome a presumption of unconstitutionality.[97] To do so, the prior restraint must take place "under procedural safeguards designed to obviate the dangers of a censorship system."[98]

In *Freedman v. Maryland,*[99] a state censorship statute required that before publicly showing a film, the would-be exhibitor must first submit the film to the Maryland State Board of Censors for a finding that the film

---

[93] *See, e.g.,* FW/PBS, Inc. v. City of Dallas, 837 F.2d 1298 (5th Cir. 1988) (applying *Renton* test to adult business licensing ordinance), *aff'd in part, rev'd in part, vacated in part, and remanded,* 493 U.S. 215 (1990) (applying prior restraint analysis to procedural components of licensing ordinance).

[94] *See, e.g.,* Smith v. Cnty. of Los Angeles, 29 Cal. Rptr. 2d 680 (1994); Landover Books, Inc. v. Prince George's Cnty., 566 A.2d 792 (Md. Ct. Spec. App. 1989).

[95] Alexander v. United States, 509 U.S. 544, 550 (1993) (quoting M. NIMMER, NIMMER ON FREEDOM OF SPEECH, § 4.03, pp. 4–14 (1984) (emphasis added)).

[96] O'Connor v. City and Cnty. of Denver, 894 F.2d 1210, 1220 (10th Cir. 1990) (citing Near v. Minnesota ex rel. Olson, 283 U.S. 697, 713 (1931)).

[97] *See* Se. Promotions, Ltd. v. Conrad, 420 U.S. 546 (1975).

[98] *Id.* at 559.

[99] 380 U.S. 51 (1965).

was not obscene. Because the board's business was to eliminate expression based on its content, the *Freedman* court invalidated the statute because necessary procedural safeguards were lacking.[100] *Freedman* held that for a prior restraint to pass constitutional muster: (1) any restraint prior to judicial review can be imposed only for a specified, brief period during which the status quo must be maintained; (2) prompt judicial review of that decision must be available; and (3) the censor must bear the burden of going to court to suppress the film, magazine, or speech and must bear the burden of proof in court.[101]

Although *Freedman* required three procedural safeguards for statutes that authorize censorship of the content of expression, a 1990 Supreme Court decision unexpectedly applied a variation of this standard to regulations that did not permit government review of speech. In *FW/PBS v. City of Dallas*,[102] the Court reviewed an ordinance that required adult businesses to obtain licenses before operating and prohibited individuals convicted of certain crimes from working in those businesses. In a badly divided opinion, a plurality of three justices ruled that two of the three *Freedman* standards should apply to the Dallas ordinance; three justices believed that all three *Freedman* standards should apply; and three opined that the Dallas ordinance was a time, place, and manner regulation, making *Freedman* inapplicable.[103]

Justice O'Connor's controlling plurality opinion held that two *Freedman* elements were "essential": (1) the initial licensing decision must be made within a brief, specified period during which the status quo is maintained; and (2) the licensing decision must be subject to prompt judicial review. The plurality concluded that the Dallas ordinance failed to provide these safeguards. First, although the ordinance required a licensing decision within thirty days of submission of a completed application, it also required that certain inspections be completed by the city before a license could issue. Because the ordinance, on its face, did not require the city to complete the inspections within the thirty-day period, the plurality concluded that "the

---

[100] *Id.* at 57–58.
[101] *Id.* at 58–60.
[102] 493 U.S. 215 (1990).
[103] *Id.*

city's regulatory scheme allows indefinite postponement of the issuance of a license."[104] Second, the plurality concluded—without much discussion—that the Dallas ordinance failed to provide "the possibility of prompt judicial review in the event that the license is erroneously denied."[105] It was thus invalid on that ground as well.

Justice O'Connor nevertheless drew a significant distinction between the censorship statute in *Freedman* and the licensing ordinance in Dallas. Under the latter, Dallas did not directly censor the content of expression; rather, "the city reviews the general qualifications of each license applicant, a ministerial action that is not presumptively invalid."[106] "Because of these differences, we conclude that the First Amendment does not require that the city bear the burden of going to court to effect the denial of a license application or that it bear the burden of proof once in court."[107]

For more than a decade, *FW/PBS*'s plurality opinion fostered substantial confusion in the lower courts, especially over the meaning of the "prompt judicial review" requirement. By the time the Court offered clarification, the federal circuits had become deeply split over the issue. The Fourth, Sixth, and Ninth Circuits held that when a city denies an adult business a license, its ordinance must guarantee a prompt judicial decision on the merits—*by a court*—within a brief, specified period of time.[108] The First, Fifth, Seventh, and Eleventh Circuits held, based on the plurality opinion, that "prompt judicial review" is satisfied if the ordinance allows for prompt access to the courts.[109]

The Supreme Court resolved the circuit split in *City of Littleton v. Z.J. Gifts D-4, L.L.C.* by specifically "modify[ing] *FW/PBS*, withdrawing

---

[104] *Id.* at 227.

[105] *Id.* at 228.

[106] *Id.*

[107] *Id.* at 240 (quoting Bantam Books v. Sullivan, 372 U.S. 58, 66 (1963)).

[108] *See* 11126 Baltimore Boulevard, Inc. v. Prince George's Cnty., 58 F.3d 988 (4th Cir. 1995); Lounge Mgmt., Inc. v. City of Paducah, 202 F.3d 884 (6th Cir. 2000); Baby Tam & Co., Inc. v. City of Las Vegas, 154 F.3d 1097 (9th Cir. 1998) (*Baby Tam I*); 4805 Convoy, Inc. v. City of San Diego, 183 F.3d 1108 (9th Cir. 1999) (extending *Baby Tam I* rationale to suspension and revocation proceedings); *but see* City News & Novelty, Inc. v. City of Waukesha, 531 U.S. 278 (2001) (indicating that a suspension or revocation proceeding after the business has been licensed and "speaking" does not raise "prompt judicial review" issue).

[109] *See* Jews for Jesus v. Mass. Bay Transp. Auth., 984 F.2d 1319 (1st Cir. 1993); TK's Video v. Denton Cnty., 24 F.3d 705 (5th Cir. 1994); Graff v. City of Chicago, 9 F.3d 1309 (7th Cir. 1993); Boss Capital, Inc. v. City of Casselberry, 187 F.3d 1251 (11th Cir. 1999).

its implication that *Freedman's* special judicial review rules apply in this case."[110] The Court gave four reasons for this conclusion. "First, ordinary court procedural rules and practices, in Colorado as elsewhere, provide reviewing courts with judicial tools sufficient to avoid delay-related First Amendment harm."[111] Second, the Court saw "no reason to doubt the willingness of Colorado's judges to exercise these powers wisely so as to avoid serious threats of delay-induced First Amendment harm."[112]

Third, *Freedman* "considered a Maryland statute that created a Board of Censors, which had to decide whether a film was 'pornographic,' tended to 'debase or corrupt morals,' and lacked 'whatever other merits.'"[113] In contrast, "the ordinance at issue here does not seek to censor material. And its licensing scheme applies reasonably objective, nondiscretionary criteria unrelated to the content of the expressive materials that an adult business may sell or display."[114] Fourth, "nothing in *FW/PBS* or in *Freedman* requires a city or a State to place judicial review safeguards all in the city ordinance that sets forth a licensing scheme . . . . [which] is not surprising given the fact that many cities and towns lack the state-law legal authority to impose deadlines on state courts."[115] The Court ultimately held: "Where (as here and as in *FW/PBS*) the regulation simply conditions the operation of an adult business on compliance with neutral and nondiscretionary criteria . . . and does not seek to censor content, an adult business is not entitled to an unusually speedy judicial decision of the *Freedman* type."[116]

In the wake of *City of Littleton*, courts have rejected claims that adult business licensing ordinances have failed to supply "prompt judicial review" for adverse licensing decisions.[117]

---

[110] 541 U.S. 774, 781 (2004).

[111] *Id.* at 782.

[112] *Id.*

[113] *Id.* at 782 (quoting Freedman v. Maryland, 380 U.S. 51, 52 (1965).

[114] *Id.* at 783.

[115] *Id.* at 784.

[116] *Id.* at 784.

[117] *See, e.g.,* Dream Palace v. Cnty. of Maricopa, 384 F.3d 990, 1004 (9th Cir. 2004) ("In short, the ordinance in this case is similar in every relevant aspect to the ordinance upheld by the Supreme Court in *City of Littleton.* . . . Arizona's rules of procedure . . . satisfy the First Amendment."); Deja Vu of Cincinnati, L.L.C. v. Union Twp. Bd. of Trustees, 411 F.3d 777, 787–88 (6th Cir. 2005) (holding that because the law at issue "applies reasonably objective, nondiscretionary criteria," the "resolution fulfills *Littleton's* requirements for prompt judicial review") (internal citations and quotation marks omitted).

B. The Essential Rule: Avoid Amorphous Standards and Undue Delay

The Constitution requires any licensing requirement for speech-related activity to be governed by narrow, definite, and objective criteria in order to avoid prior restraint problems. [118] The plurality in *FW/PBS, Inc.* noted that the Supreme Court's prior restraint cases have identified "two evils that will not be tolerated in such schemes."[119] The first is unbridled discretion in the hands of a government official to deny a license; such discretion makes room for censorship. The second is a failure to place a time limit on when the licensing decision must be made; impermissible delay produces the same result as overt censorship.

The Dallas ordinance in *FW/PBS*, discussed previously, illustrates the second failure well. The ordinance required government inspections without specifying, on the face of the ordinance, the timeframe in which the government had to perform the inspections. Thus, the ordinance created a *risk* of undue delay even though it ostensibly required a licensing decision to be made within thirty days after a completed application was submitted. [120] Lower courts have similarly scrutinized adult business licensing ordinances for failure to ensure an initial decision within a specified period of time. [121]

Several adult business ordinances have also had language that suffers from the first defect. [122] In *Broadway Books, Inc. v. Roberts*, [123] the city's ordinance required adult business applicants to be "of good moral character." The court invalidated this standard, holding that it "would permit a prior restraint on [F]irst [A]mendment rights through the

---

[118] *See* City of Lakewood v. Plain Dealer Publ'g Co., 486 U.S. 750 (1988) (invalidating ordinance making news rack permits subject to "such other terms and conditions deemed necessary and reasonable to the Mayor"); Shuttlesworth v. Birmingham, 394 U.S. 147, 150–51 (1969); Saia v. New York, 334 U.S. 558 (1948).
[119] *Id.* at 225 (plurality opinion).
[120] FW/PBS, Inc. v. City of Dallas, 493 U.S. 215, 227 (1990) (plurality opinion).
[121] *See, e.g.*, Baby Tam & Co., Inc. v. City of Las Vegas, 199 F.3d 1111, 115 (9th Cir. 2000); Lady J. Lingerie, Inc. v. City of Jacksonville, 176 F.3d 1358 (11th Cir. 2000); Redner v. Dean, 29 F.3d 1495 (11th Cir. 1994); 11126 Baltimore Blvd., Inc. v. Prince George's Cnty., 58 F.3d 988 (4th Cir. 1995); *cert. denied sub nom.* Prince George's Cnty. v. 11126 Baltimore Blvd., Inc. 116 S. Ct. 567 (1995).
[122] *See, e.g.*, Entm't Concepts v. Maciejewski, 631 F.2d 497 (7th Cir. 1980), *cert. denied*, 450 U.S. 919 (1981) (striking "in his sound discretion"); Evansville Book Mart v. City of Indianapolis, 477 F. Supp. 128 (S.D. Ind. 1979) (same); 754 Orange Ave., Inc. v. City of W. Haven, 761 F.2d 105 (2d Cir. 1985) (failure to define "adult bookstore" amounted to unbridled discretion).
[123] 642 F. Supp. 486 (E.D. Tenn. 1986).

application of an amorphous standard requiring the licensing authority to exercise unguided subjective judgment."[124] Similarly, in *East Brooks Books, Inc. v. City of Memphis*,[125] a federal court of appeals struck down a provision that allowed the city to deny a license if the applicant had a "demonstrated inability to manage the business in a law-abiding manner."

While recognizing that amorphous standards are not to be tolerated, several courts have also acknowledged that "celestial precision" is not required.[126] In *Baby Tam & Co., Inc. v. City of Las Vegas*,[127] the city had amended its licensing and zoning ordinances to cure prior restraint problems identified in earlier litigation.[128] The plaintiffs continued to challenge the ordinance, claiming that the definition of "adult" material conferred too much discretion on the city's licensing official. The court rejected this argument, explaining that

> [t]he ordinance is specific in spelling out what sexual acts and what parts of the human body and what sexual toys qualify as sexual. No set of regulations can be applied without a modicum of judgment being exercised by the regulators. This ordinance cabins their discretion and directs their judgment and therefore passes constitutional muster.[129]

The business in the *Baby Tam* cases also challenged the ordinance's failure to specify how the inventory was to be taken. The court was unpersuaded: "A ministerial function of this kind is not the stuff of constitutional objection. We assume that the City will measure inventory in a standard way. On the face of the ordinance there is nothing wrong in leaving the matter to standard practice."[130]

---

[124] *Id.* at 494.

[125] 48 F.3d 220 (6th Cir. 1995).

[126] *See, e.g.,* Hart Book Stores, Inc. v. Edmisten, 612 F.2d 821 (4th Cir. 1979); 15192 Thirteen Mile Rd., Inc. v. City of Warren, 626 F. Supp. 803 (E.D. Mich. 1985); Fantasy World, Inc. v. Greensboro Bd. of Adjustment, 496 S.E.2d 825 (N.C. Ct. App. 1998); Tily B, Inc. v. City of Newport Beach, 81 Cal. Rptr.2d 6 (Cal. Ct. App. 1998).

[127] 247 F.3d 1003 (9th Cir. 2001) (*Baby Tam III*).

[128] *See Baby Tam I,* 154 F.3d 1097 (9th Cir. 1998) (identifying "prompt judicial review" problem); Baby Tam & Co., Inc. v. City of Las Vegas, 199 F.3d 1111 (9th Cir. 2000) (*Baby Tam II*) (identifying "indefinite delay" problem).

[129] Baby Tam III, 247 F.3d at 1008.

[130] *Id.* (citing Artistic Entm't, Inc. v. City of Warner Robins, 223 F.3d 1306, 1310 (11th Cir. 2000)).

In the zoning context, conditional use and special use permit standards—like their business licensing counterparts—have often been deemed to grant unbridled discretion to the zoning authority.[131] Typically, conditional use zoning ordinances operate as licensing schemes and allow the denial of a use permit based on the zoning board's finding that the proposed use will have adverse effects on adjacent and surrounding uses. Because the negative secondary effects of adult businesses constitute the very reason for regulating them more stringently than other land uses, a number of courts have invalidated conditional use permitting schemes as applied to adult businesses.[132]

In *Dease v. City of Anaheim*,[133] the reviewing federal court held that the city's conditional use permitting process failed to avoid prior restraint problems. The court noted that before granting a permit, the planning commission must first determine that the business would not be detrimental to the "peace, health, safety, and general welfare" of the surrounding neighborhood. The planning commission could also attach conditions to the permit, including "such conditions as it may determine to be reasonably necessary to safeguard" the public good. The court concluded that such ambiguous criteria gave the commission "the power to make decisions on any basis at all, including an impermissible basis, such as content based regulation of speech."[134]

Cases such as *Dease* stand for the proposition that when municipalities place special permitting requirements on adult uses, they "must set objective standards and guidelines for the zoning board to follow in deciding whether to grant or deny the permit."[135] A few conditional use ordinances have been

---

[131] *See, e.g.*, Univ. Books & Videos, Inc. v. Miami-Dade Cnty., 132 F. Supp. 2d 1008 (S.D. Fla. 2001); Lady J. Lingerie, Inc. v. City of Jacksonville, 176 F.3d 1358, 1361 (11th Cir. 1999); T & A's, Inc. v. Town Bd. of the Town of Ramapo, 109 F. Supp. 2d 161 (S.D.N.Y. 2000); Jersey's All-American Sports Bar v. Wash. State Liquor Control Bd., 55 F. Supp. 2d 1131 (W.D. Wash. 1999); 801 Conklin St. Ltd. v. Town of Babylon, 38 F. Supp. 2d 228 (E.D.N.Y. 1999).

[132] *See, e.g.*, Landover Books, Inc. v. Prince George's Cnty., 566 A.2d 792 (Md. Ct. App. 1989); Smith v. Cnty. of Los Angeles, 29 Cal. Rptr. 2d 680 (Cal. Ct. App. 1994).

[133] 826 F. Supp. 336 (C.D. Cal. 1993).

[134] *Id.* at 344.

[135] 801 Conklin Street Ltd. v. Town of Babylon, 38 F. Supp. 2d 228, 244 (E.D.N.Y. 1999); *see also* Nakatomi Invs., Inc. v. City of Schenectady, 949 F. Supp. 988, 1002 (N.D.N.Y. 1997); Charette v. Town of Oyster Bay, 159 F.3d 749, 754 (2d Cir. 1998); Town of Islip v. Caviglia, 532 N.Y.S.2d 783 (App. Div. 1988), *aff'd*, 540 N.E.2d 215 (N.Y. 1989).

found to meet this requirement and pass constitutional muster,[136] but the more common and better practice is to specify where adult uses will be permitted as of right, subject to separation requirements from each other and from sensitive land uses such as churches, schools, and residences.

C. Substantial Government Interests in Licensing Adult Businesses

Various substantial government interests, including the prevention of criminal activity by those recently convicted of certain crimes, are advanced by the licensing of sexually oriented enterprises.[137] Requiring licenses of owners and employees of the business not only serves to identify participants in the enterprise but also helps to prevent the employment of minors in adult businesses.[138] Thus, courts have routinely upheld requirements that applicants provide their names, addresses,[139] and identifying documents that substantiate their ages.[140]

In *Schultz v. City of Cumberland*,[141] the Seventh Circuit—although rejecting criminal disqualifier provisions[142]—articulated the straightforward reasons why the city required "identification" information:

> We also uphold the Section XI required disclosures of the following: the applicant's name; proof of the applicant's age; the type of license for which the applicant is applying; the proposed location, address

---

[136] *See, e.g.*, Mom N Pops, Inc. v. City of Charlotte, 162 F.3d 1155 (4th Cir. 1998); Marty's Adult World of Enfield, Inc. v. Town of Enfield, 20 F.3d 512 (2d Cir. 1994) (emphasizing that adult businesses were permitted as of right in other zoning districts); Steakhouse, Inc. v. City of Raleigh, 166 F.3d 634 (4th Cir. 1999).

[137] *See* TK's Video, Inc. v. Denton Cnty., 24 F.3d 705 (5th Cir. 1994).

[138] *See, e.g.*, Deanna Boyd, *Club Owner Arrested for Nude Dance; Two Girls, 15, Observed Performing for Patrons*, THE FORT WORTH STAR-TELEGRAM, Mar. 13, 2001, at 7.

[139] At least one court has drawn a distinction between requiring a business address and a residential address, striking down the latter requirement as unconstitutional. *See* Schultz v. City of Cumberland, 228 F.3d 831 (7th Cir. 2000).

[140] *See, e.g.*, Genusa v. City of Peoria, 619 F.2d 1203 (7th Cir. 1980); TK's Video, Inc. v. Denton Cnty., 24 F.3d 705 (5th Cir. 1994); Broadway Books, Inc. v. Roberts, 642 F. Supp. 486 (E.D. Tenn. 1986); World Wide Video, Inc. v. City of Tukwila, 816 P.2d 18 (Wash. 1991); Kev, Inc. v. Kitsap Cnty., 793 F.2d 1053 (9th Cir. 1986).

[141] Schultz v. City of Cumberland, 228 F.3d 831 (7th Cir. 2000).

[142] *Id.*; *but see* Tee & Bee, Inc. v. City of W. Allis, 936 F. Supp. 1479, 1487 (E.D. Wis. 1996) (holding that civil disability provisions constitute a narrowly tailored means of preventing crime in adult businesses).

and descriptions of the business premises; identifying personal data. All this information allows Cumberland to regulate the time, place or manner of adult entertainment without censoring expression. This data enables Cumberland to administer licenses and monitor compliance with its zoning requirements, which the plaintiffs do not challenge. Likewise, requiring proof of employee age legitimately relates to the government's interest in preventing underage performers from engaging in adult entertainment.[143]

A separate question regarding disclosures concerns who must be disclosed on a business's application for a sexually oriented business license. Courts generally will not allow required disclosure of all shareholders of a corporation. In *East Brooks Books*,[144] the court invalidated such a requirement, opining that although the city can require disclosure of those "legally accountable" for the business or those who have "a controlling or significant share" in the business, requiring every shareholder to sign the application is impermissibly broad.[145]

In upholding disclosure provisions for employees, courts have recognized the government's need to obtain "stage names" or aliases of dancers and operators to facilitate enforcement of the ordinance.[146] "The record shows that police have found the adult-oriented establishment operators to be using aliases. The City is certainly entitled to know who is operating these establishments."[147] Complete identification of sexually oriented business employees is essential to preventing prostitution and other illicit sexual activity.[148]

Relatedly, interior configuration standards and prohibitions on certain conduct—often included in adult business licensing regulations— prevent illicit sexual activity and protect public health from the problems

---

[143] *Schultz*, 228 F.3d at 852.

[144] 48 F.3d 220 (6th Cir. 1995).

[145] *See also* DLS, Inc. v. City of Chattanooga, 894 F. Supp. 1140, 1145–47 (E.D. Tenn. 1995) (invalidating required disclosure of 5% stockholders), *aff'd*, 107 F.3d 403 (6th Cir. 1997).

[146] Broadway Books, Inc. v. Roberts, 642 F. Supp. 486 (E.D. Tenn. 1986).

[147] *Id.* at 492.

[148] *See, e.g.*, Kev, Inc. v. Kitsap Cnty., 793 F.2d 1053 (9th Cir. 1986) (upholding required disclosure of aliases at erotic dance studios).

associated with peep-show booths[149] and nude dancing establishments.[150] A number of cases establish that prostitution, indecent exposure, masturbation, and other illicit sexual activities frequently occur on the premises of adult businesses.[151] In addition to prohibitions on complete nudity and paid sexual performances such as "lap dances" and "couch dances,"[152] several cities have enacted interior configuration requirements to prevent sexual activity in peep-show booths inside sexually oriented businesses.[153] Cities have imposed requirements that such booths (1) have no doors and remain open and visible from the store's public area, (2) have only one person at a time, (3) have no holes in the walls that facilitate illicit sex acts between booths, and (4) have sufficient lighting to ensure that the booth's interior is visible. Such requirements have been repeatedly upheld.[154]

These substantive regulations in adult business ordinances must still pass the intermediate scrutiny test; that is, they must be narrowly tailored to serve a substantial government interest.[155] Thus, for every regulation

---

[149] *See, e.g.*, Bamon Corp. v. City of Dayton, 923 F.2d 470 (6th Cir. 1991) (public sex acts in peep-show booths); O'Connor v. City and Cnty. of Denver, 894 F.2d 1210 (10th Cir. 1990) (same); Berg v. Health & Hosp. Corp., 865 F.2d 797 (7th Cir. 1989) (same); Ellwest Stereo Theater, Inc. v. Wenner, 681 F.2d 1243 (9th Cir. 1982) (same).

[150] *See, e.g.*, State v. Marren, 890 F.2d 924, 926 (7th Cir. 1989) (prostitution associated with nude dancing establishment); United States v. Doerr, 886 F.2d 944, 949 (7th Cir. 1989) (same); DCR, Inc. v. Pierce Cnty., 964 P.2d 380 (Wash. Ct. App. 1998) (sexual contact between dancers and patrons); DLS, Inc. v. City of Chattanooga, 107 F.3d 403 (6th Cir. 1997) (prostitution).

[151] *See, e.g.*, Nobby Lobby, Inc. v. City of Dallas, 970 F.2d 82 (5th Cir. 1992); O'Connor v. City and Cnty. of Denver, 894 F.2d 1210 (10th Cir. 1990); N.W. Enters. v. City of Houston, 27 F. Supp. 2d 754 (S.D. Tex. 1998); People v. Perrine, 120 Cal. Rptr. 640 (Cal. Ct. App. 1975) (upholding Los Angeles arcade regulations, noting that peep-show booth conduct includes offensive, dangerous, and unlawful acts); EWAP, Inc. v. City of Los Angeles, 158 Cal. Rptr. 579 (Cal. Ct. App. 1979) (citing unsanitary acts in video booths); City of National City v. Wiener, 838 P.2d 223 (Cal. 1993).

[152] *See, e.g.*, DLS, Inc. v. City of Chattanooga, 103 F.3d 403 (6th Cir. 1997); Colacurcio v. City of Kent 163 F.3d 545 (9th Cir. 1998).

[153] *See, e.g.*, Arcara v. Cloud Books, Inc., 478 U.S. 697 (1986); Ellwest Stereo Theatres, Inc. v. Wenner, 681 F.2d 1243 (9th Cir. 1982); Wall Distributors, Inc. v. City of Newport News, 782 F.2d 1165 (4th Cir. 1986); Chez Sez VIII, Inc. v. Poritz, 688 A.2d 119 (N.J. Super. 1997).

[154] *See, e.g.*, Spokane Arcade, Inc. v. City of Spokane, 75 F.3d 692 (7th Cir. 1196); Wall Distribs., Inc. v. City of Newport News, 782 F.2d 1165 (4th Cir. 1986); Matney v. Cnty. of Kenosha, 86 F.3d 692 (7th Cir. 1996); Chez Sez VIII, Inc. v. Poritz, 688 A.2d 119 (N.J. App. 1997); Berg v. Health and Hospital Corp., 865 F.2d 797 (7th Cir. 1989); City of Lincoln v. ABC Books, 470 N.W.2d 760 (Neb. 1991).

[155] *See, e.g.*, Broadway Books, Inc. v. Roberts, 642 F. Supp. 486 (E.D. Tenn. 1986); Wall Distribs., Inc. v. City of Newport News, 782 F.2d 1165 (4th Cir. 1986).

that a city seeks to apply to an adult business, the city should be ready to articulate a corresponding negative secondary effect that it seeks to prevent by that regulation.

D. License Fees

The common practice of charging an adult business a reasonable licensing fee has been upheld by a number of courts.[156] The test is whether the fee is "revenue neutral"[157]—that is, not punitive but intended to defray the costs of administering the ordinance. Essentially, this means that the amount of the fee must be narrowly tailored: "Government cannot tax First Amendment rights, but it can exact narrowly tailored fees to defray administrative cost of regulation."[158]

In *Cox v. New Hampshire*,[159] the Supreme Court upheld a parade licensing fee because it was established to defray the costs of city services related to traffic management, police services, and waste removal. However, the Court has been quick to invalidate fees if they amount to a tax on constitutional rights[160] or are variable based on the content of the speech being licensed.[161]

Generally, cities should keep licensing fees low because the cost of litigating the fee amount can often exceed the revenue that the fee generates. Nevertheless, if the government produces evidence justifying the amount of the fee, a reviewing court is likely to uphold it.[162]

---

[156] *See, e.g.*, Schultz v. City of Cumberland, 228 F.3d 831 (7th Cir. 2000) ($100); Genusa v. City of Peoria, 619 F.2d 1203 (7th Cir. 1980) ($100); Bayside Enterprises v. Carson, 470 F. Supp. 1140 (M.D. Fla. 1979) ($400); Borrago v. City of Louisville, 456 F. Supp. 30 (W.D. Ky. 1978); Airport Book Store v. Jackson, 248 S.E.2d 623 (Ga. 1978) ($500). *See also Baby Tam III*, 247 F.3d 1003, 1007 (9th Cir. 2001).
[157] *Schultz*, 228 F.3d at 852 ("[W]e uphold the Ordinance requirement of a revenue-neutral license application fee to defray the costs of administration.").
[158] TK's Video, Inc. v. Denton Cnty., 24 F.3d 705, 710 (5th Cir. 1994) (upholding, under *Cox*, license fees of $500 for businesses and $50 for individuals)
[159] Cox v. New Hampshire, 312 U.S. 569 (1941).
[160] *See* Murdock v. Pennsylvania, 319 U.S. 105 (1943).
[161] *See* Forsyth Cnty. v. Nationalist Movement, 505 U.S. 123 (1992).
[162] *See* Blue Movies, Inc. v. Louisville-Jefferson Cnty. Metro Gov't, 317 S.W.3d 23, 35–36 (Ky. 2010) (upholding $1,000 fee based on government's evidence "regarding the costs of dealing with adult entertainment businesses and their secondary effects").

E. Defining Adult Uses to Avoid Vagueness and Overbreadth Problems

Questions often arise as to what type of establishment constitutes an "adult business." The American landscape has an abundance of commercial enterprises that carry some amount of sexually explicit materials, although not all such enterprises would properly be classified as sexually oriented businesses. Retail businesses, by their nature, are dynamic and flexible, and this fluidity is enhanced by the fact that many owners and managers will change their business operations to circumvent sexually oriented business ordinances.[163] Although a regulation must not require people of normal intelligence to guess as to its meaning,[164] the prohibition against excessive vagueness, rooted in the Due Process Clause, "does not invalidate every statute which a reviewing court believes could have been drafted with greater precision."[165]

For example, Detroit defined "adult motion picture theater" as follows:

> An enclosed building with a capacity of 50 or more persons used for presenting material distinguished or characterized by their emphasis on matter depicting, describing or relating to "Specified Sexual Activities" or "Specified Anatomical Areas," (as defined below), for observation by patrons therein.[166]

The plaintiffs claimed that adult theater operators had to guess at when a film would cross the threshold amount of sexual activity to require the theater showing it to be licensed under the ordinance. The Supreme Court rejected this argument, noting that the plaintiff adult businesses fell

---

[163] *See, e.g.,* New York City v. Les Hommes, 743 N.E.2d 368 (N.Y. 1999) (holding that video store avoided regulation as adult business by maintaining sufficient non-adult stock); Stringfellow's of N. Y., Ltd. v. City of New York, 2001 N.Y. LEXIS 628 (N.Y. March 29, 2001) (rejecting topless bar's attempt to avoid adult business classification by admitting minors).

[164] Grayned v. City of Rockford, 408 U.S. 104, 108 (1972).

[165] Rose v. Lock, 423 U.S. 87, 94 (1975); *see also* Boyce Motor Lines v. United States, 342 337, 340 (1952) ("[N]o more than a reasonable degree of certainty can be demanded. Nor is it unfair to require that one who deliberately goes perilously close to an area of proscribed conduct shall take the risk that he may cross the line.").

[166] Young v. Am. Mini-Theatres, Inc., 427 U.S. 50, 53 n. 5 (1976).

clearly within the ambit of the definition because they regularly offered "adult" fare. In the final analysis, the Court concluded:

> [T]he only amount of vagueness in the ordinances relates to the amount of sexually explicit activity that may be portrayed before the material can be said to be "characterized by an emphasis" on such matter. For most films the question will be readily answerable; to the extent that an area of doubt exists, we see no reason why the ordinances are not "readily subject to a narrowing construction by the state courts.". . . [W]e think this is an inappropriate case in which to adjudicate the hypothetical claims of persons not before the Court.

This portion of the opinion was joined by all five members of the majority, and it outlines the deference that federal courts should give to cities in applying definitions to sexually oriented businesses.

Nevertheless, improper interpretation of ordinance terms by local officials can lead to invalidation of adult business regulations. In *Tollis v. San Bernardino County*,[167] a county official interpreted the county's adult use ordinance to apply to mainstream theaters even if the theaters showed pornographic films only on one occasion. The plaintiff challenged the ordinance on the grounds that, as interpreted, it was unconstitutionally overbroad. The district court agreed and granted a permanent injunction. On appeal, the Ninth Circuit affirmed, but instead of couching its decision in terms of overbreadth, it concluded that the ordinance was not narrowly tailored to serve a substantial government interest because the category of regulated establishments went beyond adult businesses and reached establishments not associated with secondary effects: "Here, the County has presented no evidence that a single showing of an adult movie would have any harmful secondary effects on the community."[168]

It is wise to include the term "regularly" in the definitions of adult theater and adult cabaret to eliminate the possibility of a "single-use" interpretation like the one that led to the invalidation of the ordinance in *Tollis*. On several occasions, courts have rejected challenges to ordinances

---

[167] 827 F.2d 1329 (9th Cir. 1987).
[168] *Id.* at 1333.

that define establishments as adult businesses, and thus subject to regulation, because they "regularly" offer or feature nudity, semi-nudity, or some other form of adult entertainment.[169]

F. "Time" Regulations—Restricting Adult Businesses' Hours of Operation

One of the simplest and yet most effective ways to prevent the negative secondary effects of sexually oriented businesses is through the first element of time, place, and manner regulation—time. Although the U.S. Supreme Court has not specifically ruled on limitations of hours of operation as applied to adult businesses, such laws have been upheld by a number of courts, including seven federal courts of appeals.[170]

After the Supreme Court's *Alameda Books* decision, several adult businesses challenged restrictions on hours of operation based on that decision. With one exception,[171] appellate courts have continued to uphold the regulation of the hours of operation for adult businesses.[172]

VI. Conclusion

The regulation of adult businesses can be a challenging task, often involving different local political groups, neighbors, and attitudes. The First Amendment adds yet another layer of complication. However, local governments that follow the recommendations identified throughout this chapter will be in a strong position to mitigate risk and successfully control the unwanted effects of adult business establishments.

---

[169] *See, e.g.*, Schultz v. City of Cumberland, 228 F.3d 831 (7th Cir. 2000); 84 Video/Newsstand, Inc. v. Sartini, 455 Fed. App'x 541, 560 (6th Cir. 2011); MJJG Rest., LLC v. Horry Cnty., 11 F. Supp. 3d 541, 557 (D.S.C. 2014); Gold Diggers, LLC v. Town of Berlin, 469 F. Supp. 2d 43, 62 (D. Conn. 2007).
[170] *See, e.g.*, Star Satellite, Inc. v. City of Biloxi, 779 F.2d 1074 (5th Cir. 1986); Ben Rich Trading, Inc. v. City of Vineland, 126 F.3d 155 (3rd Cir. 1997); Nat'l Amusements v. Town of Dedham, 43 F.3d 731 (1st Cir. 1995); Richland Bookmart, Inc. v. Nichols, 137 F.3d 435 (6th 1998); DiMa Corp. v. Town of Hallie, 185 F.3d 823 (7th Cir. 1999); Lady J. Lingerie v. City of Jacksonville, 176 F.3d 1358 (11th Cir. 1999); L.J. Concepts, Inc. v. City of Phoenix, 215 F.3d 1333, No. 99-17270/17271, WL 338963 (9th Cir. 2000) (unpublished opinion).
[171] *See* Annex Books, Inc. v. City of Indianapolis, 740 F.3d 1136, 1138 (7th Cir. 2014).
[172] *See, e.g.*, Ctr. for Fair Pub. Pol'y v. Maricopa Cnty., 336 F.3d 1153, 1159, 1162–63 (9th Cir. 2003); Ocello v. Koster, 354 S.W.3d 187, 213–14 (Mo. 2011); Deja Vu of Cincinnati, L.L.C. v. Union Twp., 411 F.3d 777 (6th Cir. 2005) (*en banc*); Andy's Rest. & Lounge, Inc. v. City of Gary, 466 F.3d 550 (7th Cir. 2006).

8

First Amendment Limitations on the Regulation of Sexually Oriented Entertainment

Robert Allen Sedler
Distinguished Professor of Law
Wayne State University
Detroit, Michigan

I. Introduction

Chapter 7 of this book addresses, in broad terms, the First Amendment limitations on regulation of sexually oriented businesses, with a special focus on what is commonly referred to as the "secondary effects" doctrine. This chapter follows up on the discussion in chapter 7 by specifically addressing the subset of legal issues associated with the regulation of sexually oriented entertainment. Whereas chapter 7 addresses zoning and licensing issues associated with sexually oriented businesses, this chapter provides some discussion of the regulation of the activities that occur within sexually oriented establishments.

Sexually oriented entertainment generally takes the form of erotic dancing, commonly known as "striptease" dancing. The dancer removes some or all of her clothing, emphasizes the sexual parts of her body, and makes gestures and moves her body in such a way as to convey a message of sexuality. The dancer ends up partially nude, that is, topless, displaying her bare breasts and buttocks, wearing only a G-string that covers her pubic area and anus, and/or wearing "pasties" over her nipples and areolas while the rest of her breast is exposed, or completely nude, exposing her vagina and anus.[1]

Sexually oriented entertainment takes place in adult entertainment establishments, which, depending on their mode of operation, are commonly called "strip joints," "strip clubs," or "gentlemen's clubs." Some of these establishments are licensed to serve liquor; others are not. From the perspective of law enforcement and state regulation, sexually oriented entertainment is part of the commercial sex industry. The clientele wants to see nude or partially nude women dancing and acting in a sexual manner. They may also want to interact with the dancers in various ways. These ways range from a table dance, in which the dancer performs at the customer's table, to a lap dance, in which the dancer gyrates on the customer's lap and makes contact with his body, to sexual activity that takes place in a private room on the premises. Stated simply, sexually oriented entertainment is much more about sex than it is about entertainment.

Because sexually oriented entertainment is a part of the commercial sex industry, many localities would like to ban adult entertainment establishments entirely. But because adult entertainment establishments are engaged in the business of expression, states and local governments cannot ban them entirely, and local government efforts to regulate them are constrained to some extent by the First Amendment. The First Amendment protects the expressive or entertainment component of erotic dancing but leaves local governments free to suppress or, in certain ways, prohibit the sexual component of sexually oriented entertainment.

Precisely because there is a sexual component to sexually oriented entertainment, states and localities are understandably concerned with preventing the undesirable secondary effects associated with the operation of adult entertainment establishments. These undesirable secondary

---

[1] Although there are some adult entertainment establishments offering erotic dancing by male dancers, all of the reported cases involve female dancers.

effects include sexual activity between dancers and customers, drug use, and the impact that the operation of adult entertainment establishments may have on nearby businesses and adjacent residential areas. Because sexually oriented entertainment is a part of the commercial sex industry and may have these undesirable secondary effects, states and localities *can* impose some degree of regulation on sexually oriented entertainment and adult entertainment establishments. And because the First Amendment protects only the message of sexuality conveyed by sexually oriented entertainment, it does not matter that the extensive regulation of sexually oriented entertainment and adult entertainment establishments may have a significant economic impact and may make the operation of adult entertainment establishments economically infeasible. In practice although the operators of adult entertainment establishments and the states and localities seeking to regulate them are arguing about the meaning and application of the First Amendment, the real question is whether states and localities will be able to "regulate sexually oriented entertainment out of business."

This chapter discusses governmental regulation that specifically deals with sexually oriented entertainment and the operation of adult entertainment establishments featuring such entertainment. However, the constitutional doctrine that the courts have promulgated in dealing with zoning and licensing of adult entertainment establishments relating to the prevention of undesirable secondary effects has carried over to the regulation of sexually oriented entertainment itself, and the reader is therefore advised to read this chapter along with chapter 7 to fully understand the doctrine.

II. Constitutional Doctrine

Generally speaking, entertainment is a quintessential First Amendment–protected activity.[2] The First Amendment protects nudity in live theatrical performances, such as in plays like *Hair, Equus,* and *Six Degrees of*

---

[2] *See* Schad v. Borough of Mount Ephraim, 452 U.S. 61, 65 (1981) ("Entertainment, as well as political and ideological speech, is protected; motion pictures, programs broadcast by radio and television, and live entertainment, such as musical and dramatic works, fall within the First Amendment guarantee."); Se. Promotions, Ltd. v. Conrad, 420 U.S. 546 (1975).

Separation, and in productions of lesser cultural or artistic value,[3] because nudity is related to the subject of the performance, and the performance takes place in a closed venue before a willing audience. There is no valid interest in prohibiting the use of nudity as a part of the performance, and a law prohibiting all nudity in any theatrical performance or prohibiting all nudity in "any public place," without exception, is void on its face for overbreadth.[4]

The U.S. Supreme Court has taken a different approach toward nudity in connection with sexually oriented entertainment and, in fact, toward all other matters involving sexually oriented entertainment and the operation of adult entertainment establishments. The Court has held that erotic or "striptease" dancing is "expressive conduct within the outer perimeters of the First Amendment."[5] This means that states and local governments cannot ban erotic dancing because of disagreement with the message of sexuality that erotic dancing conveys.[6] However, the state can extensively regulate erotic dancing performances and the operation of adult entertainment establishments that provide erotic dancing. The Supreme Court has held that such extensive regulation is constitutionally permissible because sexually oriented entertainment is a part of the commercial sex industry and because there may be undesirable secondary effects associated with the operation of adult entertainment facilities.[7] This being so, the Court has held that regulation of erotic dancing at these facilities, when challenged as violating the First Amendment, is evaluated only under an intermediate standard of scrutiny.[8]

---

[3] *Schad,* 452 U.S. at 66 ("Nor may an entertainment program be prohibited solely because it displays the nude human figure. '[N]udity alone' does not place otherwise protected material outside the mantle of the First Amendment.") (internal citations omitted); California v. LaRue, 409 U.S. 109, 118 (1975) ("[W]e agree that at least some of the [nude] performances to which these regulations address themselves are within the limits of the constitutional protection of freedom of expression").

[4] *Id.; see also* Doran v. Salem Inn, 422 U.S. 922, 933–34 (1975); Triplett Grille v. City of Akron, 40 F.3d 129, 136 (6th Cir. 1994). These cases generally hold that general bans on nudity in public places sweep First Amendment protected speech within their ambit, thus resulting in invalidation of the bans.

[5] Barnes v. Glen Theatre, Inc., 501 U.S. 560, 566 (1991).

[6] *See* City of Erie v. Pap's A.M., 529 U.S. 277, 289 (2000); *Barnes,* 501 U.S. at 565.

[7] *See, e.g.,* City of Los Angeles v. Alameda Books, Inc., 535 U.S. 425, 434 (2002); City of Renton v. Playtime Theatres, Inc., 475 U.S. 41, 49 (1986).

[8] *See, e.g., Alameda Books,* 535 U.S. at 443.

Three consequences follow from the use of the intermediate standard of scrutiny when regulating sexually oriented entertainment on the basis of such entertainment's secondary effects. First, the state may enact regulations specifically applicable to erotic dancing at adult entertainment establishments, so long as these regulations are not directed at the message of sexuality that erotic dancing conveys. Second, regulations directed at combating the undesirable secondary effects associated with erotic dancing at adult entertainment establishments are evaluated under the symbolic speech doctrine, which applies when both speech and conduct are combined in the same activity. Under the symbolic speech doctrine, a regulation will be sustained if (1) it is within the constitutional power of government, (2) it furthers a substantial governmental interest, (3) the governmental interest is unrelated to the suppression of freedom of expression, and (4) the incidental restriction on expression is no greater than is necessary to the furtherance of that interest.[9] Third, regulations directed at the time or location of the erotic dancing or the manner in which it takes place are evaluated under the reasonable time, place, and manner doctrine. Under this doctrine, which in practice is very similar and sometimes interchangeable with the symbolic speech doctrine, the regulation will be upheld if it is content neutral, serves a significant governmental interest, and leaves open ample alternative avenues of communication.[10]

As is discussed more extensively in chapter 7, the Supreme Court first applied intermediate scrutiny to uphold state and municipal zoning laws specifically applicable to adult entertainment establishments, such as those requiring that they be dispersed from each other, on the ground that there could be undesirable secondary effects resulting from the concentration of adult entertainment establishments in particular areas.[11] In subsequent decisions, the Court has applied intermediate scrutiny to address the constitutionality of state and local government laws regulating

---

[9] United States v. O'Brien, 391 U.S. 367, 377 (1968). Under this doctrine, a sufficiently important governmental interest in regulating the "nonspeech" elements of the activity may justify "incidental" restrictions on expression.

[10] *See, e.g.,* Ward v. Rock Against Racism, 491 U.S. 781, 791 (1989); Heffron v. Int'l Soc'y for Krishna Consciousness, Inc., 452 U.S. 640 (1981).

[11] *See* Young v. American Mini Theatres, Inc., 427 U.S. 50, 71 (1976).

the state of undress of erotic dancers, finding that there were undesirable secondary effects resulting from dancers appearing in a state of total nudity.[12] Following these decisions, the lower courts have upheld numerous restrictions on the operation of adult entertainment establishments purportedly designed to avoid unnecessary secondary effects, such as bans on the serving of alcohol in these establishments[13] and prohibitions on physical contact between dancers and customers.[14] The practical result of the Supreme Court's application of the intermediate standard of scrutiny to the regulation of erotic dancing at adult entertainment establishments is that such regulation is much more likely to be upheld than most other regulation of expressive activity that is protected by the First Amendment.

III. Specific Issues

A. Bans on Erotic Dancing, Overbroad Laws, and Evidence of Undesirable Secondary Effects

As stated previously, erotic dancing falls at the outer limits of First Amendment protection.[15] Because erotic dancing is entitled to First Amendment protection, under the principle of content neutrality, local governments cannot ban erotic dancing simply because of disagreement with the message of sexuality that erotic dancing conveys.[16] Although local governments can extensively regulate erotic dancing in adult entertainment establishments

---

[12] *See Pap's A.M.*, 529 U.S. at 291 ("[T]he ordinance prohibiting public nudity is aimed at combating crime and other negative secondary effects caused by the presence of adult entertainment establishments like Kandyland and not at suppressing the erotic message conveyed by this type of nude dancing. Put another way, the ordinance does not attempt to regulate the primary effects of the expression, i.e., the effect on the audience of watching nude erotic dancing, but rather the secondary effects, such as the impacts on public health, safety, and welfare, which we have previously recognized are 'caused by the presence of even one such' establishment."); *Barnes*, 501 U.S. at 584 ("[T]he State of Indiana could reasonably conclude that forbidding nude entertainment of the type offered at the Kitty Kat Lounge and the Glen Theatre's 'bookstore' furthers its interest in preventing prostitution, sexual assault, and associated crimes.").

[13] *See* the discussion, *infra*, note 22, and accompanying text.

[14] *See* the discussion, *infra*, notes 23–27, and accompanying text.

[15] *See Pap's A.M.*, 529 U.S. at 289.

[16] *See, e.g.*, Reed v. Town of Gilbert, 135 S. Ct. 2218, 2227 (2015) ("Government regulation of speech is content based if a law applies to particular speech because of the topic discussed or the idea or message expressed.").

because of the undesirable secondary effects associated with erotic dancing at such establishments, a jurisdiction cannot, in the guise of regulation, effectively prohibit erotic dancing in adult entertainment facilities.[17]

In cases involving regulation of sexually oriented entertainment, the government bears the burden of demonstrating that the purpose of the regulation in issue is to address those undesirable secondary effects and not to prevent erotic dancing. If it fails to make such a showing, the regulation violates the First Amendment.[18] Moreover, the state can regulate nudity only in adult entertainment establishments; nudity in theatrical performances is fully protected by the First Amendment. Yet, under the overbreadth doctrine, if the state attempts to apply a law prohibiting all nudity in public places to an adult entertainment venue, the establishment can successfully challenge the law on its face for overbreadth, although the local government could constitutionally prohibit total nudity in adult entertainment establishments.[19]

With respect to the state's burden of demonstrating undesirable secondary effects associated with the operation of adult entertainment facilities, the state must provide some concrete evidence sufficient to demonstrate a reasonable belief that there is a causal relationship between the activity being regulated, such as the dancer's state of undress or the serving of alcohol at an adult entertainment establishment, and the resulting undesirable secondary

---

[17] *See, e.g.*, *Pap's A.M.*, 529 U.S. at 292.

[18] *See, e.g.*, Palmetto Props. v. Cnty. of Du Page, 160 F. Supp. 2d 876 (N.D. Ill. 2001) (finding state law prohibiting "strip clubs" from operating within one thousand feet of forest preserve violated the First Amendment, where the area in which the proposed "strip club" would operate was undeveloped and was not accessible to the general public, the effect of the law would prevent "strip clubs" from operating in any unincorporated area of the county, and there was no evidence of undesirable secondary effects associated with the operation of "strip clubs" near forest preserve areas); Nakatomi Inv., Inc. v. City of Schenectady, 949 F. Supp. 988 (N.D.N.Y. 1997) (holding effective ban on erotic dancing by requiring the covering of pubic areas, buttocks, and breasts below the areola, as opposed to only requiring that the dancers wear pasties and G-strings, was not targeted at secondary effects and did not provide ample alternative channels for communication); R.W.B. of Riverview, Inc. v. Stemple, 111 F. Supp. 2d 748 (S.D. W. Va. 2000) (purpose of state law requiring licensing of juice bars that provide nude dancing was to reduce the number of establishments providing nude dancing, not the regulation of secondary effects).

[19] *See* Broadrick v. Oklahoma, 413 U.S. 601 (1973). The overbreadth doctrine is designed to prevent a chilling effect on the exercise of First Amendment rights. Any party subject to a law regulating or applicable to acts of expression can challenge the law on its face for substantial overbreadth, regardless of whether the party's activity itself is protected by the First Amendment.

effects.[20] However, the state or municipality has a great deal of leeway in producing such evidence.[21] It is not required to conduct independent studies regarding undesirable secondary effects and may rely on evidence from other municipalities, provided that a suitable effort is made to control for other variables.[22] And it may rely on earlier studies demonstrating undesirable secondary effects without also affirmatively demonstrating that the studies remain viable.[23] Once the government produces its evidence, the burden shifts to the plaintiff to cast doubt on that evidence by showing that it does not support a finding of undesirable secondary effects.[24] If the plaintiff can make such a showing, the burden shifts back to the government to provide additional evidence to justify the regulation.[25]

Although the government is likely to prevail on its showing of undesirable secondary effects in most cases, it is possible in some cases that the plaintiff, armed with empirical study, could successfully challenge the local government's findings and thus avoid the regulation. For example, in *Flanigan's Enterprises, Inc. v. Fulton County*, the county banned totally nude dancing in establishments that were licensed to serve alcoholic beverages.[26] The court found that the evidence did not establish a causal connection between undesirable secondary effects and the combination of alcohol and totally nude dancing.[27] In *Flanagan's*, the county had conducted a study on the secondary effects of alcohol consumption in adult establishments in the

---

[20] *See, e.g., Alameda Books*, 535 U.S. at 438–49 ("The municipality's evidence must fairly support the municipality's rationale for its ordinance."); Foxxxy Ladyz Adult World, Inc. v. Vill. of Dix, 779 F.3d 706, 716–17 (7th Cir. 2015) ("To pass constitutional muster, [the local government] must provide some concrete evidence indicating that public nudity generates adverse secondary effects").

[21] *See Alameda Books*, 535 U.S. at 438 ("In *Renton*, we specifically refused to set such a high bar for municipalities that want to address merely the secondary effects of protected speech. We held that a municipality may rely on any evidence that is 'reasonably believed to be relevant' for demonstrating a connection between speech and a substantial, independent government interest.").

[22] *See Foxxxy Ladyz*, 779 F.3d at 717 ("[T]he [local government] retains considerable flexibility in identifying evidentiary support.... [The local government] is not required to conduct independent studies regarding undesirable secondary effects, but rather may rely on evidence from other municipalities...").

[23] *See, e.g., City of Renton*, 475 U.S. at 51; *Foxxxy Ladyz*, 779 F.3d at 717.

[24] *See Alameda Books*, 535 U.S. at 438–39.

[25] *See id.*

[26] 242 F.3d 976 (11th Cir. 2001).

[27] *See id.* at 987.

county that featured nude dancing. The establishments, which had operated in the county for nearly a decade, also conducted their own studies. Both sets of studies led to the conclusion that there was no statistical correlation showing an increase in crime at adult entertainment establishments that both featured nude dancing and served alcoholic beverages. In fact, there were more police calls and crime at other establishments that served alcohol and did not present nude dancing. Both studies found high occupancy, high rental rates, and high property values in the properties adjacent to the adult entertainment establishments in question. In this case, then, there could be no justification for the county's ban on nude dancing in adult entertainment establishments serving alcoholic beverages because the evidence clearly showed that there were no undesirable secondary consequences associated with alcohol and nude dancing at these establishments.[28]

B. State of Undress

The Supreme Court held in *Barnes* and *Pap's A.M.* that the government can prohibit totally nude dancing in adult entertainment establishments. Both of these cases involved state public nudity laws that had been interpreted by state officials to require that female dancers in such establishments must wear pasties and G-strings. Although the Court was badly fragmented in these cases, a Court majority agreed that these requirements did not violate the First Amendment.[29] The Court had earlier upheld zoning laws requiring adult uses, such as adult theaters and adult bookstores, to be located at some distance from each other, on the ground that the concentration of adult uses could create undesirable secondary effects on the surrounding neighborhood.[30] In *Barnes* and, later, in *Pap's A.M.*, the Court carried over the rationale of the zoning cases of "preventing undesirable secondary effects" as a permissible regulation of erotic dancing in adult entertainment establishments. Applying this rationale and the intermediate scrutiny of the symbolic speech doctrine, the Court held that the government could find that totally nude

---

[28] *Id.* at 986.
[29] *See Pap's A.M.*, 529 U.S. at 294; *Barnes*, 501 U.S. at 571.
[30] *Young*, 427 U.S. at 71; *City of Renton*, 475 U.S. at 54.

erotic dancing in adult entertainment establishments created undesirable secondary effects, such as crime, prostitution, sexual activity, and spread of sexually transmitted diseases.[31] The regulation satisfied the symbolic speech doctrine because (1) the regulation furthered the substantial governmental interest in preventing these undesirable secondary effects; (2) the regulation was unrelated to the suppression of free expression because it was not directed at the erotic message conveyed by the dance; and (3) the requirement that the dancers wear G-strings and pasties was a minimal restriction and left ample opportunity for the dancer to convey the message of sexuality by her dance.[32] The dancer would still be nude except for a G-string covering her pubic area and anus and pasties covering her nipples and areolas. Her nude breasts and buttocks would still be displayed, she could continue her gyrations and movements, and this amount of nudity would contribute to the erotic message conveyed by her dancing. The Court has thus resolved the question of an erotic dancer's state of undress, and the First Amendment permits the state to require that an erotic dancer at an adult entertainment establishment must wear some minimum amount of clothing.[33]

C. Bans on Serving Alcohol in Adult Entertainment Establishments

As a general proposition, laws prohibiting the serving of alcohol in adult entertainment establishments presenting nude or seminude erotic dancing do

---

[31] See Barnes, 501 U.S. at 584; Pap's A.M., 529 U.S. at 293.

[32] See id. at 292–93.

[33] Although the law usually requires only that the dancer cover her nipples and areolas with "pasties," a requirement that she appear in a "bikini top" has also been upheld. See Baby Dolls Topless Saloons, Inc. v. City of Dallas, 295 F.3d 471 (5th Cir. 2002); 35 Bar & Grille, LLC v. City of San Antonio, 943 F. Supp. 2d 706 (W.D. Tex. 2013) (addressing "bikini top" requirement imposed after city held hearings and found that amendment to the "pasties" exception was necessary to address undesirable secondary effects in adult entertainment establishments). For contrary results, see Nakatomi Inv., Inc. v. City of Schenectady, 949 F. Supp. 988 (N.D.N.Y. 1997) (finding that regulation effectively banned erotic dancing and therefore violated the First Amendment by requiring the covering of pubic areas, buttocks, and breasts below the areola, as opposed to only requiring that the dancers wear pasties and G-strings). The result in the latter case seems more consistent with the Supreme Court's application of the symbolic speech doctrine in Erie and Barnes. The fact that the dancer cannot display her nude breasts, except for pasties, seriously detracts from the message of sexuality conveyed by the dance because her full breast is no longer nude, and she is not displaying any part of her breast that cannot be seen in public outside of the adult entertainment establishment.

not violate the First Amendment. The government can conclude that (1) the ban is not targeted at the message conveyed by erotic dancing, (2) there are undesirable secondary effects associated with the combination of alcohol and erotic dancing at adult entertainment establishments, and (3) the ban allows for ample alternative avenues of communication because any adult entertainment venue can present erotic dancing so long as it does not serve alcohol.[34] However, if the state does permit adult entertainment establishments to serve alcohol, the First Amendment requirements applicable to the regulation of erotic dancing in adult entertainment establishments that do not serve alcohol are equally applicable to those that are licensed to serve alcohol.

D. Regulation of the Manner of Erotic Dancing and the Operation of Adult Entertainment Establishments

The government may additionally conclude that there are undesirable secondary effects relating to sexual interaction between the erotic dancers and the customers, and the government may prohibit any form of sexual contact between the erotic dancers and their customers, including in the form of lap dancing or simply in the touching of body parts.[35] Not only does the state have a substantial interest in preventing any form of sexual contact between dancers and customers,[36] but the dancer may convey her message of sexuality

---

[34] The cases upholding such bans are numerous. *See e.g.,* Sammy's of Mobile, Ltd. v. City of Mobile, 140 F.3d 993 (11th Cir. 1998); Pancakes, Biscuits and More, LLC v. Pendleton Cnty. Comm'n, 996 F. Supp. 2d 438 (N.D. W.Va. 2014); Combs v. Tex. Entm't Ass'n, 347 S.W.2d 277 (Tex. 2011). *See also* J.L. Spoons, Inc. v. Dragani, 538 F.3d 379 (6th Cir. 2008), (rejecting an overbreadth challenge by an adult entertainment establishment to a state law precisely defining "nudity" and "sexual activity," and providing that any establishment holding a liquor permit may not knowingly or willfully allow nudity or sexual activity on its premises.) If the law were invoked against a legitimate theater serving alcohol that featured a play including some nudity, the application of the law in this circumstance could be held to violate the First Amendment as applied. But see *Town of Lyndon v. Beyer,* 627 N.W.2d 548 (Wis. 2001), where a law prohibiting nude dancing in liquor licensed establishments was found to be unconstitutionally overbroad.
[35] *See, e.g.,* DLS, Inc. v. City of Chattanooga, 107 F.3d 403, 409 (6th Cir. 1997); Hang On, Inc. v. City of Arlington, 65 F.3d 1248, 1253 (5th Cir. 1995) ("[I]ntentional contact between a nude dancer and a bar patron is conduct beyond the expressive scope of the dancing itself. The conduct at that point has overwhelmed any expressive strains it may contain. That the physical contact occurs while in the course of protected activity does not bring it within the scope of the First Amendment.").
[36] *See DLS,* 107 F.3d at 410 (finding that a "buffer zone" around performers at sexually oriented entertainment establishments "furthers the important state interests of the prevention of crime and the prevention of disease.").

without gyrating on the customer's lap or engaging in sexual touching with him. Moreover, in order to prevent the possibility of sexual touching, the state may require that the dancers perform at a reasonable distance from the customer or that they perform on a raised stage.[37] The state may also require that all of the dancing take place in open view and under the observation of an employee of the establishment[38] or with an unobstructed view of every area of the premises for law enforcement personnel.[39]

Finally, as regards the dancer's performance itself, restrictions on the dancer's performance, such as a ban on "simulated sexual acts" or touching of the buttocks, genitals, and breasts, are targeted at the message of sexuality conveyed by erotic dancing itself. Such a restriction, as one court has put it, "deprives the performer of a repertoire of expressive elements with which to craft an erotic, sensual performance and thereby interferes substantially with the dancer's ability to communicate her erotic message," and therefore violates the First Amendment.[40]

One way by which states and localities can try to make adult entertainment establishments featuring erotic dancing less profitable is to limit their hours of operation, especially by requiring them to close during the

---

[37] The cases upholding these requirements are numerous. *See e.g., id.* at 411–12 (buffer zone and stage requirements); *Hang On,* 65 F.3d at 1254 (5th Cir. 1995) (no-touch rule); Krontz v. City of San Diego, 136 Cal. App. 4th 1126, (2006) (buffer zone and no touch rule); Fantasy Ranch, Inc. v. City of Arlington, 459 F.3d 546 (5th Cir. 2006) (upholding buffer zone and stage requirements, including requirement that dancers be physically separated from customers by solid, clear, unbreakable glass or Plexiglas wall with no openings that would permit physical contact with customers); Deja Vu of Nashville v. Metro. Gov't of Nashville & Davidson Cnty., 274 F.3d 377 (6th Cir. 2001), *cert. den.,* 535 U.S. 1073 (2002) (buffer zone and no-touch rule).

[38] *See, e.g.,* Bonhower v. City of Va. Beach, 76 F. Supp. 2d 681 (E.D. Va. 1999). *See also* Lady J. Lingerie v. City of Jacksonville, 176 F.3d 1358 (11th Cir. 1999), (upholding a requirement that rooms in adult entertainment establishments be at least one thousand square feet in area, based on a finding that "illegal and unhealthy activities take place in small rooms at adult entertainment establishments.").

[39] *See, e.g.,* LLEH, Inc. v. Wichita Cnty., 289 F.3d 358 (5th Cir. 2002).

[40] Schultz v. City of Cumberland, 228 F.2d 831, (7th Cir. 2000). *See also* Conchatta, Inc., v. Miller, 458 F.3d 258 (3d Cir. 2006); Centerfolds, Inc. v. Town of Berlin, 352 F. Supp. 2d 183 (E.D. Conn. 2004). But see *Giovani Carandola, Ltd. v. Fox,* 470 F.3d 1074 (4th Cir. 2006), where the Court upheld, on the basis of preventing "undesirable secondary effects," a ban on "simulated sexual acts" and "fondling of buttocks, genitals, and breasts," interpreted as prohibiting only simulated sexual acts that give the realistic impression or illusion that a sexual act is being performed and only the manipulation of specified erogenous zones. The result seems questionable and depends on a very narrow reading of these prohibitions. Compare *Legend Night Club v. Miller,* 637 F.3d 291 (4th Cir. 2011), where a similar law was invalidated on its face because it was not limited to adult entertainment establishments.

late evening hours. A limitation on the hours of operation can be sustained as a reasonable time, place, and manner limitation if (1) the state shows that there are undesirable secondary effects associated with the operation of such establishments during the late evening hours, and (2) if the establishments are permitted to stay open for a substantial number of hours so that they will have ample time to convey their message of sexuality and eroticism. In practice, the courts have upheld all of the challenged regulations pertaining to hours of operation, including some that have required a midnight closing.[41]

IV. Conclusion

Emerging from the extensive litigation involving governmental regulation of erotic dancing is the effective separation of the message of sexuality conveyed by erotic dancing from the undesirable secondary effects associated with the operation of adult entertainment establishments featuring erotic dancing. Or, to put it another way, these decisions have effectively separated the communicative message of sexuality, protected by the First Amendment, from the commercial sex industry, of which erotic dancing is a very important part. The states may not prohibit erotic dancing in adult entertainment facilities or prevent the dancer from conveying her erotic message in the dance itself. But the states' extensive regulation of activity taking place in adult entertainment establishments will be upheld against First Amendment challenge, so long as the particular regulation can be shown to be related to preventing undesirable secondary effects associated with erotic dancing in adult entertainment facilities.

The government may require that the dancer must wear a minimum amount of clothing, typically represented by a "G-string and pasties" requirement. The government may prohibit the serving of alcohol in adult entertainment establishments. The government may prohibit any sexual

---

[41] *See e.g.,* Schultz v. City of Cumberland, 228 F.3d at 831 (10:00 A.M. to midnight, Monday through Saturday); Deja Vu of Cincinnati, LLC v. Union Twp. Board of Trustees, 411 F.3d 777 (6th Cir. 2005) (midnight closure; open 12 hours a day, 6 days a week); Commonwealth v. Jameson, 215 S.W.2d 9 (Ky. 2006) (closure between 1:00 A.M. and 6:00 A.M.); Lady J. Lingerie v. City of Jacksonville, 176 F.3d 1158 (11th Cir.1999) (noon to 2:00 A.M. daily).

contact between the dancers and customers and may require that there be a buffer zone between them and that the dancer performed on a raised stage. And the government may impose reasonable limitations on hours of operation for adult entertainment establishments, including that they close at midnight. In the final analysis, what the First Amendment protects is only the erotic dancing itself, performed by a dancer on a raised stage, wearing a minimum amount of clothing, such as G-strings and pasties, in an establishment that does not serve alcohol and that must close at a particular time.

Such a result is consistent with the core values of the First Amendment. The First Amendment protects the message, and the First Amendment protects the performance of the erotic dancer as she conveys her message of sexuality and eroticism.

V. Suggestions for Practice

These suggestions are formulated with reference to First Amendment doctrine relating to adult entertainment facilities. They do not include questions of state law and state constitutional provisions that may also be applicable to adult entertainment facilities in the particular state. They are directed toward lawyers representing adult entertainment facilities and lawyers representing state and local governments. They are set forth in terms of what the government may and may not do under the First Amendment.

- The government may not prohibit erotic or "striptease" dancing in adult entertainment facilities.
- The government may extensively regulate erotic dancing in adult entertainment facilities. However, the particular regulation must expressly apply only to adult entertainment facilities. Where the government attempts to regulate erotic dancing in adult entertainment facilities by a more general law, such as a law prohibiting "public nudity" or a woman appearing in public with "bare breasts," that law by its terms could be applicable beyond adult entertainment facilities, such as to theatrical performances, and could be successfully

challenged as void on its face for overbreadth, in violation of the First Amendment. The overbreadth challenge can be asserted by an adult entertainment establishment when the state attempts to apply the law in question to an adult entertainment establishment, although it would be constitutional for the government to apply the law only to adult entertainment establishments.

- The government can extensively regulate erotic dancing performances and the operation of adult entertainment establishments that provide erotic dancing. The constitutionality of state and local regulation of erotic dancing performances at and the operation of adult entertainment establishments is evaluated under the intermediate scrutiny of the symbolic speech doctrine. The regulation must be shown to be directed at preventing undesirable secondary effects associated with the operation of adult entertainment establishments. The government has the burden of demonstrating that the purpose of the particular regulation was to deal with those undesirable secondary effects and of producing concrete evidence sufficient to demonstrate a reasonable belief that there is a causal relationship between the activity being regulated, such as the dancer's state of undress or the serving of alcohol at the adult entertainment establishment. However, the state or local government has a great deal of leeway in producing such evidence, such as relying on studies from other places or older studies showing undesirable secondary effects. Although the operator of the adult entertainment establishment can challenge the government's evidence and can litigate the matter of undesirable secondary effects, this is a very difficult challenge to make, and the government is very likely to prevail on the matter of undesirable secondary effects.

- The government may prohibit totally nude dancing in adult entertainment establishments and may require that the dancers wear a minimum amount of clothing, such as G-strings, covering the pubic area and anus, and pasties, covering the nipples and areola.

- The government may prohibit the serving of alcohol in adult entertainment establishments presenting nude or seminude dancing.

However, if the government does permit adult entertainment establishments to serve alcohol, then the same First Amendment requirements applicable to the regulation of erotic dancing in adult entertainment establishments that do not serve alcohol are equally applicable to those that are licensed to serve alcohol.

- The government can prohibit any form of sexual contact between the erotic dancers and their customers, including a "no-touch" rule, a requirement that there be a "buffer zone" between dancers and customers, and a requirement that the dancers perform on a raised stage.

- Under the First Amendment, the government cannot impose restrictions on the dancer's performance itself, such as by imposing a ban on "simulated sexual acts" or the dancer's touching of her buttocks, genitals, and breasts.

- Under the reasonable time, place, and manner doctrine, the government can regulate the hours of operation of adult entertainment establishments by requiring them to close during the late evening hours, such as after midnight, if (1) the government shows that there are undesirable secondary effects associated with the operation of such establishments during the late evening hours and (2) if the establishments are permitted to stay open for a substantial number of hours so that they will have ample time to convey their message of sexuality. In practice, the courts have upheld all of the challenged regulations regarding hours of operation, including some that have required a midnight closing.

9

Regulation of Speech on Government Property:
The Government Speech Doctrine

Gerald C. Hicks
Supervising Deputy City Attorney
Joseph Cerullo
Senior Deputy City Attorney
Sacramento City Attorney's Office
Sacramento, California

I. Introduction

This chapter analyzes speech by the government on public property. Other chapters address speech by private individuals and organizations on both public and private property: Chapter 2 addresses the placement of signs by private individuals and organizations on private property, chapters 5 and 6 discuss religious speech by individuals or organizations on private property, and chapters 10 and 11 address speech by private individuals and organizations on public property.

Generally, as several of the other chapters discuss, the First Amendment prohibits government from regulating private speech based on the speech's content unless the government can show that the regulation is narrowly tailored to serve a compelling governmental interest. In practical terms, this means that government cannot restrict speech simply because it dislikes the message.

And since 1939, the U.S. Supreme Court has applied a "forum analysis" to determine whether the government's regulation of speech on public property is constitutional.[1] First the Court determines the nature of the property, or forum, where the speech is occurring. Then the Court applies the test appropriate to that forum. The Court has identified four types of forums:

- *Traditional public forums* consist of streets, sidewalks, and parks that "have immemorially been held in trust for the use of the public and, time out of mind, have been used for the purposes of assembly, communicating thoughts between citizens, and discussing public questions."[2] In traditional public forums, reasonable time, place, and manner restrictions are allowed, but restrictions based on the content of speech must be narrowly tailored to serve a compelling government interest, and restrictions based on viewpoint are prohibited.[3]
- *Designated public forums* consist of "government property that has not traditionally been regarded as a public forum but is intentionally opened up for that purpose."[4] Regulation of speech in designated public forums is subject to the same standards that apply to traditional public forums. Government entities are not required to create or maintain designated public forums and may close them at any time for any reason.[5]
- *Limited public forums* consist of government property that is not a traditional public forum but has been opened "to use by certain groups or dedicated solely to the discussion of certain

---

[1] *See* Hague v. Comm. for Indus. Org., 307 U.S. 496, 504–05 (1939).

[2] Perry Educ. Assn. v. Perry Local Educ. Assn., 460 U.S. 37, 45 (1983) (internal quotation marks omitted). Utility poles and other facilities that are *part* of a street or sidewalk are not considered traditional public forums. *See, e.g.,* Members of City Council of Los Angeles v. Taxpayers for Vincent, 466 U.S. 789, 793 (1984) (holding that utility poles are not traditional public forums). But they may become designated public forums if government allows the placement of signs or banners on them.

[3] *See, e.g., Perry Ed. Ass'n,* 460 U.S. at 45.

[4] Pleasant Grove City v. Summum, 555 U.S. 460, 469 (2009) (internal quotation marks omitted).

[5] *See, e.g., Perry Ed. Ass'n,* 460 U.S. at 46; Sons of Confederate Veterans v. City of Lexington, 722 F.3d 224, 231 (4th Cir. 2014).

subjects."[6] In a limited public forum, government may impose content based restrictions on speech that are reasonable in light of the forum's purposes, but the restrictions must not discriminate against speakers because of their viewpoints on the permitted subjects.[7]

- **Nonpublic forums** consist of public property "which is not by tradition or designation a forum for public communication."[8] In such a forum, government may impose restrictions on speech that are reasonable in light of the property's intended purposes and viewpoint neutral.[9]

The forum analysis applies when government acts to regulate the speech of others on government property.

Under a more recent Supreme Court analysis, however, the First Amendment does not apply when the government itself is the speaker.[10] Indeed, "it is the very business of government to favor and disfavor points of view."[11] According to the Court, the primary constraint on government speech is the ballot box.[12] "When the government speaks, for instance to promote its own policies or to advance a particular idea, it is, in the end, accountable to the electorate and the political process for its advocacy. If the citizenry objects, newly elected officials later could espouse some different or contrary position."[13] It is also important to recognize that government, unlike many private citizens, may "speak" in many different ways, including the selective funding of favored programs. In addition, government "may exercise this same freedom to express its views when it receives assistance from private sources for the purpose of delivering a

---

[6] *Perry Ed. Ass'n*, 460 U.S. at 45, n.7.
[7] *See, e.g., Summum*, 555 U.S. at 470.
[8] *See, e.g., Perry Ed. Ass'n*, 460 U.S. at 45–46.
[9] *Id.* at 46.
[10] See *Summum*, 555 U.S. at 467 (2009); Walker v. Tex. Div., Sons of Confederate Veterans, 135 S. Ct. 2239, 2250 (2015).
[11] Nat'l Endowment for the Arts v. Finley, 524 U.S. 569, 598 (1998) (Scalia, J., concurring).
[12] *See* Johanns v. Livestock Marketing Assn., 544 U.S. 550, 563 (2005).
[13] Bd. of Regents of the Univ. of Wisc. Sys. v. Southworth, 529 U.S. 217, 235 (2000).

government controlled message."[14] Although the Free Speech Clause of the First Amendment does not apply to government speech, there are other legal constraints on government speech, such as the Establishment Clause of the First Amendment and statutory prohibitions on government's ability to engage in political advocacy.[15]

II. Development of the Government Speech Doctrine

Two hundred years after the ratification of the Bill of Rights, the Supreme Court decided *Rust v. Sullivan*,[16] commonly recognized as the origin of the government speech doctrine. In *Rust*, the federal government authorized funds for family planning services but prohibited the funds from being used to discuss abortion as a method of family planning. The grantees and doctors who received the funds argued that the prohibition violated their First Amendment rights. The Court disagreed, holding that government may "refus[e] to fund activities, including speech, which are specifically excluded from the scope of the project funded."[17] *Rust* is noteworthy in that

---

[14] *Summum*, 555 U.S. at 468.

[15] *See id.* at 468–69 (noting that "government speech must comport with the Establishment Clause" and that "[t]he involvement of public officials in advocacy may be limited by law, regulation, or practice"); Felix v. City of Bloomfield, 841 F.3d 848, 855 (10th Cir. 2016) ("The Establishment Clause constrains government speech only."); *see also, e.g.,* CAL. GOV'T CODE § 54964(a) (2016) ("An officer, employee, or consultant of a local agency may not expend or authorize the expenditure of any of the funds of the local agency to support or oppose the approval or rejection of a ballot measure, or the election or defeat of a candidate, by the voters."); 10 ILL. COMP. STAT. 5/9-25.1(b) (2016) ("No public funds shall be used to urge any elector to vote for or against any candidate or proposition, or be appropriated for political or campaign purposes to any candidate or political organization.").

[16] 500 U.S. 173 (1991).

[17] Nine years after *Rust*, the court reached a different result in *Legal Services Corporation v. Velazquez*, 531 U.S. 533 (2001). In *Velazquez*, the federal government established the Legal Services Corporation (LSC) to distribute funds to organizations "for the purpose of providing financial support for legal assistance in noncriminal proceedings or matters to persons unable to financially afford legal assistance." LSC funding could not be used, however, for legal representation that sought to amend or otherwise challenge existing welfare law. Even though the issue was remarkably similar to the issue in *Rust*, the Court invalidated the restriction of use of funding, noting that the LSC program in *Velazquez*, unlike the family planning program in *Rust*, "was designed to facilitate private speech, not to promote a governmental message," *id.* at 542, and that the restriction on use of LSC funding would constitute a "severe impairment of the judicial function," *id.* at 546.

the government was speaking by controlling the message through private agents rather than through governmental employees.[18]

The Court next applied the doctrine in *National Endowment for the Arts v. Finley*.[19] The National Endowment for the Arts (NEA) awarded funding to artists who demonstrated "artistic excellence and artistic merit." In selecting recipients, the NEA would "tak[e] into consideration general standards of decency and respect for the diverse beliefs and values of the American public." Artists who were denied funding challenged the funding criteria as viewpoint discrimination in violation of the First Amendment. The Court ruled in favor of the NEA, noting that "the Government may allocate competitive funding according to criteria that would be impermissible were direct regulation of speech or a criminal penalty at stake."[20]

In *Johanns v. Livestock Marketing Association*,[21] two associations representing beef producers objected to mandatory assessments used by the federal government to fund an advertising campaign promoting beef. The associations argued that the assessment violated the First Amendment because it compelled them to subsidize speech they found objectionable, and the government countered that the advertisements constituted government speech. The associations then argued that the advertisements could not constitute government speech because they were designed and delivered by private parties and were represented to the public as funded by "America's Beef Producers." Finding that the advertisements were government speech, the Court noted that "[t]he message set out in the beef promotions is from beginning to end the message established by the Federal Government."[22] Moreover, "[w]hen, as here, the government sets the overall message to be communicated and approves every word that is

---

[18] In a subsequent case, *Rosenberger v. Rectors & Visitors of the Univ. of Va.*, 515 U.S. 819 (1995), the Court held that the University of Virginia violated the First Amendment when it declined to fund a student organization's newspaper because it was a "religious activity." The distinction between *Rust* and *Rosenberger* is that *Rust* involved government funding of *its* program (government speech), whereas in *Rosenberger*, the speech (the student newspaper) was private.

[19] 524 U.S. 569 (1998).

[20] *Id.* at 587–88.

[21] 544 U.S. 550 (2005).

[22] *Id.* at 560.

disseminated, it is not precluded from relying on the government-speech doctrine because it solicits assistance from nongovernmental sources in developing specific messages."[23] Finally, in responding to the argument that the government must disclose that it is the speaker, the Court noted that "whether or not the reasonable viewer would identify the speech as the government's" was of no consequence in determining if the government speech doctrine applied.[24]

In 2009, the Court decided *Pleasant Grove City v. Summum*,[25] perhaps the first clear and formal articulation of the government speech doctrine. Pleasant Grove City, Utah, had placed various monuments in a city park, including one displaying the Ten Commandments. Summum, a religious organization, sought the city's permission to erect a stone monument, similar in size and nature to the Ten Commandments monument, that celebrated the "Seven Aphorisms of Summum." The city declined the request, and Summum sued, asserting that the city's acceptance of the Ten Commandments monument and rejection of the Summum monument violated the First Amendment. Summum argued that the city park was subject to the rules for regulating speech in a traditional public forum; the city argued that the issue was one of government speech. The Court agreed with the city: "There may be situations in which it is difficult to tell whether a government entity is speaking on its own behalf or is providing a forum for private speech, but this case does not present such a situation. Permanent monuments displayed on public property typically represent government speech."[26] In response to Summum's argument that a governmental agency accepting a privately donated monument must go through a formal process adopting the message that the monument conveys, the Court observed that a monument may mean different things to different people and that the "message" the governmental entity wishes to convey by accepting the

---

[23] *Id.* at 562.

[24] *Id.* at 564, n. 7. The Court distinguished a very similar case involving assessments for advertising mushrooms, *United States v. United Foods, Inc.*, 533 U.S. 405 (2001), because the government had waived the argument that the mushroom-advertising campaign was government speech. *Id.* at 448–49.

[25] 555 U.S. 460 (2009).

[26] *Id.* at 470.

monument may differ from the message the creator of the monument wished to convey. "By accepting such a monument, a government entity does not necessarily endorse the specific meaning that any particular donor sees in the monument."[27]

In 2015, the Supreme Court again applied the government speech doctrine in *Walker v. Texas Division, Sons of Confederate Veterans, Inc.*[28] At issue in *Walker* was whether specialty license plates issued by Texas constituted government speech. Private individuals and private entities that wanted specialty license plates could submit their designs to the State for approval, and the State could disapprove a proposed specialty plate by finding that the "design might be offensive to any member of the public. . . ." The case arose when Texas rejected a design for a specialty plate that included a Confederate battle flag.

Relying almost exclusively on *Summum*, the Court sided with Texas and held that the specialty plates constituted government speech.[29] This was so because of history, public perception, and government control:

- "First, the history of license plates shows that, insofar as license plates have conveyed more than state names and vehicle identification numbers, they long have communicated messages from the States."[30]
- "Second, Texas license plates 'are often closely identified in the public mind with the [State].'"[31]
- "Third, Texas maintains direct control over the messages conveyed on specialty plates."[32]

---

[27] *Id.* at 476–77.
[28] 135 S. Ct. 2239 (2015).
[29] *But see* Matwyuk v. Johnson, 22 F. Supp. 3d 812 (W.D. Mich. 2014) (finding that personalized license plates were not government speech); Mitchell v. Md. Motor Vehicle Admin., 126 A.3d 165 (Md. Ct. App. 2015) (finding that message on vanity license plates was not government speech).
[30] *Id.* at 2248.
[31] *Id.* at 2248 (quoting *Summum*, 555 U.S. at 472).
[32] *Id.* at 2249.

III. Application of the Government Speech Doctrine to Government Websites and Social Media

One of the primary areas where government speaks today is the Internet. Government websites and government communication through electronic mail, texting, Facebook, Twitter, YouTube, and other social media provide resources for apprising the public of current events, applicable laws, services, pertinent documents and publications, and employment opportunities. In addition, some government websites offer blogs or discussion boards for public discussion. To date, no reported cases have addressed First Amendment issues with respect to government blogs, discussion boards, or other electronic forums. But some federal appellate courts have begun addressing government's use of websites for conveying information and advocating government-supported positions. Three decisions from these courts illustrate how local governments benefit when speech regulations are analyzed under the government speech doctrine rather than by applying the forum analysis. Application of the government speech doctrine to cases involving government websites is, in part, due to difficulties in applying a public forum analysis to websites.[33]

The Putnam Pit, Inc. v. City of Cookeville[34] concerned a small tabloid, *The Putnam Pit*, that was the self-appointed "eye on government corruption" in Cookeville, Tennessee. Cookeville maintained a website on which it had permitted hyperlinks to several business entities. When *The Putnam Pit* requested that the city install a hyperlink for *The Putnam Pit*'s website, the city refused. *The Putnam Pit* sued, alleging the city's website was a designated public forum and that the city's refusal to add a link to *The Putnam Pit*'s website constituted viewpoint discrimination in violation of the First Amendment. Applying a forum analysis, the Court of Appeals for the Sixth Circuit found that Cookeville's website was a nonpublic forum, so Cookeville's refusal to add *The Putnam Pit*'s link would be constitutional

---

[33] *See* Sutliffe v. Epping Sch. Dist., 584 F.3d 314, 334 (1st Cir. 2009) ("The public forum doctrine is not a natural fit for the issues raised in this case.").

[34] 221 F.3d 834 (6th Cir. 2000).

only if both reasonable and viewpoint neutral. The court remanded the case to the trial court for further findings on the issue of viewpoint neutrality.

Had the Sixth Circuit applied the government speech doctrine in *The Putnam Pit*, the outcome might have been different, as the next two cases show.

In *Page v. Lexington County School District One*,[35] the school district used its website, e-mail, and other forms of communication to express opposition to a bill pending in the South Carolina legislature that proposed tax credits for private and home schooling. The district had included links to nondistrict websites on its website and included nondistrict materials in its e-mails. A proponent of the bill requested access to the district's information-distribution system, and when the district refused, the proponent filed suit against the district, asserting a violation of his First Amendment rights. The proponent argued that the district's information-distribution system was a public forum and that the district engaged in viewpoint discrimination by excluding viewpoints in opposition to the bill. The district argued that its communications through the system were government speech. Agreeing with the district and citing *Johanns*, the Court of Appeals for the Fourth Circuit held that the communications disseminated through the system were indeed the district's speech: "[T]he government established the message; maintained control of its content; and controlled its dissemination to the public. Moreover, . . . the form of the message was, in part, *adopted by the government* from private sources."[36]

Sutliffe v. Epping School District[37] involved similar allegations that a school district had created a public forum and engaged in viewpoint discrimination. The underlying dispute centered on government spending in the Town of Epping, New Hampshire. The town used its own newsletters, mass mailings, and website, which included hyperlinks to town-friendly websites, to garner approval for budgets and spending for town and school purposes. As in *Page*, the plaintiff sought equal access by the placement of a hyperlink to an opposing website. The town refused. Relying primarily

---

[35] 531 F.3d 275 (4th Cir. 2008).
[36] *Id.* at 282 (emphasis added).
[37] 584 F.3d 314 (1st Cir. 2009).

on *Summum*, the Court of Appeals for the First Circuit concluded that "the Town defendant's actions, in setting up and controlling a town website and choosing not to allow the hyperlinks, constituted government speech."[38] The First Circuit noted that "*Summum* makes it clear that when the government uses its discretion to select between the speech of third parties for presentation through communication channels owned by the government and used for government speech, this in itself may constitute an expressive act by the government that is independent of the message of the third-party speech."[39]

IV. Requirements for Application of the Government Speech Doctrine

The government speech doctrine is "recently minted," and the Supreme Court has not yet articulated a clear test for deciphering what is and is not government speech.[40] Even so, the Court's opinions in *Johanns*, *Summum*, and *Walker* indicate that the government speech doctrine will likely apply when (1) the means used to communicate the government's message has historically been used to deliver government messages, (2) the means used to communicate the government's message is "closely identified in the public mind with the [governmental agency]", and (3) the governmental agency controls the content of the message.[41]

---

[38] *Id.* at 329.

[39] *Id.* at 330.

[40] *See* Pleasant Grove City v. Summum, 555 U.S. 460, 481 (2009) (Stevens, J., concurring).

[41] Walker v. Tex. Div., Sons of Confederate Veterans, Inc., 135 S. Ct. 2239, at 2248–49 (2015); *see also* Johanns v. Livestock Marketing Assn., 544 U.S. 550, 560–62 (2005). Recent appellate cases have found that transit advertising does not constitute government speech, ostensibly because the advertising does not meet the first two criteria. *See, e.g.*, Seattle Mideast Awareness Campaign v. King Cnty., 781 F.3d 489, 496 (9th Cir. 2015); Coleman v. Ann Arbor Transp. Auth., 904 F. Supp. 2d 670, 685–90 (E.D. Mich. 2012). Additional recent cases include *Felix v. City of Bloomfield*, 841 F.3d 848 (10th Cir. 2016) (finding Ten Commandments monument in city hall square to be government speech, but violative of Establishment Clause); *Freedom From Religion Foundation, Inc. v. Abbott*, No. A-16-CA-00233-SS, 2016 WL 7388401 (W.D. Tex. Dec. 20, 2016) (finding that private displays in Texas state capitol rotunda do not constitute government speech); *Dawson v. City of Grand Haven*, No. 329154, 2016 WL 7611556 (Mich. Ct. App. Dec. 29, 2016) (finding cross monument on city-owned land to constitute government speech).

In addition, the Fourth, Eighth, Ninth, and Tenth Circuits have employed four factors for distinguishing government speech from private speech: "(1) the central 'purpose' of the program in which the speech in question occurs; (2) the degree of 'editorial control' exercised by the government or private entities over the content of the speech; (3) the identity of the 'literal speaker'; and (4) whether the government or the private entity bears the 'ultimate responsibility' for the content of the speech. . . ."[42] In applying this analysis, appellate courts have determined that permanent monuments donated to governmental entities and displayed on public property are examples of government speech.[43]

V. Government Signs

When a government speaks through signs on its own property, it does not act as a regulator, so the First Amendment does not apply. Government entities thus may use signs to say whatever they want.[44] As Justice Alito recently explained in *Reed v. Town of Gilbert*, "government entities may . . . erect their own signs consistent with the principles that allow governmental speech. They may put up all manner of signs to promote safety, as well as directional signs and signs pointing out historic sites and scenic spots."[45] To be sure, government speech is not completely unrestrained. "[G]overnment speech must comport with the Establishment Clause [of the First Amendment]. The involvement of public officials in advocacy may be limited by

---

[42] Ariz. Life Coal., Inc. v. Stanton, 515 F.3d 956, 964–65 (9th Cir. 2008). The cases adopting the test from the Fourth, Eighth, and Tenth Circuits are *Planned Parenthood of S.C. Inc. v. Rose*, 361 F.3d 786, 792 (4th Cir. 2004); *Knights of the Ku Klux Klan v. Curators of the Univ. of Mo.*, 203 F.3d 1085, 1093–94 (8th Cir. 2000); and *Wells v. City and Cnty. of Denver*, 257 F.3d 1132, 1141 (10th Cir. 2001).

[43] *See* Felix v. City of Bloomfield, 841 F.3d 848, 855 (10th Cir. 2016) (holding that Ten Commandments monument in city hall lawn constituted government speech but violated Establishment Clause); Red River Freethinkers v. City of Fargo, 764 F.3d 948 (8th Cir. 2014) (stating that Ten Commandments monument located on City-owned land was government speech and did not violate the Establishment Clause); Am. Atheists, Inc. v. Davenport, 637 F.3d 1095, 1114 (10th Cir. 2010); *see also* Freedom from Religion Found., Inc. v. City of Warren, 707 F.3d 686, 696–97 (6th Cir. 2013) (citing *Wells*, 257 F.3d at 1137, 1143–44) (holding that city's temporary holiday display constituted government speech).

[44] *See Summum*, 555 U.S. at 467. *See also* Newton v. LePage, 700 F.3d 595, 604 (1st Cir. 2012) (finding that mural in a governmental building constituted government speech and government could remove the same).

[45] Reed v. Town of Gilbert, 135 S. Ct. 2218, 2233 (2015) (Alito, J., concurring).

laws, regulation, or practice. And of course, a government entity is ultimately 'accountable to the electorate and the political process for its advocacy.'"[46]

VI. Practice Tips

- Generally, the greater control the governmental agency exercises over the message, the more likely the message will be determined to be government speech. Ideally, this means that the message has been approved by the legislative body of the governmental agency. Delegation of approval authority by the legislative body may also demonstrate control and be more practical in ongoing programs requiring governmental approval.
- The more editorial input the governmental agency has with respect to the message, the greater the likelihood that the message will be determined to be that of the government.

VII. Conclusion

Unlike the public forum doctrine, which rests on the principle that citizens have a right to express their opinions in a public forum even if the government disagrees with those opinions, the government speech doctrine rests on the pragmatic understanding that "it is the very business of government to favor and disfavor points of view."[47] Thus, the gist of the government speech doctrine can be simply stated: when the government speaks, the First Amendment does not apply. But because the government speech doctrine is of recent vintage, with its contours still being determined, identifying when particular speech comes within the doctrine can be difficult.

---

[46] *Summum*, 555 U.S. at 468.
[47] Nat'l Endowment for the Arts v. Finley, 524 U.S. 569, 598 (1998) (Scalia, J., concurring).

Sidewalk Distribution of Protected Speech and Expression

J. Thomas Macdonald

Otten Johnson Robinson Neff + Ragonetti, P.C.
Denver, Colorado

I. Introduction

Streets, sidewalks, and public parks are optimum locations for anyone who wishes to communicate with fellow citizens inexpensively. Indeed, they may be the only possible locations for a panhandler exercising "the right to engage fellow human beings with the hope of receiving aid and compassion."[1] Thus, individuals and groups frequently take to the streets to engage in activities such as leafleting, solicitation, panhandling, preaching, education, counseling, street performance, sales of artwork or religious products, targeted picketing, and attempts to communicate with the patrons of a particular facility, such as an abortion clinic. The regulation of large groups engaging in such activities and the requirement of a proper permitting process for those activities are discussed at length in chapter 11. The same principles that govern a proper permitting scheme for a group demonstration also apply when

---

[1] See McLauglin v. City of Lowell, 140 F. Supp. 3d 177, 184 (D. Mass. 2015) (quoting Benefit v. City of Cambridge, 679 N.E.2d 184, 190 (Mass. 1997)).

the government regulates the use of newspaper racks and other physical structures located in public rights of way to facilitate communication.[2] This chapter will focus on the specific First Amendment issues raised by regulation of expressive activity by individuals or small groups in parks or on sidewalks, as well as the other aspects of the regulation of newspaper racks and other physical structures used to distribute expressive materials. Although courts use a common framework in addressing challenges to regulation of expressive conduct by large or small groups, application of that framework to individuals and small groups presents some unique issues.

II. Early Twentieth-Century Approach

In *Commonwealth v. Davis*, an opinion authored by Justice Oliver Wendell Holmes in 1897, the Massachusetts Supreme Court upheld the conviction of a man for preaching a sermon in the Boston Common without first obtaining a permit.[3] The opinion stated:

> For the legislature absolutely or conditionally to forbid public speaking in a highway or public park is no more an infringement of the rights of a member of the public than for the owner of a private house to forbid it in his house. When no proprietary rights interfere, the legislature may end the right of the public to enter upon the public place by putting an end to the dedication to public uses. So it may take the less step of limiting the public use to certain purposes.[4]

The U.S. Supreme Court affirmed the decision, quoting the passage just set forth with approval.[5]

---

[2] *See, e.g.*, City of Lakewood v. Plain Dealer Publ'g Co., 486 U.S. 750, 761 (1988) (for purposes of analyzing permitting schemes in public fora, proper analogy for newspaper racks is with leafleting, not with soda machines).

[3] Commonwealth v. Davis, 39 N.E. 113 (Mass. 1895).

[4] *Id.*

[5] Davis v. Massachusetts, 167 U.S. 43, 47 (1897).

Forty-two years later, in *Hague v. Committee for Industrial Organization*, the Court articulated a far different conception of the right of the legislature to regulate expressive activity in public streets and parks:[6]

> Wherever the title of streets and parks may rest, they have immemorially been held in trust for the use of the public and, time out of mind, have been used for purposes of assembly, communicating thoughts between citizens, and discussing public questions. Such use of the streets and public places has, from ancient times, been a part of the privileges, immunities, rights, and liberties of citizens. The privilege of a citizen of the United States to use the streets and parks for communication of views on national questions may be regulated in the interest of all; it is not absolute, but relative, and must be exercised in subordination to the general comfort and convenience, and in consonance with peace and good order; but it must not, in the guise of regulation, be abridged or denied.[7]

The principle that the government holds the streets in trust, as opposed to as a proprietor, was developed in a remarkable series of World War II–era cases recognizing that the use of public spaces for religious and political discourse is "essential to free government."[8] The view expressed in those cases is now settled law. "The protections afforded by the First Amendment are nowhere stronger than in streets and parks, both categorized for First Amendment purposes as traditional public fora. In such fora, the government's right 'to limit expressive activity [is] sharply circumscribed.'"[9] "Such areas occupy a 'special position in terms of First Amendment protection' because of their historic role as sites for discussion and debate."[10] As the Supreme Court recently noted, public streets and sidewalks remain one of the few places where a speaker can be confident of speaking to listeners who

---

[6] *See,* 307 U.S. 496, 515–16 (1939).

[7] *Id.*

[8] Thornhill v. Alabama, 310 U.S. 88, 95 (1940).

[9] Berger v. City of Seattle, 569 F.3d 1029, 1035–36 (9th Cir. 2009) (citation omitted) (alteration in original) (quoting Perry Educ. Ass'n v. Perry Local Educ. Ass'n, 460 U.S. 37, 45 (1983)).

[10] McCullen v. Coakley, 134 S. Ct. 2518, 2529 (2014) (quoting United States v. Grace, 461 U.S. 171, 180 (1983)).

might disagree, and it characterized the listener's encounter with "speech he might otherwise tune out" as a "virtue, not a vice" in light of the First Amendment's purpose of preserving an uninhibited marketplace of ideas.[11]

But it is equally settled that "[g]overnmental authorities have the duty and responsibility to keep their streets open and available for movement,"[12] and therefore the use of streets, sidewalks, parks and other public facilities for expressive activity is subject to "reasonable restrictions on the time, place, or manner of protected speech, provided the restrictions 'are justified without reference to the content of the regulated speech, that they are narrowly tailored to serve a significant governmental interest, and that they leave open ample alternative channels for communication of the information.'"[13] Additionally, the government's right as a proprietor to restrict expressive activity retains viability with respect to limited public fora such as the internal sidewalks of a public university[14] or a nonpublic forum such as a military base.[15]

Ever since the World War II–era cases firmly established the right to use streets and public spaces for expressive activity, legislatures and courts have wrestled with the issues that arise when such expressive activity interferes with traffic flow or other uses of the public areas. How the courts have resolved the tension between these competing uses has depended on the nature and intended use of the public property; the size of the group engaging in expressive activity; other physical characteristics of the expressive activity, such as sound amplification or use of a physical structure; and whether the ordinance in question is content neutral.

III. World War II–Era Principles

In 1947, the Massachusetts Supreme Court again considered a fine imposed on an individual for "'mak[ing] an oration' on Boston Common without a permit from the mayor" and one imposed for distributing pamphlets on the Common

---

[11] *Id.*

[12] Cox v. Louisiana, 379 U.S. 536, 554–55 (1965).

[13] *McCullen*, 134 S. Ct. at 2529 (quoting Ward v. Rock Against Racism, 491 U.S. 781, 791 (1989)).

[14] *See, e.g.*, Bloedorn v. Grube, 631 F.3d 1218, 1232–34 (11th Cir. 2011).

[15] Greer v. Spock, 424 U.S. 828, 838 (1976).

without a permit.[16] Although urged by the Commonwealth to uphold the fines based on the precedent of *Davis*, and noting that it had difficulty reconciling its decision with the *Davis* case,[17] the court said it was "compelled [to overturn the fines] by the broad sweep of principles set forth in great amplitude in more recent decisions of the Supreme Court of the United States."[18] It noted that the U.S. Supreme Court had mentioned its own decision affirming *Davis* in both *Hague*[19] and in *Jamison v. Texas*,[20] but neither followed nor expressly overruled it, and stated, "[w]e are not sure that we fully comprehend the ground on which *Davis v. Massachusetts* has been distinguished."[21] To paraphrase more bluntly, the intervening decisions had dramatically changed the ability of the legislature to restrict expressive activity on sidewalks and parks. Those intervening decisions introduced the principles that continue to govern constitutional limits on a state's right to regulate expressive activity in public spaces.

Permitting schemes that vest too much discretion in public officials were an early target of the U.S. Supreme Court. In 1938, the Court overturned the conviction of Alma Lovell for distributing religious pamphlets and magazines in the City of Griffin without first obtaining a license.[22] Noting that "[t]he struggle for freedom of the press was primarily directed against the power of the licensor" and that pamphlets and leaflets, such as those by Thomas Paine, have been historic weapons in defense of liberty, the Court held that the ordinance requiring a permit to distribute literature anywhere within the municipality "would restore the system of license and censorship in its baldest form."[23] The following year, in *Hague*, the Court ruled that an ordinance that vested an official with discretion as to whether to grant a permit for a public assembly in a public space was unconstitutional on its face.[24] Since *Hague*, the Court has repeatedly affirmed that although the government may impose a permit requirement

---

[16] Commonwealth v. Gilfedder, 73 N.E.2d 241, 241 (Mass. 1947).
[17] *Id.* at 245.
[18] *Id.*
[19] 307 U.S. 496 (1939).
[20] 318 U.S. 413 (1943).
[21] *Gilfedder*, 73 N.E.2d at 245.
[22] Lovell v. City of Griffin, 303 U.S. 444 (1938).
[23] *Id.* at 451–52.
[24] 307 U.S. at 516.

to regulate competing uses of a public forum, it "may not delegate overly broad licensing discretion to a government official."[25]

That the use of streets and parks for expressive activities is essential to protect liberty received early recognition.[26] Accordingly, outright prohibitions of expressive activity have been viewed with suspicion. In *Schneider v. New Jersey*, the Court held unconstitutional three separate ordinances that contained an outright prohibition of the distribution of leaflets in public streets and that lower courts had upheld as valid efforts to prevent littering.[27] In another case, it rejected the argument that a city's plenary control of its streets gave it the right to prohibit all dissemination of information by handbills, stating that "one who is rightfully on a street which the state has left open to the public carries with him there as elsewhere the constitutional right to express his views in an orderly fashion. This right extends to communication of ideas by handbills and literature as well as by the spoken word."[28] However, relying on a now partially discredited distinction between commercial and other speech, the Court did not extend the right to distribute handbills to commercial handbills.[29] In *McCullen v. Coakley*, the Court recently reiterated the principles of these cases, stating that the government's ability to restrict speech on streets and sidewalks is very limited and that it has no power to restrict speech in such areas based on its message.[30]

The willingness of the Court in *Schneider* to assess the significance of the government's interest in preventing litter and to balance the means used to achieve that interest against the First Amendment rights at stake is reflected in the now familiar formula for testing content neutral time, place, and manner regulations of expressive activity.[31] That formula is set

---

[25] *See, e.g.*, Forsyth Cnty. v. Nationalist Movement, 505 U.S. 123, 130 (1992) (ordinance allowing official to vary cost of assembly and fee based upon estimated cost of maintaining public order). For a recent application of *Lovell* and *Forsyth* by a lower court, see Working Am., Inc. v. City of Bloomington, 142 F. Supp. 3d 823, 833 (D. Minn. 2015) (ordinance allowing denial of solicitor's license on grounds that applicant is not of good moral character or repute).

[26] *Hague*, 307 U.S. at 515–16.

[27] Schneider v. New Jersey, 308 U.S. 147 (1939).

[28] Jamison v. Texas, 318 U.S. 413, 416 (1943).

[29] Valentine v. Chrestensen, 316 U.S. 52 (1942). The evolution of the treatment of commercial speech is described in RODNEY A. SMOLLA, 2 SMOLLA & NIMMER ON FREEDOM OF SPEECH §§ 20.1 to 20.9 (2016).

[30] McCullen v. Coakley, 134 S. Ct. 2518, 2529 (2014).

[31] *Schneider*, 308 U.S. at 162.

forth earlier in the text and was recently utilized by the Court in *McCullen* to find the statute in question unconstitutional because it was not narrowly tailored to serve a significant governmental interest.[32] Obviously, that willingness is also reflected in the strict scrutiny standard applicable to content based regulations, which requires that in order to survive such scrutiny, the regulation must be the least restrictive means of serving a compelling governmental interest.[33] Finally, it is reflected in the standard for evaluating regulation of commercial speech, which provides that regulation of commercial speech concerning lawful activity that is not misleading must serve a substantial governmental interest and be done by means that are reasonably fitted to the governmental interest.[34]

The World War II–era cases also emphasized the protection of unpopular or potentially offensive speech. As long as a speaker's deportment is not "noisy, truculent, overbearing or offensive," the government's legitimate interest in maintaining peace does not allow it to punish messages that may offend or incite a listener:[35]

> In the realm of religious faith, and in that of political belief, sharp differences arise. In both fields the tenets of one man may seem the rankest error to his neighbor. To persuade others of his own point of view, the pleader, as we know, at times, resorts to exaggeration, to vilification of men who have been, or are, prominent in church or state, and even to false statement. But the people of this nation have ordained in the light of history, that, in spite of the probability of excesses and abuses, these liberties are, in the long view, essential to enlightened opinion and right conduct on the part of the citizens of a democracy.[36]

This principle that the government may not, in a public forum, selectively shield the public from speech that might be offensive remains firmly embedded in First Amendment jurisprudence.[37]

---

[32] 134 S. Ct. at 2534–41.
[33] *Id.* at 2530.
[34] *See, e.g.*, City of Cincinnati v. Discovery Network, Inc., 507 U.S. 410, 414 (1993).
[35] Cantwell v. Connecticut, 310 U.S. 296, 309–10 (1940).
[36] *Id.* at 310.
[37] *See, e.g., McCullen*, 134 S. Ct. at 2529; Forsyth Cnty. v. Nationalist Movement, 505 U.S. 123, 134 (1992).

In the World War II–era cases, the right to use the streets for persuasion was also extended to the right to canvas door-to-door. "Door to door distribution of circulars is essential to the poorly financed causes of little people."[38] Handbills and leaflets "have been historic weapons in the defense of liberty."[39] "And perhaps the most effective way of bringing them to the notice of individuals is their distribution at the homes of people."[40] Even when distribution is combined with the solicitation of money, the governmental interest in the prevention of fraud does not justify an outright prohibition of such distribution or subjecting it to the discretionary approval of the government.[41] Nor does it allow the government to impose a flat license fee for the privilege of distributing door-to-door.[42] "[A] person cannot be compelled 'to purchase, through a license fee or a license tax, the privilege freely granted by the constitution.'"[43]

In a 2002 case striking down an ordinance requiring door-to-door canvassers to first register with the mayor and receive a permit, the Court commented on these early cases:

> The rhetoric used in the World War II-era opinions that repeatedly saved petitioners' coreligionists from petty prosecutions reflected the Court's evaluation of First Amendment freedoms that are implicated in this case. The value judgment that then motivated a united democratic people fighting to defend those very freedoms from totalitarian attack is unchanged. It motivates our decision today.[44]

The principles developed in these early cases continue to provide the framework by which the regulation of expressive activity in streets and parks is evaluated by courts today.

---

[38] Martin v. City of Struthers, 319 U.S. 141, 146 (1943).

[39] Lovell v. City of Griffin, 303 U.S. 444, 452 (1938).

[40] Schneider v. New Jersey, 308 U.S. 147, 164 (1939).

[41] *Id.*

[42] Murdock v. Pennsylvania, 319 U.S. 105, 114 (1943).

[43] *Id.* (quoting Blue Island v. Kozul, 41 N.E.2d 515, 519 (Ill. 1942)).

[44] Watchtower Bible and Tract Soc'y of N.Y., Inc. v. Vill. of Stratton, 536 U.S. 150, 169 (2002).

IV. Nature and Use of Public Property

Public places historically associated with the free exercise of expressive activities are considered to be public fora.[45] Such places include streets, sidewalks, and parks.[46] But what about other government property? "The [g]overnment may ban the entry on to public property that is not a 'public forum' of all persons except those who have legitimate business on the premises."[47] Just as many of the World War II–era cases involved the activities of the Jehovah's Witnesses because door-to-door canvassing and public teaching are mandated by the religion,[48] many of the cases addressing whether a particular government property is a public forum have involved the International Society for Krishna Consciousness, Inc. ("ISKCON"), whose members perform the ritual of sankirtan, which consists of "going into public places, disseminating religious literature and soliciting funds to support religion."[49] Thus, ISKCON cases have led to Supreme Court rulings that airport terminals are nonpublic fora[50] and that a state fairgrounds is a limited public forum.[51]

The public forum doctrine and the classification of government property as traditional public fora, designated public fora, limited public fora, and nonpublic fora are discussed in depth in chapter 11. For the purposes of this chapter, only a few points need to be kept in mind.

First, because streets, sidewalks, and parks have been "historically associated with the free exercise of expressive activity," they are "considered, without more," to be public fora.[52] As noted previously, in public fora, "the government's ability to permissibly restrict expressive conduct is very limited: the government may enforce reasonable time, place and manner regulations as long as the restrictions 'are content neutral, are narrowly tailored to serve a significant government interest, and leave open ample

---

[45] United States v. Grace, 461 U.S. 171, 177 (1983).
[46] *Id.*
[47] *Id.* at 178.
[48] *See Watchtower Bible*, 536 U.S. at 160–61.
[49] Int'l Soc'y for Krishna Consciousness, Inc. v. Lee, 505 U.S. 672, 674–75 (1992).
[50] *Id.* at 679.
[51] Heffron v. Int'l Soc'y for Krishna Consciousness, Inc., 452 U.S. 640, 655 (1981).
[52] *Grace*, 461 U.S. at 177.

alternative channels of communication.'"[53] The same limitation applies in a designated public forum.[54]

Second, although the treatment of sidewalks as public fora extends to sidewalks adjacent to important public buildings that are not public fora, such as the sidewalks surrounding the Supreme Court[55] and sidewalks adjacent to the U.S. Capitol Building,[56] it does not necessarily extend to certain publicly owned, special-purpose sidewalks. For example, a sidewalk located wholly within postal service property and used for no other purpose than to provide passage between the parking lot and post office is not a public forum.[57] Similarly, the interior sidewalks of a public university are not public fora even though the adjacent exterior sidewalk is one.[58] Even within a public forum, such as the National Mall, the government may reserve a space, such as the interior of the Jefferson Memorial, as a nonpublic forum dedicated to a solemn commemorative purpose that is incompatible with the full range of expressive activity.[59]

Just as with streets, in the application of the forum analysis, not all parks are created equal. Rejecting a claim that all national parks are public fora, a federal appellate court stated that the label ascribed to a property by the government is not dispositive and that "Mount Rushmore does not become a public forum merely by being called a 'national park' any more than it would be transformed into a nonpublic forum if it were labeled a 'museum.'"[60] Similarly, "the mere physical characteristics of [government] property cannot dictate forum analysis."[61] "What makes a park a traditional public forum is not its grass and trees, but the fact that it has 'immemorially been held in trust for the use of the public and, time out of mind, ha[s] been used for purposes of assembly, communicating

---

[53] *Id.* (quoting Perry Educ. Ass'n v. Perry Local Educ. Ass'n, 460 U.S. 37, 45 (1983)).

[54] *Perry Educ. Ass'n,* 460 U.S. at 45–46.

[55] *Grace,* 461 U.S. at 180.

[56] Lederman v. United States, 291 F.3d 36, 44 (D.C. Cir. 2002).

[57] United States v. Kokinda, 497 U.S. 720, 727–30 (1990).

[58] Hershey v. Goldstein, 938 F. Supp. 2d 491, 511–12 (S.D.N.Y. 2013).

[59] Oberwetter v. Hilliard, 639 F.3d 545, 552 (D.C. Cir. 2011).

[60] Boardley v. U.S. Dep't of the Interior, 615 F.3d 508, 514–15 (D.C. Cir. 2010).

[61] *Id.* (quoting *Kokinda,* 497 U.S. at 727).

thoughts between citizens, and discussing public questions.'"[62] Applying this test, the D.C. Circuit stated that the national parks "undoubtedly include areas that meet the definition of traditional public forums" but also include large areas that have never been dedicated to free expression and public assembly.[63]

Third, if a government-owned sidewalk or park is a limited public forum, restrictions on expressive activity need only be reasonable and viewpoint neutral.[64] Reasonableness is assessed in light of the purpose of the forum.[65] So, for example, a public university may limit use of expressive areas on its campus to students, faculty, and employees and their sponsored guests without opening its campus to outside speakers.[66] A government also may distinguish on the basis of subject matter and make content based exclusions of speech that do not fall within the category of uses to which the forum has been opened, so long as the exclusions are viewpoint neutral and reasonable.[67] After determining that the Lincoln Center Plaza was a limited public forum, the Second Circuit upheld content based regulations limiting expressive uses to those that are artistic or performance related because the regulations were viewpoint neutral and reasonable in light of the fact that the Lincoln Center complex was created as an enclave for the cultural arts.[68]

Finally, if a government-owned sidewalk is a nonpublic forum, any restriction on expressive activity "must only be 'reasonable and not an effort to suppress expression merely because public officials oppose the speaker's view.'"[69]

---

[62] *Id.* at 515 (alteration in original) (quoting Perry Educ. Ass'n v. Perry Local Educ. Ass'n, 460 U.S. 37, 45 (1983)).

[63] *Id.*

[64] *Id.* at 507; Bloedorn v. Grube, 631 F.3d 1218, 1231 (11th Cir. 2011); *see also* Rosenberger v. Rector & Visitors of Univ. of Va., 515 U.S. 819, 829 (1995) (applying limited public forum analysis to distribution of student activity funds).

[65] *Bloedorn*, 631 F.3d at 1231.

[66] *Id.* at 1232–33.

[67] Hotel Emps. & Rest. Emps. Union, Local 100 v. City of N.Y. Dep't of Parks & Recreation, 311 F.3d 534, 553 (2d Cir. 2002).

[68] *Id.* at 553–54.

[69] Hershey v. Goldstein, 938 F. Supp. 2d 491, 507 (S.D.N.Y. 2013) (quoting Perry Educ. Ass'n v. Perry Local Educ. Ass'n, 460 U.S. 37, 46 (1983)).

V. Time, Place, and Manner Regulations

"[G]overnments routinely pursue public objectives in regulating the time, place and manner of speech on public fora without running afoul of the Constitution. Such legitimate objectives include public safety, accommodating competing uses of the easement, controlling the level and times of noise, and similar interests."[70] If a regulation governing when, where, or how loudly expressive activity can take place is content neutral, it will be upheld "provided the restrictions 'are justified without reference to the content of the regulated speech, that they are narrowly tailored to serve a significant governmental interest, and that they leave open ample alternative channels for communication of the information.'"[71] Content neutral regulations by no means receive a free pass. In contrast to the deferential rational basis by which many laws are reviewed, the intermediate scrutiny standard applicable to content neutral restrictions on speech "imposes meaningful limits on government."[72]

The strict dichotomy between content based and content neutral regulations does not apply to regulation of commercial speech. A regulation that applies specially to commercial speech is subject to a different intermediate scrutiny standard known as the *Central Hudson* test.[73] The Supreme Court has stated that the application of the *Central Hudson* test is substantially similar to the application of the test for validity of time, place, and manner restrictions.[74] There is not space to discuss the complex issues that arise when attempting to distinguish between commercial and noncommercial speech other than to point out that the Supreme Court has recognized that much expressive activity contains both commercial and noncommercial elements and that speech in a public forum does not lose its First Amendment protection because it may involve a solicitation to purchase or otherwise pay or contribute money.[75]

---

[70] Rodney A. Smolla, 1 Smolla & Nimmer on Freedom of Speech § 8.36 (2016) (quoting First Unitarian Church v. Salt Lake City Corp., 308 F.3d 1114, 1132 (10th Cir. 2002)).

[71] *Id.* at § 8.37 (quoting Ward v. Rock against Racism, 491 U.S. 781, 791 (1989)).

[72] *Id.* at § 3.2.

[73] *See* Bd. of Trustees v. Fox, 492 U.S. 469, 477 (1989) (discussing Cent. Hudson Gas & Elec. Corp. v. Pub. Serv. Comm'n, 447 U.S. 557, 563–64 (1980)).

[74] *See id.*

[75] *See* City of Cincinnati v. Discovery Network, Inc., 507 U.S. 410, 419–21 (1993).

No element of the time, place, and manner test has been free from confusion. Sometimes this confusion arises from disagreement between the justices of the Supreme Court. For example, in *McCullen*, there was a five-to-four split among the justices as to whether the regulations in question were content based.[76] Although all nine justices agreed that a statute making it a crime to knowingly stand on a public way or sidewalk within thirty-five feet of an entrance to any place where abortions are performed violated the First Amendment, the majority opinion determined that the regulation was content neutral, whereas four justices in two separate concurring opinions argued that the statute was a content based regulation.[77] At other times, confusion can be caused by the application of a general standard to vastly different factual situations. For example, the government's interest in ensuring the safety and convenience of park users through a permitting scheme may be a significant interest when applied to a large group but not when applied to a small group.[78]

The following discussion first addresses content neutrality in the context of regulation of sidewalk expression and then highlights certain issues that frequently occur with respect to the various elements of the time, place, and manner test when applied to small-group activities on sidewalks.

VI. Content Neutrality

A content based regulation of speech is subject to strict scrutiny.[79] A regulation subject to strict scrutiny will survive only if the government can prove that it is necessary to further a compelling interest and is narrowly tailored to achieve that interest.[80] A regulation subject to strict scrutiny is

---

[76] 134 S. Ct. 2518 (2014).

[77] *Compare id.* at 2534 ("We thus conclude that the Act is neither content nor viewpoint based. . . ."), *with id.* at 2548 (Scalia, J., concurring) ("[T]he Act should be reviewed under the strict-scrutiny standard applicable to content based legislation."), *and id.* at 2549 (Alito, J., concurring) ("I believe the law clearly discriminates on [viewpoint].").

[78] *See* Grossman v. City of Portland, 33 F.3d 1200, 1207 (9th Cir. 1994) ("[W]e simply cannot agree that six to eight people carrying signs in a public park constituted enough of a threat to the safety and convenience of park users. . . . to justify the restriction imposed on their speech. . . .").

[79] *See* Reed v. Town of Gilbert, 135 S. Ct. 2218, 2228 (2015).

[80] *See id.* at 2231.

presumptively invalid and "likely to be struck down."[81] "[I]t is the 'rare case [ ] in which a speech restriction withstands strict scrutiny.'"[82] However, the government is given "somewhat wider leeway to regulate features of speech unrelated to its content."[83] Restrictions on the time, place, or manner of speech may be imposed provided they satisfy the intermediate scrutiny test described in Section V.[84]

Although courts struggle with the concept of content neutrality, there are several types of regulations applicable to expressive conduct in the street that are generally held to be content neutral. At least as applied to larger groups, a properly designed permitting process is content neutral.[85] Limitations on the use of amplified sound in the streets or parks for purposes of noise control are generally held to be content neutral.[86] A ban of targeted picketing of a residence has been held to be content neutral and to serve the state's interest in protecting the well-being, tranquility, and privacy of a home.[87] However, each of these types of regulations may fail if not properly designed. For example, a permit requirement that applies only to political expression and not to other speech is not content neutral because it applies to only a certain subject matter.[88] Likewise, in *Saia v. New York*, the Court ruled that an ordinance that prohibited the use of amplified sound in the street unless permission was first obtained from the chief of police violated the First Amendment because the lack of objective guidelines gave a government official the discretion to discriminate based on message.[89] Finally, although stated in terms of equal protection, the Court held that a prohibition on picketing of residences that contained an

---

[81] RODNEY A. SMOLLA, 1 SMOLLA & NIMMER ON FREEDOM OF SPEECH § 4.3 (2016).

[82] *Reed*, 135 S. Ct. at 2236 (Kagan, J., concurring) (alteration in original).

[83] McCullen v. Coakley, 134 S. Ct. 2518, 2529 (2014).

[84] *Id.*

[85] *See* Thomas v. Chicago Park Dist., 534 U.S. 316 (2002) (upholding a permit requirement for park gatherings of groups of fifty or more as a valid time, place, and manner regulation).

[86] *See, e.g.*, Ward v. Rock Against Racism, 491 U.S. 781, 791–92 (1989) (upholding noise control regulations requiring use of city's sound equipment and sound engineer for performances at municipal bandshell); Kovacs v. Cooper, 336 U.S. 77, 87 (1949) (finding it permissible to bar sound trucks that emit loud and raucous sounds from public ways).

[87] *See* Frisby v. Schultz, 487 U.S. 474, 484 (1988).

[88] *See* Burk v. Augusta-Richmond Cnty., 365 F.3d 1247, 1251 (11th Cir. 2004).

[89] 334 U.S. 558 (1948).

exemption for labor picketing was invalid because it discriminated based on the subject matter of expression.[90] In his concurring opinion, Justice Stewart indicated his view that the issue was more properly analyzed under the Free Speech Clause.[91]

In its most recent effort to articulate the test for determining whether a regulation is content based, *Reed v. Town of Gilbert*, the Supreme Court described two categories of content based speech regulations.[92] The first category consists of those regulations that, on their face, draw distinctions based on the subject matter of the speech or define regulated speech by its function or purpose.[93] The second category includes regulations that, although facially content neutral, will be considered content based regulations because they cannot be justified without reference to the content of the regulated speech or were adopted by the government because of "disagreement with the message."[94] Using this approach, the Court reversed the Ninth Circuit and held that distinctions in a sign code between political, ideological, and directional signs were content based on their face and could not withstand strict scrutiny.[95]

Although *Reed* is a sign code case, it appears to reject the approach to evaluating content neutrality set forth in earlier Court decisions considering regulation of expressive activity on sidewalks. In determining that the sign code distinctions were not content based, the Ninth Circuit had relied in part on *Hill v. Colorado*, which upheld regulation of speech-related conduct within one hundred feet of the entrance to any healthcare facility.[96] The statute in question in *Hill* made it unlawful for any person to knowingly approach within eight feet of another person near the healthcare facility without consent for the purpose of passing a leaflet or handbill to, displaying a sign to, or engaging in oral protest, education, or counseling

---

[90] *See* Carey v. Brown, 447 U.S. 455, 471 (1980).

[91] *See id.* at 471–72 (Stewart, J., concurring).

[92] 135 S. Ct. 2218, 2227 (2015).

[93] *Id.; see also* Sorrell v. IMS Health, Inc., 131 S. Ct. 2653, 2664 (2011).

[94] *Id.* (quoting Ward v. Rock Against Racism, 491 U.S. 781, 791 (1989)).

[95] *Id.* at 2224, 2233.

[96] *Reed v. Town of Gilbert*, 707 F.3d 1057, 1070–71 (9th Cir. 2013) (citing Hill v. Colorado, 530 U.S. 703, 707 (2000)).

with such other person.[97] The *Hill* majority rejected the argument that the statute was content based because it drew a distinction between a person who approached others for the purpose of wishing them good morning and one who approached another for the purpose of protest, education, or counseling, even though the enforcement officer would have to examine the content of the oral statement to determine whether the statute applied.[98]

> It is common in the law to examine the content of a communication to determine the speaker's purpose. Whether a particular statement constitutes a threat, blackmail, an agreement to fix prices, a copyright violation, a public offering of securities, or an offer to sell goods often depends on the precise content of the statement. We have never held, or suggested, that it is improper to look at the content of an oral or written statement to determine whether a rule of law applies to a course of conduct. With respect to the conduct that is the focus of the Colorado statute, it is unlikely that there would often be any need to know exactly what words were spoken in order to determine whether 'sidewalk counselors' are engaging in 'oral protest, education, or counseling' rather than pure social or random conversation.[99]

In *Reed*, an ordinance that applied different treatment to signs in the same location depending on whether they were directional, political, or ideological was a content based regulation merely because it required an enforcement officer to examine the content of the communication to determine which category applied, whereas in *Hill*, an ordinance that applied different treatment to communications taking place in the same location depending on whether they were purely social or random conversation or oral protest, education, or counseling was content neutral. Despite this apparent inconsistency, the *Reed* majority did not expressly overrule *Hill*.[100]

As noted previously, in addition to ordinances that, on their face, draw distinctions based on the content of a communication, *Reed* identified another

---

[97] *See Hill*, 530 U.S. at 707.
[98] *Id.* at 720–21.
[99] *Id.* at 721.
[100] *See Reed*, 135 S. Ct. at 2218.

category of content based regulations, those that will be considered content based regulations because they cannot be justified without reference to the content of the regulated speech or were adopted by the government because of disagreement with the message.[101] In *McCullen*, the Court rejected the argument that the statute fell into this second category because it applied only outside of abortion clinics and therefore had the "inevitable effect" of restricting abortion-related speech more than speech on other topics.[102] The Court stated that the articulated purposes of the statute, public safety, patient access to healthcare, and the unobstructed use of public sidewalks and roadway, were concerns the Court had previously held to be content neutral.[103] Addressing the argument that an improper purpose should be inferred because the stated governmental interests applied to every building but the statute only applied to buildings in which abortions took place, the Court refused to make such an inference, stating: "States adopt laws to address the problems that confront them. The First Amendment does not require States to regulate problems that do not exist."[104] This drew a fierce response from Justice Scalia in the concurring opinion:

> It blinks reality to say, as the majority does, that a blanket prohibition on the use of streets and sidewalks where speech on only one politically controversial topic is likely to occur—and where that speech can most effectively be communicated—is not content based. Would the Court exempt from strict scrutiny a law banning access to the streets and sidewalks surrounding the site of the Republican National Convention? Or those used annually to commemorate the 1965 Selma-to-Montgomery civil rights marches? Or those outside the Internal Revenue Service? Surely not.[105]

Although the dissent raised an interesting question concerning the regulation of protests around political conventions, in doing so, it ignored a

---

[101] *See id.* at 2227.
[102] 134 S. Ct. 2518, 2531 (2014).
[103] *See id.*
[104] *Id.* at 2532 (quoting Burson v. Freeman, 504 U.S. 191, 207 (1992) (plurality opinion)).
[105] *Id.* at 2543 (Scalia, J., concurring).

number of lower court decisions that have uniformly upheld buffer zone restrictions around such conventions as content neutral regulations.[106]

For the present, a restriction on communication at particular locations where past events have raised concerns about public safety or congestion will be considered a content neutral regulation. But the intense tenor of concurring and dissenting opinions in abortion protest cases makes it difficult, if not impossible, to predict how long this will remain the case. The strong disagreement among the justices is exemplified by the intemperate attacks made by Justice Scalia in repeatedly accusing fellow justices of distorting First Amendment principles to favor a particular agenda, in this case, the purported agenda of suppressing anti-abortion speech.[107] The point here is not to focus on judicial manners but to highlight the uncertainty facing lawyers advising local governments and picketers with respect to whether an ordinance is content neutral.

In addition to perhaps impacting future cases addressing the regulation of protests at abortion facilities, the *Reed* decision appears to have resolved a split among circuit courts as to whether anti-panhandling ordinances that prohibit a request for money to be given immediately but allow a request for money at a later time are content neutral. The split was described in *Norton v. City of Springfield* ("*Norton I*"), which involved an ordinance that prohibited panhandling in certain areas and defined panhandling as an oral request for an immediate donation of money.[108] The ordinance allowed

---

[106] *See, e.g.*, Marcavage v. City of New York, 689 F.3d 98, 104 (2d Cir. 2012) (analyzing restrictions of protests at 2004 Republican National Convention to a restricted demonstration zone that provided little, if any, access to delegates under content neutral test); Bl(a)ck Tea Soc'y v. City of Boston, 378 F.3d 8, 11–12 (1st Cir. 2004) (same with respect to 2004 Democratic National Convention); *see also* Menotti v. City of Seattle, 409 F.3d 1113, 1128–29 (9th Cir. 2005) (upholding emergency order restricting access to areas surrounding World Trade Organization conference as a content neutral regulation).

[107] *See, e.g.*, McCullen, 134 S. Ct. at 2541 (Scalia, J., concurring) ("Today's opinion carries forward this Court's practice of giving abortion-rights advocates a pass when it comes to suppressing the free-speech rights of their opponents."); Hill v. Colorado, 530 U.S. 703, 741 (2000) (Scalia, J., dissenting) ("What is before us, after all, is a speech regulation directed against the opponents of abortion, and it therefore enjoys the benefit of the 'ad hoc nullification machine' that the Court has set in motion to push aside whatever doctrines of constitutional law stand in the way of that highly favored practice.") (quoting Madsen v. Women's Health Ctr., Inc., 512 U.S. 753, 785 (1994) (Scalia, J., concurring in part and dissenting in part)). Of course, Justice Scalia accusing other justices of pursuing a political agenda puts one in mind of a verse of Robert Burns's poem *To a Louse, On Seeing One on a Lady's Bonnet at Church*: "O wad some Pow'r the giftie gie us To see oursels as ithers see us!" *See* Robert Burns, *To a Louse, On Seeing One on a Lady's Bonnet at Church* (1786), *available at* https://en.wikipedia.org/wiki/To_a_Louse.

[108] 768 F.3d 713, 714–15 (7th Cir. 2014) (describing circuit split and listing cases).

signs requesting money as well as oral requests for money to be sent later.[109] The *Norton I* court noted that the Ninth Circuit, Fourth Circuit, and Sixth Circuit had each held a similar ordinance to be an invalid, content based regulation of expressive activity.[110] It stated that the D.C. Circuit and First Circuit had each determined that a similar regulation was content neutral and upheld the regulation,[111] although the dissent took issue with its characterization of the First Circuit decision.[112] Following *Reed*, the panel granted a petition for rehearing and reversed itself ("*Norton II*"):[113]

> The majority opinion in *Reed* effectively abolishes any distinction between content regulation and subject-matter regulation. Any law distinguishing one kind of speech from another by reference to its meaning now requires a compelling justification.[114]

Norton I relied in part on *Thayer v. City of Worcester*, in which the First Circuit upheld an ordinance against aggressive panhandling as a content neutral regulation.[115] Following its decision in *Reed*, the Supreme Court granted certiorari in *Thayer*, vacated the judgment, and remanded for further consideration in light of *Reed*.[116] On remand, the lower court ruled that an ordinance making it "unlawful for any person to beg, panhandle or solicit any other person in an aggressive manner" was content based.[117]

Several other lower courts following *Reed* have found similar panhandling ordinances to be content based regulations.[118] For example, in

---

[109] *See id.* at 714.

[110] *Id.* (citing ACLU v. City of Las Vegas, 466 F.3d 784 (9th Cir. 2006); *see, e.g.*, Clatterbuck v. City of Charlottesville, 708 F.3d 549 (4th Cir. 2013); Speet v. Schuette, 726 F.3d 867 (6th Cir. 2013)).

[111] *Norton*, 768 F.3d at 714–15 (citing ISKON of Potomac, Inc. v. Kennedy, 61 F.3d 949, 954–55 (D.C. Cir. 1995)); Thayer v. Worcester, 755 F.3d 60 (1st Cir. 2014) *vacated*, 135 S. Ct 2887 (2015)).

[112] *Id.* at 720 (Manion, J., dissenting) (noting that ordinance in *Thayer*, 755 F.3d at 71, allowed at least one verbal solicitation for money and prohibited only aggressive follow-up).

[113] Norton v. City of Springfield, 806 F.3d 411, 412–13 (7th Cir. 2015).

[114] *Id.* at 412.

[115] *Thayer*, 755 F.3d at 60. The majority opinion in *Thayer* was authored by retired Supreme Court Justice David Souter.

[116] Thayer v. City of Worcester, 135 S. Ct. 2887 (2015) (mem).

[117] Thayer v. City of Worcester, 144 F. Supp. 3d 218, 228, 233 (D. Mass. 2015).

[118] *See, e.g.*, Homeless Helping Homeless, Inc. v. City of Tampa, No. 8:15-cv-1219-T-23AAS, 2016 WL 4162882 (M.D. Fla. 2016); Browne v. City of Grand Junction, 136 F. Supp. 3d 1276, 1288–91 (D. Colo. 2015); McLaughlin v. City of Lowell, 140 F. Supp. 3d 177, 185–86 (D. Mass. 2015).

Browne v. City of Grand Junction, the court considered an ordinance that prohibited panhandling at certain times and in certain locations and that defined panhandling as follows:

> to knowingly approach, accost or stop another person in a public place and solicit that person without that person's consent, whether by spoken words, bodily gestures, written signs or other means, for money, employment or other thing of value.[119]

Although the *Browne* court had determined that the ordinance was a content based regulation in a prior ruling, it reviewed that ruling in light of *Reed, Norton II,* and the *Thayer* remand and stated that those decisions provided additional support for the correctness of its prior ruling.[120] In another example, *McLaughlin v. City of Lowell*, a federal district court in Massachusetts determined that an ordinance that distinguished between solicitations for an immediate donation from other solicitations was content based and stated that "*Reed* makes earlier cases, which had split over what forms of regulation of panhandling were content based, of limited continuing relevance."[121] *McLaughlin* also rejected the argument that the ordinance could be rendered content neutral by application of the secondary effects doctrine, which has been applied to find zoning regulations content neutral if they are targeted not at the content of adult establishments but at the effects on crime, property value, and other characteristics.[122]

VII. Governmental Interests

Under the strict scrutiny review applicable to content based regulations, the regulation must serve a compelling state interest, but under the test for content neutral regulations, a regulation must serve only a significant

---

[119] 136 F. Supp. 3d at 1288–91, 1297.
[120] *See id.* at 1288–91.
[121] *See McLaughlin*, 140 F. Supp. 3d at 185.
[122] *Id.* at 187.

or substantial government interest.[123] Unfortunately, courts have provided remarkably little guidance as how to differentiate a compelling interest from a significant one.

Most often, courts simply choose to announce or assume that an interest is significant or compelling. Thus, for example, in *Madsen v. Women's Health Center, Inc.*, the Supreme Court announced without analysis that, "[t]he State also has a strong interest in ensuring the public safety and order, in promoting the free flow of traffic on public streets and sidewalks, and in protecting the property rights of all its citizens."[124] To repurpose the oft-quoted line from Justice Potter Stewart: the Court knows a significant or compelling interest when it sees it. The doctrine has not set potential litigants entirely adrift, however, particularly with respect to the interests that emerge time and again in the context of newspaper sales, panhandling, and preaching along public rights-of-way.

A. Compelling Interest

Courts tend to acknowledge a compelling state interest after conclusory or categorical analysis,[125] yet some guidance has emerged over the years. The Court has noted, first in 2000 and then again in 2011, that to demonstrate a compelling interest, the government must "present more than anecdote and supposition"[126] and must instead "specifically identify an 'actual problem' in need of solving."[127] Thus, in *Brown v. Entertainment Merchant's Association*, the court rejected as not compelling California's interest in banning the sale of violent video games to minors without parental consent because the state could not "show a direct causal link between violent video games and harm to minors."[128] Although few courts adopted the "actual problem" standard when it was first announced, its use expanded

---

[123] *Compare* Reed v. Town of Gilbert, 135 S. Ct. 2218, 2226 (2015) (compelling interest), *with* McCullen v. Coakley, 134 S. Ct. 2518, 2534 (2014) (substantial interest).

[124] Madsen v. Women's Health Ctr., Inc., 512 U.S. 753, 768 (1994).

[125] *See, e.g.*, United States. v. Alvarez, 132 S. Ct. 2537, 2549 (2012) (plurality opinion) (observing simply that "[t]he Government is correct when it states military medals 'serve the important public function of recognizing and expressing gratitude for acts of heroism and sacrifice in military service.'").

[126] United States v. Playboy Entm't Grp., Inc., 529 U.S. 803, 822 (2000).

[127] Brown v. Entm't Merchs. Ass'n, 564 U.S. 786, 799 (2011) (quoting *Playboy*, 529 U.S. at 822).

[128] *Id.* at 2738–39.

significantly following the more recent recitation in *Brown*.[129] Still, given that this standard remains in its infancy, it is difficult to predict whether courts will choose to apply it only to novel interests or whether they will re-examine traditionally accepted rationales.

In addressing a compelling interest, the government must also ensure that it has been appropriately inclusive. If, for example, the government asserts a particular interest yet enacts regulations to serve the interest in only a few circumstances, it may indicate that the government does not consider the interest sufficiently compelling.[130] Similarly, where the government states a particular interest yet fails to regulate where the harms seem virtually identical—even if not contained within the letter of the stated interest—the interest may fall short of compelling.[131] Despite the Supreme Court's clarity on this issue when it first discussed it in 1991, courts have not since included a statement about inclusivity in the standard recitation of the strict scrutiny analysis. At best, then, it may function in the background.

Beyond these standards, compelling state interest analysis is a largely categorical affair, although it is still possible to identify some general themes. The government cannot, for instance, assert a compelling interest in privileging some kinds of protected speech over others.[132] Nor can it claim a compelling interest in prohibiting expression "simply because society finds the idea itself offensive or disagreeable."[133] On the other hand, in the context of restrictions on speech, interests related to protecting the political system as well as free and fair elections are typically compelling,[134] yet

---

[129] *See, e.g.*, Awad v. Ziriax, 670 F.3d 1111, 1131–32 (10th Cir. 2012) (considering the constitutionality of an Oklahoma constitutional amendment to prevent the application of sharia law and holding that although the state had a "valid interest" in determining the law its courts applied, its general statement of concern did not establish an actual problem supporting a compelling state interest).

[130] *See* Eugene Volokh, *Freedom of Speech, Permissible Tailoring and Transcending Strict Scrutiny*, 144 U. PA. L. REV. 2417, 2420 (1996) (discussing Simon & Schuster, Inc. v. Members of N.Y. State Crime Victims Bd., 502 U.S. 105 (1991)); *see also* Working Am., Inc. v. City of Bloomington, 142 F. Supp. 3d 823, 832 (D. Minn. 2015) (crime prevention as reason for content based regulation of door-to-door solicitation a legitimate but not compelling interest).

[131] *See* Volokh, *supra*, note 130.

[132] *See* Carey v. Brown, 447 U.S. 455, 467 (1980) (invalidating a city ordinance that barred most forms of protesting on residential sidewalks but allowed labor union picketing).

[133] *Simon & Schuster*, 502 U.S. at 118.

[134] *See* Burson v. Freeman, 504 U.S. 191, 199–200 (1992).

the government cannot place its thumb on the scales to favor a particular group, even one it considers underrepresented.[135]

B. Significant Government Interest

Although the compelling state interest analysis adheres to few guidelines, the significant government interest required for intermediate scrutiny is a veritable free for all. There, nearly anything can be a significant interest, and the ostensibly operative word *significant* is often used interchangeably with *valid*[136] or *legitimate*.[137]

In practice, the significance or legitimacy of the interest virtually never proves dispositive, and notably absent from the analysis is the "actual problem" standard applicable to compelling state interests. To date, courts have recognized as a significant government interest almost every conceivable rationale justifying regulations on expressive content in traditional public fora. Interests that have been found significant or legitimate include public safety;[138] public order; promoting free flow of traffic; protecting property rights; protecting a woman's freedom to seek pregnancy-related services;[139] traffic safety;[140] aesthetics;[141] preventing fraud, crime, and undue annoyance;[142] protecting citizens against unwelcome and excessive noise; and even "ensuring the sufficiency of sound amplification at bandshell events."[143] If the foregoing suggests anything, it is that conceiving of an illegitimate interest is likely more

---

[135] *See* Buckley v. Valeo, 424 U.S. 1, 28–29 (1976).

[136] *See, e.g.*, Heffron v. Int'l Soc'y for Krishna Consciousness, Inc., 452 U.S. 640, 650 (1981).

[137] *See, e.g.*, Ward v. Rock Against Racism, 491 U.S. 781, 798 (1989).

[138] *See, e.g.*, McCullen v. Coakley, 134 S. Ct. 2518, 2541 (2014).

[139] *See, e.g.*, Schenck v. Pro-Choice Network, 519 U.S. 357, 358 (1997) (holding that "public safety and order, promoting the free flow of traffic, protecting property rights, and protecting a woman's freedom to seek pregnancy-related services" were, in combination, "certainly significant enough to justify an appropriately tailored injunction."). Regarding traffic flow, *see also Comite de Jornaleros de Redondo Beach v. City of Redondo Beach*, 657 F.3d 936, 947–48 (9th Cir. 2011) (en banc), which stated, "It is undisputed that '[g]overnmental authorities have the duty and responsibility to keep their streets open and available for movement.'" (alteration in original) (quoting Cox v. Louisiana, 379 U.S. 536, 554–55 (1965)).

[140] *See, e.g.*, Metromedia, Inc. v. City of San Diego, 453 U.S. 490, 507–08 (1981) (plurality opinion); Solantic, LLC v. City of Neptune Beach, 410 F.3d 1250 (11th Cir. 2005).

[141] *See, e.g.*, *Metromedia*, 453 U.S. at 507–08; Members of City Council v. Taxpayers for Vincent, 466 U.S. 789, 806 (1984) (discussing *Metromedia*); *see also* Neighborhood Enters., Inc. v. City of St. Louis, 644 F.3d 728, 737–38 (8th Cir. 2011) (collecting cases).

[142] *See, e.g.*, Speet v. Schuette, 726 F.3d 867, 879–80 (6th Cir. 2013).

[143] Ward v. Rock Against Racism, 491 U.S. 781, 782 (1989).

difficult than arriving at a legitimate one. Of course, much more difficulty arises in attempting to narrowly tailor a statute to serve the proposed interest.

Even though courts rarely question whether a proposed governmental interest is significant, the government must still prove that the proposed interest is actually implicated by the regulated conduct.[144] In *Weinberg v. City of Chicago*, the plaintiff was the author of a book critical of the Chicago Blackhawks' management who attempted to sell his book outside the arena in which the team played.[145] After doing so for approximately two months, he was threatened with arrest for violating two ordinances that prohibited any person from peddling merchandise within one thousand feet of the arena and prohibited unlicensed peddlers from selling any article or service other than newspapers on any public way.[146] The city justified its prohibitions as necessary for public safety and to promote the free flow of traffic on public streets based on the testimony of police officers and security officials that peddling created congestion.[147] The Seventh Circuit acknowledged that such interests were significant but held that the city failed to show that the prohibition advanced such interests.[148] The court considered a videotape of the plaintiff's activities, made at the request of the district court, which showed no interference with any pedestrian traffic nor any congestion.[149] In light of that evidence, it then stated that conclusory testimony from an interested party in the absence of any objective evidence was insufficient to meet the government's burden of establishing a significant interest.[150] Citing *Weinberg*, the Ninth Circuit similarly held that a state agricultural association had failed to demonstrate a significant interest in preventing congestion in the parking lots and walkways around a performance facility because there was no evidence in the record that events at the facility ever attracted more than a handful of protesters.[151]

---

[144] *See* Weinberg v. City of Chicago, 310 F.3d 1029, 1038–39 (7th Cir. 2002).
[145] *Id.* at 1033–34.
[146] *Id.* at 1034.
[147] *Id.*
[148] *Id.* at 1040.
[149] *Id.* at 1038.
[150] *Id.* at 1039.
[151] *See* Kuba v. 1-A Agric. Ass'n, 387 F.3d 850, 859 (9th Cir. 2004).

A similar result is obtained under the *Central Hudson* test applicable to commercial speech. In *City of Cincinnati v. Discovery Network, Inc.*, for instance, the Supreme Court never questioned Cincinnati's interest in safety and aesthetics but instead struck down the city's attempt to require the removal of sixty-two tabloid and advertising newspaper racks while leaving in place approximately 1,500 to 2,000 newspaper racks used by newspapers that included at least some content that was not commercial because targeting only the commercial items fell woefully short of advancing the purported interests.[152]

C. Compelling Versus Significant Government Interest: Traffic Safety and Aesthetics

Although significant and compelling interests typically inhabit distinct spheres, they occasionally collide where an interest sufficient to support a content neutral regulation proves incapable of justifying one that is content based. In particular, courts have grappled with the importance of aesthetic and traffic safety rationales: the Eighth and Eleventh Circuits have both concluded that although traffic safety and aesthetics might be significant, they fall short of compelling.[153] Most recently, however, the Supreme Court in *Reed* assumed without deciding that both interests could be compelling, then struck down a city sign ordinance for lack of narrow tailoring.[154] Furthermore, the Court noted in dicta that protecting the safety of pedestrians, drivers, and passengers potentially constituted a compelling state interest.[155] For their part, the circuits making the distinction have arrived at their conclusion after little to no analysis.[156] In only one of the several cases to address the issue did the court provide a rationale, and there reasoned only that the government had provided insufficient evidence to establish a link between the content regulated and any impact on the interests proffered.[157]

---

[152] 507 U.S. 410, 424 (1993).
[153] *See* Neighborhood Enters., Inc. v. City of St. Louis, 644 F.3d 728, 737–38 (8th Cir. 2011) ("[A] municipality's asserted interests in traffic safety and aesthetics, while significant, have never been held to be compelling."); *see also* Solantic, LLC v. City of Neptune Beach, 410 F.3d 1250, 1262 (11th Cir. 2005).
[154] 135 S. Ct. 2218, 2231 (2015).
[155] *See id.* at 2232.
[156] *See Neighborhood Enters.*, 644 F.3d at 737–38; *see also Solantic*, 410 F.3d at 1262.
[157] *See* Dimmitt v. City of Clearwater, 985 F.2d 1565, 1569–70 (11th Cir. 1993).

VIII. Narrowly Tailored

For a regulation to be narrowly tailored, it must not burden substantially more speech than is necessary to further the government's significant interest.[158] A regulation need not employ the least restrictive means of validating the significant government interest.[159] But "the Government . . . bears the burden of showing that the remedy it has adopted does not 'burden substantially more speech than is necessary to further the government's legitimate interests.'"[160]

A regulation may fail the narrow tailoring test if it is geographically overinclusive. For example, a ban on solicitation of employment on all streets and sidewalks within a city was determined to be not narrowly tailored because there was evidence of traffic problems only with respect to a small number of major streets and medians.[161] Similarly, a ban on expressive activity in all medians within a city was not narrowly tailored because the evidence of incidents of traffic danger all related to a few narrow medians.[162] By contrast, in a case involving newspaper racks, *Globe Newspaper Co. v. Beacon Hill Architectural Commission*, the First Circuit upheld an outright ban on all newspaper racks within an area designated as a national historic landmark as narrowly tailored to advance the commission's aesthetic interest, relying, in part, on the fact that newspaper racks were allowed outside the district and no point within the district was more than one thousand feet from a source of publications.[163]

Although narrow tailoring does not require the government to use the least restrictive means possible, "the existence of obvious, less burdensome alternatives is 'a relevant consideration in determining whether the 'fit' between ends and means is reasonable.'"[164] In holding that a ban

---

[158] *See* McCullen v. Coakley, 134 S. Ct. 2518, 2535 (2014).

[159] *See* Ward v. Rock Against Racism, 491 U.S. 781 (1989).

[160] Turner Broad. Sys., Inc. v. FCC, 512 U.S. 622, 665 (1994) (quoting *Ward, 491 U.S. at 799*).

[161] *See* Comite de Jornaleros de Redondo Beach v. City of Redondo Beach, 657 F.3d 936, 949 (9th Cir. 2011) (en banc).

[162] *See* Cutting v. City of Portland, 802 F.3d 79, 92 (1st Cir. 2015).

[163] 100 F.3d 175, 180 (1st Cir. 1996).

[164] Berger v. City of Seattle, 569 F.3d 1029, 1041 (9th Cir. 2009) (quoting City of Cincinnati v. Discovery Network, Inc., 507 U.S. 410, 417 n. 13 (1993)).

on knowingly standing on a sidewalk or public way within thirty-five feet of an entrance or driveway to an abortion facility was not narrowly tailored to serve the government's interests in public safety, patient access to health care, and the unobstructed use of public roads and sidewalks, the *McCullen* Court pointed to anti-harassment legislation adopted by the federal government and other states and local ordinances making it a violation to obstruct free passage for travelers on a public sidewalk and stated that Massachusetts had "not shown that it seriously undertook to address the problem with less intrusive tools readily available to it."[165]

Circuit courts have taken differing views as to whether *McCullen* changed the law with respect to narrow tailoring. In reversing a preliminary injunction of an ordinance prohibiting solicitation or distribution in city roadways, the Eighth Circuit expressed doubt that the *McCullen* Court intended to change the law.[166] By contrast, in *Bruni v. City of Pittsburgh*, the Third Circuit stated, "*McCullen* represents an important clarification of the rigorous and fact-intensive nature of intermediate scrutiny's narrow-tailoring analysis." [167] Although another panel of that court had previously rejected a First Amendment challenge to Pittsburgh's ordinance establishing a fifteen-foot buffer around the entrance to healthcare facilities in *Brown v. City of Pittsburgh*,[168] the *Bruni* court reversed the lower court's dismissal of a post-*McCullen* challenge to the same ordinance and remanded the matter for a more rigorous analysis of the narrow tailoring issue:[169]

> No buffer zone can be upheld *a fortiori* simply because a similar one was deemed constitutional, since the background facts associated with the creation and enforcement of a zone cannot be assumed to be identical with those of an earlier case, even if the ordinances in the two cases happened to be the same.[170]

---

[165] McCullen v. Coakley, 134 S. Ct. 2518, 2539 (2014).
[166] *See* Traditionalist Am. Knights v. City of Desloge, 775 F.3d 969, 978 (8th Cir. 2014) ("[A]t no point did the Supreme Court announce a new rule.").
[167] Bruni v. City of Pittsburgh, 824 F.3d 353, 372 (3d Cir. 2016).
[168] Brown v. City of Pittsburgh, 586 F.3d 263 (3d Cir. 2009).
[169] *Bruni*, 824 F.3d at 375.
[170] *Id.* at 372.

Noting that *McCullen* requires a government to justify its regulation of speech by showing it had "seriously considered and reasonably rejected 'different methods that other jurisdictions have found effective'"[171] and that such proof can only be considered after discovery and the production of evidence, it went on to state that the government "will rarely be able to satisfy narrow tailoring at the pleading stage."[172]

The narrow tailoring requirement is a frequent concern when considering the application of permit requirements to small groups. "An ordinance that requires individuals or groups to obtain a permit before engaging in protected speech is a prior restraint on speech."[173] As such, there is a presumption against its constitutional validity, which must be overcome by the government.[174] But reasonable time, place, and manner regulations of expressive activity may include a permit requirement as long as they satisfy the *Ward* test.[175] When a group desiring to engage in expressive activity on a street or sidewalk or in a park is sufficiently large to present serious traffic, safety, or competing use concerns, the application of a proper permitting scheme is uncontroversial.[176] But a number of courts have considered whether a permit requirement can be constitutionally applied to a small group.

"[T]he Supreme Court has consistently struck down permitting systems that apply to individual speakers—as opposed to large groups—in the one context in which they have been put in place with some regularity: solicitation of private homes."[177] It has not addressed the validity of single-speaker

---

[171] *Id.* at 371 (quoting McCullen v. Coakley, 134 S. Ct. 2518, 2539 (2014)).

[172] *Id.* at 372.

[173] Green v. City of Raleigh, 523 F.3d 293, 300 (4th Cir. 2008) (quoting Cox v. City of Charleston, 416 F.3d 281, 284 (4th Cir. 2005)).

[174] Long Beach Area Peace Network v. City of Long Beach, 574 F.3d 1011, 1023 (9th Cir. 2009); Cmty. for Creative Non-Violence v. Turner, 893 F.2d 1387, 1390 (D.C. Cir. 1990).

[175] *Long Beach*, 574 F.3d at 1023.

[176] Although not expressly considering the size limitation, in a unanimous opinion, the Supreme Court upheld a permit requirement for park gatherings applicable to groups of fifty or more as a valid time, place, and manner regulation. *See* Thomas v. Chicago Park Dist., 534 U.S. 316 (2002). As noted previously, the requirements of a proper permitting scheme are addressed in chapter 11.

[177] Berger v. City of Seattle, 569 F.3d 1029, 1038 (9th Cir. 2009) (citing Watchtower Bible and Tract Soc. of N.Y., Inc. v. Vill. of Stratton, 536 U.S. 150, 166–67 (2002); Vill. of Schaumberg v. Citizens for a Better Env't, 444 U.S. 620, 638–39 (1980); Cantwell v. Connecticut, 310 U.S. 296, 301, 306–07 (1940); Schneider v. New Jersey, 308 U.S. 147, 163–64 (1939)).

permitting requirements for speech in a public forum.[178] But, "it stands to reason that such requirements would be at least as constitutionally suspect when applied to speech in a public park, where a speaker's First Amendment protections reach their zenith, than when applied to speech on a citizen's doorstep, where substantial privacy interests exist."[179] Not surprisingly, most circuit courts have refused to uphold registration requirements when applied to individuals or small groups in a public forum.[180]

The Fourth Circuit has held that the lack of a small-group exception in ordinances regulating assemblies, parades, processions, and exhibitions will render such ordinances facially unconstitutional.[181] Other circuits have held that a small-group exception must be included in such ordinances in order for them to be narrowly tailored.[182]

In striking down an ordinance that made it unlawful to participate in any special event without first obtaining a permit, the Sixth Circuit stated that "[p]ermit schemes and advance notice requirements that potentially apply to small groups are nearly always overly broad and lack narrow tailoring."[183] In that case, "special event" was defined to include "any walkathon, bikeathon, or jogging group, or other organized group having a common purpose or goal, proceeding along a public street or other public right-of-way."[184] The court held the definition to be overly broad because it would apply to "a group of senior citizens walking together to religious services."[185] It then noted that the ordinance lacked narrow tailoring for similar reasons because the city's "significant interest in crowd and traffic control, property maintenance, and protection of the public welfare [was] not advanced by the application of the Ordinance to small groups."[186]

---

[178] *See Berger*, 569 F.3d at 1039.
[179] *Id.*
[180] *Id.*
[181] Cox v. City of Charleston, 416 F.3d 281, 286 (4th Cir. 2005).
[182] *See* Smith v. Exec. Dir., 742 F.3d 282, 289 (7th Cir. 2014); Boardley v. U.S. Dept. of the Interior, 615 F.3d 508, 523 (D.C. Cir. 2010); Knowles v. City of Waco, 462 F.3d 430, 435–36 (5th Cir. 2006); American-Arab Anti-Discrimination Comm. v. City of Dearborn, 418 F.3d 600, 608 (6th Cir. 2005); Grossman v. City of Portland, 33 F.3d 1200, 1207–08 (9th Cir. 1994); Cmty. for Creative Non-Violence v. Turner, 893 F.2d 1387, 1392 (D.C. Cir. 1990).
[183] *American-Arab*, 418 F.3d at 608.
[184] *Id.*
[185] *Id.*
[186] *Id.*

In *Santa Monica Food Not Bombs v. City of Santa Monica*, the Ninth Circuit considered whether other elements of an ordinance regulating groups of any size could provide narrow tailoring in the absence of a small-group exception.[187] The ordinance in question imposed a permit requirement for groups engaging in expressive activities in streets and sidewalks but limited its application to only two types of events: "(1) [T]hose that 'may impede, obstruct, impair or interfere' with the free flow of traffic or (2) those that 'do[ ] not comply with the normal or usual traffic regulations or controls.'"[188] The court held that the second permit requirement was narrowly tailored even in the absence of a small-group exception because its application was limited only to events that actually implicated the governmental interest in traffic regulation.[189] Conversely, the first requirement was not narrowly tailored because of its use of the term *may*, which made it applicable to too many circumstances that do not turn out to actually implicate the governmental interest.[190]

The Seventh Circuit declined to hold that permit requirements for groups of any specified number are per se unconstitutional and remanded the matter for consideration of the constitutionality of a permit requirement "in light of the concerns that are unique to the venue in question."[191] The plaintiffs were members of a small religious group with the goal of spreading the Gospel outside of various venues at Chicago's annual Gay Games.[192] One of the venues was Gateway Park, which the court described as a "narrow bottleneck" leading to a crowded commercial pier surrounded by water on three sides, traversed by as many as eighty-five thousand people per day.[193] It noted that unique logistical concerns might make regulation necessary, but it added that it was left with the impression that "the imposition of burdensome restrictions for small groups at Gateway Park might be overreaching."[194]

---

[187] 450 F.3d 1022 (9th Cir. 2006).

[188] *Id.* at 1040 (alteration in original).

[189] *See id.*

[190] *Id.* at 1041.

[191] *See* Marcavage v. City of Chicago, 659 F.3d 626, 635 (7th Cir. 2011).

[192] *See id.* at 628.

[193] *See id.* at 634. In a prior case, the court had previously held that the pier was devoted to commercial activities and was a nonpublic forum. *See* Chicago ACORN v. Metro. Pier & Exposition Auth., 150 F.3d 695 (7th Cir. 1998).

[194] *Id.* at 635.

In *Green v. City of Raleigh*, the Fourth Circuit upheld an advance notice requirement for groups picketing on sidewalks and public ways applicable to groups of ten or more.[195] In doing so, however, it emphasized that the ordinance only applied to sidewalks and other public ways and not to parks or more capacious public fora and did not contain many of the restrictions found in most municipal regulations of public demonstrations.[196] Importantly, the ordinance did not extend any discretion to city officials to grant, deny, or set conditions on permission to demonstrate; allowed notice at any time, in person, by telephone, or by facsimile; and required officials to issue a receipt of notice immediately.[197]

Because the ordinance in *Green* allowed immediate notice by telephone, its impact on spontaneous expression was minimal.[198] As applied to small groups, a primary concern with permitting and advance notice regulations that are more onerous than the one considered by the *Green* court is the impact on spontaneous expression. In striking down an ordinance that required a permit to engage in door-to-door advocacy, the Supreme Court addressed its impact on spontaneous expression:

> [T]here is a significant amount of spontaneous speech that is effectively banned by the ordinance. A person who made a decision on a holiday or a weekend to take an active part in a political campaign could not begin to pass out handbills until after he or she obtained the required permit. Even a spontaneous decision to go across the street and urge a neighbor to vote against the mayor could not lawfully be implemented without first obtaining the mayor's permission.
>
> In this respect, the regulation is analogous to the circulation licensing tax the Court invalidated in *Grosjean v. American Press Co.,* .... In *Grosjean*, while discussing the history of the Free Press Clause of the First Amendment, the Court stated that "[t]he evils to be prevented were not the censorship of the press merely, but any action of the government

---

[195] 523 F.3d 293, 304–05 (4th Cir. 2008).
[196] *Id.* at 304.
[197] *Id.* at 301.
[198] *See id.* at 301.

by means of which it might prevent such free and general discussion of public matters as seems absolutely essential to prepare the people for an intelligent exercise of their rights as citizens."[199]

As the D.C. Circuit noted in *Boardley v. U.S. Department of Interior*,[200] the chilling of spontaneous expression by a permit or advance notice requirement falls almost exclusively on individuals and small groups because large-group activities require advance planning and generally do not occur spontaneously:

> Individuals and small groups, by contrast, frequently wish to speak off the cuff, in response to unexpected events or unforeseen stimuli. For example, if an individual comes upon a (duly licensed) anti-war protest at a national park and wishes to don a 'support the troops' pin in response, must he first apply for a permit or otherwise risk being penalized for engaging in an unlicensed 'demonstration.'? [sic] *See* C.F.R. § 2.51(a). This is a major deprivation of free speech, and it falls almost exclusively on individuals and small groups.[201]

The court expressed skepticism that application of the requirement to small groups is necessary to achieve any of the government's proffered justifications.[202]

Application of permitting and advance notice requirements to small groups also burdens the right of a speaker to remain anonymous, which has long been recognized by the Supreme Court as important to First Amendment values:

> Anonymous pamphlets, leaflets, brochures and even books have played an important role in the progress of mankind. Persecuted groups and sects from time to time throughout history have been able to criticize

---

[199] Watchtower Bible & Tract Soc'y v. Village of Stratton, 536 U.S. 150, 167–68 (2002) (alteration in original) (quoting Grosjean v. Am. Press Co., 297 U.S. 233, 249–50 (1936)).

[200] 615 F.3d 508, 523 (D.C. Cir. 2010).

[201] *Id.*

[202] *Id.* at 521–22. *See also* McDonnell v. City and Cnty. of Denver, ___ F. Supp. 3d ___, 2017 WL 698802 (D. Colo. Feb. 17, 2017) (finding, on a motion for preliminary injunction, that Denver airport permitting scheme was unreasonable as applied to small group of plaintiffs who sought to protest on short notice).

oppressive practices and laws either anonymously or not at all. The obnoxious press licensing law of England, which was also enforced on the Colonies was due in part to the knowledge that exposure of the names of printers, writers and distributors would lessen the circulation of literature critical of the government. The old seditious libel cases in England show the lengths to which government had to go to find out who was responsible for books that were obnoxious to the rulers. John Lilburne was whipped, pilloried and fined for refusing to answer questions designed to get evidence to convict him or someone else for the secret distribution of books in England. Two Puritan Ministers, John Penry and John Udal, were sentenced to death on charges that they were responsible for writing, printing or publishing books. Before the Revolutionary War colonial patriots frequently had to conceal their authorship or distribution of literature that easily could have brought down on them prosecutions by English-controlled courts. Along about that time the Letters of Junius were written and the identity of their author is unknown to this day. Even the Federalist Papers, written in favor of the adoption of our Constitution, were published under fictitious names. It is plain that anonymity has sometimes been assumed for the most constructive purposes."[203]

IX. Alternative Means

"[T]he First Amendment does not guarantee the right to communicate one's views at all times and places or in any manner that may be desired."[204] But an alternative mode of communication may be constitutionally inadequate if the speaker's "ability to communicate effectively is threatened."[205] An alternative is not ample if the speaker is not permitted to reach the "intended audience."[206]

---

[203] Talley v. California, 362 U.S. 60, 64–65 (1960) (striking down requirement that handbills must have name of person who printed, wrote, compiled, or manufactured them).

[204] Heffron v. Int'l Soc'y for Krishna Consciousness, Inc., 452 U.S. 640, 647 (1981).

[205] Members of City Council v. Taxpayers for Vincent, 466 U.S. 789, 812 (1984).

[206] Bay Area Peace Navy v. United States, 914 F.2d 1224, 1229 (1990). *See also* Students Against Apartheid Coal. v. O'Neil, 660 F. Supp. 333, 339–40 (W.D. Va. 1987) (holding university regulation prohibiting erection of protest shanties on lawn of building where Board of Visitors meets is not rendered valid by permission to erect shanties elsewhere on campus, in place not visible to members of Board, the intended audience), *aff'd*, 838 F.2d 735 (4th Cir. 1988); Dr. Martin Luther King, Jr. Movement, Inc. v. City of Chicago, 419 F. Supp. 667, 674 (N.D. Ill. 1976) (finding parade route through black neighborhood not constitutional alternative to route through white neighborhood when intended audience was white).

On the other hand, courts will weigh the ability to reach the intended audience against practical limitations:

> The ample alternative channels analysis cannot be conducted in an objective vacuum, but instead it must give "practical recognition" to the facts giving rise to the restriction on speech. . . . Thus, we must ask whether, given the particular security threat posed, the geography of the area regulated, and the type of speech desired, there were ample alternative channels of communication. To treat the ample alternative channels analysis as wholly independent disconnects it from reality and diminishes the emphasis courts have traditionally placed on the importance of the government interest.[207]

Thus, in *Citizens for Peace in Space v. City of Colorado Springs*, the Tenth Circuit held that in light of the practical requirements for providing security at a North Atlantic Treaty Organization (NATO) conference, limiting protestors to one checkpoint at which delegates would see them only briefly as their vehicles passed by constituted an ample alternative means of communication.[208] Going further, in *Marcavage v. City of New York*, the Second Circuit held that an alternative channel is adequate and therefore ample if it is in close proximity to the intended audience and need not be within sight and sound of the intended audience.[209]

Although giving lip service to the necessity of reaching the intended audience, the results in *Citizens for Peace* and *Marcavage* appear to be driven more by the practical requirements of achieving the governmental interest:

> Here, the manifold risks ranged from pedestrian gridlock to assassination. Under such circumstances, a demonstration zone one avenue from the primary entrance to the Garden was an ample alternative channel for protesters, such as Plaintiffs.[210]

When the potential of assassination and other security threats are not at issue, courts tend to focus more on whether the alternative means

---

[207] Citizens for Peace in Space v. City of Colo. Springs, 477 F.3d 1212, 1226 (10th Cir. 2007).
[208] *Id.* at 1218–19, 1226.
[209] 689 F.3d 98, 107–108 (2d Cir. 2012).
[210] *Id.* at 108.

of communication allow the speaker to reach the intended audience in a cost-effective manner. In *Weinberg v. City of Chicago*, the plaintiff was the author of a book critical of the owner of the Chicago Blackhawks who wanted to reach the audience of other Blackhawk fans.[211] The Court determined that the alternatives of selling the book via the Internet, through bookstores, or in other areas of the city were not ample, stating that the ability "to communicate his message elsewhere does not end our analysis if the intended message is rendered useless or is seriously burdened."[212] In another case involving a very specific intended audience, potential employers looking to hire day laborers, the Ninth Circuit also rejected more general means of communication. *Redondo Beach* involved a challenge by day laborers to an ordinance prohibiting solicitation of employment on streets and highways.[213] In an *en banc* ruling, the Ninth Circuit struck the ordinance as not being narrowly tailored.[214] In a concurring opinion, two judges argued that the ordinance also did not leave open alternative channels of communication because "[d]ay laborers simply cannot effectively communicate their intended message ('I am available to work today') to their intended audience (contractors, homeowners, and other potential employers) by soliciting pedestrians, canvassing door-to-door, or mailing and calling individuals and businesses directly."[215]

By contrast, when the intended audience is a broader group, more generalized forms of communication might be adequate. In *The Contributor v. City of Brentwood*, a newspaper written and sold by homeless and formerly homeless people challenged a ban on the sale or distribution of newspapers on the streets or by handing the newspaper to the occupant of a motor vehicle.[216] In upholding the ban, the Sixth Circuit found that mail subscriptions, e-mail distribution, news boxes, sales to pedestrians on sidewalks, and door-to-door sales were ample alternative channels of

---

[211] 310 F.3d 1029, 1033 (7th Cir. 2002).
[212] *Id.* at 1041.
[213] *See* Comite de Jornaleros de Redondo Beach v. City of Redondo Beach, 657 F.3d 936, 940 (9th Cir. 2011) (en banc).
[214] *See id.* at 951.
[215] *Id.* at 956 (Smith, J., concurring).
[216] 726 F.3d 861, 864 (6th Cir. 2013).

communication.[217] It distinguished *Weinberg* and *Redondo Beach* on the basis of the intended audience:

> The key distinction between *Weinberg* and *Redondo Beach* and this case is the speakers' ability to reach the intended audience. A day laborer wants to find a person who will hire him. Absent an area to meet with potential employers, the day laborer is potentially left going door-to-door or soliciting pedestrians on a needle-in-a-haystack search for work. A person selling a book decrying the reign of the Blackhawks former CEO want to find other Blackhawks' fans who dislike the person or those that might be so persuaded. Absent an opportunity to meet with Blackhawks fans where they congregate—the arena where the Blackhawks play—it would be difficult to reach the intended audience.
>
> Plaintiffs' intended audience, on the other hand, is the general citizenry of Brentwood. Plaintiffs can easily reach this audience by going door-to-door, by seeking out people on sidewalks, or by distributing *The Contributor* via the mail, email, and news boxes.[218]

The question of cost also plays a role in the consideration of whether ample alternative means of communication exist, but the fact that an alternative channel is more expensive does not render it inadequate. In the context of the posting of signs on public property, the Supreme Court has noted its "special solicitude for forms of expression that are much less expensive than feasible alternatives" but stated that such "solicitude has practical boundaries."[219] The First Circuit upheld a ban on newspaper racks in a historic district, finding that the use of street vendors constituted an adequate alternative channel.[220] In doing so, it stated that "the First Amendment does not guarantee a right to the most cost-effective means of distribution."[221] Considering a challenge to an ordinance requiring that all newspaper racks be of a uniform size and color, made from 20-gauge

---

[217] *Id.* at 866.

[218] *Id.*

[219] Members of the City Council v. Taxpayers for Vincent, 466 U.S. 789, 812 n. 30 (1984).

[220] *See* Globe Newspaper Co. v. Beacon Hill Architectural Comm'n, 100 F.3d 175, 192–94 (1st Cir. 1996).

[221] *Id.* at 193.

or thicker zinc-coated steel, and be attached to a concrete base of a certain weight, another court considered whether the $200 to $300 cost of acquiring a conforming newspaper rack deprived a publisher of ample alternative means of communication.[222] Noting that the city had modified the ordinance to allow publishers time to comply, it found that the compliance costs were not prohibitive, and therefore the use of a compliant newspaper rack was an adequate alternative means of communication.[223]

X. Conclusion and Practical Considerations

Given the special position of streets, sidewalks, and parks in First Amendment protection[224] and the ability of even the poorest among us to utilize them to solicit, preach, protest, perform, or distribute literature and other expressive products, it is perhaps unsurprising that use of such areas for expressive activity results in so much conflict and litigation. It is in such locations that those with an urgent need to proclaim their message, whether religious, political, artistic, or merely a cry for help, meet supporters, detractors, and others who just want to pass by uninterrupted and be left alone. Expressive activity can interfere with vehicular or pedestrian traffic flow, it can deter potential customers from patronizing an establishment in an area where they are likely to be solicited by panhandlers, and it can interfere with the operation of abortion clinics and other facilities. This leads to calls to government officials for regulation of such activity, and as the Supreme Court noted long ago, government officials have a duty and responsibility to keep the streets open and available for movement.[225]

The myriad forms, subject matters, and targeted audiences of expressive activity in public areas; the conflicting demands on public facilities; and the variety of governmental interests involved combine to create a plethora of different situations to which First Amendment principles must be applied by overworked courts. The resulting decisions can sometimes appear to

[222] See Lauder, Inc. v. City of Houston, 751 F. Supp. 2d 920, 924, 938–43 (S.D. Tex. 2010).
[223] See id. at 939–40.
[224] See McCullen v. Coakley, 134 S. Ct. 2518, 2529 (2014).
[225] See Cox v. Louisiana, 379 U.S. 536, 554–55 (1965).

be, and perhaps sometimes are, inconsistent. Given that apparent inconsistency, one can offer practical pointers only with a degree of trepidation.

Nevertheless, one can confidently predict that public streets, sidewalks, and parks will remain favored locations for First Amendment activity subject to the strongest protections.[226] Therefore, regulations that impose an absolute ban on expressive activity should be avoided.

One can also confidently predict that any content based regulation will almost certainly fail.[227] The most common drafting errors that render a regulation content based are the targeting of only one type of subject matter, such as requiring a permit only for political expression,[228] or the inclusion of exemptions that favor a particular speaker.[229]

With respect to content neutral regulations, a government should document the governmental interest and the manner in which the proposed regulation will actually address that need using objective evidence and should avoid relying only on the conclusory testimony of government officials.[230]

A regulation of expressive activity should be as narrow as reasonably practicable to meet the narrow tailoring requirement. If the problems creating the need for a regulation only occur in particular locations or at particular times, the regulation should apply only at those locations and times.[231] However, if the regulation is to apply only to a particular location or type of facility, the regulation still must apply equally to all expressive activity at that location or facility to avoid being content based.[232] If the problem to be addressed is present only with respect to a larger group, include a small-group exception.[233]

---

[226] *See* Berger v. City of Seattle, 569 F.3d 1029, 1035–36 (9th Cir. 2009).

[227] *See* Reed v. Town of Gilbert, 135 S. Ct. 2218, 2236 (2015) (Kagan J., concurring).

[228] *See* Burk v. Augusta-Richmond Cnty., 365 F.3d 1247, 1251 (11th Cir. 2004).

[229] *See* Carey v. Brown, 447 U.S. 455, 471 (1980) (picketing ban contained exemption for labor picketing).

[230] *See* Weinberg v. City of Chicago, 310 F.3d 1029, 1038 (7th Cir. 2002).

[231] *See, e.g.,* Cutting v. City of Portland, 802 F.3d 79, 92 (1st Cir. 2015).

[232] *Compare* McCullen v. Coakley, 134 S. Ct. 2518, 2531 (2014) (regulation that was applicable near abortion facilities but that did not draw distinctions based on content was content neutral), *with* Boos v. Barry, 485 U.S. 312, 315 (1988) (ordinance applicable near any foreign embassy and directed at messages critical of the foreign government was content based).

[233] *See* Cox v. City of Charleston, 416 F.3d 281, 286 (4th Cir. 2005).

Narrow tailoring will also leave open more alternative channels of communication.[234] As noted previously, the evaluation of alternative channels of communication is fact intensive, but evidence that alternative channels were considered as part of the legislative process is more likely to be persuasive than evidence developed only after a regulation has been challenged.

Finally, in adopting and enforcing regulations governing the use of public space, government officials should always keep in mind that the use of those spaces for religious and political discourse is "essential to free government."[235]

---

[234] *See, e.g.*, Globe Newspaper Co. v. Beacon Hill Architectural Comm'n, 100 F.3d 175, 190 (1st Cir. 1996) (holding that ability to place newspaper racks in areas adjacent to historical district was one of several alternative channels, supporting ban within district).

[235] Thornhill v. Alabama, 310 U.S. 88, 95 (1940).

11

The Regulation of Public Protest: Mass Demonstrations, Marches, and Parades

Kevin F. O'Neill

Associate Professor of Law
Cleveland-Marshall College of Law
Cleveland State University
Cleveland, Ohio

I. Introduction

Chapter 10 addressed the First Amendment protections available to individuals who engage in the unpermitted distribution of protected speech on sidewalks and in other public places, as well as the ability of local governments to regulate those activities. This chapter addresses a different but related set of circumstances: the regulation by local governments of mass demonstrations, marches, and parades, which often require the issuance of government permits. There are two lines of precedent where land use law intersects with First Amendment protection for public protest: (1) the public forum doctrine and (2) the decisions governing permits and fees for public forum expression. This chapter will address each of those subjects in turn and will provide practical suggestions to local government lawyers, managers, and others responsible for managing and enforcing regulations for these large-scale events.

II. The Public Forum Doctrine

A. Origins and Basic Principles

Access to public property for speech-related activity is governed by the public forum doctrine.[1] Although judges and scholars disagree on the doctrine's origin,[2] the U.S. Supreme Court has repeatedly[3] identified its inspiration as *Hague v. Committee for Industrial Organization*,[4] where Justice Owen Roberts, finding a constitutional right to use "streets and parks for communication of views,"[5] based that right on the fact that "streets and parks ... have immemorially been held in trust for the use of the public and, time out of mind, have been used for the purposes of assembly, communicating thoughts between citizens, and discussing public questions."[6]

But the right to engage in public protest has never entailed free access to all types of government property.[7] The government, no less than a private property owner, "'has the power to preserve the property under its control for the use to which it is lawfully dedicated.'"[8] Nothing in the Constitution "requires the Government freely to grant access to all who wish to exercise their right to free speech on every type of Government

---

[1] *See* Capitol Square Review & Advisory Bd. v. Pinette, 515 U.S. 753, 761 (1995).

[2] *Compare* Irish Subcomm. of the R.I. Heritage Comm'n v. R.I. Heritage Comm'n, 646 F. Supp. 347, 353 n. 3 (D.R.I. 1986) (tracing the doctrine to *Hague v. Comm. for Indus. Org.*, 307 U.S. 496 (1939), and describing it as a "response to increasing efforts by government to cut back, restrict, and close off access to forums which were historically, traditionally, and, perhaps, inherently wide open for all types of expression"), *with* Robert C. Post, *Between Governance and Management: The History and Theory of the Public Forum*, 34 UCLA L. REV. 1713, 1718–19 (1987) (tracing the doctrine to an article by Harry Kalven, *The Concept of the Public Forum: Cox v. Louisiana*, 1965 SUP. CT. REV. 1, later cited by the Supreme Court in *Police Dep't v. Mosley*, 408 U.S. 92, 95 n. 3, 99 n. 6 (1972)).

[3] Int'l Soc'y for Krishna Consciousness, Inc. v. Lee, 505 U.S. 672, 679 (1992); Frisby v. Schultz, 487 U.S. 474, 480–81 (1988); Members of City Council v. Taxpayers for Vincent, 466 U.S. 789, 813–14 (1984); Perry Educ. Ass'n v. Perry Local Educ. Ass'n, 460 U.S. 37, 45 (1983); Carey v. Brown, 447 U.S. 455, 460 (1980).

[4] 307 U.S. 496 (1939) (striking down ordinances that, *inter alia*, imposed a flat ban on public distribution of printed materials, and required a permit—issued at the uncontrolled discretion of the public safety director—for all public meetings and demonstrations).

[5] *Id.* at 515–16.

[6] *Id.* at 515.

[7] *See Capitol Square*, 515 U.S. at 761; Cornelius v. NAACP Legal Defense & Educ. Fund, Inc., 473 U.S. 788, 799 (1985).

[8] Greer v. Spock, 424 U.S. 828, 836 (1976) (quoting Adderly v. Florida, 385 U.S. 39, 47 (1966)). *See also Krishna Consciousness*, 505 U.S. at 679–80.

property without regard to the nature of the property or to the disruption that might be caused by the speaker's activities."[9] The First Amendment has never meant that people who want to engage in public protest "have a constitutional right to do so whenever and however and wherever they please."[10]

B. The Supreme Court's Division of Public Property into Four Discrete Categories: Traditional, Designated, Limited, and Nonpublic Fora

In light of these principles, the Supreme Court has adopted a "forum-based" approach to assessing restrictions that the government seeks to place on the use of its property.[11] Government-owned property has been divided into four[12] categories for purposes of forum analysis: (1) traditional public fora, (2) designated public fora, (3) limited public fora, and (4) nonpublic fora—with the last category comprising all of the government property not specifically embraced by the first three.[13]

---

[9] *Cornelius*, 473 U.S. at 799–800.

[10] *Greer*, 424 U.S. at 836 (quoting *Adderly*, 385 U.S. at 47–48).

[11] *Krishna Consciousness*, 505 U.S. at 678 (reaffirming the Court's commitment to a "forum-based" analysis).

[12] Under current law, there are now *four*, no longer just three, categories of government property under the public forum doctrine. Traditional public fora and nonpublic fora are defined today exactly as they were before. What has changed? The Supreme Court now draws a distinction between two terms—"designated" and "limited" public fora—that it used interchangeably for so long that lower courts took note. *See* Currier v. Potter, 379 F.3d 716, 728 n. 8 (9th Cir. 1994) (stating that the terms "designated" and "limited" public fora may be used "interchangeably"); Sons of Confederate Veterans v. City of Lexington, 894 F. Supp. 2d 768, 773 n.2 (W.D. Va. 2012) ("The terms 'designated public forum' and 'limited public forum' have generally been employed interchangeably."), *aff'd*, 722 F.3d 224 (4th Cir. 2013); Act Now to Stop War and End Racism Coal. v. Dist. of Columbia, 798 F. Supp. 2d 134, 144 (D.D.C. 2011) (treating "designated" and "limited" public fora as synonymous). When did the Supreme Court effect this change? In footnote 11 of *Christian Legal Soc'y v. Martinez*, 130 S. Ct. 2971, 2984 n. 11 (2010). And the lower courts have recognized this change. *See* Wright v. Incline Vill. Gen. Improvement Dist., 665 F.3d 1128, 1134 (9th Cir. 2011) (recognizing four discrete categories of public forum property); R.O. *ex rel.* Ochshorn v. Ithaca City Sch. Dist., 645 F.3d 533, 539 (2d Cir. 2011) (recognizing four discrete categories of public forum property). Confirming the shift from three to four, the Supreme Court recently performed a public forum analysis in which it carefully delineated all four categories of public forum property. *See* Walker v. Tex. Div., Sons of Confederate Veterans, 135 S. Ct. 2239, 2250–51 (2015).

[13] *Krishna Consciousness*, 505 U.S. at 678–79 (after describing traditional, designated, and limited public fora, the Court introduces the nonpublic forum by stating, "Finally, there is all remaining public property.").

Traditional public fora are places that "by long tradition or by government fiat have been devoted to assembly and debate."[14] They are largely confined to public parks, squares, streets, and sidewalks.[15]

Designated and limited public fora come into existence when the government takes public property that is not a traditional public forum and intentionally opens it up for expressive purposes.[16] A designated public forum is opened for all speakers and all topics.[17] A limited public forum is opened for a limited range of speakers (e.g., student groups[18]) or a limited range of topics (e.g., school board business[19]).[20]

Nonpublic fora are places that, by tradition, nature, or design, "are not appropriate platforms for unrestrained communication"[21]—including, for example, military bases[22] and federal workplaces,[23] "'[w]here the

---

[14] Perry Educ. Ass'n v. Perry Local Educ. Ass'n, 460 U.S. 37, 45 (1983).

[15] *Cornelius*, 473 U.S. at 802. *See* Frisby v. Schultz, 487 U.S. 474, 480–81 (1988) (holding that *residential* streets are no less a traditional public forum than their downtown counterparts—so that restrictions on residential picketing must be judged under the same stringent standards that govern the regulation of speech in a traditional public forum); United States v. Grace, 461 U.S. 171 (1983) (striking down statutory prohibition against leafleting or displaying signs on the U.S. Supreme Court's sidewalk and holding that a traditional public forum cannot be transformed by government fiat into a nonpublic forum).

[16] *Sons of Confederate Veterans*, 135 S. Ct. at 2250; Christian Legal Soc'y v. Martinez, 130 S. Ct. 2971, 2984 n. 11 (2010).

[17] *Krishna Consciousness*, 505 U.S. at 678.

[18] *See* Widmar v. Vincent, 454 U.S. 263 (1981).

[19] *See* City of Madison Joint Sch. Dist. v. Wisc. Employment Relations Comm'n, 429 U.S. 167 (1976).

[20] *Sons of Confederate Veterans*, 135 S. Ct. at 2250; *Christian Legal Soc'y*, 130 S. Ct. at 2984 n. 11.

[21] Paulsen v. Cnty. of Nassau, 925 F.2d 65, 69 (2d Cir. 1991) (holding that county coliseum where leafleting took place was a designated public forum, such that county could not impose a total ban on leafleting conducted outside the facility).

[22] *See* Greer v. Spock, 424 U.S. 828 (1976) (holding that military bases are nonpublic fora and rejecting challenge to base regulation that banned all speeches and demonstrations of a partisan political nature); United States v. Albertini, 472 U.S. 675 (1985) (reaffirming that "[m]ilitary bases are not generally public fora," and that "[t]here is 'no generalized constitutional right to make political speeches or distribute leaflets' on military bases, even if they are generally open to the public") (quoting *Greer v. Spock*, 424 U.S. at 838).

[23] *See* Sefick v. Gardner, 164 F.3d 370 (7th Cir. 1998) (holding that the lobby of a federal courthouse is a nonpublic forum, the court rejects First Amendment claim by sculptor who was prevented from displaying in the lobby of Chicago's federal courthouse a satirical, life-sized sculpture of a judge astride a white horse); United States v. Sachs, 679 F.2d 1015 (5th Cir. 1982) (upholding conviction of anti-draft protester who sat down in federal building elevator and obstructed its use); United States v. Shiel, 611 F.2d 526 (4th Cir. 1979) (affirming defendant's conviction for lying down in Pentagon passageway during nuclear arms protest); Arbeitman v. Dist. Ct. 522 F.2d 1031 (2d Cir. 1975) (rejecting First Amendment defense asserted by Vietnam War protester who blocked entrance to federal building); United States v. Jones, 365 F.2d 675 (2d Cir. 1966) (affirming disorderly conduct convictions of

(*footnote continued on next page*)

government is acting as a proprietor, managing its internal operations.'"[24] In a series of famous decisions, the Supreme Court likewise identified the following types of property as nonpublic fora: utility poles,[25] residential letterboxes,[26] an interschool mail system,[27] and a workplace charity drive aimed at government employees.[28]

C. How the Level of Judicial Scrutiny Hinges on Whether the Property Is Deemed a Traditional, Designated, Limited, or Nonpublic Forum

In forum analysis, the government's power to impose speech restrictions depends on how the affected property is categorized; the level of judicial scrutiny hinges on whether the property is deemed a traditional, designated, limited, or nonpublic forum.[29]

(footnote continued from previous page)

civil rights protesters who chained themselves to federal courthouse entranceway); United States v. Sroka, 307 F. Supp. 400 (E.D. Wis. 1969) (rejecting First Amendment defense by anti-war protesters who assembled in a federal building corridor to read the names of soldiers killed in Vietnam and, upon the close of business at 5:00, refused to leave the building); United States v. Akeson, 290 F. Supp. 212 (D. Colo. 1968) (rejecting First Amendment defense by anti-war protesters who ventured into a government building to interfere with the processing of individuals being admitted into the military).

[24] *Sons of Confederate Veterans*, 135 S. Ct. at 2251 (quoting Int'l Soc'y for Krishna Consciousness, Inc. v. Lee, 505 U.S. 672, 678–79 (1992)).

[25] *See* Members of the City Council v. Taxpayers for Vincent, 466 U.S. 789 (1984) (addressing political candidate's unsuccessful challenge to an ordinance banning the posting of signs on public property, which effectively proscribed his practice of attaching campaign signs to utility pole crosswires and holding that the property covered by the ordinance—which included utility poles, lampposts, curbstones, fire hydrants, and tree trunks—is not a public forum).

[26] *See* U.S. Postal Serv. v. Council of Greenburgh Civic Ass'ns, 453 U.S. 114 (1981) (holding that residential letterboxes do not constitute a public forum, the Court rejected a First Amendment challenge to a federal statute prohibiting the deposit of unstamped mailable matter in such letterboxes).

[27] *See* Perry Educ. Ass'n v. Perry Local Educ. Ass'n, 460 U.S. 37 (1983) (holding that teacher mailboxes and interschool mail system constituted a nonpublic forum, so granting access to exclusive bargaining representative of teachers' union—and denying access to rival union—did not violate First Amendment rights of rival union).

[28] *See* Cornelius v. NAACP Legal Defense & Educ. Fund, Inc., 473 U.S. 788 (1985) (distinguishing between designated public fora and nonpublic fora, the Court held that a charity drive aimed at federal employees is a *nonpublic* forum and ruled that the federal government did not violate the First Amendment rights of legal defense and political advocacy organizations by excluding them from participation in the drive).

[29] *See Krishna Consciousness*, 505 U.S. at 678–79.

Traditional public fora may be regulated only by content neutral time, place, and manner restrictions.[30] To survive judicial scrutiny, such restrictions must be "justified without reference to the content of the regulated speech," must be "narrowly tailored to serve a significant governmental interest," and must "leave open ample alternative channels for communicati[ng] the information."[31] Governmental restrictions on the *content* of speech in a traditional public forum are presumptively unconstitutional;[32] they will be struck down unless shown to be "necessary, and narrowly drawn, to serve a compelling state interest."[33] Chapter 2 discusses content neutrality in the context of outdoor sign regulation; the same analysis applies in the context of the public forum doctrine.

These same standards govern the second category—restrictions on speech in *designated* public fora.[34] Content based restrictions here are subject to strict scrutiny, whereas content neutral regulations are governed by the same three-prong test outlined previously.[35]

The rules are different for the third category—restrictions on speech in *limited* public fora. The three-prong intermediate scrutiny test does *not* apply here; instead, a *reasonableness* test prevails, and only viewpoint discrimination is forbidden.[36] Although the government is free to restrict access to a limited range of speakers or a limited range of topics,[37] its restrictions must be applied evenhandedly to all similarly situated parties.[38]

---

[30] *See* Paulsen v. Cnty. of Nassau, 925 F.2d 65, 69 (2d Cir. 1991). *See also* Capitol Square Review and Advisory Bd. v. Pinette, 515 U.S. 753, 761 ("[In a traditional public forum], a State's right to limit protected expressive activity is sharply circumscribed: it may impose reasonable, content-neutral time, place, and manner restrictions . . . but it may regulate expressive content only if such a restriction is necessary, and narrowly drawn, to serve a compelling state interest.").

[31] Ward v. Rock Against Racism, 491 U.S. 781, 791 (1989) (quoting Clark v. Cmty. for Creative Non-Violence, 468 U.S. 288, 293 (1984)). *Accord* United States v. Grace, 461 U.S. 171, 177 (1983).

[32] Rosenberger v. Rector & Visitors of the Univ. of Va., 515 U.S. 819, 828 (1995).

[33] *Pinette*, 515 U.S. at 761. *See also Krishna Consciousness*, 505 U.S. at 678; United States v. Kokinda, 479 U.S. 720, 726 (1990); *Cornelius*, 473 U.S. at 800; *Grace*, 461 U.S. at 177; *Perry*, 460 U.S. at 45.

[34] *See* Christian Legal Soc'y v. Martinez, 561 U.S. 661, 679 n. 11 (2010).

[35] *Id.*; *Krishna Consciousness*, 505 U.S. at 678–79.

[36] *Christian Legal Society*, 561 U.S. at 669 n. 11.

[37] *Id.*

[38] *Rosenberger*, 515 U.S. at 829–30 ("The necessities of confining a forum to the limited and legitimate purposes for which it was created may justify the State in reserving it for certain groups or for the

(footnote continued on next page)

In the fourth and final category—*nonpublic* fora—the same deferential standard prevails. So long as the government does not engage in forbidden viewpoint discrimination, its regulation of speech in a nonpublic forum will be analyzed under a reasonableness test.[39] In a nonpublic forum, it is permissible for the government to prohibit *all* protest activities. Thus, the First Amendment afforded no defense to anti-war protesters who occupied a nonpublic forum (a corridor in a federal office building) to read aloud the names of fallen soldiers.[40]

Because the level of judicial scrutiny varies so widely from category to category, many public forum cases feature a battle over how to categorize the property in question. The resulting case law offers guidance on how to differentiate the four categories.

Traditional public fora are so narrowly defined by the Supreme Court that we may safely confine them to public parks, squares, streets, and sidewalks.[41] They "are places which 'by long tradition or by government fiat have been devoted to assembly and debate'"[42]—places whose "principal purpose . . . is the free exchange of ideas."[43] Under this narrow conception,

---

(footnote continued from previous page)

discussion of certain topics. Once it has opened a limited forum, however, the State must respect the lawful boundaries it has itself set. The State may not exclude speech where its distinction is not 'reasonable in light of the purpose served by the forum,' nor may it discriminate against speech on the basis of its viewpoint. Thus, in determining whether the State is acting to preserve the limits of the forum it has created so that the exclusion of a class of speech is legitimate, we have observed a distinction between, on the one hand, content discrimination, which may be permissible if it preserves the purposes of that limited forum, and, on the other hand, viewpoint discrimination, which is presumed impermissible when directed against speech otherwise within the forum's limitations.") (citations and internal quotation marks omitted).

[39] Perry Educ. Ass'n v. Perry Local Educ. Ass'n, 460 U.S. 37, 46 (1983).

[40] *See* United States v. Sroka, 307 F. Supp. 400 (E.D. Wis. 1969) (rejecting First Amendment defense by anti-war protesters who assembled in a federal building corridor to read the names of soldiers killed in Vietnam and, upon the close of business at 5:00, refused to leave the building).

[41] Cornelius v. NAACP Legal Defense & Ed. Fund, Inc., 473 U.S. 788, 802 (1985). To this very short list, we might add the curtilage of legislative seats. *See* Capitol Square Review & Advisory Bd. v. Pinette, 515 U.S. 753, 761 (1995) (Ohio statehouse grounds where Ku Klux Klan sought to erect a Christian cross constituted a traditional public forum). But the Supreme Court "has rejected the view that traditional public forum status extends beyond its historic confines." Walker v. Tex. Div., Sons of Confederate Veterans, 135 S. Ct. 2239, 2250 (2015) (quoting Ark. Educ. Television Comm'n v. Forbes, 523 U.S. 666, 678 (1998)).

[42] *Cornelius*, 473 U.S. at 802 (quoting *Perry*, 460 U.S. at 45).

[43] *Cornelius*, 473 U.S. at 800.

traditional public forum status has eluded such heavily frequented public spaces as airport terminals,[44] state fairgrounds,[45] post office sidewalks,[46] public housing complexes,[47] Chicago's municipally owned pier,[48] and the interior of the Jefferson Memorial.[49]

In determining whether public property is a designated or limited public forum—and therefore *not* a nonpublic forum—the most important factor is whether the government took affirmative steps to *dedicate* the property to expressive purposes.[50] The government does not create such a forum "by inaction,"[51] or by allowing the public "'freely to visit,'"[52] or by "permitting limited discourse"[53] there; instead, such a forum is created only where the government "'intentionally open[s] a nontraditional forum for public discourse.'"[54] Absent these intentional, affirmative steps by the government, the property in question will be deemed a *nonpublic* forum.

This factor—examining the government's "policy and practice"[55] toward the property—was decisive in *Widmar v. Vincent;*[56] *Southeastern*

---

[44] *See* Int'l Soc'y. for Krishna Consciousness, Inc. v. Lee, 505 U.S. 672 (1992); Stanton v. Fort Wayne-Allen Cnty., 834 F. Supp. 2d 865 (N.D. Ind. 2011).

[45] Heffron v. Int'l Soc'y. for Krishna Consciousness, Inc., 452 U.S. 640, 655 (1981).

[46] United States v. Kokinda, 497 U.S. 720, 727 (1990).

[47] Daniel v. City of Tampa, 38 F.3d 546 (11th Cir. 1994).

[48] Chicago ACORN v. Metro. Pier & Exposition Auth., 150 F.3d 695 (7th Cir. 1998).

[49] Oberwetter v. Hilliard, 639 F.3d 545 (D.C. Cir. 2011).

[50] *Kokinda*, 497 U.S. at 730 (stressing that a designated public forum is not created unless it is "expressly dedicated" by the government to "expressive activity"); Walker v. Tex. Div., Sons of Confederate Veterans, 135 S. Ct. 2239, 2250 (2015) (holding that to create a designated public forum, the government must have "intentionally opened up" the property for expressive purposes; to create a limited public forum, the government must have "reserved a forum" for particular groups or topics of discussion) (citations, brackets, and internal quotation marks omitted).

[51] Int'l Soc'y for Krishna Consciousness, Inc. v. Lee, 505 U.S. 672, 680 (1992); Cornelius v. NAACP Legal Defense & Ed. Fund, Inc., 473 U.S. 788, 802 (1985).

[52] *Krishna Consciousness*, 505 U.S. at 680 (quoting Greer v. Spock, 424 U.S. 828, 836 (1976)). *Accord* United States v. Grace, 461 U.S. 171, 177 (1983).

[53] *Cornelius*, 473 U.S. at 802.

[54] *Krishna Consciousness*, 505 U.S. at 680 (quoting *Cornelius*, 473 U.S. at 802). *Accord Kokinda*, 497 U.S. at 730 (stressing that governmental acquiescence is not enough, that "a practice of allowing some speech activities on [the] property do[es] not add up to the dedication of [that] property to speech activities").

[55] *Cornelius*, 473 U.S. at 803.

[56] 454 U.S. 263 (1981) (finding that state university that makes its facilities generally available for the activities of registered student groups violates the First Amendment by closing its facilities to a registered student group desiring to use the facilities for religious worship and religious discussion).

Promotions, Ltd. v. Conrad;[57] *Lehman v. City of Shaker Heights;*[58] and *Perry Education Association v. Perry Local Educators' Association.*[59] In *Conrad* and *Widmar*, respectively, the Supreme Court deemed a municipal auditorium to be a designated public forum and deemed a university meeting center to be a limited public forum because in each case the government affirmatively dedicated the facilities to expressive uses.[60] *Perry* and *Lehman*, by contrast, featured well-established policies disfavoring, respectively, access to a school district's internal mail system and access to advertising spaces on city transit vehicles.[61] The Court deemed each, accordingly, a nonpublic forum.

Another factor to distinguish nonpublic fora from designated and limited public fora is whether the property is by nature "compatib[le] with expressive activity."[62] The Supreme Court has stressed: "We will not . . . infer that the government intended to create a public forum when the nature of the property is inconsistent with expressive activity."[63] This factor proved pivotal in *International Society for Krishna Consciousness v. Lee,*[64] *Cornelius v. NAACP,*[65] *Greer v. Spock,*[66] and *Adderly v. Florida,*[67] where the Supreme

---

[57] 420 U.S. 546 (1975) (holding that municipal board's refusal to permit the performance of *Hair* was a prior restraint that violated the First Amendment because it was effected under a licensing scheme that gave unfettered discretion to the board and afforded applicants no procedure for prompt judicial review); *id.* at 555 (holding that the municipal auditorium and city-leased theater here were "public forums designed for and dedicated to expressive activities").

[58] 418 U.S. 298, 304 (1974) (upholding city's refusal to accept any political advertising for placement in or upon city's rapid transit vehicles and holding that advertising spaces in and upon a city's transit system vehicles do not constitute a public forum).

[59] 460 U.S. 37 (1983) (holding that teacher mailboxes and interschool mail system constituted a nonpublic forum, so granting access to exclusive bargaining representative of teachers' union—and denying access to rival union—did not violate First Amendment rights of rival union).

[60] *See* Cornelius v. NAACP Legal Defense & Ed. Fund, Inc., 473 U.S. 788, 802–03 (1985) (analyzing the two cases).

[61] *Id.* at 803–04.

[62] *Id.* at 802.

[63] *Id.* at 803.

[64] 505 U.S. 672 (1992).

[65] 473 U.S. 788, 799–800 (1985).

[66] 424 U.S. 828 (1976).

[67] 385 U.S. 39 (1966) (rejecting First Amendment defense to trespass convictions of student civil rights protesters who entered upon jailhouse grounds, blocked vehicular traffic, and refused to leave—where there was no evidence that any protesters had ever previously been permitted to gather in the jailhouse curtilage and where there was no evidence that defendants' message, rather than their physical intrusion, prompted their arrest); *id.* at 47–48 (suggesting that jailhouse curtilage is not a public forum and holding that "people who want to propagandize protests or views [do not] have a constitutional right to do so whenever and however and wherever they please").

Court held to be nonpublic fora, respectively, an airport terminal, a federal workplace charity drive, a military base, and jailhouse grounds. Each of these cases turned on the Court's declared "reluctan[ce]" to recognize a designated or limited public forum "where the principal function of the property would be disrupted by expressive activity."[68]

Finally, there is an important point to remember about designated and limited public fora. After opening such a forum, there is no requirement that the government *keep* it open indefinitely.[69] But there is very little case law governing the *closure* of a designated or limited public forum.[70] It appears that the government may close such a forum whenever it wants to, with no offense to the First Amendment,[71] and its *motive* for closing the forum is irrelevant.[72] When a designated or limited public forum is closed, it reverts back to the status of a nonpublic forum.[73]

D. Content Based Restrictions on Public Forum Expression

"It is axiomatic," the Supreme Court has stressed, "that the government may not regulate speech based on its substantive content or the message it

---

[68] *Cornelius*, 473 U.S. at 804.

[69] *See Perry*, 460 U.S. at 45–46 and n. 7.

[70] The leading case is *Sons of Confederate Veterans v. City of Lexington*, 722 F.3d 224 (4th Cir. 2013), affirming the district court's 12(b)(6) dismissal of a complaint filed by the Sons of Confederate Veterans, whose desire to display Confederate flags from city-owned flagpoles was thwarted when the city enacted a new ordinance permitting the flag poles to be used only for displaying three specific flags: the flag of the United States, the state flag of Virginia, and the local municipal flag—even though the city *previously* allowed the Confederate and other privately owned flags to be displayed. *See id.* at 229–32 (holding that the city created a designated public forum when it previously allowed privately owned flags to be displayed from city-owned flagpoles—but a designated public forum need not be kept open indefinitely, and the city's new ordinance effectively *closed* the designated public forum, which reverted back to being a nonpublic forum; closing the forum did not violate the First Amendment, held the court, and the city's *motive* for closing the forum is irrelevant).

[71] *See id.* at 231; *accord* Currier v. Potter, 379 F.3d 716, 728 (9th Cir. 2004) (observing that government may close a designated public forum "whenever it wants"); Make the Road by Walking, Inc. v. Turner, 378 F.3d 133, 143 (2d Cir. 2004) (asserting that a "government may decide to close a designated public forum"); United States v. Bjerke, 796 F.2d 643, 647 (3d Cir. 1986) (observing that "officials may choose to close . . . a designated public forum at any time").

[72] *See Confederate Veterans*, 722 F.3d at 231–32.

[73] *See id.* at 231.

conveys."[74] In regulating speech, the government may not favor one speaker over another;[75] discrimination against speech because of its message "is presumed to be unconstitutional."[76]

When the government targets not subject matter but, even more narrowly, particular *views* on a given subject, the First Amendment violation "is all the more blatant."[77] Viewpoint discrimination is thus "an egregious form of content discrimination."[78] Accordingly, the government "must abstain from regulating speech when the specific motivating ideology or the opinion or perspective of the speaker is the rationale for the restriction."[79]

Impermissible content based restrictions appear in a variety of guises; these include the following:

1. Where the government categorically suppresses or favors a particular topic or message[80]—as, for example, in *Boos v. Barry*,[81] where a District of Columbia statute banned the display of any sign criticizing a foreign government within five hundred feet of its embassy;
2. Where the government serves as a content conscious *gatekeeper*, selectively blocking access to a forum based on the speaker's intended message[82]—as, for example, in *Mahoney v.*

---

[74] Rosenberger v. Rector & Visitors of the Univ. of Va., 515 U.S. 819, 828 (1995); *accord* Reed v. Town of Gilbert, 135 S. Ct. 2218, 2228 (2015); Police Dep't v. Mosley, 408 U.S. 92, 96 (1972).

[75] *See Rosenberger*, 515 U.S. at 828; Members of City Council v. Taxpayers for Vincent, 466 U.S. 789, 804 (1984).

[76] *Rosenberger*, 515 U.S. at 828; *accord* Turner Broad. Sys., Inc. v. FCC, 512 U.S. 622, 641 (1994).

[77] *Rosenberger*, 515 U.S. at 829; *accord* R.A.V. v. City of St. Paul, 505 U.S. 377, 391 (1992).

[78] *Rosenberger*, 515 U.S. at 829.

[79] *Id.*; *accord Perry*, 460 U.S. at 46.

[80] *See, e.g.*, Carey v. Brown, 447 U.S. 455, 460–61 (1980) (striking down—as a content based restriction on public forum speech—a statute that banned the picketing of residences or dwellings but exempted from its prohibition the picketing of any place of employment involved in a labor dispute); Police Dep't v. Mosley, 408 U.S. 92 (1972) (striking down—as a content based restriction on public forum speech—an ordinance that prohibited all picketing within 150 feet of a school, except for picketing of any school involved in a labor dispute).

[81] 485 U.S. 312, 318–19, 321–22 (1988) (striking down a District of Columbia statute that criminalized the display of any sign criticizing a foreign government within five hundred feet of its embassy).

[82] *See, e.g.*, Lamb's Chapel v. Ctr. Moriches Union Free Sch. Dist., 508 U.S. 384, 393 (1993) ("[I]t discriminates on the basis of viewpoint to permit school property to be used for the presentation of all views about family issues and child-rearing except those dealing with the subject matter from a religious standpoint."); Widmar v. Vincent, 454 U.S. 263 (1981) (finding that state university that makes its facilities generally available for the activities of registered student groups violates the First

(footnote continued on next page)

Babbitt,[83] where the National Park Service sought to prevent anti-abortion protesters from displaying banners along the route of President Clinton's inaugural parade;

3. Where the government subjects unpopular speakers to a higher fee for using a forum[84]—as, for example, in *Forsyth County v. Nationalist Movement,*[85] where, under a local parade permit scheme, the fee for police protection could be increased if the speaker was likely to generate controversy;

4. Where the government withholds a service or subsidy to which the speaker would otherwise be entitled if not for the speaker's message—as, for example, in *Rosenberger v. Rector & Visitors of the University of Virginia,*[86] where a student religious journal was denied the same subsidy for printing costs that the university furnished to all other student publications; and

5. Where the government alters the speaker's intended message as the price for use of a forum[87]—as, for example, in *Hurley v. Irish-American*

(footnote continued from previous page)

Amendment by closing its facilities to a registered student group desiring to use the facilities for religious worship and religious discussion); Congregation Lubavitch v. City of Cincinnati, 997 F.2d 1160 (6th Cir. 1993) (finding viewpoint discrimination in restricting access to a traditional public forum); ACT-UP v. Walp, 755 F. Supp. 1281, 1289 (M.D. Pa. 1991) (holding that police, in their effort to shield governor from criticism and thwart planned protest by AIDS activists, violated First Amendment by closing state legislature's public gallery for the first time ever during a governor's annual address).

[83] 105 F.3d 1452, 1457–58 (D.C. Cir. 1997) (refusing "[to] permit the government to destroy the public forum character of the sidewalks along Pennsylvania Avenue by the ipse dixit act of declaring itself a permittee").

[84] *See, e.g.,* Cent. Fla. Nuclear Freeze Campaign v. Walsh, 774 F.2d 1515, 1525 (11th Cir. 1985) (striking down—both facially and as applied—an Orlando ordinance that required persons wishing to demonstrate in city streets and parks to prepay the cost of additional police protection, to be determined at police chief's discretion).

[85] 505 U.S. 123, 134–35 (1992) (striking down ordinance permitting government administrator to vary the fee for assembling or parading to reflect the estimated cost of maintaining public order; holding that the ordinance unconstitutionally required the administrator to examine the *content* of the prospective speaker's message—and to charge a higher fee for controversial viewpoints).

[86] 515 U.S. 819, 831 (1995) (holding that a student religious journal was entitled to the same subsidy from student activity funds that the university furnishes to secular student journals).

[87] *See, e.g.,* City of Cleveland v. Nation of Islam, 922 F. Supp. 56 (N.D. Ohio 1995) ("[Minister Farrakhan has] one message for male constituents, another for female constituents. If the City is allowed to make the public accommodation law requir[e] Minister Farrakhan to speak to a mixed audience, the content and character of the speech will necessarily be changed."); N.Y. Cnty. Bd. of Ancient Order

(footnote continued on next page)

Gay, Lesbian & Bisexual Group of Boston,[88] where, as the price for securing their parade permit, the private organizers of a St. Patrick's Day parade were compelled by the government to include a contingent of gay and lesbian marchers, whose very presence would impart a message that the organizers did not wish to convey.

E. Regulating the Time, Place, and Manner of Public Forum Expression

Time, place, and manner restrictions are content neutral limitations imposed by the government on how, when, and where expressive activity may be conducted. Such restrictions come in many forms: imposing limits on the noise level of speech,[89] capping the number of protesters who may occupy a given forum,[90]

(footnote continued from previous page)

of Hibernians v. Dinkins, 814 F. Supp. 358 (S.D.N.Y. 1993) (finding city's ordering of private parade sponsor to include a gay and lesbian group was a content based alteration of sponsor's message and thus offended the First Amendment); Invisible Empire of the Knights of the Ku Klux Klan v. Mayor of Thurmont, 700 F. Supp. 281, 289 (D. Md. 1988) (holding that town officials unconstitutionally denied KKK a parade permit where issuance of the permit hinged on a never–before–imposed "nondiscrimination condition" that effectively entitled blacks to march in the Klan's parade).

[88] 515 U.S. 557, 570 (1995) (holding that Massachusetts could not invoke its public accommodations law to force private organizers of St. Patrick's Day Parade to include a contingent of Irish gays and lesbians who would impart a message that the organizers did not wish to convey; compelling the inclusion of this group effectively altered the expressive content of the organizers' parade, thereby violating the First Amendment).

[89] *See, e.g.*, Ward v. Rock Against Racism, 491 U.S. 781 (1989) (rejecting First Amendment challenge by rock concert promoter to New York City's use guidelines for its bandshell in Central Park; the guidelines—upheld here as a reasonable time, place, and manner restriction—were designed to limit the noise level of band shell concerts by requiring the performers to use a sound system and sound technician furnished by the city; the technician, while deferring to the performers as to sound mix, retained sole control over sound volume); Grayned v. City of Rockford, 408 U.S. 104 (1972) (upholding— as a reasonable time, place, and manner restriction—an anti-noise ordinance prohibiting a person while on grounds adjacent to a school building from willfully making a noise or diversion that tends to disturb classes in session); Kovacs v. Cooper, 336 U.S. 77 (1949) (upholding ordinance prohibiting use on city streets of sound trucks emitting "loud and raucous" noises); Stokes v. City of Madison, 930 F.2d 1163 (7th Cir. 1991) (demonstrators protesting U.S. policy toward El Salvador were arrested when they attempted to use sound amplification equipment to address a rally without first having obtained the requisite permit for use of such equipment; court upholds the sound amplification ordinance as a reasonable time, place, and manner restriction); Medlin v. Palmer, 874 F.2d 1085 (5th Cir. 1989) (upholding—as a legitimate time, place, and manner regulation—a noise ordinance prohibiting the use of any handheld amplifier within 150 feet of an abortion clinic or other medical facility).

[90] *E.g.*, Blasecki v. City of Durham, 456 F.2d 87 (4th Cir. 1972) (upholding ordinance that prohibited more than fifty people from assembling in a small downtown park).

barring early-morning or late-evening demonstrations,[91] and restricting the size or placement of signs on government property.[92] Such regulations are frequently upheld and represent a common part of the regulatory landscape in most cities.

Time, place, and manner analysis is governed by a three-part test, from *Ward v. Rock Against Racism*,[93] requiring separate inquiry into three distinct issues: (1) whether the regulation is truly content neutral, (2) whether the regulation is narrowly tailored to serve a significant government interest, and (3) whether the regulation leaves open ample alternative channels for communicating the information.[94] In the next three subsections, those issues are addressed in turn.

1. Assessing "Content Neutrality"

The first prong, requiring content neutrality, will be violated by any regulation that describes permissible expression in terms of its subject matter.[95] So the first step in content neutrality analysis is to check the face of the statute.[96] *Police Department of Chicago v. Mosley* provides an example of a time, place, and manner regulation that, on its face, failed the content neutrality requirement.[97] In *Mosley*, an ordinance prohibited all picketing within 150 feet of any school building while classes were in session, but picketing was allowed if the school was involved in a labor dispute. Writing for the Court, Justice Thurgood Marshall observed that the ordinance "describes impermissible picketing not in terms of time, place, and manner, but in terms of subject matter. The

---

[91] *E.g.,* Abernathy v. Conroy, 429 F.2d 1170 (4th Cir. 1970) (upholding ordinance that limited parades to the hours between 8:00 a.m. and 8:00 p.m.).

[92] *E.g.,* United States v. Musser, 873 F.2d 1513 (D.C. Cir. 1989) (rejecting First Amendment challenge to federal regulation prohibiting unattended signs in Lafayette Park); White House Vigil for the ERA Comm. v. Clark, 746 F.2d 1518 (D.C. Cir. 1984) (upholding—as reasonable time, place, and manner restrictions on demonstrations taking place on the White House sidewalk—regulations that limited the size, construction, and placement of signs on the sidewalk; restricted, but did not prohibit, demonstrations within the "center zone" of the sidewalk; and prohibited the placement, except momentarily, of parcels upon the sidewalk); *see id.* at 1520 n. 4 (listing an array of violent incidents in D.C. that prompted a tightening of security restrictions in all government buildings).

[93] 491 U.S. 781 (1989).

[94] *Id.* at 791.

[95] *See* Boos v. Barry, 485 U.S. 312 (1988).

[96] *See* Reed v. Town of Gilbert, 135 S. Ct. 2218, 2228 (2015).

[97] 408 U.S. 92 (1972).

regulation thus slips from the neutrality of time, place, and circumstance into a concern about content. This is never permitted."[98]

Mosley does not exemplify the only way that a speech restriction can violate the content neutrality requirement. Even if the regulation does not expressly discriminate on the basis of subject matter, as in *Mosley*, it can run afoul of the content neutrality requirement if the circumstances surrounding its enactment reveal a governmental intent to favor or punish particular messages.[99]

But speech restrictions will be deemed content neutral even if they impinge more severely on a particular speaker or message so long as they are *facially* content neutral and so long as the government can credibly justify its regulation as serving purposes that have nothing to do with the content of speech. A good example of this may be found in *Community for Creative Non-Violence v. Kerrigan*,[100] where a federal regulation banned the overnight maintenance of any "props" on the U.S. Capitol grounds. This regulation effectively thwarted a plan by homeless advocates to erect, as part of a seven-day vigil, a five-hundred-pound clay statue of a man, woman, and child huddled over a steam grate. The homeless advocates complained that the overnight ban would require them to dismantle their statue every evening and rebuild it each morning, which, over the course of their seven-day vigil, would cause the statue to disintegrate. Thus, they complained, the regulation was content based because it imposed a special hardship on their capacity to communicate their message. The court flatly disagreed, noting that neither the text nor the enforcement history of the regulation indicated any content based animus by the government. Instead, the government offered a credible, content neutral justification for the ban: by requiring the nightly removal of homemade signs and other props from Capitol Hill, the regulation simply gave the

---

[98] *Id.* at 99 (internal quotation marks and footnote omitted).

[99] *Reed*, 135 S. Ct. at 2227 ("Our precedents have also recognized a separate and additional category of laws that, though facially content neutral, will be considered content based regulations of speech: laws that cannot be justified without reference to the content of the regulated speech, or that were adopted by the government because of disagreement with the message [the speech] conveys.") (internal quotation marks omitted).

[100] 865 F.2d 382 (D.C. Cir. 1989).

government meaningful day-to-day control over the Capitol grounds so that they could be cleared of debris and cleaned each night. Given this content neutral justification, the court held that the regulation could not be deemed content based.

To sum up, here are the basic steps and lessons to remember about content neutrality analysis, as set forth by the Supreme Court in *Reed v. Town of Gilbert*.[101] The first step is to check whether the law is content based on its face.[102] A law is facially content based if it applies to particular speech because of the topic discussed or the idea, message, or viewpoint expressed.[103] A speech restriction that is facially content based is subject to strict scrutiny *regardless* of the government's reason for enacting it.[104] Even if a law is content *neutral* on its face, it will be governed by strict scrutiny if the government had content based *motives* in adopting it.[105] So if a law is content neutral on its face, the second step is to examine the government's *reason* for enacting it.[106] Strict scrutiny can be avoided only if the government can credibly justify the law as serving purposes unrelated to the content of the regulated speech.[107]

2. Assessing the Requisite "Narrow Tailoring"

We move now from the first to the second prong of *Ward's* three-prong test for time, place, and manner restrictions. The second prong requires

---

[101] 135 S. Ct. 2218 (2015).

[102] *See id.* at 2228.

[103] *See id.* at 2227, 2230. "Government discrimination among viewpoints . . . is a more blatant and egregious form of content discrimination. . . . Thus, a speech regulation targeted at specific subject matter is content based even if it does not discriminate among viewpoints within that subject matter." *Id.* at 2230 (citations and internal quotation marks omitted).

[104] *See id.* at 2228 ("A law that is content based on its face is subject to strict scrutiny regardless of the government's benign motive, content-neutral justification, or lack of animus toward the ideas contained in the regulated speech. . . . In other words, an innocuous justification cannot transform a facially content based law into one that is content neutral.") (citations and internal quotation marks omitted).

[105] *See id.* at 2227.

[106] *See id.* at 2228 ("[W]e have repeatedly considered whether a law is content neutral on its face *before* turning to the law's justification or purpose.") (emphasis in original); *id.* ("Because strict scrutiny applies either when a law is content based on its face or when the purpose and justification for the law are content based, a court must evaluate each question before it concludes that the law is content neutral and thus subject to a lower level of scrutiny.").

[107] *See id.*

that the regulation must be narrowly tailored to serve a significant governmental interest.[108]

The Supreme Court has stressed that this prong does *not* require time, place, and manner restrictions to be the least restrictive or least intrusive means of achieving the government's end.[109] But to satisfy the narrow tailoring requirement, a speech restriction "must not 'burden substantially more speech than is necessary to further the government's legitimate interests.'"[110]

Until very recently, when the Supreme Court decided *McCullen v. Coakley*, the narrow tailoring requirement was not stringently enforced. Instead, lower courts adopted a relaxed approach to narrow tailoring, based on one particular sentence in *Ward*: "[T]he requirement of narrow tailoring is satisfied 'so long as the . . . regulation promotes a substantial government interest that would be achieved less effectively absent the regulation.'"[111] Viewed in isolation, that lone statement suggests a deferential role for the courts in reviewing time, place, and manner restrictions. But viewed in context, the statement appears in a much more nuanced discussion of narrow tailoring, where the Supreme Court also says: "Government may not regulate expression in such a manner that a substantial portion of the burden on speech does not serve to advance its goals."[112] Years later, in *McCullen*, Chief Justice Roberts invigorated the narrow tailoring requirement by delving back into *Ward* and dredging up that quotation, plus other speech-protective statements that accompanied it.[113]

In the years prior to *McCullen*, the case law reflects a relaxed conception of narrow tailoring. Regulations *failing* this test invariably featured broad restraints on traditional[114] forms of expressive activity, imposing, for example,

---

[108] *See* Ward v. Rock Against Racism, 491 U.S. 781, 791 (1989).

[109] *See id.* at 798–99.

[110] McCullen v. Coakley, 134 S. Ct. 2518, 2535 (2014) (quoting *Ward*, 491 U.S. at 799).

[111] *Ward*, 491 U.S. at 799 (quoting United States v. Albertini, 472 U.S. 675, 689 (1985)).

[112] *Ward*, 491 U.S. at 799.

[113] *McCullen*, 134 S. Ct. at 2535.

[114] Where the regulation targeted an *unconventional* mode of expressive activity, courts readily upheld even a sweeping prohibition. *See, e.g.*, Roulette v. City of Seattle, 97 F.3d 300 (9th Cir. 1996) (rejecting a First Amendment challenge brought by homeless advocates, street musicians, and other political organizations, the Ninth Circuit here upheld a prohibition against sitting or lying on sidewalks); ACORN v. City of Phoenix, 798 F.2d 1260 (9th Cir. 1986) (upholding ordinance that banned soliciting funds from the occupants of motor vehicles stopped at intersections).

sweeping prohibitions on parades,[115] demonstrations,[116] residential picketing,[117] door-to-door leafleting,[118] or public handbilling.[119] Then as now, the narrow tailoring requirement is violated by a categorical ban on any of the foregoing methods of expressive conduct. It is also violated by a restriction that substantially deprives citizens of any of those methods. So, for example, an ordinance would violate the narrow tailoring requirement by banning parades anywhere within the city's central business district on all workdays because it would allow parades only when the downtown streets are bereft of onlookers.[120] Absent a

---

[115] *See, e.g.*, United Food & Commercial Workers Union v. City of Valdosta, 861 F. Supp. 1570, 1582 (M.D. Ga. 1994) (striking down outright ban on parades in residential zones); Sixteenth of September Planning Comm., Inc. v. City and Cnty. of Denver, 474 F. Supp. 1333 (D. Colo. 1979) (striking down, for lack of narrow tailoring, a time, place, and manner restriction on parades in downtown Denver; the regulation banned parades anywhere within the seven-square-block central business district on all workdays from 7:00 a.m. to 6:00 p.m.).

[116] *See, e.g.*, *United Food*, 861 F. Supp. at 1580–81 (striking down outright ban on public assemblies in all public and quasi-public places other than parks, a prohibition that swept within its ambit all demonstrations on streets, roads, highways, sidewalks, driveways, and alleys).

[117] *See, e.g.*, Kirkeby v. Furness, 52 F.3d 772 (8th Cir. 1995) (holding that anti-abortion protesters were entitled to preliminary injunction barring enforcement of a Fargo, North Dakota, ordinance that banned picketing within two hundred feet of a residential dwelling and authorized year-long, neighborhood-wide "non-picketing zones"); Vittitow v. City of Upper Arlington, 43 F.3d 1100 (6th Cir. 1995) (striking down, on overbreadth grounds, city's outright ban on residential picketing); Pursley v. City of Fayetteville, 820 F.2d 951 (8th Cir. 1987) (striking down ordinance that imposed outright ban on all residential picketing).

[118] *See, e.g.*, Martin v. City of Struthers, 319 U.S. 141, 146 (1943) (striking down outright ban on all door-to-door leafleting and observing that door-to-door leafleting "is essential to the poorly financed causes of little people").

[119] *See, e.g.*, Lederman v. United States, 291 F.3d 36 (D.C. Cir. 2002) (striking down, for lack of narrow tailoring, a total ban on leafleting and other expressive activities on the sidewalk at the base of the U.S. Senate steps, which the court held to be a traditional public forum); Krantz v. City of Fort Smith, 160 F.3d 1214, 1222 (8th Cir. 1998) (striking down for lack of narrow tailoring an ordinance that banned placing handbills on unattended vehicles parked on public property); Gerritsen v. City of Los Angeles, 994 F.2d 570 (9th Cir. 1993) (striking down—as invalid time, place, and manner restrictions on public forum speech—city's outright ban on handbill distribution in specified areas of a public park and its permit scheme for handbill distribution in all other areas of the park); Henderson v. Lujan, 964 F.2d 1179 (D.C. Cir. 1992) (striking down, for lack of narrow tailoring, a National Park Service regulation banning all leafleting on the sidewalks surrounding the Vietnam Veterans Memorial, where the sidewalks, even at their closest, were more than one hundred feet from the memorial's wall); Ramsey v. City of Pittsburgh, 764 F. Supp. 2d 728 (W.D. Pa. 2011) (striking down Pittsburgh's flat ban on leafleting; city's anti-littering justification for the ban failed to satisfy the narrow tailoring requirement because the city already had a littering ordinance, and 70 percent of the city's litter was composed of pizza boxes and other types of nonliterature); *United Food*, 861 F. Supp. at 1581–82 (striking down outright ban on picketing and handbilling in streets, alleys, roads, highways, or driveways).

[120] *See* Sixteenth of September Planning Comm., Inc. v. City and Cnty. of Denver, 474 F. Supp. 1333 (D. Colo. 1979).

categorical or substantial ban on a traditional method of expressive activity, before 2014, courts routinely upheld time, place, and manner restrictions as satisfying the narrow tailoring requirement.[121]

In *McCullen*, the Supreme Court strengthened the narrow tailoring requirement, striking down, for *lack* of narrow tailoring, a Massachusetts statute that barred speakers from entering fixed thirty-five-foot buffer zones at abortion clinics. The legislature enacted this statute when police found it difficult to enforce an earlier statute, one that imposed a floating six-foot buffer zone surrounding patients as they came within eighteen feet of abortion clinics.[122] Writing the majority opinion, Chief Justice Roberts stressed that the government's power to restrict speech in a traditional public forum is "very limited,"[123] and that: "[T]o be narrowly tailored," a speech restriction "must not 'burden substantially more speech than is necessary to further the government's legitimate interests.'"[124] "[B]y demanding a close fit between ends and means, the tailoring requirement prevents the government from too readily 'sacrific[ing] speech for efficiency.'"[125] To satisfy the narrow tailoring requirement, he insisted, the government "'may not regulate expression in such a manner that a substantial portion of the burden on speech does not serve to advance its goals.'"[126] Another way of expressing this last requirement is that it is not enough for speech regulators to recite a governmental interest that is significant in the abstract; the regulation must be narrowly tailored to *achieve* that governmental interest, with a real nexus between the regulation and the government's ostensible objective.[127]

---

[121] *See, e.g.*, Nationalist Movement v. City of Cumming, 92 F.3d 1135 (11th Cir. 1996) (upholding ordinance banning Saturday morning parades as a reasonable time, place, and manner regulation).

[122] *See McCullen*, 134 S. Ct. at 2525–26.

[123] *Id.* at 2529 (quoting United States v. Grace, 461 U.S. 171, 177 (1983)).

[124] *McCullen*, 134 S. Ct. at 2535 (quoting Ward v. Rock Against Racism, 491 U.S. 781, 799 (1989)).

[125] *McCullen*, 134 S. Ct. at 2534–35 (quoting Riley v. Nat'l Fed'n of the Blind, 487 U.S. 781, 795 (1988)).

[126] *McCullen*, 134 S. Ct. at 2535 (quoting *Ward*, 491 U.S. at 799).

[127] Two recent cases advance this conception of narrow tailoring. In *Johnson v. Minneapolis Park & Recreation Board*, 729 F.3d 1094 (8th Cir. 2013), the Eighth Circuit struck down, for lack of narrow tailoring, a municipal park board's restriction on distributing literature inside a public park during an annual gay pride festival. This case arose after years of conflict in which the gay pride festival organizers tried to exclude the plaintiff, an evangelical Christian who wanted to distribute Bibles during the festival. The park board adopted a regulation banning the distribution of all literature except from booths approved by the festival organizers. What governmental interest did the board invoke to support this ban? To prevent

(*footnote continued on next page*)

Perhaps the most significant feature of *McCullen's* narrow tailoring analysis is the following requirement that it imposes on the government: "To meet the requirement of narrow tailoring, the government must *demonstrate* that alternative measures that burden substantially less speech would fail to achieve the government's interests, not simply that the chosen route is easier."[128] To *satisfy* that requirement, "it is not enough for [the government] simply to say that other approaches have not worked."[129]

There is some evidence already that *McCullen* has shifted the legal landscape, prompting judges to perform a more searching analysis of the narrow tailoring requirement. Two recent cases, one decided before *McCullen*, the other decided after, provide a good example. Both cases pose the same question: Does the narrow tailoring requirement allow the government to impose a total ban on stepping into the street and approaching the occupants of motor vehicles stopped at traffic lights to solicit money or sell newspapers? The pre-*McCullen* decision upholds the ordinance with no hesitation; the parties actually *stipulated* that the law was narrowly tailored.[130] The

---

(*footnote continued from previous page*)

crowding and congestion. The court responded skeptically to this congestion justification, observing that the board left street performers completely unrestricted, even though street performers often produce significant congestion. Ultimately, *id.* at 1099, the court stressed that narrow tailoring requires a genuine nexus between the speech restriction and the governmental interest it purports to achieve. Here that nexus was dubious, so the board failed to satisfy the narrow tailoring requirement. In *Defending Animal Rights Today & Tomorrow v. Washington Sports & Entertainment*, 821 F. Supp. 2d 97 (D.D.C. 2011), the court granted summary judgment against animal rights activists who protested animal cruelty outside an arena where a circus was performed. The activists positioned themselves just outside the exit doors as nine thousand audience members were trying to leave the building. The activists claimed their First Amendment rights were violated when security guards ordered them to move away from the exit doors, a distance of less than twenty feet. The court held that this order was content neutral and narrowly tailored to advance the government's substantial interest in ensuring the free flow of audience members out of the building; moreover, the order left open multiple alternative channels for communicating the protesters' message because the activists were allowed to wear signs, to use megaphones to amplify their spoken comments, and to display images on the side of the building with a video projector. The court observed: "The narrow tailoring inquiry requires that there be a '*real nexus* between the challenged regulation and the significant governmental interest sought to be served by the regulation. . . . It is not enough . . . that a governmental interest is significant; rather, it must be shown that a reasonable regulation is narrowly tailored *to substantially serve* a significant government interest.'" *Id.* at 107 (quoting Cmty. for Creative Non-Violence v. Kerrigan, 865 F.2d 382, 388 (D.C. Cir. 1989) (emphasis in original)).

[128] *McCullen*, 134 S. Ct. at 2540 (emphasis added).

[129] *Id.*

[130] *See* The Contributor v. City of Brentwood, 726 F.3d 861 (6th Cir. 2013) (upholding a local ordinance that banned selling newspapers and other printed matter to the occupants of any motor vehicle that

(*footnote continued on next page*)

post-*McCullen* decision strikes the law down for lack of narrow tailoring.[131] The key difference between these cases is that the post-*McCullen* decision gives great weight to *McCullen's* requirement that the government must affirmatively *demonstrate* that alternative measures burdening substantially less speech would fail to achieve the government's goal. Given the overwhelming government interest in promoting pedestrian and traffic safety that comes into play whenever people enter roadways, many judges, even in *McCullen's* wake, will be inclined to uphold such an ordinance.[132] But after *McCullen*, their narrow tailoring analysis won't be quite so deferential as before.

3. Assessing the Sufficiency of "Alternative Channels" of Communication

Under *Ward's* third prong, the regulation must leave open ample alternative channels for communicating the speaker's message.[133] Two different themes run through the cases that construe this requirement.

First, the Supreme Court has shown a "special solicitude" for *inexpensive* methods of communication (e.g., leaflets or homemade signs).[134] Accordingly, a speech restriction may run afoul of this requirement if it

---

(footnote continued from previous page)

is on a street; the parties stipulated that the ordinance was content neutral and narrowly tailored; the court held that this ordinance afforded adequate alternative channels of communication, which included selling such materials to people on public sidewalks).

[131] *See* Reynolds v. Middleton, 779 F.3d 222, 230 (4th Cir. 2015) (siding with a homeless panhandler, the court ruled that county government failed to demonstrate that its total ban on roadway solicitation was narrowly tailored because the ban applied "not just [to] the busiest or most dangerous roads and intersections, but [to] *all* roadways and medians in the County, without regard to whether solicitation could be safely conducted there"). This decision is significant for interpreting *McCullen* as imposing on the government a heretofore unrecognized duty to *demonstrate* narrow tailoring—that is, "requir[ing] the government to present actual evidence supporting its assertion that a speech restriction does not burden substantially more speech than necessary." 779 F.3d at 229.

[132] *See* Traditionalist Am. Knights of the Ku Klux Klan v. City of Desloge, 775 F.3d 969 (8th Cir. 2014) (upholding, post-*McCullen*, a ban on soliciting money and distributing leaflets in public roadways, holding that the ordinance was narrowly tailored to the city's strong interest in promoting pedestrian and traffic safety and finding that there was no obvious, less burdensome alternative that the city could have selected).

[133] Ward v. Rock Against Racism, 491 U.S. 781, 791 (1989). In applying this requirement, it must be borne in mind that "one is not to have the exercise of his liberty of expression in appropriate places abridged on the plea that it may be exercised in some other place." Schneider v. New Jersey, 308 U.S. 147, 163 (1939).

[134] Members of City Council v. Taxpayers for Vincent, 466 U.S. 789, 812–13 n. 30 (1984).

precludes forms of expression that are much less expensive than feasible alternatives.[135]

Second, the ample alternative channels requirement most commonly arises when the speaker identifies one particular *place* as uniquely suited to conveying his or her message, but the government insists that the speaker take up position in an alternative location.[136] The basic test for gauging

---

[135] Martin v. City of Struthers, 319 U.S. 141 (1943) (striking down outright ban on all door-to-door leafleting); *id*. at 146 (observing that door-to-door leafleting "is essential to the poorly financed causes of little people"); City of Ladue v. Gilleo, 512 U.S. 43, 54–55, 57 (1994) (unanimously striking down a "visual clutter" ordinance that barred homeowners from displaying signs—even *political* signs—on their property and stressing the special importance of preserving *inexpensive* modes of communication).

[136] *See, e.g.*, Bay Area Peace Navy v. United States, 914 F.2d 1224 (9th Cir. 1990) (affirming that 75-yard security zone established around viewing stand and vessels in naval parade violated First Amendment rights of demonstrators who, by sailing past the onlooking dignitaries, hoped to present an anti-war message); *id*. at 1229 (the court concluded that the government's suggested alternatives—passing out pamphlets or demonstrating on land—could not substitute for a water-borne procession past the viewing stand because the Peace Navy's intended audience (the invited dignitaries who occupied that stand) were not accessible from land-based positions); *id*. (holding that a governmental restriction on speech does *not* leave open ample alternative channels of communication if the speaker is left unable to reach the intended audience); Nationalist Movement v. City of Boston, 12 F. Supp. 2d 182, 191–93 (D. Mass. 1998) (holding that city officials violated the First Amendment in denying a parade permit to plaintiff organization, a self-styled "pro-democracy, pro-majority" group viewed by its critics as racist, anti-Semitic, and anti-gay, because the city flunked the ample alternative channels test when it required the plaintiff to hold its parade in downtown Boston rather than the plaintiff's requested site in South Boston, stressing that the downtown alternative was constitutionally inadequate because it thwarted plaintiff's access to its target audience in South Boston and because plaintiff's selected site, the route of the traditional St. Patrick's Day Parade, was part and parcel of its pro-majority message: "To change the [parade's] location, however, was to change the character of the message. . . . [T]he specific place where a message is communicated may be important to the message and, consequently, of constitutional significance itself."); Students Against Apartheid Coal. v. O'Neil, 660 F. Supp. 333, 339–40 (W.D. Va. 1987) (granting injunctive relief to student protesters who challenged university's lawn-use regulations, under which they had been barred from erecting symbolic shanties to protest South African apartheid and to urge the university's governing body to adopt a divestment policy toward South Africa, and holding that the alternative channels of communication offered by the university—erecting the shanties "beyond earshot or clear sight of the Rotunda"—were constitutionally inadequate because they thwarted the students' ability to reach their intended audience: the university's governing body, which meets on campus only four times a year and gathers only in the Rotunda); Dr. Martin Luther King, Jr. Movement, Inc. v. City of Chicago, 419 F. Supp. 667, 673–74 (N.D. Ill. 1976) (where civil rights organization sought to march through white neighborhood, its previous foray there having been curtailed when bystanders pelted the procession with rocks, bricks, and explosive devices, city officials violated the First Amendment in denying organizers a permit for a second march through the same neighborhood, proposing instead an alternate route through an all-black neighborhood; because the whole point of plaintiffs' march was to publicize and protest a pattern of violence against blacks attempting to reside in or travel through the specified neighborhood, the city's proposal for an alternative route—taking plaintiffs *away from* that neighborhood and *away from* their intended audience—was constitutionally inadequate as an alternative channel of communication).

the sufficiency of alternative channels is whether the speaker is afforded a forum that is accessible and where the intended audience is expected to pass.[137] In performing this analysis, a court should take account of (1) the speaker's intended audience and (2) the extent to which the speaker's chosen location contributes to his or her message.[138]

A speech restriction does *not* leave open ample alternative channels if the speaker is left unable to reach the intended audience.[139] A good example of this is *Million Youth March, Inc. v. Safir,*[140] where New York City denied a permit request by the Nation of Islam to hold a massive rally in Harlem, insisting that the rally be held instead on Randall's Island. Located in the middle of the East River between Manhattan and Queens, Randall's Island was inaccessible by bus or subway and was virtually uninhabited. The Nation of Islam brought suit under the First Amendment, challenging the city's imposition of Randall's Island as the only permissible site for the rally. In an extensive and instructive prong-three analysis, a federal judge ruled that the city had violated the ample alternative channels requirement. The court stressed that the Randall's Island alternative was constitutionally inadequate because it thwarted the plaintiff's access to its target audience, the residents of Harlem, and because holding the rally in Harlem was part and parcel of the plaintiff's message—a message that focused on ways to improve the lives of African Americans.[141]

In contrast to *Million Youth March*, the speech restriction in *United States v. Fee*[142] was upheld as affording sufficient alternative channels of communication. In *Fee*, nine environmental protesters were convicted of willfully defying a special order of the National Forest Service that closed a sector of the San Juan National Forest to permit logging activity. The defendants had entered the closed sector of the forest to protest the cutting

---

[137] *Students Against Apartheid*, 660 F. Supp. at 339; *Bay Area Peace Navy*, 914 F.2d at 1229.
[138] *See* Million Youth March, Inc. v. Safir, 18 F. Supp. 2d 334, 347–48 (S.D.N.Y. 1998).
[139] *See* United States v. Baugh, 187 F.3d 1037, 1044 (9th Cir. 1999); *Bay Area Peace Navy*, 914 F.2d at 1229; Serv. Employee Int'l Union v. City of Los Angeles, 114 F. Supp. 2d 966, 972 (C.D. Cal. 2000); *Students Against Apartheid*, 660 F. Supp. at 339–40; *Dr. Martin Luther King, Jr. Movement*, 419 F. Supp. at 673–74.
[140] 18 F. Supp. 2d 334 (S.D.N.Y. 1998).
[141] *See id.* at 348.
[142] 787 F. Supp. 963 (D. Colo. 1992).

of ancient trees there. Rejecting the protesters' First Amendment defense, the court upheld the special order, which banned all expressive activity within the closed sector during a ninety-day period of active logging, as a reasonable time, place, and manner restriction. The order had been precipitated by prior protests in which demonstrators occupied a tree for twelve days, locked themselves to a cattle guard, blocked motor vehicles, rolled logs into the road, and surrounded both loggers and trees to prevent cutting.[143] In upholding the order, the court concluded that it left open sufficient alternative channels by which the protesters could communicate their message. Although the protesters wanted to demonstrate "where the trees were endangered,"[144] they *had* been permitted to take up position inside the forest, at the very point where the road entered the logging area.[145] This, the court held, was constitutionally sufficient; it afforded these speakers the requisite platform by which to convey their outrage at the felling of ancient trees.[146]

The guiding principle that reconciles these cases is that a speech restriction will be struck down as failing to afford sufficient alternative channels of communication if it largely impairs a speaker's capacity to reach his or her intended audience.[147] When courts fall short of fulfilling

---

[143] *See id.* at 964, 969.

[144] *Id.* at 969.

[145] *See id.*

[146] *See id.* at 969–70.

[147] *Compare* United States v. Baugh, 187 F.3d 1037, 1044 (9th Cir. 1999) (holding that park service violated the First Amendment rights of protesters by restricting them to an area 150 to 175 yards away from a visitor's center that housed the intended audience because "[s]uch distancing of the demonstrators from the intended audience does not provide a reasonable alternative means for communicati[ng] the protesters'] views"), *and* Serv. Employee Int'l Union v. City of Los Angeles, 114 F. Supp. 2d 966, 972 (C.D. Cal. 2000) (holding that a speech restriction fails to afford sufficient alternative channels of communication "if the speakers are not permitted to reach their intended audience" and striking down, for failure to afford adequate alternative channels of communication, an "Official Demonstration Site" that kept protesters 260 yards away from the 2000 Democratic National Convention; at so great a distance, wrote the court, "only those delegates with the sharpest eyesight and most acute hearing have any chance of getting the [protesters'] message"; although city officials claimed that the protesters would be visible to delegates entering the conventional hall, the court noted that the sight line would be blocked by a "media village" housing ten thousand members of the press), *with* The Coalition to March on the RNC and Stop the War v. City of St. Paul, 557 F. Supp. 2d 1014 (D. Minn. 2008) (upholding the constitutionality of a parade permit issued by the City of St. Paul to demonstrators who sought to protest the war in Iraq by parading within sight and sound of the 2008 Republican

(footnote continued on next page)

this standard in rejecting a protester's challenge, it is usually because the facts in the case present extreme overcrowding[148] or violence.[149]

(footnote continued from previous page)
National Convention), *and* Defending Animal Rights Today & Tomorrow v. Wash. Sports & Entertainment, 821 F. Supp. 2d 97 (D.D.C. 2011) (granting summary judgment against animal rights activists who protested animal cruelty outside an arena where circus was performed; the activists positioned themselves just outside the exit doors as nine thousand audience members were trying to leave the building; the activists claimed their First Amendment rights were violated when security guards ordered them to move away from the exit doors, a distance of less than twenty feet; court held that this order was content neutral and narrowly tailored to advance the government's substantial interest in ensuring the free flow of audience members out of the building; moreover, the order left open multiple alternative channels for communicating the protesters' message because the activists were allowed to wear signs, to use megaphones to amplify their spoken comments, and to display images on the side of the building with a video projector).

[148] *See, e.g.*, Marcavage v. City of New York, 689 F.3d 98 (2d Cir. 2012) (upholding New York City's time, place, and manner restrictions on protest activity outside Madison Square Garden for the 2004 Republican National Convention; the restrictions banned protesting on the sidewalk across the street from the Garden's entrance and created a large demonstration zone one block away that was not visible to delegates entering and exiting the convention). Although these restrictions seem excessive, and therefore unlikely to satisfy the narrow tailoring and ample alternative channels requirements, the decision makes sense given the enormous congestion problems with the site: 50,000 people were attending the convention, tens of thousands more were expected to protest, and Madison Square Garden sits atop the Penn Station transportation hub, which accommodates 1,300 trains and 600,000 riders every day. *See also* We've Carried the Rich for 200 Years, Let's Get Them Off Our Backs-July 4th Coalition v. City of Philadelphia, 414 F. Supp. 611 (E.D. Pa. 1976) (refusing to allow two massive parades to be conducted simultaneously within twelve blocks of each other in downtown Philadelphia on the date of the Bicentennial, and upholding city's denial of parade permit to plaintiffs, "an amalgam of self-styled dissidents," who sought to conduct a massive counter-demonstration in close proximity to the Bicentennial's "official" celebration, an eight-hour parade with fifty thousand participants, a speech by the U.S. President, and an estimated throng of three hundred thousand spectators), *aff'd mem.*, 538 F.2d 322 (3d Cir. 1976). This opinion can best be explained by the huge number of people involved and the physical impossibility of juxtaposing two massive events in one place.

[149] *See, e.g.*, Menotti v. City of Seattle, 409 F.3d 1113 (9th Cir. 2005) (upholding as a content neutral time, place, and manner restriction an emergency order issued by the mayor of Seattle that barred entry to a section of downtown where the World Trade Organization [WTO] was meeting); *id.* at 1120–23 (fifty thousand protesters, some of them extremely violent, flooded the city; some protesters started fires and then blocked fire trucks from reaching the scene; others barraged police with rocks, bottles, metal spikes, ball bearings, and chunks of concrete; still others vandalized and looted stores, physically attacked WTO delegates, and threatened the security of the conference sites; the district court, *id.* at 1120 n. 7, described "an emergency situation marked by pervasive vandalism, theft, arson, and assault that overwhelmed law enforcement resources"); *id.* at 1128–43 (given these extreme facts, the court credibly held that the emergency order did not violate the intermediate scrutiny test—(1) the order was content neutral in creating a secure zone to restore civic order for the WTO delegates, the president of the United States, and other world leaders attending the conference; (2) although the secure zone covered several blocks of downtown Seattle and lasted for two days, it was narrowly tailored because it carved out just enough space to allow the delegates and the president to move safely from their hotels to the conference site, and it lasted only until the conference ended; (3) the order afforded adequate alternative channels by allowing the protesters to demonstrate directly across the street from the convention center and three of the four hotels where delegates were staying).

4. Injunctions That Impose Time, Place, and Manner Restrictions

Ward's three-prong test governs time, place, and manner regulations imposed by *legislative* bodies. Judicial *injunctions* that impose content neutral time, place, and manner restrictions are subject to a heightened form of intermediate scrutiny under a test that is slightly more stringent than that for legislation.[150] Observing that "[i]njunctions . . . carry greater risks of censorship and discriminatory application than do general ordinances," the Supreme Court held in *Madsen v. Women's Health Center* that content neutral injunctions should be subjected by appellate courts to more "stringent" First Amendment scrutiny than comparable legislation—that, "when evaluating a content neutral *injunction*, we think that our standard time, place, and manner analysis is not sufficiently rigorous."[151] Announcing a new standard of review for *judicially* imposed time, place, and manner restrictions, the Court held that *Ward's* three-prong test would be modified by making the second prong more demanding. Rather than inquiring (per *Ward*) whether the order is *narrowly tailored* to serve a significant governmental interest, the Court held that "[w]e must ask instead whether the challenged provisions of the injunction *burden no more speech than necessary* to serve a significant government interest."[152] Thus, for judicially imposed time, place, and manner restrictions, *Madsen* requires a modified version of *Ward's* three-prong test in which the second prong is transformed into a least-restrictive-means requirement.

Some courts have applied the heightened *Madsen* test to police directives and protocols that specifically target particular groups of protesters, reasoning that those individualized speech restrictions are more like injunctions than generally applicable statutes.[153]

---

[150] *See* Madsen v. Women's Health Center, Inc., 512 U.S. 753 (1994).

[151] *Id.* at 764–65 (emphasis added).

[152] *Id.* at 765 (emphasis added).

[153] *See, e.g.*, McTernan v. City of York, 564 F.3d 636, 655 (3d Cir. 2009) ("We conclude that a police directive, issued by officers in the field, poses risks similar to those presented by an injunction, warranting heightened scrutiny."); Zalaski v. City of Hartford, 838 F. Supp. 2d 13, 38–42 (D. Conn. 2012) (applying the *Madsen* test to an oral police directive, not an injunction, that sought to move animal

(footnote continued on next page)

III. Permits and Fees

For mass demonstrations, marches, and parades, restrictions on public forum access are usually imposed by means of a licensing scheme that requires the prospective speaker to secure a permit and pay a fee.[154] The Supreme Court has long acknowledged that requiring permits and fees as a precondition to speaking, marching, or assembling in a traditional public forum is a prior restraint on speech.[155] Although any prior restraint bears a "heavy presumption" against its validity,[156] the Court has recognized that in order to regulate competing uses of public fora, governments may require permits and fees of those wishing to hold a march, parade, or rally.[157] The proper target of a licensing scheme is any mass demonstration or procession, not protest activity by a few individuals.[158]

(footnote continued from previous page)

rights protesters several feet away from their desired location), *aff'd in part, vacated in part on other grounds*, 723 F.3d 382, 385 n. 2 (2d Cir. 2013); Ross v. Early, 899 F. Supp. 2d 415, 422 (D. Md. 2012) (applying the *Madsen* standard to a *protocol*, not an injunction, that the City of Baltimore developed for demonstrations at an arena).

[154] *See, e.g.*, Eric Neisser, *Charging for Free Speech: User Fees and Insurance in the Marketplace of Ideas*, 74 GEORGETOWN L.J. 257 (1985); David Goldberger, *A Reconsideration of* Cox v. New Hampshire: *Can Demonstrators Be Required to Pay the Costs of Using America's Public Forums?* 62 TEX. L. REV. 403 (1983).

[155] *See, e.g.*, Forsyth Cnty. v. Nationalist Movement, 505 U.S. 123, 130 (1992); Shuttlesworth v. City of Birmingham, 394 U.S. 147, 150–51 (1969); Niemotko v. Maryland, 340 U.S. 268, 271 (1951).

[156] Bantam Books, Inc. v. Sullivan, 372 U.S. 58, 70 (1963).

[157] *See Forsyth*, 505 U.S. at 130.

[158] Courts are hostile to permit requirements for small assemblies. *See, e.g.*, Smith v. Exec. Dir. of Ind. War Mem'ls Comm'n, 742 F.3d 282 (7th Cir. 2014) (striking down, for lack of narrow tailoring, a public forum permit scheme that required an advance permit from groups numbering as few as fifteen people; for advertised events, the ordinance required an advance permit even if *fewer* than fifteen people showed up—in this case, the permit requirement was enforced against only *two* people (the plaintiff and his son), who were expelled from the site for lack of a permit); Berger v. City of Seattle, 569 F.3d 1029, 1037–40 (9th Cir. 2009) (en banc) (striking down single-speaker permit requirement governing individual street performers' access to large public park); Santa Monica Food Not Bombs v. City of Santa Monica, 450 F.3d 1022, 1039–40 (9th Cir. 2006) (striking down, for lack of narrow tailoring, a permit scheme that governed expressive activity in the city's outdoor public spaces because the ordinance lacked a numerical floor and therefore applied to small groups of speakers); American-Arab Anti-Discrimination Comm. v. City of Dearborn, 418 F.3d 600, 608 (6th Cir. 2005) (striking down parade permit ordinance because it applied to groups of *any* size—even to "group[s] of two or more persons"—and therefore violated the narrow tailoring requirement); Cox v. City of Charleston, 416 F.3d 281 (4th Cir. 2005) (striking down municipal parade permit ordinance for its failure to contain any exemption for small groups of protesters); Douglas v. Brownell, 88 F.3d 1511, 1524 (8th Cir. 1996) (striking down a parade permit ordinance for imposing a five-day advance

(footnote continued on next page)

The constitutionality of any such licensing scheme will hinge on three basic inquiries. The first goes to the barrier of *cost* that the fee creates for prospective speakers.[159] The second goes to the degree of *discretion* that the scheme vests in the licensing official.[160] The third goes to the procedural *timeframe* in which applications to demonstrate must be entertained.[161] The following three sections correspond to these three inquiries.

A. Limits on Government Power to Impose User Fees on Public Forum Speakers

Municipal licensing schemes typically require a prospective speaker not only to obtain a permit before using a public forum but also to pay some sort of fee in connection with that permit.[162] License fees have been imposed

---

(footnote continued from previous page)

registration requirement, the court observed that the permit requirement was applicable "to groups as small as ten persons," which "compounds our conclusion that the parade permit ordinance is not narrowly tailored"); Grossman v. City of Portland, 33 F.3d 1200 (9th Cir. 1994) (striking down, for lack of narrow tailoring, an ordinance that required a permit for *any* demonstration, no matter how small, to be conducted in any public park).
[159] *See, e.g.,* Murdock v. Pennsylvania, 319 U.S. 105 (1943) (rejecting the application of a peddler's license fee to sidewalk and house-to-house sales of religious literature by Jehovah's Witnesses); Cox v. New Hampshire, 312 U.S. 569 (1941) (upholding parade permit scheme that authorized the imposition of fees as high as $300); Int'l Women's Day March Planning Comm. v. City of San Antonio, 619 F.3d 346, 365–68 (5th Cir. 2010) (upholding parade permit scheme that required applicant to pay fees for traffic control and cleanup; the regulation did not violate the First Amendment because it imposed sufficient control over police discretion in calculating the fees).
[160] The Supreme Court has consistently struck down licensing schemes that vested unfettered discretion in the licensing authority, *see, e.g.,* City of Lakewood v. Plain Dealer Publ'g Co., 486 U.S. 750, 759–60 (1988), including schemes that allowed the licensor to vary the fee based on the controversial nature of the speaker's message or its potential for inspiring a hostile response, *see* Forsyth Cnty. v. Nationalist Movement, 505 U.S. 123, 134 (1992).
[161] The Court will treat as "a species of unbridled discretion" any failure by a licensing scheme to place limits on the *time frame* within which the decision-maker must grant or deny the permit. FW/PBS, Inc. v. City of Dallas, 493 U.S. 215, 223–24 (1990).
[162] *See* Neisser, *supra* note 154, at 258–60 and nn. 1–3; Goldberger, *supra* note 154, at 404 and nn. 6–9. Even when the government imposes a permit requirement with *no* accompanying fee, the courts do not necessarily uphold the scheme. *Compare* United States v. Kistner, 68 F.3d 218 (8th Cir. 1995) (upholding permit requirement imposed by National Park Service as prerequisite to distribution of printed matter within a national park) (defendant, who was passing out religious pamphlets at the base of the Arch in St. Louis, refused to obtain the requisite permit, even though such permits were routinely processed in thirty-five minutes, without any fee, and were available every day on the Arch grounds), *with* Cmty. for Creative Non-Violence v. Turner, 893 F.2d 1387 (D.C. Cir. 1990) (striking down for lack of narrow tailoring a transit authority regulation requiring an advance permit, obtainable without a fee, for any person seeking to engage in any "free speech activity" in the above-ground plazas of Washington's subway system).

on a broad range of expressive activities, including marches,[163] parades,[164] assemblies in public parks,[165] the sidewalk sale of newspapers[166] and religious

---

[163] *See, e.g.,* Int'l Women's Day March Planning Comm. v. City of San Antonio, 619 F.3d 346 (5th Cir. 2010); E. Conn. Citizens Action Grp. v. Powers, 723 F.2d 1050 (2d Cir. 1983) (striking down state transportation department's $750,000 liability insurance requirement and its $200 administrative fee for a proposed march along an abandoned railroad bed in which plaintiffs sought to express their belief that a proposed interstate highway should be replaced by rail transportation); Collin v. Smith, 578 F.2d 1197, 1206–208, 1211 (7th Cir. 1978) (declaring unconstitutional an array of ordinances enacted by the Village of Skokie with a view toward prohibiting Nazi marches, including a provision that required $300,000 in liability insurance as a precondition to marching).

[164] *See, e.g.,* Cox v. New Hampshire, 312 U.S. 569 (1941) (upholding parade permit scheme that authorized the imposition of fees as high as $300); iMatter Utah v. Njord, 774 F.3d 1258 (10th Cir. 2014) (striking down, for lack of narrow tailoring, parade permit requirements compelling the applicant to obtain liability insurance and sign an indemnification agreement protecting the government, noting: (1) the government completely failed to justify the required minimum level of insurance coverage—$1 million per occurrence and $2 million in aggregate—and failed to demonstrate any alignment between the costs borne by the applicant in securing a permit and the expenses incurred by the government in hosting a parade; and (2) the indemnification provision was far broader than necessary to protect the government from financial loss if an accident occurred during the parade); *id.* at 1264 (holding that the First Amendment does not require a parade permit regulation to contain an indigency exception so long as it provides for cost-free alternative methods of expression, such as using the sidewalks); Sullivan v. City of Augusta, 511 F.3d 16 (1st Cir. 2007) (assessing the constitutionality of several provisions in a municipal parade permit ordinance, the court held: (1) a thirty-day advance registration requirement violates the First Amendment; (2) to satisfy the Constitution, a parade permit ordinance need not contain an indigency exception for applicants who cannot pay the required fee, especially if public sidewalks are available for free; and (3) the provision requiring applicants to pay the costs of traffic control and cleanup did not delegate too much discretion to the police chief in setting the fee, even though the chief was authorized to estimate the number of police officers and vehicles necessary for handling the parade, and the ordinance contained no factors or "formula" to guide the chief's estimate); Stonewall Union v. City of Columbus, 931 F.2d 1130 (6th Cir. 1991) (rejecting First Amendment challenge by gay rights organization to ordinance governing parades; plaintiffs argued unsuccessfully that the ordinance violated the Constitution by imposing "user fees" far in excess of a nominal sum as a precondition to the exercise of First Amendment freedoms).

[165] *See, e.g.,* Transp. Alts., Inc. v. City of New York, 340 F.3d 72 (2d Cir. 2003) (invalidating municipal permit scheme requiring payment of fee for special group events in public parks because it vested the parks commissioner with unbridled discretion in assessing fees); Invisible Empire Knights of the Ku Klux Klan v. City of West Haven, 600 F. Supp. 1427, 1432–33 (D. Conn. 1985) (granting injunctive relief to KKK in its facial challenge to an ordinance restricting expressive activity in public parks).

[166] *See, e.g.,* Northeast Ohio Coal. for the Homeless v. City of Cleveland, 105 F.3d 1107 (6th Cir. 1997) (rejecting First Amendment challenge, bought by indigent vendors of homeless and Nation of Islam "street" newspapers, to city's imposition of a flat fifty-dollar-per-vendor license fee, charged as a precondition to the sidewalk sale of plaintiffs' newspapers); Hull v. Petrillo, 439 F.2d 1184, 1185–86 (2d Cir. 1971) (recognizing that city could not constitutionally apply its peddler's license fee to sidewalk sales of the Black Panther Party's newspaper because to do so would offend the First Amendment); Gall v. Lawler, 322 F. Supp. 1223 (E.D. Wis. 1971) (rejecting under the First Amendment the application of a peddler's license fee to sidewalk sales of an "underground" newspaper).

literature,[167] charitable solicitations,[168] the operation of sound trucks,[169] and the display of political signs.[170]

Such a fee is constitutionally permissible if it is directly linked to, and serves to defray, the administrative expenses incurred by the government in regulating the speaker's expressive activity.[171] This principle has been extended to parade permit fees that require the applicant to pay for the police officers who furnish traffic control.[172] More controversial are provisions that force speakers

---

[167] *See, e.g.,* Follett v. Town of McCormick, 321 U.S. 573 (1944) (rejecting the application of a peddler's license fee to sidewalk and house-to-house sales of religious literature by Jehovah's Witnesses); Murdock v. Pennsylvania, 319 U.S. 105 (1943) (rejecting the application of a peddler's license fee to sidewalk and house-to-house sales of religious literature by Jehovah's Witnesses).

[168] *See, e.g.,* Dayton Area Visually Impaired Persons, Inc. v. Fisher, 70 F.3d 1474, 1478, 1490 (6th Cir. 1995) (affirming the denial of preliminary injunctive relief to nonprofit organizations and professional contribution solicitors who challenged provisions of the Ohio Charitable Solicitation Act that imposed a $25,000 bonding requirement on professional solicitors and required nonexempt charities to pay a sliding-scale registration fee of $50 to $200 based on the amount of contributions they received).

[169] *See, e.g.,* NAACP v. City of Chester, 253 F. Supp. 707, 714–15 (E.D. Pa. 1966) (striking down a $25-per-day fee for permit to operate a sound truck after the city offered no evidence linking the fee and the cost of enforcing the ordinance); Pennsylvania v. Winfree, 182 A.2d 698, 703 (Pa. 1962) (sustaining a $25-per-day permit fee for the use of a sound truck because the city showed that the amount of the fee was reasonable given the costs of regulating such activity); United States Labor Party v. Codd, 527 F.2d 118, 119–20 (2d Cir. 1975) (upholding a $5-per-day permit fee for using a bullhorn because the sum it collected was much less than the administrative costs associated with enforcing the licensing scheme).

[170] *See, e.g.,* Baldwin v. Redwood City, 540 F.2d 1360, 1371 and n. 31 (9th Cir. 1976) (striking down a $1-per-sign nonrefundable inspection fee imposed on the temporary display of political campaign signs; observing that the ordinance effectively required "a $500 fee for inspecting 500 identical political posters," the court concluded that "[t]he absence of apportionment suggests that the fee is not in fact reimbursement for the cost of inspection but an unconstitutional tax upon the exercise of First Amendment rights").

[171] *Compare* United States Labor Party v. Codd, 527 F.2d 118, 119–20 (2d Cir. 1975) (upholding $5-per-day permit fee for using sound amplification equipment because the sum collected by this fee was much less than the administrative costs associated with enforcing the licensing scheme), *with* E. Conn. Citizens Action Grp. v. Powers, 723 F.2d 1050, 1056 (2d Cir. 1983) (striking down imposition of $200 permit fee against prospective marchers because the fee's size could not be justified as confined to defraying the state's administrative expenses), *and* Fernandes v. Limmer, 663 F.2d 619, 632–33 (5th Cir. 1981) (invalidating $6-per-day permit fee for solicitation at airport where government "did not demonstrate a link between the fee and the costs of the licensing process").

[172] *See* Int'l Women's Day March Planning Comm. v. City of San Antonio, 619 F.3d 346 (5th Cir. 2010); Sullivan v. City of Augusta, 511 F.3d 16 (1st Cir. 2007) (assessing the constitutionality of several provisions in a municipal parade permit ordinance, court held that provision requiring applicants to pay the costs of traffic control and cleanup did not delegate too much discretion to the police chief in setting the fee, even though the chief was authorized to estimate the number of police officers and vehicles necessary for handling the parade, and the ordinance contained no factors or "formula" to guide the chief's estimate); Nationalist Movement v. City of York, 481 F.3d 178, 184–87 (3d Cir. 2007) (striking down parade permit fee ordinance under *Forsyth Cnty. v. Nationalist Movement,* 505 U.S. 123 (1992), because the ordinance contained a reimbursement provision that allowed the city to

(footnote continued on next page)

to pay insurance costs associated with the forum's use.[173] Likewise unsettled is just how *heavy* these pecuniary burdens may be. The Supreme Court has offered no real guidance on any of these questions since the 1940s, when it decided a cluster of cases involving license fees for parading and leafleting.[174] In the intervening years, the Court has almost entirely neglected the subject of public forum user fees,[175] leaving the lower courts to fend for themselves.

Any examination of public forum permit fees must start with the seminal decisions of the 1940s. Among these, the principal authority is *Cox v. New Hampshire*,[176] which approved charging fees to demonstrators in order to recoup government expenses caused by speech activity.[177] *Cox* rejected a First Amendment challenge by Jehovah's Witnesses to a licensing scheme that required demonstrators to obtain a permit and pay a fee of up to $300

(*footnote continued from previous page*)

impose extra charges for police protection based on the applicant's unpopularity and the likely hostility of counter-demonstrators); Stonewall Union v. City of Columbus, 931 F.2d 1130 (6ᵗʰ Cir. 1991) (rejecting First Amendment challenge by gay rights organization to ordinance governing parades; plaintiffs argued unsuccessfully that the ordinance violated the Constitution by imposing "user fees" far in excess of a nominal sum as a precondition to the exercise of First Amendment freedoms); Yates v. Norwood, 841 F. Supp. 2d 934 (E.D. Va. 2012) (rejecting First Amendment challenge to municipal parade permit ordinance that required applicant to pay the cost of all police vehicles and off-duty officers needed for policing the applicant's parade; specifically, the court held that this licensing scheme did not grant excessive discretion to the administrator charged with calculating the fee, as she was required to consider the size and location of the proposed parade in estimating the necessary number of officers and vehicles, and she was required to obey a fixed cost schedule for each officer and vehicle); Gay & Lesbian Servs. Network, Inc. v. Bishop, 841 F. Supp. 295 (W.D. Mo. 1993) (assessing parade sponsors the cost of *traffic* control is a permissible component of parade permit fees, so long as no fee for *crowd* control is included, to the extent that crowd control costs vary depending upon hostility toward the speaker, such fees run afoul of *Forsyth*).

[173] *See* iMatter Utah v. Njord, 774 F.3d 1258 (10ᵗʰ Cir. 2014); E. Conn. Citizens Action Grp. v. Powers, 723 F.2d 1050 (2d Cir. 1983); Collin v. Smith, 578 F.2d 1197, 1206–08, 1211 (7ᵗʰ Cir. 1978); Houston Peace Coal. v. Houston City Council, 310 F. Supp. 457, 461–63 (S.D. Tex. 1970) (striking down liability insurance requirement for parades because it bestowed unfettered discretion upon city attorney to grant or withhold parade permits).

[174] *See* Follett v. Town of McCormick, 321 U.S. 573 (1944); Murdock v. Pennsylvania, 319 U.S. 105 (1943); Jones v. Opelika, 319 U.S. 103 (1943); Cox v. New Hampshire, 312 U.S. 569 (1941).

[175] The Court has offered only the most fleeting elaboration on the meaning of its user fee precedents. *See* Forsyth Cnty. v. Nationalist Movement, 505 U.S. 123 (1992); Jimmy Swaggart Ministries v. Bd. of Equalization, 493 U.S. 378 (1990) (holding that the religion clauses of the First Amendment do not prevent a state from imposing a generally applicable sales and use tax on the distribution of religious materials by a religious organization); Minneapolis Star & Tribune Co. v. Minnesota Comm'r of Revenue, 460 U.S. 575 (1983) (upholding newspaper's First Amendment challenge to a state tax on ink and paper products used in the production of periodical publications).

[176] 312 U.S. 569 (1941).

[177] *See* Goldberger, *supra* note 154, at 404–05.

before marching on public streets or sidewalks.[178] The Court upheld the fee requirement, which authorized sliding-scale adjustments depending on the size of the procession, because it allowed the government to recoup only those expenses directly attributable to the applicant's speech activities.[179] Two years earlier, in *Schneider v. New Jersey*,[180] the Court had rejected the notion that a speech activity might be banned if it generated excessive cleanup costs for the government.[181] Following in *Schneider's* wake, *Cox* suggested that the government, although powerless to *ban* speech activities due to their costs, might nevertheless *shift* those costs back to the speakers who generated them.

But in the years immediately following *Cox*, the Court emphatically restricted the power of government to foist user fees on public forum speakers. In *Murdock v. Pennsylvania*[182] and *Follett v. Town of McCormick*,[183] the Court struck down the assessment of a flat peddler's license fee imposed as a precondition to sidewalk and house-to-house sales of religious literature by Jehovah's Witnesses. Identifying the constitutional flaw in this type of regulatory scheme and distinguishing it from the permit fee upheld in *Cox*, the *Murdock* Court observed:

> [T]he issuance of the permit [here] is dependent on the payment of a license tax. And the license tax is fixed in amount and unrelated to the scope of the [applicants' expressive activities] or to their realized revenues. It is not a nominal fee imposed as a regulatory measure to defray the expenses of policing the activities in question. It is in

---

[178] 312 U.S. at 571 n. 1.

[179] *See id.* at 577 (suggesting that to be valid, such a fee must be levied to recoup, and should not exceed, "the expense incident to the administration of the act and to the maintenance of public order in the matter licensed") (quoting the lower court opinion, State v. Cox, 16 A.2d 508, 513 (N.H. 1940)).

[180] 308 U.S. 147 (1939).

[181] In *Schneider*, the government attempted to justify broad restrictions on leafleting on the grounds that they were necessary to prevent littering. The Court rejected this argument, holding that cleanup costs could not justify a ban on the distribution of leaflets. *Id.* at 162. The Court stressed that "the purpose to keep the streets clean and of good appearance is insufficient to justify an ordinance which prohibits a person rightfully on a public street from handing literature to one willing to receive it. Any burden imposed upon the city authorities in cleaning and caring for the streets as an indirect consequence of such distribution results from the constitutional protection of the freedom of speech and press." *Id.*

[182] 319 U.S. 105 (1943).

[183] 321 U.S. 573 (1944).

no way apportioned. It is a flat license tax levied and collected as a condition to the pursuit of activities whose enjoyment is guaranteed by the First Amendment. Accordingly, it restrains in advance those constitutional liberties of press and religion and inevitably tends to suppress their exercise. That is almost uniformly recognized as the inherent vice and evil of this flat license tax.[184]

Unfortunately, the Court has rarely bothered to elaborate on this language in the intervening decades.[185] The most that may be gleaned from this passage and the Court's subsequent pronouncements is the three characteristics that distinguish a flat license tax from the permit fee approved in *Cox*: A license tax of the sort struck down in *Murdock* and *Follett* is (1) unapportioned and unrelated either to the government's regulatory expenses or to the scope of the licensee's expressive activity,[186] and it is exacted (2) in advance of, and (3) as a condition precedent to, permitting the applicant to speak.[187]

Even in striking down the challenged fees in *Murdock* and *Follett*, the Supreme Court was careful to stress the continued vitality of *Cox*, observing that First Amendment freedoms are by no means immune "from all financial burdens of government"[188] and that municipalities retain the power to collect reasonable fees "imposed as a regulatory measure to defray the expenses of policing [expressive] activit[y]."[189]

---

[184] *Murdock*, 319 U.S. at 113–14 (footnote omitted).

[185] *See supra* note 175.

[186] What makes the *Murdock* and *Follett* fees unconstitutional, and what distinguishes them from the fee upheld in *Cox*, is that they were "unrelated to the receipts or income of the speaker or to the expenses of administering a valid regulatory scheme." Minneapolis Star & Tribune Co. v. Minn. Comm'r of Revenue, 460 U.S. 575, 587 n. 9 (1983). Thus, it wasn't the *size* of the *Murdock/Follett* fees that made them unconstitutional but their lack of any *linkage* either to the government's regulatory expenses or to the scope of the speakers' expressive activities. *See* Forsyth Cnty. v. Nationalist Movement, 505 U.S. 123, 137 (1992) (observing that *Murdock* "does not mean that an invalid fee can be saved if it is nominal, or that only nominal charges are constitutionally permissible. . . . The tax at issue in *Murdock* was invalid because it was *unrelated* to any legitimate state interest, not because it was of a particular size.") (emphasis added).

[187] *See* Jimmy Swaggart Ministries v. Bd. of Equalization, 493 U.S. 378, 387 (1990) (observing that the constitutional flaw in the *Murdock* and *Follett* ordinances was that by imposing a flat license tax "as a *precondition*" to the exercise of First Amendment freedoms, "they operated as prior restraints") (emphasis in original); Minneapolis Star & Tribune Co. v. Minn. Comm'r of Revenue, 460 U.S. 575, 587 n. 9 (1983) (the *Murdock* and *Follett* fees were invalid because, *inter alia*, they were imposed "as a *condition* of the right to speak") (emphasis added).

[188] *Follett*, 321 U.S. at 577.

[189] *Murdock*, 319 U.S. at 114.

Never squarely addressed by these cases is the question of fee *afford-ability*. What if a fee is set so high as to be financially oppressive to ordinary citizens? What if a demonstrator claims that he or she cannot afford to pay a given fee? Can the *size* of a fee, by itself, offend the First Amendment? On these questions, *Cox* and its progeny afford no express guidance.[190] At most, they offer hints. *Murdock* and *Follett* both evince a genuine concern that First Amendment freedoms not be conditioned on a citizen's ability to pay.[191] *Murdock* cautioned that itinerant preachers might be especially vulnerable to the "cumulative effect" of fee requirements as they traveled from town to town[192] and that the financial resources of a religious organization might be seriously depleted by imposing charges on its expressive activities.[193] Although *Murdock* spoke in passing of "nominal" fees as constitutionally acceptable,[194] the Supreme Court has since asserted that the flaw in the *Murdock* fee was not its *size* (i.e., its failure to be "nominal") but its lack of any *linkage* to the government's regulatory expenses.[195] Nevertheless, *Schneider* makes clear that the government cannot *ban* speech just because it poses administrative expenses,[196] and because there is no effective difference between banning speech and making it financially unaffordable, *Schneider* suggests that the government cannot fix public forum user fees at exorbitant levels.[197]

Taken together, *Cox*, *Schneider*, *Murdock*, and *Follett* stand for a basic principle: "[T]he state may recoup the actual costs of governmental services

---

[190] Goldberger, *supra* note 154, at 407–08.

[191] *Murdock*, 319 U.S. at 111 ("Freedom of speech, freedom of the press, freedom of religion are available to all, not merely to those who can pay their own way."); *Follett*, 321 U.S. at 576 ("Freedom of religion is not merely reserved for those with a long purse.").

[192] 319 U.S. at 115 ("Itinerant evangelists moving throughout a state or from state to state would feel immediately the cumulative effect of [fee] ordinances as they became fashionable. . . . This method of disseminating religious beliefs can be crushed and closed out by the sheer weight of the toll or tribute which is exacted town by town, village by village.").

[193] *Id.* at 112–14.

[194] Describing the challenged assessment, the *Murdock* Court observed: "It is not a nominal fee imposed as a regulatory measure to defray the expenses of policing the activities in question." *Id.* at 113–14.

[195] *Forsyth Cnty.*, 505 U.S. at 137 (observing that *Murdock* "does not mean that an invalid fee can be saved if it is nominal, or that only nominal charges are constitutionally permissible. . . . The tax at issue in *Murdock* was invalid because it was *unrelated* to any legitimate state interest, not because it was of a particular size.") (emphasis added).

[196] *See* 308 U.S. at 162. Nor can the government unduly restrict the *number* of available permits. *See* Bery v. City of New York, 97 F.3d 689 (2d Cir. 1996).

[197] Goldberger, *supra* note 154, at 410.

that are generated by the use of public property for speech activities, so long as the charge is not so great as to appear to the judiciary to be oppressive or completely preclusive of speech."[198] This principle accurately describes the approach that lower courts have taken in the decades since *Cox*.[199] They have been largely *consistent* in requiring a *linkage* between any fee and the regulatory expenses it purportedly defrays,[200] but due to the lack of Supreme Court guidance, they have been *inconsistent* on the question of fee *affordability*.[201] The lower courts are split on whether a licensing scheme must contain an indigency exception.[202] Given the confusion that its silence has produced, the Supreme Court should not wait *another* half century before addressing the cost barriers erected by public forum user fees.

B. Limits on Administrative Discretion in Issuing Permits and Fees

There are two distinct lines of precedent in this area: (1) decisions invalidating permit schemes that vest "unfettered discretion" in the licensing official; and (2) decisions invalidating permit schemes that allow the licensor to consider the controversial nature of a speaker's message or its potential for inspiring a hostile response.

1. Permit Schemes That Vest "Unfettered Discretion" in the Licensing Official

Courts have consistently invalidated permit schemes vesting government officials with "unfettered discretion" to forbid or allow certain speech activities,

---

[198] *Id.* at 409–10.

[199] *Id.* at 410, n. 42.

[200] *See supra* note 172 and accompanying text.

[201] Goldberger, *supra* note 154, at 411, n. 43.

[202] *Compare* Cent. Fla. Nuclear Freeze Campaign v. Walsh, 774 F.2d 1515, 1523–24 (11th Cir. 1985) *and* Invisible Empire Knights of the Ku Klux Klan v. City of W. Haven, 600 F. Supp. 1427, 1435 (D. Conn. 1985) *with* iMatter Utah v. Njord, 774 F.3d 1258, 1264 (10th Cir. 2014) *and* Sullivan v. City of Augusta, 511 F.3d 16 (1st Cir. 2007) *and* Stonewall Union v. City of Columbus, 931 F.2d 1130, 1136–37 (6th Cir. 1991) (holding that parade permit ordinance was not constitutionally invalid for failing to provide an indigency exception because the public sidewalks remained a free and entirely acceptable alternative forum for "indigent paraders"). *Cf.* Northeast Ohio Coal. for the Homeless v. City of Cleveland, 105 F.3d 1107 (6th Cir. 1997).

striking down discretionary limits on parades[203] and demonstrations;[204] sidewalk preaching,[205] performing,[206] and leafleting;[207] rallies in public parks;[208] and the use of sound amplification equipment.[209]

Any scheme that vests arbitrary discretion in the licensing official "has the potential for becoming a means of suppressing a particular point

---

[203] *See, e.g.*, Shuttlesworth v. City of Birmingham, 394 U.S. 147, 150–53 (1969) (striking down a parade permit scheme whose administration effectively vested unfettered discretion in licensing officials); Invisible Empire of the Knights of the Ku Klux Klan v. Mayor of Thurmont, 700 F. Supp. 281, 285 (D. Md. 1988) (holding that town officials unconstitutionally denied KKK a parade permit where licensing officials were vested with unfettered discretion).

[204] *See, e.g.*, Hague v. Comm. for Indus. Org., 307 U.S. 496 (1939) (striking down ordinances that, *inter alia*, imposed a flat ban on public distribution of printed materials and required a permit, issued at the uncontrolled discretion of the public safety director, for all public meetings and demonstrations).

[205] *See, e.g.*, Kunz v. New York, 340 U.S. 290 (1951) (striking down an ordinance vesting discretionary power in the city police commissioner to control in advance the right of citizens to speak on religious matters in the streets of New York); Furr v. Town of Swansea, 594 F. Supp. 1543, 1547–49 (D.S.C. 1984) (holding, in facial challenge brought by Anabaptist ministers to ordinance requiring permit for sidewalk preaching and public speaking, that permit scheme offends First Amendment by vesting town council with unfettered discretion in granting or denying permits).

[206] *See* Pence v. City of St. Louis, 958 F. Supp. 2d 1079 (E.D. Mo. 2013) (granting preliminary injunction that blocked enforcement of licensing scheme as a prior restraint).

[207] *See, e.g.*, Schneider v. New Jersey, 308 U.S. 147, 164 (1939) ("[W]e hold a municipality cannot . . . require all who wish to disseminate ideas to present them first to police authorities for their consideration and approval, with a discretion in the police to say some ideas may, while others may not, be . . . disseminate[d].''); Lovell v. City of Griffin, 303 U.S. 444 (1938) (striking down as a prior restraint a municipal licensing scheme that required advance permission from city manager before distributing circulars, pamphlets, or literature of any kind and vested city manager with unfettered discretion in granting or denying such permission).

[208] *See, e.g.*, Niemotko v. Maryland, 340 U.S. 268, 271 (1951) (reversing disorderly conduct conviction of Jehovah's Witnesses convicted on the grounds that they used a public park for Bible talks without first obtaining a permit from city officials even though there existed no statute or ordinance *imposing* a permit requirement); ACORN v. City of Tulsa, 835 F.2d 735 (10th Cir. 1987); Rubin v. City of Santa Monica, 823 F. Supp. 709 (C.D. Cal. 1993) (striking down permit scheme governing demonstrations in public parks because it vested undue discretion in the licensing official; under the challenged ordinance, demonstrations of thirty-five or more people were permissible only if they fell within an undefined exception for "First Amendment Activities," and the licensor had unbridled discretion to inquire into the content of applicant's speech in determining whether to grant a permit under the exception); Invisible Empire Knights of the Ku Klux Klan v. City of West Haven, 600 F. Supp. 1427 (D. Conn. 1985).

[209] *See, e.g.*, Saia v. New York, 334 U.S. 558 (1948) (striking down ordinance prohibiting use of loudspeaker in public places without permission of police chief, whose discretion was unlimited); Friedrich v. City of Chicago, 619 F. Supp. 1129, 1147–48 (N.D. Ill. 1985) (holding, *inter alia*, that provision forbidding street performers from using sound amplification equipment unless granted a special permit issued by city council violated First Amendment because the ordinance did not specify how to obtain such a permit and set no standards or guidelines concerning issuance of such permits).

of view."[210] If a regulation leaves room for assessing the speaker's viewpoint in deciding whether or not to grant a permit, "'the danger of censorship and abridgment of our precious First Amendment freedoms is too great' to be permitted."[211]

These principles are so firmly grounded in precedent that a district judge, confronted fifty years ago with the suppression of Vietnam War protesters, observed even then that

> [i]t is established beyond need for an extended discussion that municipalities cannot validly leave decision-making for allowance of peaceful parades or demonstrations to the unbridled discretion or mere opinion of a local official. The lodging of any such broad discretion in a public official would permit such official to say which expressions of view . . . will be permitted [—] a power fraught with possibilities for selective administration that would in effect deprive some groups of the equal protection of the laws.[212]

Accordingly, a permit scheme will survive constitutional scrutiny only if it employs content neutral criteria[213] and only if it contains "narrowly drawn, reasonable, and definite standards for the officials to follow."[214] A permit scheme fails this test if it "'involves appraisal of facts, the exercise of judgment, [or] the formation of an opinion' by the licensing authority."[215] Without such standards, "post hoc rationalizations by the licensing official and the use of shifting or illegitimate criteria are far too easy, making it

---

[210] Forsyth Cnty. v. Nationalist Movement, 505 U.S. 123, 130 (1992) (quoting Heffron v. Int'l Soc'y for Krishna Consciousness, Inc., 452 U.S. 640, 649 (1981)).

[211] *Forsyth*, 505 U.S. at 131 (quoting Se. Promotions, Ltd. v. Conrad, 420 U.S. 546, 553 (1975)).

[212] Hurwitt v. City of Oakland, 247 F. Supp. 995, 1000–01 (N.D. Cal. 1965) (enjoining city officials from prohibiting a parade intended to protest U.S. military intervention in Vietnam).

[213] *See* Gay & Lesbian Services Network, Inc. v. Bishop, 832 F. Supp. 270, 275 (W.D. Mo. 1993) (striking down, under *Forsyth*, a Kansas City Police Department policy governing parade permits that authorized the assessment of a crowd control fee that would vary depending on the level of hostility likely to be generated by the speaker or message).

[214] *See* Niemotko v. Maryland, 340 U.S. 268, 271 (1951); Shuttlesworth v. City of Birmingham, 394 U.S. 147, 151 (1969) (holding that "a law subjecting the exercise of First Amendment freedoms to the prior restraint of a license, without narrow, objective, and definite standards to guide the licensing authority, is unconstitutional").

[215] *Forsyth Cnty.*, 505 U.S. at 131 (quoting Cantwell v. Connecticut, 310 U.S. 296, 305 (1940)).

difficult for courts to determine in any particular case whether the licensor is permitting favorable, and suppressing unfavorable, expression."[216]

In 2002, when the Supreme Court revisited the law governing public forum permit schemes, it confirmed that these "unfettered discretion" precedents are still good law.[217]

2. Permit Schemes That Allow the Licensing Official to Consider the Controversial Nature of a Speaker's Message or Its Potential for Inspiring a Hostile Response

Closely akin to the "unfettered discretion" cases are those in which the permit scheme allows licensing officials to consider either the controversial nature of a speaker's message or its potential for inspiring a hostile response. These schemes are struck down just as readily—and for the same reason—as the schemes affording unbridled discretion. In both contexts, the First Amendment flaw is the same: public forum access is left to hinge on the *popularity* of a speaker's message.

The permit schemes in this line of precedent are of two (equally fatal) types: (1) those allowing the licensor to forbid or restrict speech activities based on concerns that the speaker's message will inspire a hostile response[218]

---

[216] City of Lakewood v. Plain Dealer Publ'g Co., 486 U.S. 750, 758 (1989).

[217] In *Thomas v. Chicago Park District*, 534 U.S. 316 (2002), the Supreme Court held that the "extraordinary procedural safeguards" required by *Freedman v. Maryland*, 380 U.S. 51, 58–60 (1965), which were designed for motion picture censorship schemes, do *not* apply to municipal permit schemes governing expressive access to public parks. The *Freedman* safeguards, held the Court, apply only to content based regulations; they do not apply to content neutral time, place, and manner restrictions on use of a public forum. This means that content neutral public forum permit schemes need *not* contain *Freedman's* requirement that the government, every time it denies a permit, must rush into court to enjoin the applicant's speech. *Thomas*, 534 U.S. at 322. But *Thomas* makes clear that the law remains the same in two important respects: (1) content neutral permit schemes governing expressive use of a public forum are *still* unconstitutional if they vest the licensing official with *unfettered discretion* to grant or deny the permit (*id.* at 323), and (2) content neutral permit schemes governing expressive use of a public forum are *still* unconstitutional if they do not contain a brief and specific *timeframe* in which the licensor must grant or deny the permit (*id.* at 322).

[218] *See, e.g.*, Christian Knights of Ku Klux Klan Invisible Empire, Inc. v. Dist. of Columbia, 972 F.2d 365 (D.C. Cir. 1992) (even though KKK's previous rallies in Washington, D.C., had been cut short by violent crowds, resulting in brick-throwing, injuries, and multiple arrests, the D.C. Circuit here affirmed the grant of an injunction to the Klan, allowing it to march the full eleven-block route that it had requested rather than the truncated four-block route for which D.C. police had granted a permit) (because

(footnote continued on next page)

and (2) those allowing the licensor to charge a higher police protection fee based on the anticipated level of hostility among onlookers.[219]

The first category is famously exemplified by cases in which Ku Klux Klansmen and Nazis were denied permits to march. In *Village of Skokie v. National Socialist Party of America*,[220] the court declined to enjoin a group of Nazis from marching through an Illinois suburb populated by hundreds of Holocaust survivors.[221] Even though it was "a virtual certainty" that the appearance of parading Nazis would prompt "thousands of irate Jewish citizens [to] physically attack [them],"[222] the court refused to prevent the march, holding that the possibility of a violent audience reaction is an impermissible consideration in granting an injunction or withholding a permit.[223] In *Christian Knights of the Ku Klux Klan Invisible*

(*footnote continued from previous page*)

the District's place restriction, resting as it did on concerns about a violent reaction to a controversial speaker, was content based, it could be sustained only if necessary to advance a compelling interest, and it could not be sustained where the district court found that the threat of violence, although substantial, was not beyond reasonable control); Beckerman v. City of Tupelo, 664 F.2d 502, 509–10 (5ᵗʰ Cir. 1981) (striking down provision authorizing police chief to deny parade permit if he determined that issuance would "provoke disorderly conduct"; on its face, this section was an unconstitutional prior restraint on free speech because it sanctioned permit denial on basis of heckler's veto); Collin v. Chicago Park Dist., 460 F.2d 746, 754–55 (7ᵗʰ Cir. 1972) (holding that Nazis were entitled to injunctive relief after city officials denied their application for permit to hold demonstration in public park); Hurwitt v. City of Oakland, 247 F. Supp. 995, 1001 (N.D. Cal. 1965) (enjoining city officials from prohibiting a parade intended to protest U.S. military intervention in Vietnam, even though plaintiffs' previous marches had been disrupted by angry spectators, including the Hell's Angels, who hurled tear gas bombs, broke through a police cordon, ripped banners, and disabled loudspeakers, where plaintiffs and their followers had always remained nonviolent); Williams v. Wallace, 240 F. Supp. 100, 109 (M.D. Ala. 1965) (granting civil rights activists injunctive relief ordering the State of Alabama to permit, and not to interfere with, plaintiffs' plans to march from Selma to Montgomery).

[219] *See, e.g.*, Forsyth Cnty. v. Nationalist Movement, 505 U.S. 123 (1992); Cent. Fla. Nuclear Freeze Campaign v. Walsh, 774 F.2d 1515 (11ᵗʰ Cir. 1985); Gay & Lesbian Servs. Network, Inc. v. Bishop, 832 F. Supp. 270 (W.D. Mo. 1993) (striking down, under *Forsyth*, a Kansas City Police Department policy governing parade permits that authorized the assessment of a crowd control fee that would vary depending on the level of hostility likely to be generated by the speaker or message).

[220] 366 N.E.2d 347 (Ill. App. Ct. 1977), *aff'd in part, rev'd in part*, 373 N.E.2d 21 (Ill. 1978) (holding that appellate court correctly refused to enjoin the Nazi march but erred in barring the Nazis from wearing their uniforms).

[221] *See* 366 N.E.2d at 349.

[222] *Id.* at 353.

[223] *Id.* (citing, *inter alia*, Collin v. Chicago Park Dist., 460 F.2d 746 (7ᵗʰ Cir. 1972) (holding that Nazis were entitled to injunctive relief after city officials denied their application for permit to hold demonstration in public park); Dr. Martin Luther King, Jr. Movement, Inc. v. City of Chicago, 419 F. Supp. 667 (N.D. Ill. 1976) (where civil rights organization sought to march through white

(*footnote continued on next page*)

Empire, Inc. v. District of Columbia,[224] the Ku Klux Klan (KKK) obtained an injunction permitting it to march in Washington, D.C.,[225] even though its previous rallies there had been cut short by violent crowds,[226] resulting in brick-throwing, injuries, and multiple arrests.[227] Evincing little enthusiasm for its result,[228] the D.C. Circuit nevertheless affirmed the Klan's injunction, holding that permit denials are content based if grounded on concerns about audience hostility,[229] and they therefore cannot be sustained where the threat of violence, even if substantial, is "not beyond reasonable control."[230]

This first category of precedent stretches back through the Vietnam War and civil rights era, where we find permit denials invalidated on factual

---

(footnote continued from previous page)

neighborhood, its previous foray there having been curtailed when bystanders pelted the procession with rocks, bricks, and explosive devices, city officials violated the First Amendment in denying organizers a permit for a second march through the same neighborhood, proposing instead an alternate route through an all-black neighborhood).

[224] 972 F.2d 365 (D.C. Cir. 1992).

[225] Under the injunction, the Klan was allowed to march the full eleven-block route that it had requested, rather than the truncated four-block route for which D.C. police had granted a permit. *Id.* at 368, 376.

[226] *See id.* at 367.

[227] *See id.* at 369.

[228] Expressing sympathy with the government's response here—rather than *denying* the Klan a permit, police had reduced the *scope* of the Klan's march from eleven to four blocks—the D.C. Circuit draws a distinction between limiting and refusing a permit, asserting that the government must be afforded *some* leeway in restricting the parameters of a demonstration when confronted with "the prospect of a violent response." *Id.* at 374. Rejecting more absolutist approaches urged by counsel and scholars—for example, (1) that restrictions may be imposed only where the threatened violence is "truly real and substantial and beyond reasonable control," (2) that "the fear of a hostile audience is never to be considered in ruling upon permit applications," and (3) that authorities may impose restrictions "only on the scene in response to a clear and present danger of violence"—the court arrives at a position that is more indulgent of the government: "We cannot agree that a threat of violence 'is an impermissible ground even for a time, place, and manner limitation.' When the choice is between an abbreviated march or a bloodbath, government must have some leeway to make adjustments necessary for the protection of participants, innocent onlookers, and others in the vicinity." *Id.*

[229] *See id.* at 374.

[230] *Id.* at 375. In rejecting the contention by D.C. police that the Klan's march had to be reduced from eleven blocks to four blocks or the threat of violence would be beyond reasonable control, the district court relied on testimony by the National Park police that the greatest confrontation was expected to occur at the assembly point of the march, that planned force levels at the assembly point were sufficient to overcome any violent attempts to stop the march, and that planned force levels along the proposed eleven-block route were sufficient to assure a reasonable level of safety—notwithstanding testimony by D.C. police that they would not have been able to control violence if the march were to span the full eleven blocks. *Id.*

records bristling with violence. Even where prior marches were greeted with great hostility, where Vietnam War protests were derailed by tear gas bombs,[231] and civil rights processions were pelted with rocks, bricks, and explosive devices,[232] the courts consistently held that such speakers could not be denied a permit based on the antagonism that their message would likely inspire.[233] "This is so," explained one court, "because under such a doctrine, unpopular political groups might be rendered virtually inarticulate."[234] The alternative, explained another, would leave the exercise of First Amendment freedoms "depend[ent] on the dictates of those willing to resort to violence."[235]

The second category of precedent in this area is prominently exemplified by *Forsyth County v. Nationalist Movement*,[236] where the Supreme Court struck down a licensing scheme that permitted the administrator to vary the fee for assembling or parading to reflect the estimated cost of maintaining public order.[237] The ordinance had been enacted "[a]s a direct result"[238] of two violent demonstrations in which civil rights activists, protesting racial discrimination in a rural Georgia county, were confronted by hostile residents. The first march was brought to a premature halt when four hundred KKK members, shouting racial slurs, began throwing rocks and beer bottles.[239] The second march featured twenty thousand marchers, one thousand counterdemonstrators, and three thousand law enforcement officers.[240] It was punctuated (although not halted) by rock-throwing and produced sixty arrests.[241]

---

[231] *See* Hurwitt v. City of Oakland, 247 F. Supp. 995 (N.D. Cal. 1965).
[232] Dr. Martin Luther King, Jr. Movement, Inc. v. City of Chicago, 419 F. Supp. 667 (N.D. Ill. 1976).
[233] *See Martin Luther King Movement*, 419 F. Supp. at 675; *Hurwitt*, 247 F. Supp. at 1001; Williams v. Wallace, 240 F. Supp. 100 (M.D. Ala. 1965).
[234] *Hurwitt*, 247 F. Supp. at 1001.
[235] *Martin Luther King Movement*, 419 F. Supp. at 675.
[236] 505 U.S. 123 (1992).
[237] *See id.* at 126–27.
[238] *Id.* at 126.
[239] *See id.* at 125.
[240] *Id.* at 125–26.
[241] *Id.*

Although these facts presented an "emotional" context in which to review the county's response,[242] its ordinance vested the administrator with the same unfettered discretion that invariably proves fatal in licensing schemes.[243] Here, that discretion came into play in fixing police protection fees on an applicant-by-applicant basis: "The fee assessed will depend on the administrator's measure of the amount of *hostility* likely to be created by the speech based on its content. Those wishing to express views unpopular with bottle-throwers, for example, may have to pay more for their permit."[244] In striking down the ordinance, the Court concluded: "Speech cannot be financially burdened, any more than it can be punished or banned, simply because it might offend a hostile mob."[245]

C. Limits on the Timeframe for Issuing a Permit

Courts will treat as "a species of unbridled discretion" any failure by a licensing scheme to place limits on the *timeframe* within which the decision-maker must grant or deny the permit.[246] There are two ways in which a licensing scheme may run afoul of this requirement: (1) by failing to impose a brief and specific timeframe for the licensor's decision and (2) by imposing advance registration requirements that build into the application process a lengthy delay before the licensee may speak.

---

[242] *Id.* at 124.

[243] On this point, the Court observed: "Based on the county's implementation and construction of the ordinance, it simply cannot be said that there are any 'narrowly drawn, reasonable, and definite standards' guiding the hand of the Forsyth County administrator. The decision as to how much to charge for police protection or administrative time, or even whether to charge at all, is left to the whim of the administrator. There are no articulated standards either in the ordinance or in the county's established practice. The administrator is not required to rely on any objective factors. He need not provide any explanation for his decision, and that decision is unreviewable. Nothing in the law or its application prevents the official from encouraging some views and discouraging others through the arbitrary application of fees. The First Amendment prohibits the vesting of such unbridled discretion in a government official." *Id.* at 132–33 (quoting Niemotko v. Maryland, 340 U.S. 268, 271 (1951) (citations and footnotes omitted)).

[244] *Forsyth*, 505 U.S. at 134 (emphasis added).

[245] *Id.* at 134–35.

[246] FW/PBS, Inc. v. City of Dallas, 493 U.S. 215, 223–24 (1990). *FW/PBS* struck down the licensing scheme in an ordinance regulating sexually oriented businesses because it lacked "an effective limitation on the time within which the licensor's decision must be made." *Id.* at 229. In performing its analysis, the Court identified "two evils" in speech licensing schemes "that will not be tolerated": vesting "unbridled discretion" in the licensing authority and "fail[ing] to place limits on the time within which the decision-maker must issue the license." *Id.* at 225–26.

1. Requiring the Licensor's Decision Within a Brief and Specific Timeframe

Courts consistently invalidate speech licensing schemes that fail to impose a brief and specific timeframe within which the licensor must grant or deny the permit.[247] This failure to impose a time limit offends the First Amendment because it leaves the government free to ignore any permit application that it does not wish to grant. Rather than denying the permit, which would prompt an immediate lawsuit by the disappointed applicant, the government is free to withhold its decision indefinitely, forcing the applicant to wait until he or she no longer wishes to speak. As one court observed, the failure to impose a time limit "impermissibly places the fate of a parade application in official limbo, both chilling and freezing the applicant's free speech intentions and expectations."[248]

The law in this area used to be dominated by the Supreme Court's 1965 decision in *Freedman v. Maryland*,[249] but that changed in 2002 when the Court handed down *Thomas v. Chicago Park District*.[250] Let's begin with *Freedman* and then cover the changes wrought by *Thomas*.

Freedman held that speech licensing systems must contain the following procedural safeguards:

1. Burden of proof is on the *licensor* to demonstrate that the applicant's speech is *unprotected* expression.
2. There must be a specified and brief timeframe in which the licensor must either issue the license *or go to court to restrain the applicant's expression.*
3. The procedure must also assure a prompt and final *judicial decision.*[251]

---

[247] *See, e.g., FW/PBS*, 493 U.S. at 226–27; Collin v. Chicago Park Dist., 460 F.2d 746 (7th Cir. 1972); MacDonald v. Safir, 26 F. Supp. 2d 664 (S.D.N.Y. 1998); Long Beach Lesbian & Gay Pride, Inc. v. City of Long Beach, 17 Cal. Rptr. 2d 861 (Cal. Ct. App. 1993) (holding that ordinance was unconstitutional for its failure to impose a specific time limit for granting or denying the permit).
[248] *Long Beach Lesbian & Gay Pride*, 17 Cal. Rptr. at 872.
[249] Freedman v. Maryland, 380 U.S. 51 (1965).
[250] Thomas v. Chicago Park District, 534 U.S. 316 (2002).
[251] *Freedman*, 380 U.S. at 58–60 (emphasis added).

In *Thomas*, the Supreme Court held that the "extraordinary procedural safeguards"[252] required by *Freedman*, which were designed for motion picture censorship schemes, do *not* apply to municipal permit schemes governing expressive access to public parks.[253] The *Freedman* safeguards, held the Court, apply only to content based regulations; they do not apply to content neutral time, place, and manner restrictions on the use of a public forum.[254] This means that content neutral public forum permit schemes need *not* contain *Freedman's* requirement that the government, every time it denies a permit, must rush into court to enjoin the applicant's speech.[255]

But *Thomas* did not abolish the requirement that public forum permit schemes must contain a specific timeframe in which the licensor must grant or deny the permit.[256] Those precedents remain good law.

2. Advance Registration Requirements

Because a speech licensing scheme must contain limits on the timeframe for issuing permits,[257] courts are consistently hostile toward schemes that impose advance registration requirements of any significant duration.[258] Such requirements are vulnerable to First Amendment challenge because they build into the application process a mandatory delay before the licensee may speak. The problem with any built-in delay, as Justice Harlan once observed, is that "timing is of the essence in politics. It is almost impossible to predict the political future; and when an event occurs, it is often necessary to have one's voice heard promptly, if it is to be considered

---

[252] *Thomas*, 534 U.S. at 323.

[253] *Id.* at 322.

[254] *Id.*

[255] *Id.*

[256] In explaining why the permit scheme did *not* offend the First Amendment, the *Thomas* Court observed that the ordinance imposed a specific timeframe for issuing the decision and did not otherwise afford the licensor unfettered discretion. *Id.* at 324.

[257] *See FW/PBS*, 493 U.S. at 223–24.

[258] *See, e.g.*, Sullivan v. City of Augusta, 511 F.3d 16 (1st Cir. 2007); American-Arab Anti-Discrimination Comm. v. City of Dearborn, 418 F.3d 600 (6th Cir. 2005); Douglas v. Brownell, 88 F.3d 1511 (8th Cir. 1996); Grossman v. City of Portland, 33 F.3d 1200 (9th Cir. 1994); NAACP v. City of Richmond, 743 F.2d 1346 (9th Cir. 1984); Int'l Brotherhood of Teamsters v. City of Rocky Mount, 672 F.2d 376 (4th Cir. 1982); Serv. Employee Int'l Union v. City of Los Angeles, 114 F. Supp. 2d 966, 973–74 (C.D. Cal. 2000); Long Beach Lesbian & Gay Pride, Inc. v. City of Long Beach, 17 Cal. Rptr. 2d 861, 871 (Cal. Ct. App. 1993).

at all."[259] In *NAACP v. City of Richmond*,[260] the death of a black man in police custody prompted immediate plans for a protest march, but city officials thwarted the march by invoking a twenty-day advance registration requirement in the city's parade permit ordinance.[261] Rejecting the ordinance as effectively "outlaw[ing] spontaneous expression,"[262] the Ninth Circuit stressed that

> simple delay may permanently vitiate the expressive content of a demonstration. A spontaneous parade expressing a viewpoint on a topical issue will almost inevitably attract more participants and more press attention, and generate more emotion, than the "same" parade [twenty] days later. The later parade can never be the same. Where spontaneity is part of the message, dissemination delayed is dissemination denied.[263]

Advance registration requirements have been invalidated in a broad range of contexts, including permit schemes for parading,[264] demonstrating,[265] picketing,[266] and leafleting.[267] Because parades and demonstrations create greater congestion than picketing or leafleting, they necessarily require more lead time,[268] but even for parades and demonstrations, the courts

---

[259] Shuttlesworth v. Birmingham, 394 U.S. 147, 163 (1969) (striking down parade permit scheme in context of thwarted civil rights march) (Harlan, J., concurring). *Accord* Carroll v. President & Comm'rs of Princess Anne, 393 U.S. 175 (1968) (invalidating speech-restrictive injunction imposing ten-day freeze on demonstrations by white supremacist group); *id.* at 182 (asserting that a delay "of even a day or two" may be intolerable when applied to "'political' speech in which the element of timeliness may be important").

[260] 743 F.2d 1346 (9th Cir. 1984).

[261] *Id.* at 1349.

[262] *Id.* at 1355.

[263] *Id.* at 1356.

[264] *See* Sullivan v. City of Augusta, 511 F.3d 16 (1st Cir. 2007) (striking down thirty-day advance registration); American-Arab Anti-Discrimination Comm. v. City of Dearborn, 418 F.3d 600 (6th Cir. 2005) (striking down thirty-day advance registration); Douglas v. Brownell, 88 F.3d 1511 (8th Cir. 1996) (striking down five-day advance registration); NAACP v. City of Richmond, 743 F.2d 1346 (9th Cir. 1984) (striking down twenty-day advance registration); Long Beach Lesbian & Gay Pride, Inc. v. City of Long Beach, 17 Cal. Rptr. 2d 861 (Cal. Ct. App. 1993) (striking down thirty-day advance registration).

[265] *See* Grossman v. City of Portland, 33 F.3d 1200 (9th Cir. 1994) (striking down seven-day advance registration).

[266] *See* Int'l Brotherhood of Teamsters v. City of Rocky Mount, 672 F.2d 376 (4th Cir. 1982) (striking down seventy-two-hour advance registration).

[267] *See* Rosen v. Port of Portland, 641 F.2d 1243 (9th Cir. 1981) (striking down one-business-day advance registration).

[268] *See Rosen*, 641 F.2d at 1247–48.

have consistently rejected advance registration requirements beyond two days.[269] Thus, if a speech licensing scheme imposes a built-in delay of more than two days, it will be especially vulnerable to constitutional challenge.

IV. Conclusion

In closing, here are some important, practical points to be borne in mind by local government regulators when dealing with mass demonstrations, marches, and parades:

- Courts are hostile to permit requirements for small assemblies. A permit requirement is most applicable to speakers who are massing or traveling in large groups on public streets or sidewalks. Such a requirement is almost certain to be struck down if it applies to groups of twenty or fewer individuals.
- For mass demonstrations and parades, a permit fee will be upheld if it is directly linked to, and serves to defray, the administrative expenses incurred by the government in regulating the speaker's expressive activity. This principle has been extended to parade permit fees that require the applicant to pay for the police officers who furnish traffic control.
- Courts have consistently invalidated permit schemes vesting government officials with "unfettered discretion" to forbid or allow

---

[269] *See City of Richmond*, 743 F.2d at 1357. *Compare* Douglas v. Brownell, 88 F.3d 1511 (8th Cir. 1996) (striking down parade permit scheme imposing five-day advance registration requirement), *and* Int'l Brotherhood of Teamsters v. City of Rocky Mount, 672 F.2d 376 (4th Cir. 1982) (striking down picketing permit scheme imposing 72-hour advance registration requirement), *with* A Quaker Action Grp. v. Morton, 516 F.2d 717, 735 (D.C. Cir. 1975) (upholding forty-eight-hour advance registration requirement for demonstrations near the White House but holding that the regulation must be revised to specify that the permit must be deemed granted if not acted on within the forty-eight-hour period), *and* Bayless v. Martine, 430 F.2d 873 (5th Cir. 1970) (upholding forty-eight-hour advance registration requirement for on-campus demonstrations), *and* Powe v. Miles, 407 F.2d 73, 84 (2d Cir. 1968) (upholding forty-eight-hour advance registration requirement for on-campus demonstrations), *and* Serv. Empl. Int'l Union v. Port Auth. of N. Y., 3 F. Supp. 2d 413, 422 (S.D.N.Y. 1998) (upholding a thirty-six-hour waiting period for permits to stage protests at the World Trade Center and Port Authority Bus Terminal), *and* Jackson v. Dobbs, 329 F. Supp. 287 (N.D. Ga. 1970) (upholding ordinance requiring marchers to obtain a permit by 4:00 p.m. on the day preceding a march), *aff'd*, 442 F.2d 928 (5th Cir. 1971). *But see* Progressive Labor Party v. Lloyd, 487 F. Supp. 1054, 1059 (D. Mass. 1980) (approving a three-day advance filing requirement in the context of a broader challenge to parade permit ordinance).

certain speech activities, especially if the regulation leaves room for assessing the speaker's viewpoint in deciding whether or not to grant a permit.

- Courts will strike down any permit scheme that allows the licensing official to consider either the controversial nature of the speaker's message or its potential for inspiring a hostile response.

- Courts consistently invalidate speech licensing schemes that fail to impose a brief and specific timeframe within which the licensor must grant or deny the permit.

- In a speech licensing scheme, an advance registration requirement of more than two days is likely to be struck down if challenged in court.

- A time, place, and manner restriction, even if facially content neutral, will be vulnerable to constitutional challenge if the circumstances surrounding its enactment or enforcement reveal a governmental intent to favor or punish particular messages.

- The Supreme Court appears to have created a new requirement for time, place, and manner regulations: "To meet the requirement of narrow tailoring, the government must *demonstrate* that alternative measures that burden substantially less speech would fail to achieve the government's interests, not simply that the chosen route is easier."[270] To *satisfy* that requirement, "it is not enough for [the government] simply to say that other approaches have not worked."[271]

- The Supreme Court has shown a "special solicitude" for *inexpensive* methods of communication.[272] Accordingly, municipalities should avoid imposing broad restrictions on leaflets, homemade signs, and other inexpensive means of expression.

- A speech restriction will be struck down as failing to afford sufficient alternative channels of communication if it largely impairs a speaker's capacity to reach the intended audience.

---

[270] McCullen v. Coakley, 134 S. Ct. 2518, 2540 (2014) (emphasis added).
[271] *Id.*
[272] Members of City Council v. Taxpayers for Vincent, 466 U.S. 789, 812–13 n. 30 (1984).

12

Some Concluding Thoughts on the Effect of the First Amendment in Land Use Law

Nancy E. Stroud

Lewis, Stroud & Deutsch, P.L.
Boca Raton, Florida

I. Introduction

Land use regulation is a primary means by which local governments ensure that their communities are "beautiful as well as healthy, spacious as well as clean."[1] Although First Amendment freedoms are some of the most deeply held values—especially of those who act in the political realm, including elected officials—local government officials generally do not think first of First Amendment concerns when making land use decisions. The economic effect of regulation on property values tends to overshadow local land use discussions. However, First Amendment concerns permeate several aspects of local land use planning and regulation, especially in the already difficult areas relating to signs, religious uses, and sexually oriented businesses.

Land use practitioners must become more versed in the First Amendment in order to ensure that in their effort to create more livable communities, local governments also adhere to First Amendment values. Admittedly, this

---

[1] Berman v. Parker, 348 U.S. 26, 33 (1954).

is no easy task. To a large extent, the difficulty arises because the protected status of First Amendment freedoms requires that public officials change their normal orientation and assume a greater burden to support and tailor their decisions to the problem they seek to address. Another difficulty arises from the fact that the judicial guidelines for what constitutes a supportable land use decision are broadly stated and are constantly reinterpreted as applied to the particulars of those decisions. Witness the difficulty that the federal courts have had in deciding what is appropriate for religious displays on public lands.[2] The badly split court pronouncements on these issues only add to the unpredictability of judicial interpretations. Indeed, the definition of what is protected "speech" has expanded over the years and may include, for example, donation bins[3], tattoos,[4] and panhandling.[5] Finally, the federal courts' increasing interest in expanding First Amendment protections to commercial entities in the last decade in such areas as political speech[6] and religious expression[7] will no doubt encourage more litigation and require the local government attorney to pay even closer attention to the risks of regulating in this arena.[8]

Given these difficulties, what is a land use lawyer to do? Aside from reading and referring to this book and other valuable resources on the subject, it is vital to stay abreast of the changing case law. In addition to the traditional legal research methods, the computer-literate attorney will find a number of listservs and websites that highlight current issues and cases, including those of special-interest groups, professionals, and academia. Certain land use topics—signs, panhandling, religious uses,

---

[2] *See* notes 30–32, *infra*.

[3] *See* Planet Aid v. City of St. Johns, 782 F.3d 318 (6th Cir. 2015).

[4] *See* Jucha v. City of North Chicago, 63 F. Supp. 3d 820 (N.D. Ill. 2014).

[5] *See* Norton v. City of Springfield, 806 F.3d 411 (7th Cir. 2015).

[6] *See, e.g.,* Citizens United v. FEC, 558 U.S. 310 (2009) (corporations are associations of citizens and thus have the same political speech rights of the members of the corporation).

[7] *See, e.g.,* Burwell v. Hobby Lobby Stores, Inc., 134 S. Ct. 2751 (2014) (finding a for-profit corporation to be a "person" engaged in the "exercise of religion" within the meaning of the federal Religious Freedom Restoration Act).

[8] Indeed, Justice Breyer has expressed concern that the Supreme Court's shift to grant corporations more First Amendment protection is akin to the Court's discredited striking down of public laws regulating business during the "Lochner era" of the early twentieth century, through the use of the Constitution's Due Process Clause. *See* Sorrell v. IMS Health, Inc., 131 S. Ct. 2653, 2675 (2011).

and so forth—should always be approached with the extra care required by the First Amendment to justify regulation.

This concluding chapter highlights some of the ways in which the First Amendment has impacted the practice of land use law, both procedurally and substantively, especially from the perspective of the local government lawyer.

II. General Procedural Pitfalls

When entering into First Amendment territory, land use practitioners must be vigilant about obeying the more stringent procedural rules established by the courts to ensure that the right of free speech is not more restricted than necessary, under the court's "strict scrutiny" review. The first rule regarding free speech is that the government will not be given the benefit of the doubt about the constitutionality of the land use regulation. Unlike other typical land use regulation, that affecting free speech will not be presumed constitutional, and the burden of sustaining the regulation against a constitutional challenge will fall on the local government. The second rule is that the regulation must be carefully tailored to achieve its legitimate public purpose; related to this premise is the rule that standards that are vague or regulations that are overbroad will be not tolerated. Finally, the land use permitting requirements must provide for a specific and speedy decision by the licensing body to avoid being an invalid "prior restraint" on speech.

The regulation of religious uses restricting religious expression requires the same procedural considerations unless such regulation is considered to be a neutral law of general applicability. Land use regulation until relatively recently was considered to be a neutral law of general applicability, unless overtly discriminatory among religious denominations. Since the publication of the first edition of this book, the First Amendment protections for religious expression have been supplemented—and in many ways, overshadowed—by the federal Religious Land Use and Institutionalized Persons Act (RLUIPA),[9] which imports the procedural requirements of

---

[9] 42 U.S.C. § 2000cc *et seq.*

strict scrutiny to any land use regulation that imposes "a substantial burden on the religious exercise" of a person, including a religious assembly or institution. Perhaps more than any other land use issue, the regulation of religious use in the last decade has generated extensive legal angst and litigation as RLUIPA has been interpreted and applied by the courts. On the other hand, no particular procedural niceties apply where the complaint is that the land use regulation violates the Establishment Clause of the First Amendment. In this relatively rare circumstance—discussed later in this chapter with regard to religious displays on public property—the courts' focus is on the purpose and the effect of the government action and whether it involves the government in "excessive entanglement" with religion.[10]

A. No Presumption of Constitutionality

The general presumption that statutes are constitutional does not apply in the case of regulations affecting free speech rights. Instead, the burden of proving the constitutionality of a law shifts to the government. This exception to the general rule also applies to certain other types of land use regulations. Thus, the presumptive shift will apply where a land use regulation intentionally affects a "suspect classification," such as a racial classification, under equal protection guarantees.[11] The U.S. Supreme Court also requires local governments to justify the imposition of conditions to land development approvals, such as land dedication or mitigation fees.[12] However, the presumptive shift is most broadly applied in land use regulations where free speech principles are at stake.

The practical effect of this shift is that local government must change the way in which they prepare land use regulations affecting free speech and religious uses—that is, with an eye toward carrying a greater burden of proof if challenged in court. For the most careful local government, this could mean that it commissions planning studies to support the type and content of the regulation, holds hearings that present this information, and documents the information for future use. This adds time and expense to

---

[10] Lemon v. Kurtzman, 408 U.S. 602 (1971).

[11] Vill. of Arlington Heights v. Metro Hous. Dev. Corp., 429 U.S. 252 (1977).

[12] *See* Koontz v. St. Johns River Water Mgmt. Dist., 133 S. Ct. 2586 (2013).

the promulgation of local law, but it avoids the greater expense of defending the law after the fact. The local government should most certainly prepare a substantial statement of purpose for any ordinance affecting free speech and religious uses. It should also refrain from borrowing regulations "whole cloth" from other jurisdictions. Instead, the local government should carefully consider to what extent those regulations have been judicially tested and how applicable the judicial decisions are to the circumstance of its community. Additionally, the local government should invite the comments of the affected interests early in the process to understand the potential challenges and to adjust the regulations appropriately to meet legitimate concerns.

Ideally, of course, these steps should be taken for any land use regulation, as many professional planners and land use lawyers would advocate. In the press of time and politics, the ideal is difficult to meet. Nevertheless, it is especially important—for example, in the case of ordinances that regulate sexually oriented businesses—that a record be developed before the adoption of the ordinance, even if the record is composed only of studies conducted in similar jurisdictions.[13]

B. Narrowly Tailored Regulations

Regulations that are directed to a particular viewpoint or content expressed by speech are subject to strict scrutiny by the courts. The courts demand that the government demonstrate a compelling interest for such regulations and that the least restrictive means to serve that interest be used. The difficulty is determining whether the regulation is content based, and that determination has been made more difficult by the U.S. Supreme Court's very recent decision in *Reed v. Town of Gilbert*.[14] *Reed* broadly applied the strict scrutiny standard to strike down the Town of Gilbert's sign regulations, rejecting a heretofore accepted argument that as long as a sign code is viewpoint neutral, the code would not trigger strict scrutiny review.[15] The fallout from the case is yet to be fully developed, but it appears that the standard of "intermediate level" of scrutiny for viewpoint neutral

---

[13] *See* City of Renton v. Playtime Theatres, Inc., 475 U.S. 1 (1986).
[14] 135 S. Ct. 2218 (2015).
[15] *See, e.g.,* Ward v. Rock Against Racism, 491 U.S. 781 (1989).

regulations now will not be available to support land use regulations that regulate on the basis of category or content. The result will be that land use regulations will more than ever need to be narrowly tailored to achieve the regulatory interest to be served.

Regulations that are overbroad, where their application casts too wide a net to cover constitutionally protected speech, will not be tolerated under the strict requirement of narrow tailoring. In a related fashion, regulations that are vague and do not give adequate notice of what conduct or speech is prohibited will fail as well. Because the courts have also relaxed the standing requirements for facial challenges to these First Amendment speech defects, the consequences of a vague or overbroad regulation can be substantial as measured in litigation risk.[16]

Prior to *Reed*, if a land use regulation restricted time, place, and manner rather than viewpoint, the Court required that the regulation be "no greater than necessary" to protect the "substantial governmental interest sought to be advanced" and specified that the regulation "need not be the least restrictive or least intrusive means of doing so."[17] The regulation would not be overturned "simply because there is some imaginable alternative that might be less burdensome on speech," but if "the means chosen are not substantially broader than necessary to achieve the government's interest . . . the regulation will not be invalid simply because a court concludes that the government's interest could be adequately served by some less speech-restrictive alternative."[18] The standard under *Reed*, however, will be more exacting, although at this time it is difficult to predict how it will be applied. Even before *Reed*, the federal decisions applying this standard were fractured and case specific as courts attempted to determine whether there was an adequate fit between the purpose of the regulation and its operation. The practitioner must pay close attention to the evolving case law and to precedent in regard to specific types of regulations. Local government officials justifiably feel that these uncertainties contribute to the "judicialization" of their land use actions, making their actions more

---

[16] *See, e.g.*, Vill. of Schaumburg v. Citizens for a Better Environment, 444 U.S. 620 (1980).

[17] *Ward*, 491 U.S. at 798.

[18] *Id.* at 799.

subject to legal challenge and delay. Ultimately, it may discourage all but the most case-tested ordinances from being enacted.

C. Prior Restraint

Because land use regulations are essentially permitting and licensing regulations, the First Amendment protection against prior restraints of speech imposes substantial restraints on the type of land use procedures available to local governments. To avoid prior restraint problems, the government must provide clear standards that guide the local decision-making; the local official must decide on the permit within a specific and brief period, during which the status quo must be preserved; and the regulation must provide an express and prompt judicial review procedure in the case of a denial.

The obvious result for land use regulations is that those affecting First Amendment rights must establish a prompt procedure for permit decisions, placing signs, adult businesses, newsracks, and the like in a priority process over other land uses. The reasonableness of the review period will be necessarily determined on a case-by-case basis, but the burden will be on the local government to justify the length of time. Local governments are not in control of the period of judicial review, but the Court has required that there be access to prompt judicial review and a prompt judicial decision.[19] Another important effect of the prior restraint doctrine is to discourage conditional use permits in favor of permits issued "as of right." Typically, a conditional use permit requires the application of discretion from the permitting agency or board. It is thus subject to the criticism that the standards for issuance are vague and nonspecific. The favored criterion in many conditional use regulations, that a use must be shown to be compatible with the neighborhood, is particularly subject to this criticism. Applicants must be asked for information that is definitive and readily reviewable. Thus, local land development regulations affecting First Amendment issues must be carefully drafted to include specific application requirements, review standards, and specific and timely review procedures. The administering agencies must be advised and trained to treat

---

[19] *See* City of Littleton v. Z.J. Gifts D-4, L.L.C., 541 U.S. 774 (2004). In this instance, the Court found that the normal judicial processes of the Colorado state court were sufficient to meet the standard.

the applications with particular expedition and attention. The importance of the prior restraint doctrine permeates the entire way in which the government does business in this area of land use.

III. Sensitive Topic Areas

The constraints of the First Amendment as applied to land use problems promise local government lawyers that they will never be bored by routine. Land use law, including regulation of signs, sexually oriented businesses, and religious use issues, is a dynamic and challenging area that enjoys high public interest. This section discusses some of the issues that are of particular current interest.

A. Signs and the Commercial/Ideological Distinction

Since *Central Hudson Gas and Electric v. Public Service Commission*,[20] the federal courts have recognized a hierarchy of speech under which regulation of political or ideological speech is subject to strict scrutiny while commercial speech regulation is subject to a balancing of interests between free speech rights and other substantial public interests. Under the *Central Hudson* formula, commonly referred to as "intermediate scrutiny," restrictions on commercial speech must serve a substantial government interest, directly advance that interest, and be no more extensive than necessary to serve that interest. Prior to *Reed*, this hierarchy recognized that, for example, signs with political content (e.g., "Support Proposition 2") are given greater protection than commercial signs. In an often-quoted explanation, Justice Stewart once described the differences between commercial speech and ideological communication:

> Ideological expression, be it oral, literary, pictorial, or theatrical, is integrally related to the exposition of thought—thought that may shape our concepts of the whole universe of man. Although such expression may convey factual information relevant to social and individual decision-making, it is protected by the Constitution, whether or not it contains factual representations and

---

[20] 447 U.S. 557 (1980).

even if it includes inaccurate assertions of fact. . . . Commercial price and product advertising differs markedly from ideological expression because it is confined to the promotion of specific goods or services. The First Amendment protects the advertisement because of the "information of potential interest and value" conveyed, rather than because of any direct contribution to the interchange of ideas.[21]

The elimination of visual clutter created by unregulated signage is one of the most effective ways for local governments to improve the aesthetic quality of the community. The Supreme Court has recognized that aesthetics and safety are substantial government interests that support commercial sign regulation.[22] For this reason, any indication that the Court might be amenable to providing even greater protection to commercial signs, equivalent to that of political or ideological speech, is a worrisome development. Justice Thomas's opinion in *Reed* simply did not address the commercial–noncommercial distinction, and thus the impact of the Court's most recent pronouncement on signs leaves this issue unclear. Justice Alito's concurring opinion in the case sets out the types of sign regulation that three justices, at least, believe are not content based, but it does not address commercial signs per se. Justice Breyer's opinion, concurring in the result, argues that the Court should not abandon intermediate scrutiny but points out that the Court recently applied strict scrutiny in a case involving commercial speech, *Sorrell v. IMS Health, Inc.*[23]

Up to now, the Court has not explicitly abandoned its commercial–noncommercial distinctions in addressing land use cases. In *Lorillard Tobacco Co. v. Reilly*,[24] the Supreme Court granted certiorari to Lorillard Tobacco Company and other petitioners in their challenge to a Massachusetts law restricting the advertisement of tobacco on signs near schools and playgrounds. The tobacco companies urged that the established constitutional test, which provides lesser protection based on the content of their

---

[21] Va. State Bd. of Pharmacy v. Va. Citizens Consumer Council, Inc., 425 US. 748, 779–80 (1976) (Stewart, J., concurring) (internal citations and punctuation omitted).

[22] *See* Metromedia, Inc. v. City of San Diego, 453 U.S. 490, 507–08 (1981).

[23] 131 S. Ct. 2653 (2011). *Sorrell* struck down Vermont's Prescription Confidentiality Law under a heightened judicial scrutiny test; the law prohibited the sale or disclosure of information about prescribers without the prescriber's consent.

[24] 121 S. Ct. 2404 (2001).

commercial and economic speech, is adverse to the First Amendment. If commercial messages have the same constitutional protection as "core value speech," communities will be considerably restricted in their ability to control the proliferation of signs, to the detriment of the community and, arguably, even to commercial activity itself. The Court rejected a change in the test by deciding *Lorillard* on federal preemption grounds, yet subsequent decisions show a course that arguably moves commercial speech closer to strict scrutiny protection.

Practitioners in the field should be particularly concerned because of the Supreme Court's decision confusing the distinction in the context of newsrack regulation, in *Discovery Network, Inc. v. City of Cincinnati.*[25] In that case, the city prohibited newsracks that displayed commercial newspapers but allowed noncommercial newspapers. The Court found that the distinction was not reasonable under *Central Hudson.* Arguably, the case is limited to the specific facts, especially because the Court stated that the city possibly could build a record to justify differential treatment.

The Supreme Court rejected another invitation to grant commercial speech more protection, in *Greater New Orleans Broadcasting Ass'n, Inc. v. United States,*[26] where the Court reversed a ban on the broadcasting of advertisements for legal gambling at area casinos. Because it found that there was not a sufficient relationship to a legitimate governmental purpose, the Court stated that there was "no need to break new ground. *Central Hudson,* as applied in the Court's more recent commercial speech cases, provides an adequate basis for decision."[27] However, the issue is not likely to go away, considering the economic interests of the various media in a change of the rule and the Court's shift in *Reed.*

B. Sexually Oriented Businesses and the Small Community

Another area of particular concern to local governments is the regulation of sexually oriented businesses, otherwise referred to as adult entertainment uses. The cases have established that nonobscene adult entertainment

---

[25] 507 U.S. 410 (1993).
[26] 527 U.S. 173 (1999).
[27] *Id.* at 184.

is a protected First Amendment activity for which the local government must make sites reasonably available. The question for small communities is whether they should be required to make sites available at all, especially where adult uses otherwise may be located within geographic proximity to the jurisdiction, although not within its political boundaries. Not surprisingly, local officials find it incredible that the First Amendment might require that sexually oriented businesses be able to locate within a small community, whereas, evidently, there is no constitutional prohibition against excluding places of worship (except that RLUIPA requires that houses of worship not be excluded).

Arguably, the Supreme Court has held open the possibility that not every small jurisdiction must allow sexually oriented businesses. In *Schad v. Borough of Mount Ephraim*,[28] involving an adult bookstore with "peep shows," a majority of the Court (three concurring and two dissenting justices) indicated that some communities may be able to regulate or ban all commercial live entertainment. The plurality opinion also stated:

> [The borough] suggest[s] that if there were countywide zoning, it would be quite legal to allow live entertainment in only selected areas of the county and to exclude it from primarily residential communities. . . . This may very well be true, but the [b]orough cannot avail itself of that argument in this case.[29]

Some courts have taken encouragement from *Schad*, even though the composition of the Supreme Court has significantly changed since then. For example, in *Boss Capital, Inc. v. City of Casselberry*,[30] the Eleventh Circuit raised, but did not address, the question. In determining the relevant real estate market, however, the court considered the availability of sites for adult entertainment, including those as far as 1.25 miles south of the city limits. Two years earlier, the same court noted that the Supreme Court had not decided that "every unit of local government entrusted with zoning

---

[28] 452 U.S. 61 (1981).
[29] *Id.* at 76.
[30] 187 F. 3d 1251 (11th Cir. 1999).

responsibilities must provide a commercial zone in which [protected activity] is permitted."[31]

Often, the problem with adult uses does not become an issue until the adult use locates itself in the jurisdiction. At that point, the city attorney often scrambles to consult with other jurisdictions that have dealt with the issue, borrowing studies and ordinance language. The reality is that when faced with an increasingly sophisticated and well-funded adult entertainment industry, this is an area of First Amendment law where a small local government is likely to perceive itself to be a David facing Goliath. The issue needs to be settled, but small communities are the least likely to have the resources to litigate the issue to its conclusion.

C. Religious Uses

In the case of religious uses, local governments must tread a fine line between land use regulations that can be used to favor religion and those that impermissibly interfere with the free exercise of religion. As a practical matter, local governments are buffeted on both sides by interest groups—for example, by those that challenge traditional activities, such as the display of nativity scenes on public property,[32] and by religious groups that urge various accommodations for locating and operating religious facilities. Decisions from a badly split Supreme Court on religious establishment questions could cause one to despair of finding predictability in the laws regarding the Establishment Clause. For example, the Court has found that posting the Ten Commandments in a Kentucky courthouse violated the Establishment Clause, whereas a monument with the Ten Commandments at the Texas Capitol did not.[33] Recent decisions do little to add clarity.[34]

---

[31] Digital Props., Inc. v. City of Plantation, 121 F. 3d 586, n. 2 (11th Cir. 1997). *See also* Keego Harbor Co. v. City of Keego Harbor, 657 F.2d 94, 99 (6th Cir. 1981), saying "[w]e do not hold that every unit of government, however small, must provide an area in which adult fare is allowed."

[32] For example, *see* Cnty. of Allegheny v. ACLU, 492 U.S. 573 (1989) (unconstitutional to display nativity scene at a county courthouse, but the display of a menorah next to a Christmas tree outside public building did not appear to endorse religion).

[33] *Compare* McCreary Cnty. v. ACLU, 545 U.S. 844 (2005) and Van Orden v. Perry, 545 U.S. 677 (2005).

[34] For example, *see* Capitol Square Review and Advisory Bd. v. Pinette, 115 S. Ct. 2440 (1995), where five separate opinions were written on the issue of whether a cross could be erected at Christmas by

(footnote continued on next page)

On the other hand, the general principles applied to the Free Exercise Clause seem to fit the character of land use regulations very nicely, and there are few federal cases striking down those regulations on the basis that they interfere with the free exercise right of the Constitution. The general principle is that neutral laws of general applicability will not require proof of a compelling interest if they place only incidental burdens on the exercise of religion.[35] Zoning laws, which typically control matters such as setbacks, height controls, or other locational factors, would seem to be relatively safe from such constitutional challenges. However, the landscape of religious exercise challenges changed dramatically in 2000 with the adoption of RLUIPA, which gives religious institutions a federal cause of action where local governments enact or apply zoning or historic landmark laws to property owned or used by religious institutions in a manner that substantially burdens the exercise of religion, denies religious institutions equal treatment, or discriminates against religious uses in favor of similar secular uses. It also does not permit a local jurisdiction to totally exclude religious uses from its boundaries, much like adult entertainment uses presumably cannot be excluded.

The legislative response in RLUIPA was portended in earlier state legislation exempting religious entities from certain zoning, such as that of California Assembly Bill 133. A.B. 133 created an exemption from the California historic landmark preservation law for "noncommercial property owned by any association or corporation that is religiously affiliated and not organized for private profit, whether the corporation is organized as a religious corporation, or as a public benefit corporation."[36] For the exemption to apply, the association must determine "in a public forum" that landmarking of its property would cause "a substantial hardship, which is likely to deprive the association . . . of economic return on its property,

---

(footnote continued from previous page)

the Ku Klux Klan in the Ohio statehouse square. *See* more recently in Salazar v. Buono, 130 S. Ct. 1803 (2010), the multiple opinions of the justices in explaining the Establishment Clause implications in a case where Congress mandated a land transfer of national preserve property on which a Latin cross was displayed.

[35] *See* Emp't Div. v. Smith, 494 U.S. 872 (1990).

[36] CAL GOV'T CODE § 25373(d).

the reasonable use . . . (or) appropriate use of its property in furtherance of its religious mission."[37] Against a challenge that the legislative exemption violated the federal Establishment Clause, a split California Supreme Court upheld the legislation; religiously affiliated uses in California are now free to exempt themselves from historic landmark laws.[38] The U.S. Supreme Court refused to grant certiorari,[39] placing the issue squarely back in the state courts.

RLUIPA, as a civil rights statute, packs a big punch because a successful challenge will provide attorney's fees to the plaintiff. Also, the federal Department of Justice and religious interest attorneys have been very active in pursuing challenges to local land use regulations under the statute. The form of religious exercise under the statute does not have to be mandated by the adherent's faith, and the statute defines religious exercise to include the "use, building, or conversion of real property for the purpose of religious exercise."[40] Thus, when a group seeks land use permission to build or expand a church or to establish a home-based religious activity in a residential neighborhood, the protections of RLUIPA come into play. Although it does not require the government to exempt religious uses from ordinary zoning processes, the statute compels the local government to ensure that the zoning regulation does not substantially burden religious activity—in effect, to be prepared to show that there are other reasonable alternatives to the religious group's request. It requires the local government to not treat religious assembly uses more stringently than secular assembly uses, such as theaters, schools, and private clubs; this provision alone has required the reassessment of zoning district use regulations in many cities and counties throughout the country. The federal circuits have evolved somewhat different interpretations of RLUIPA, so the practitioner must be aware of the local distinctions in judicial interpretation as government seeks to accommodate religious land uses.

---

[37] Cal. Gov't Code §§ 37361(c) and 25373(d), applying to California cities and counties, respectively.
[38] E. Bay Asian Local Dev. v. California, 13 P.3d 1122, 1141 (Cal. 2000).
[39] See 121 S. Ct. 1735 (2001).
[40] 42 U.S.C. § 2000cc-5(7)(B).

IV. Conclusion

Land use law is practiced in the most public of arenas—that of local government. Inevitably, land use issues will involve First Amendment concerns, and the issue will often be a matter of important public debate.

First Amendment issues require the local government to be thoroughly prepared to support its action in the case of a legal challenge. For the unsuccessful defendant, there is a high cost involved in the litigation of constitutional rights, including damages and attorney's fees under 42 U.S.C. §§ 1983 and 1988. The uncertainties in the law require the land use practitioner to study carefully and keep current with developments in the area of First Amendment legal restrictions. Reviewing this book should be considered an important first step in doing so.

Table of Cases

Index